011 42 555 055025

Suleman Chacho.

FUSION
Analysis

FUSION
Analysis

MERGING FUNDAMENTAL, TECHNICAL, BEHAVIORAL, AND QUANTITATIVE ANALYSIS FOR RISK-ADJUSTED EXCESS RETURNS

V. John Palicka CFA CMT

New York   Chicago   San Francisco   Lisbon   London
Madrid   Mexico City   Milan   New Delhi   San Juan
Seoul   Singapore   Sydney   Toronto

1 2 3 4 5 6 7 8 9 0   DOC/DOC   1 6 5 4 3 2 1

ISBN: 978-0-07-162938-6
MHID: 0-07-162938-6

e-ISBN: 978-0-07-176310-3
e-MHID: 0-07-176310-4

This publication is designed to provide accurate and authoritative information in regard to the subject matter covered. It is sold with the understanding that neither the author nor the publisher is engaged in rendering legal, accounting, securities trading, or other professional services. If legal advice or other expert assistance is required, the services of a competent professional person should be sought.
> —*From a Declaration of Principles Jointly Adopted by a Committee of the American Bar Association and a Committee of Publishers and Associations*

McGraw-Hill books are available at special quantity discounts to use as premiums and sales promotions or for use in corporate training programs. To contact a representative, please e-mail us at bulksales@mcgraw-hill.com.

This book is printed on acid-free paper.

CONTENTS

ACKNOWLEDGMENTS

As a special thanks, I would like to mention some of my early mentors at Prudential. In the first few years, my first boss was Ray Kurtz, who was an excellent analyst and technician. Bill Rankin, our lead senior analyst, offered good analytical leadership, and we had great academic guidance from Ed Zinbarg, who helped write leading financial textbooks. Once Bill left and Ray passed away, I took over the funds and enhanced a fusion process that we were using. I thank all the support staff and analysts who worked on the funds at Prudential. I am also grateful for the support I got from my family, especially my wife Cindy, and the many students who took my Fusion courses around the world. I also wish to thank Pat Sparacio who as head of NYIF's courses gave me the opportunity to teach my Fusion course. I also wish to thank my friend Esam Hassanyeh who helped me take the course overseas and who also plays a great game of tennis. Speaking of tennis, I wish to thank my daily partners such as Rich, Ernie and Zoran whose questions helped me shape some of the paths to the end conclusions. Naturally, any errors are mine.

INTRODUCTION

What is the best way to make money when investing?

This question is one any investor asks, no matter if he or she is an "ordinary" investor, a professional money manager, an academic, or a fund consultant. Some of these people are naive and know little about investing, while others are very knowledgeable. Their objectives and investment processes range from the most conservative and sound to the most speculative.

For the most part, money is actively managed. While index funds and their similar exchange-traded funds (ETFs) cousins are rapidly growing, investors still seek active management in the hopes of getting an edge on the market returns, called seeking risk-adjusted excess returns, leading to the selection of an investment discipline. Investment disciplines should then lead to better returns than that of the market. Putting aside hot tips, indexing, hunches, and so on, professional money managers will seek such an investment discipline. Managers check their investment disciplines against benchmarks, such as an index, to see if the results are any good. The starting point in this process involves fundamentals or the use of accounting and other financial information to create valuation. These may include earnings or even qualitative factors like brand images of consumer companies.

However, results are not too good for those managers who only rely on the fundamentals, as the vast majority cannot beat their benchmarks, especially when one adjusts returns for the risk they take. As we shall see, the market gets rather efficient as many professionals seek the best returns. There are also statistical issues that surprise us. For example, we got faked out by the devastation of Hurricane Katrina. The event and eventual damage were much greater than anyone expected, and therefore the insurance companies were under-reserved against the potential.

Not Just Fundamentals

An increasing number of portfolio managers have now realized that fundamental analysis alone often does not make the best investment approach and have therefore begun to utilize technical, behavioral, and quant analyses as well. Proper use of fundamental techniques is required for selecting investments that are designed to generate risk-adjusted excess returns. However, users of technical analysis, from institutional investors to short-term traders, must use non-fundamental information to get another perspective in activities such as market timing and the minimization of transaction costs.

Fundamental analysts have increased their caution when taking reported financial numbers—consider the large audited firm Enron that went up in smoke with fraud in 2001. So which numbers can, and do, you trust? For example, is China's success for real or is the government fudging numbers?

Technical analysis includes the study of charts, volume, and other market statistics, and uses little if any fundamentals. Behavioral analysis is the study of moods and emotions. In more recent years, these analyses, and not fundamentals, have become the drivers of investment decisions. Technicals also utilize investor moods (technicians call this sentiment). At times, technical and behavioral analysis can be close cousins. Quants use numbers in some mathematical formula to make a decision.

There is also a feeling that the market is not rational and that there are emotions which drive investment decisions, hence the interest in behavioral and technical. For this reason quant is also popular, as it is felt that quant can eliminate these emotions by just investing on the numbers. Of course, behaviorally, managers may start to make exceptions at times, and this could lead them into trouble.

Another reason why managers have sought areas outside fundamentals is that the markets can be volatile. Fundamentals can't seem to capture these swings, as we saw in 2008 and 2009. The news looks good, but the market falls, and then the news looks bad, but the market sharply rallies. For some, technicals can take advantage of this type of situation, more so than fundamentals. With all of these options, the numbers can be blended, based on fundamentals, technical, and behavioral measures. Thus, trading markets have increasingly focused attention on somehow incorporating the proper blend of technical analysis.

Fusion Analysis

This book describes the blending of major investment disciplines into one. This approach is not commonly used in mainstream investing, but, in my opinion, it can offer advantages to investors that each discipline on its own cannot. The investment discipline includes the proprietary blending of fundamental, technical, and behavioral disciplines into a quant model. I call this investment process *Fusion analysis* (not to be confused with other uses of the word "fusion" that permeate the world today in areas such as making lipstick, cars, and cuisines). The Fusion blending is both exciting and challenging, as it covers uncharted territory.

When some investors say they find it hard to justify using technicals with fundamentals, one can only be amused. Some fundamental strategies already incorporate technicals, behavioral, and quant through the back door. For example, a value low P/E strategy already has a quant criteria. The low P/E could be low because investors are already cautious of the fundamental outlook and their pessimism means they will not bid up the price. And high P/E could be the opposite, as great expectations and bullishness mean that they may be willing to bid up the prices beyond the true fundamental requirements.

Some investors then claim, "We tried fundamentals and we tried technicals and putting them together, they don't work. We'll just stick with fundamentals." Such a statement is akin to a football coach saying, "I tried offense and I tried defense, but putting them together they don't work. So I will only do offense." Most likely the blending of analyses didn't work for these investors because, at times, technicals and fundamentals will contradict each other. When the fundamental news is bad, the technicals may be very good. Investors therefore need to know how to blend these analyses, and for this reason, I use quant. Think of it this way: If you have a button and fabric, they will not magically be joined together. You'll need the *thread* to sew the button to the fabric. Consider that thread the quant portion of the Fusion process.

For Whom?

Is this book for the highly trained professional or the beginner? Good question. It is really designed for serious investors who already have knowledge of the capital markets. However, the beginner may get the most value, as Fusion hopes to show that the "Hawaiian shirt" approach of investing is better left to the cable stations and not to the serious investor. Fusion is for the professional on the offense of getting true economic returns. It is also a good shield to new investors who are attempting to wrestle with the concept of investing. It is expected that the minimum body of knowledge will include some of the expected Learning Outcome Statements of Level 1 CFA and CMT programs. In the book, however, I try to give training wheels in some areas for the novices while still keeping the professional engaged in the discussions.

Fusion analysis will be geared mostly for the equity investor but will cover some other asset classes such as fixed income, real estate, foreign exchange, and commodities. It will then attempt to blend the best of all approaches to a successful investment strategy. Of course, there are no guarantees but hopefully the logic of this approach will appeal to investors.

My Background

So what do I bring to the table and why should you care about my opinions and knowledge on Fusion?

From the start of my investing career in the 1970s, the blend of fundamental and technical analysis, along with the inclusion of behavioral and quant has played an important role for me in small-cap investing. I was the Chief Portfolio Manager of small-cap stocks at Midco Investors, a subsidiary of The Prudential Insurance Company (now called Prudential Financial, Inc.), where my team and I managed over $1.5 billion for 11 years. At Prudential, my team and I managed billions, with top rankings and significant premiums to the index. I doubled client money approximately every four years. We grew about $50 million in U.S. small-cap stocks into $1.5 billion over 11 years, with a return of 600 basis points per annum over the Russell 2000 Index and competitors (as past performance is no guarantee of future results). Take a look at the appendix material, where you will find my earliest fusion recommendations in situation reports on the Mite Corporation and on FCA International LTD. As you will see, I have been using the fusion analysis method since the 1970s. These reports were created before I joined Prudential.

After Midco, I started my own company, Global Emerging Growth Capital (GEGC), where I continued my Fusion approach with my own funds. In 1990, I started my own asset management activities with GEGC, which has generated per-annum returns of 13.7 percent – through September 30, 2011. GEGC was designed to enter other financial activities, and hence its assets are very small relative to those of Prudential. This return also well outperformed representative benchmarks of 8.3 percent for the S&P Global Small Cap Index and 7.4 percent for the Lipper Global Small Cap funds. The S&P 500 index return of 8.3 percent was also substantially exceeded. So, I am pleased that at least I not only kept up with the benchmarks but also exceeded them. Of course, no guarantees going forward. So I have done both academic and actual management over a long period of time.

I practice Fusion in my investments. More importantly, I have taught on the topic and other subjects that are intrinsic to Fusion at intern programs of leading investment firms, business schools, and open courses for various levels of students, both in the United States and abroad. The peer group reviews over the years have been very positive based on my class evaluations. These courses include the actual Fusion one, but also some of the "parts that make the whole," such as portfolio theory, corporate finance, technical analysis, and security analysis. It also includes my specialized courses in global small-cap investing, fund evaluation, stealth and algorithmic trading, portable wealth investing, and gold investing. Also, the course materials from my teaching candidates who wish to earn the CMT and CFA charterholder designations have also been an intrinsic part of the Fusion process. We shall see some features of these courses throughout the book.

Growing Fusion Support

The evidence in the growing interest in Fusion-type analysis is considerable. The number of managers, especially dealing with hedge funds, using approaches beyond just fundamentals has increased and become more pronounced. Some prominent hedge funds use various types of quant and are gaining more publicity in doing so. More applicants are taking the CFA exam for fundamental analysis and the CMT exam for technical analysis. A great number of people are also earning both professional CFA and CMT designations. In addition, quant managers are taking their own certifications for financial engineering. There are also growing financial engineering programs within business schools where fundamentals have been relied on for years.

Further distrust of accounting and other fundamental issues has led investors to more probing courses on accounting and finance. For example, I did a free cash flow course for a major accounting firm who adjusts fundamental accounting numbers into more real economic ones, which is a part of Fusion analysis. Fusion does not necessarily take fundamental numbers at face value but, instead, adjusts them for economic reality in the same way.

Growing academic evidence supports the use of technical/behavioral analysis as well. These studies are done not necessarily by technicians but finance professionals. Hence, there is less "having an axe to grind syndrome." Recently, a Nobel Prize in economics recognized the contribution of behavioral finance. Increased successful investment strategies use mostly quant approaches. There are also many mutual funds and hedge funds that run by quant or a type of robo investing.

Most major MBA schools and leading textbooks now devote specific sections to technical analysis. When I have taught at Columbia or Baruch, the course book used was Bodie, Kane, and Marcus, *Investments*, which has a whole chapter devoted to behavioral and technical analysis. Even the CFA Level 1 exam introduces the candidate to technical analysis.

Skill Set

Few are skilled in both technical and fundamental analysis, not to mention behavioral and quant. Even New York City has relatively few people who have both the CFA and CMT designation, although the number is growing. While the desire is there to combine both approaches, the course offerings and textbooks are virtually nonexistent. In fact, academic journals don't analyze results on a Fusion approach but rather are more specific on one type of investment approach, be it fundamental or behavioral.

Accomplishment Goals

Moving forward, I will be introducing investment ideas throughout the book, then utilize cases to illustrate Fusion topics. I will also discuss other issues that are not always considered part of the normal investment process, to help provide perspective on Fusion's capabilities. This book is not necessarily meant to be a course in learning all the basic modules of investing knowledge, though we shall occasionally brush up on our fundamental and technical tools via breakout analysis. Then to get direction, potential problems will be discussed. Again, others are better suited to provide the specifics of each investment topic in their own separate textbooks. So when I show how to hammer in a nail to hang a picture, I will leave the stress tests of the nail's composition to the engineers.

By the end of this book, you should realize the limitations of only using just fundamental or behavioral or quant or technical knowledge. Instead, you will understand the power that can be harnessed through the blending, the fusion, of these approaches. You should also be able to better time investment decisions using Fusion analysis. Fundamental valuation techniques and technical tools will be used to create price objectives. Quant models will provide investment opportunities and help avoid the mistakes of behavioral finance pitfalls. Overall, Fusion analysis can better maximize your profitable trades, execute capital preservation techniques, and outperform the market on a risk-adjusted basis, leading you to making money through your investments.

Let's get started.

FUSION
Analysis

Part 1

THE BIG PICTURE

The stock market correlates closely with the growth of the GDP. All the companies in the S&P 500 Index are a good reflection of the economy, even though some large private companies are not in the index. The index is compiled of a diverse mix of industries such as finance, technology, and consumer. In the United States, we have a rich diversity of companies, but the larger exposure is to service companies. Some might even say that going forward we will develop more data and intellectual types of companies. I call these "right inflection" companies, as the job requirements to work in these companies will require skills beyond the first standard deviation on many standardized tests. While important skills requiring sales and creativity will not go away, it is possible that less demanding skills may increasingly be handled through automation or outsourced to low-wage countries.

Other countries may not have as broad a mixture of industries in their index. Emerging markets could be tied more to commodities, such as Chile with copper or Russia, where the stock index is composed mostly of energy and mineral companies. However, it is likely that these countries will develop skills to enhance their growth in other industries, including "right inflection" jobs.

Top-Down and Bottom-Up Analysis

A rising market lifts all ships and a falling market naturally drags them down. This is usually called a top-down analysis. In order to make use of top-down analysis, we must first make an accurate forecast of the economy. Experiencing a recession in a period when one forecasted a boom will likely mean that stocks will go down, not up. Thus, using top-down investing will have losses in the stock market.

Top-down analysis forecasts the broad economic picture, identifies the industries that would do best in that picture, and finally selects the appropriate, individual companies. For example, if you feel that an economic boom is on the way, you might identify the consumer industries of transportation and housing, and then select the better auto players and home-building companies. By doing this, you would overweight these industries in the index. So, if consumer discretionary stocks are 20 percent of the index, you might place a larger weight of, say, 25 percent.

Now, if you feel that a recession is on the way, you may choose to identify defensive industries, such as health care or consumer staples, and then select a particular company, like Kellogg, for example. Kellogg would be expected to have more stable sales and profits in a recession and not decline as much as the market. In this case, you would overweight the staples and underweight the consumer discretionary industries.

While it is still possible that some fantastic company like the next Google or Apple will buck the economic trend, the companies will prosper because of their products and service innovations that rapidly gain market share. Most likely these companies would be analyzed bottoms up.

In bottom-up analysis, you forecast the health of a company's prospects. While there may be some economic influence on the company's earnings, the outlook of its own products may be the key or dominant factor in a future stock price move. For example, a biotech company that provides a cure for a disease may see its stock soar upon FDA approval. However, on the date of the announcement, the market may actually be down due to general economic conditions. So, while bottom-up companies may be buffeted by the economic winds, most likely their fortunes will be tied to their own products. In this example, the cure for a disease could prove to be a big winner in a seemingly stagnant economy.

In the past, we've had companies like FedEx, Wrigley, and Coca-Cola emerge from economically weak scenarios to become major corporations that hired thousands of people. It seems that the future of true GDP growth lies in the encouragement and fostering of new, dynamic companies. I call these companies "sunrise" companies, as compared to "sunset" companies that have seen better days. Some sunrise companies are more easily understood using top-down analysis than others, but long term, they create a large market that tends to overcome the fluctuations caused by the economy.

Knowing which is a sunrise or sunset company is not always easy to do. Even stock experts are faked out. Consider past peaches like Dell, Citibank, and GM, all of which later turned into prunes. Many investors missed Apple and McDonald's in their early stages. Are these companies now in their latter stages ready to become prunes as well?

1

FORECASTING
THE ECONOMY

The economy can be forecasted by observing the growth or decline of GDP or by studying past trends and economic boom and bust scenarios. Usually one forecasts refinements of an already perceived direction. For example, you may forecast GDP growth of 3.2 percent versus an expert consensus estimate of 3.0 percent. This means the level of the stock market is estimated a bit too high or too low, depending on the actual growth of the economy. If the S&P 500 Index is at 1200 and the estimate is off by only 10 points, the level of error is small—a scenario much more pleasant than being way off by something like 300 points. If you are off by a few hundred points on the downside, you will have forecasted a boom when, in fact, a deep recession will occur, forcing the stock market to plunge.

Since most investment firms use a top-down approach, forecasting GDP (and thus corporate profits) can be a major challenge. Talking heads on TV channels like CNBC may share their financial expertise with the public, only to have an important market guru provide a different or dissenting opinion. The guru may be a well-respected, longtime market observer giving more accurate information or he may be a "flavor of the month" strategist or economist who has only been hot for a brief time. With so much information from so many different sources, it is hard to know who or what to follow. Sometimes forecasting the future economy may just end up with the blind leading the blind.

Challenge or not, it is understandable why firms tend to use a top-down approach. Most companies in a major index such as the S&P 500 Index are mature and not necessarily cutting-edge as they grow larger in size.

They are therefore used to track the health of the economy. This means that much of the trillions of dollars under asset management must be invested in such companies. While some firms may splinter their funds between top-down and bottom-up funds, others use some blend of both strategies. For example, a fund manager may have a large cap fund that has an average market cap of over $10 billion and, at the same time, have a small-cap growth fund that has an average market cap under $1 billion. The large-cap fund can manage several billions of dollars, but the small-cap fund may manage only a few hundred million dollars. While the small-cap funds may have more weight on bottom up, some may use more weight on top down. Based on my experience meeting managers, many funds have some of both.

Market Timing

Evidence shows that market timing is not easy and there is no magic formula that will tell an investor if the market is overvalued or cheap (indicating if it will soon plunge or rise). Whether economists, strategists, or fund managers, the experts usually get market timing wrong. Often, too much fund cash is held at bottoms and too little at tops. Fund betas tend to be low at bottoms and high at tops, but the reverse should actually be done in order to capitalize on the eventual market direction. If you expect the market to rise, then you should be fully invested and not have a drag from parking cash. Likewise, all things being equal, higher beta stocks would go up more than lower beta stocks. So, flavor-of-the-month experts and talking heads who formerly looked great are all of a sudden shown to be totally wrong.

Compounding the problem to make correct market timing calls is the fact that news tends to be good at tops and bad at bottoms. Naturally, one feels better when the news is good and will therefore have more confidence in buying stocks. Bad news causes people to become cautious with their finances and if not sell their stocks, then at least not buy any.

Fundamental strategists have models to show how bad things are and to convince investors to stay out of the market; this happened in the fall of 2002. On the other hand, news may be good and strategists might try to convince investors to buy on the hopes that the economy is entering a "new era of prosperity," which happened in 1929 and again in 2000. In 1929, Irving Fisher, a leading economist, stated, "The nation is marching along a permanently high plateau of prosperity." Five days later, the market crashed. Similarly, one can reminisce about the late-2007 positive outlook on the economy, just before the market dropped from around 14,000 to under 7000 in a period that was only a bit longer than a year.

Technicians and users of behavioral analysis may actually provide opposing advice. Behaviorialists might state that too much euphoria indicates the market should be sold and not bought. Technicians may use contrary opinion to help define market turning points. Thus, while the economic news may be very good, the giddy psychology of stock buyers may indicate too much bullishness. This situation would indicate to the technicians that a turning point in the market's upward direction would soon present itself to investors.

All of these crosscurrents between fundamental and technical indicators understandably can lead to conflicting signals. Which ones do you believe? Also, as Martin J. Pring mentioned in his book *Technical Analysis Explained*, investing is based on probabilities and not certainties, Even if we have an indicator that has generally worked in the past, we cannot assume it will be 100 percent accurate for the future. In addition, you wonder if there are even more factors that must be analyzed.

Fundamentalists may have to revise their models. For example, using just-reported price earnings ratios to determine market attractiveness may not be enough. Such earnings might have to be adjusted due to the potential impact of nonrecurring or extraordinary events that distort true returns.

Technicians also wonder if using contrary opinion is enough. It is generally felt that while contrary opinion is useful at estimating market turning points, the exact timing and magnitude of the change is not as predictable. Thus, a technician may use a chart pattern such as Head and Shoulders to get a better estimate of market direction and to help answer questions on the magnitude of a price change. Behavioralists may sense excesses but not have tools to measure price objectives. Different approaches may result in different price objectives.

Where to begin and what to do? Investors may feel frustrated. Fusion will attempt to tackle this.

Modeling

One way to begin the top-down decision process is to compare the returns over time of various asset classes—namely, stocks and bonds. Usually you can find this information in textbooks that are compiled from several sources. In addition, there are professors who have their own calculations, as well as organizations led by such pioneers as Roger Ibbotson and Rex Sinquefield that deal in this type of analysis.

When looking at data that begins with some long historical period of time and is then updated on a regular basis, you may see something like Table 1.1, which shows the yearly returns of stocks, bonds, and Treasury bills (T-bills). T-bills are considered risk-free, as the U.S. government is not expected to default, and in any case, it can always print more money. For valuation purposes, U.S. long-term government bonds are considered at a risk-free rate because they have a maturity of 10 years, which better coincides with investment requirements. However, because of their length of exposure to fluctuating interest rates, bonds do have more volatility risk than T-bills, which have much shorter maturities (a year or less). In addition, note in the table the return that the assets generate compared to T-bills.

In looking at this table, we want to focus on two things in particular: return (and excess return), and risk. In other words, looking at reward or the return is only part of the story. You must also look at the risk, which in the table is the standard deviation. The standard deviation is the volatility, up or down from the average, that can be adjusted in a mathematical way. The larger the standard deviation or the volatility, the more risk is shown.

TABLE 1.1 Rates of Return and Risk Statistics, 1926–2005

	U.S. Small Stocks	U.S. Large Stocks	World Large Stocks	U.S. Long-Term Treasury Bonds	U.S. T-Bills	U.S. Inflation
Geometric Average	12.01	10.17	9.85	5.38	3.70	3.13
Arithmetic Average	17.95	12.15	11.46	5.68	3.75	3.18
Standard Deviation	38.71	20.26	18.57	8.09	3.15	4.29
Excess Average Returns to T-Bills	14.20	8.39	N/A	1.93	N/A	N/A

Source: Bodie, Kane, Marcus. *Investments*, New York: McGraw-Hill/Irwin, 7th Edition, 2008, pp. 132, 146, 148. Above data is stated in percentage terms; U.S. geometric inflation return is an estimate.

We can see that U.S. small stocks have the highest return of 17.95 percent (arithmetic) and 12.01 percent (geometric) return. But they also have the most risk with the largest standard deviation. Geometric calculations show lower returns, as they reflect a geometric compounding effect; arithmetic calculations overstate returns, as they are simple averages. Asset management firms typically use geometric return calculations to follow mutual funds. This method is required for performance measurement of traditional funds under Global Investment Performance Standards (GIPS) of the CFA Institute.

The CFA Institute administers a program that enables candidates to earn the Chartered Financial Analyst (CFA) designation. Various requirements include passing three levels of exams that cover many business topics in areas such as accounting, economics, statistics, and finance. (The CFA exams are discussed in detail in Part 4, Chapter 18.)

We know T-bills are a safer investment than U.S. small stocks, but as shown in the table, while the safest investment is U.S. T-bills, they return only 3.70 percent (geometric) and 3.75 percent (arithmetic). The volatility of returns is the least, as the standard deviation is 3.15 percent. U.S. small stocks show 38.71 percent standard deviation. In other words, one may lose a lot of money in U.S. small stocks in just a short period of time. Reflecting on the year 2008 in particular refreshes our memory of these kinds of losses, when the small-cap stock indices were down sharply and the Russell 2000 Index showed losses 33.8 percent.

So what you see here is the classic case of investing: One can eat well or one can sleep well, but not both. Higher returns require the assumption of higher levels of risk. The excess average returns to T-bills increases as one goes from bills to bonds to stocks. Notice that bonds are in the middle, as long-term U.S. Treasury bonds return 5.38 percent (geometric) and 5.68 percent (arithmetic), which is lower than stocks (large and small) but more than U.S. T-bills. However, the standard deviation of U.S. long-term Treasury bonds is 8.09 percent, which means more risk than U.S. T-bills, but less risk than stocks.

Higher reward means higher risk. It would be ideal, of course, if you could get higher returns but with less risk.

The Sharpe Ratio

Some methods allow us to calculate a trade-off between risk and reward, such as the Reward to Variability, commonly called the Sharpe ratio. This ratio takes the excess return of the asset to the risk-free rate and divides by the standard deviation of the asset—or Return-Risk–Free/Standard Deviation. The higher the number, the better the deal on the trade-off.

When we do this we get the following:[1]

Investment	The Sharpe Ratio
U.S. Small Stocks	0.36
U.S. Large Stocks	0.41
World Large Stocks	0.41
Long-Term U.S. Treasury Bonds	0.24

So large-cap stocks are a better deal, as they have a higher Sharpe ratio than U.S. small stocks and U.S. long-term Treasury bonds. In general, while stocks look better than bonds, there are other risks that may affect a decision, such as liquidity and skewness. Skewness indicates how asymmetrical downside returns compare to upside returns. Negative skewness would indicate more downside risk than positive skewness, so this also needs to be considered in the risk equation. The small stock have less negative skewness of −0.22 to U.S. large of −0.80 and world stocks of −0.61. The bonds have a positive skewness of 0.23.

Still, it appears that stocks have a higher Sharpe than bonds. Thus, if bond returns are equal to or even higher than those of stocks, and all the risks are equal, then bonds would be a better deal, and vice versa. This argument has been made to determine whether you should invest in emerging market stocks or emerging market bonds. The same argument can be used in making other comparisons with various asset classes.

Subjectively, bonds have less risk but lower yield and stocks have higher returns but carry more risk, whatever the final measure of risk may be. This is a good place to start when you are trying to determine the best plan for asset allocation. Next we need to become familiar with various valuation methods such as the Fed model

The Fed Valuation Model

The Fed Valuation model compares the returns of stocks with those of long-term U.S. government bonds. It gives a signal to either buy or sell stocks based on the returns one can make in the bonds. When the forward earnings yield on the S&P 500 is less than the 10-year bond yield, stocks have begun to get too expensive. The model was made popular by Ed Yardeni when he was economist for Prudential Securities. Though based on his examination of prior Fed analyses, it is not officially endorsed by the federal government.

Technicians find the appeal of comparing earnings yields to fixed income yields as a proxy for sentiment. When investors are bullish on stocks, the stock price index will rise more sharply than the earnings, causing the stock yield to fall. If, simultaneously, investors shun bonds, you have a perfect storm as bond prices fall and bond yields rise, causing low yields on stocks and high yields on bonds. Of course, there can still be a sharp drop in stock yields, even if bond yields don't rise, initiating a rather unattractive stock yield to bond yield.

Fundamental Tools

One of the fundamental tools used for analysis is the price/earnings ratio (P/E ratio). It is derived by taking the stock price of a company or an index of companies and dividing it by the earnings. So, for example, if XYZ trades at $10 a share and it earns $1.00 a share, its price earnings ratio would be 10. Assuming all things are equal, high P/E ratios indicate that stocks are expensive and one is paying too much for earnings; low P/E ratios indicate good bargains. Investors could justify paying higher P/E ratios if earnings growth was also higher. However, this feeling may lead to overvaluations, and likewise to undervaluations with low P/E ratios.

This same type of analysis can be used on a price-to-book value ratio (P/B ratio). Equity (sometimes called book) is balance sheet assets minus all balance sheet liabilities. In this case, one would divide the stock price by the equity per share. High P/B ratios (flip this ratio upside down and call it low book-to-market values) indicate that one is paying too much for net assets and the stock is expensive. Low P/B ratios indicate there is more substance behind the stock price, as one is getting the stock near, or perhaps even below, net asset values. Again, there is nothing wrong with paying high P/B ratios, if you expect rising cash flows down the road. Conversely, if lower cash flows are expected, then one may pay lower P/B ratios.

Many fundamentalists use P/E and P/B ratios, along with other factors, to identify levels that would be attractive for determining valuations. Some prominent works in this area are the studies of academic professionals Eugene Fama and Kenneth French, who created the Fama–French model describing market behavior. They have shown that a blend of low P/B ratios and the size of company (with smaller company sizes in terms of market capitalization offering better growth prospects) are also good ingredients for valuation considerations. Some or perhaps all of the measures (Fed model, P/E ratios, and P/B ratios) can be massaged by analysts to get a better slant on the general direction of the market.

In addition to determining whether the market is cheap or expensive, one may also want to determine if small companies are a better deal than large companies. In this arena, we can use the T. Rowe Price P/E model for small stocks. While there are variations of this approach using other market indices, here one can compare the P/E of a small-cap index to of a large-cap index. For many years T. Rowe Price has had a mutual fund composed of small-cap companies. Today, with the expansion of small-cap indices, you can use the same thought process and compare the Russell 2000 Index with its larger-cap brother of another large-cap index, like the S&P 500 Index. (In addition, you might also consider beta analysis or the volatility of a stock to the market index.)

Technical Tools

For technical analysis, we can explore the use of chart patterns such as the Head and Shoulders. Technicians could also use other patterns like Double and Triple Tops/Bottoms, Triangles and Rectangles, and the Selling Climax. These stock patterns often tell a story of bullishness or bearishness. They can reflect the struggle between the bulls and bears that make lines in the sand, or a pattern. Resolution of the patterns then indicates the next direction of an index or a security price. In addition, we shall explore similar concepts such as trends, support/resistance, moving averages, fund flows, and sentiment measures.

Just as there are varied schools of thought in fundamental approaches, such as discounting cash flows versus comparative analysis, there are various schools of thought in technical analysis. Some technicians use patterns, some sentiment, some momentum, and some use more exotic measures such as Gann and Elliott Wave (discussed further in Chapters 11 and 12, respectively). Some even use a blend of several approaches, but again, there is a difference of opinion on how much to weight each factor and which factor to use. In addition, financial behaviorists would complement some of the technical approaches by attempting to analyze investor psychology.

The combination of all these tools, fundamental and technical, will be applied to both short- and longer-term investors. This creates further challenges, as long-term outlooks may conflict with short-term opportunities. Before starting an analysis of all of these factors, using a discussion of the Fed model as our springboard, you must decide whether or not analysis is worth it. If you do top-down analysis, will it be successful?

ternative? Should you spend precious time (and
market turns, or should this activity be entrusted
to a discussion of the Efficient Market Hypothesis
do better than the returns offered by the market?

Efficient Market Hypothesis

Generally, an efficient market is one where prices reflect all available information and the corresponding risk. Therefore, it is not possible to get a
bargain. A security that *appears* cheap is either damaged goods or it is not
cheap. It only has the illusion of being cheap, but soon the investor finds
that it was properly priced. (It was priced down because it was not as good
as it appeared.) The same analysis can be made on expensive securities.
While every investor tries to find a bargain, it is unlikely that you will find
it in a market that has a large number of participants who analyze the
information in the same manner. Why should you be the lucky one to get
this bargain? Maybe the answer is already in the question. You are perhaps
lucky and happened to stumble on it.

The efficient market analysis for stock shopping can be compared
to shopping for another item, say, clothes. For example, customers always
want to buy clothes at a bargain—that is, purchasing the clothing item
below the normal retail price. Let's assume you are shopping for a green
IZOD shirt that sells on Madison Avenue for $80. You can wait for a sale
and get 20 percent off, but sales are not always certain and they may only
occur at certain times of the year. You need the shirt for this weekend, so
you try to find it elsewhere.

Another store might give you a discount if you charge a certain
amount on its credit card, but you hate to get the card, as you might buy
things you really want but don't need. You decide to pass on that retailer,
but you hear about an outlet store that carries designer clothing lines at
good discounts. They usually carry IZOD shirts for $50. But it is not close.
You will need some kind of transportation.

After playing all of these scenarios in your mind, you may decide to
pay the full market price on Madison Avenue and be done with it. In this

way, you get the item, even at full price, and save time and weariness on your body traveling. In financial terms, you might say that you avoided the transaction costs and got what you wanted but you did not beat the market. You paid the "market" price.

So what can we conclude? In an efficient market, it is unlikely that we can locate an easy bargain for desirable goods. It is possible, but when we add transaction costs and the possibility of emotional shopping actions, we may not really get a bargain. We face similar challenges in security selection. Seeking information on cheap stocks may entail transaction costs, such as the cost of research. And remember the transportation costs? We can compare that to liquidity constraints, as we may not be able to buy and sell without some friction.

So, the Efficient Market Hypothesis tends to show the market as so efficient that we cannot get a bargain easily, or in economic terms, risk-adjusted excess returns to that of the market.

EMH Forms of Information

The EMH has three forms that address specific types of information: Weak, Semi-Strong, and Strong.

The Weak form states that past charts and volume figures cannot make future price predictions worthwhile. Thus, this type tends to dismiss technical analysis. The argument is that all prices are random (based on the theory by Burton Malkiel in his book *Random Walk Down Wall Street*). Malkiel believes that random prices cannot be predicted, as they can only react to future news. Clearly, Burton Malkiel is not a fan of technical analysis.[2]

Of course, not all agree that news is random and that one cannot take advantage of random-walk prices. Some prices exhibit serial correlation or start momentums and trends. This is because not all assimilate the information equally. While the market produces information, not all investors massage the information in the same manner. Some may not be knowledgeable enough on their own to interpret the information properly and so choose to wait for others to make the interpretation, such as in a news release. As more people jump on board, a trend begins. One could say that at first we have the innovators, then the imitators,and finally the idiots. Technicians say, "Stay with the trend until it's broken." Thus, things that are cheap may get cheaper, and things that are expensive may get more expensive.

The Semi-Strong form states that fundamental, historical information, such as brokerage reports, annual reports, and SEC documents, are not useful. The market will already assimilate the data and adjust the prices, so that by the time you read the reports, it is too late to acquire a bargain. There is evidence that brokerage reports do not produce risk-adjusted returns after transaction costs.[3] In addition, other users of public, fundamental information don't fare as well. These others could be mutual funds that tend to underperform their benchmarks as a group, although individually there are some excellent performers.

The Strong form states that the market is so efficient that even if you had illegal, nonpublic inside information, you still could not outperform the market. This is the strictest form. While economists seem to believe in the Weak and Semi-Strong forms, they tend to disagree on the Strong form. For this reason, insider information is well regulated and carries severe penalties for violators. Professional money managers would like to collect management fees to shepherd assets, while skeptics would dismiss such fees as nonproductive. They would recommend that investors just index their returns to a benchmark, pay lower fees, and even get more transparency than that shown by a manager.

Various studies show exceptions to the EMH that provide opportunities for performance-oriented investors. In the weak form, serial correlation has been found in small-cap and emerging market stocks. In addition, technicians using the 200-day moving average to create buy and sell signals has found some academic support. In its most simplistic form, when stock prices rise above the 200-day moving average, one has a buy signal; when prices fall below the 200-day average, one has a sell signal. When studied by academics, this concept showed risk-adjusted excess returns. (It was also quoted in standard finance textbooks by Nobel Prize winner Sharpe.)[4] Based on 25,000 trading days, using the Dow Jones Industrial Average (DJIA), the difference between buy and sell decisions was 16.8 percent, statistically significant from zero. Other technical indicators, such as the Head and Shoulders pattern, have been studied and found to have predictable outperformance as well.[5]

In the Semi-Strong form, it has been found that financial factors can predict risk-adjusted excess returns. For example, the works of Fama and French have shown that using factors such as a company's size and its P/B value ratio is a way to generate risk-adjusted excess returns. Also, some events such as earnings announcements don't always adjust immediately and investors have time to take advantage of the news.

In the Strong form, corporate insiders and stock specialists who work on the exchange floor have generated above-average returns; however, as stated earlier, they are heavily regulated.

Academic literature has measured many types of investments, resulting in ping-pong studies going back and forth on the EMH. Such studies tend to be more sophisticated than just measuring returns against an index, and also include various ways to properly measure true risks. For example, a hedge fund proclaims it beat the S&P 500 Index return of 10 percent with its own return of 12 percent. While on the surface this may seem good, there may be factors that indicate the fund's returns actually prove poor results. The hedge fund could use large leverage, so in an up market you would expect that the increased risk would generate better returns than that of the market. If you adjust for the leverage, you can perhaps see underperformance, especially if the leverage is 2:1. The hedge fund may have a wide dispersion of returns that are negatively skewed in relation to the market return. In downturns the fund may produce results that are much more negative than that of the market.

One measure that can be used to capture these returns on a risk-adjusted basis is the Sharpe ratio. It measures the excess returns of the fund to a risk-free rate and then divides that by the fund's standard deviation. Thus, it is possible if the excess returns are divided by a large standard deviation, the Sharpe is lower and it reflects a poorer measure of performance. For example, an excess return of 7 percent (12 − 5 percent) to the risk-free rate divided by a standard deviation of the fund of 28 percent would yield 0.25. This would be worse than the market's excess return of 5 percent divided by a 15 percent market standard deviation. The market would then show a Sharpe ratio that is higher at 0.33.

In addition, behaviorists could cast doubt on the efficiency of the EMH. The Capital Asset Pricing Model (CAPM) is used to calculate expected returns against the market. It is a basic benchmark of risk-adjusted excess returns used by many financial firms. In this case, the returns that would be adjusted for risk would be the beta. The beta is the volatility of a security to the market—the greater the volatility, the greater the risk.

CAPM measures risk-adjusted excess returns by this formula: Expected returns are equal to the risk-free rate plus the product of the beta multiplied by the excess market return. So, if the risk-free rate is 5 percent and the beta is 2, and excess market return to the risk-free rate is 6 percent, you would get an expected return of 5 percent + 2(6 percent), or 17 percent.

So far, that is easy. However, what is controversial is how the beta is measured. How far back does one go to measure the volatility? There could be new circumstances that change the volatility (such as management changes). In addition, there is a formula where beta is equal to the covariance of the security to the market divided by the variance of the market. This means there is a standard deviation calculation in the formula. Ah, there is the rub. The deviation above the expected return may not equal the deviation below the return. In other words, the volatility and its expectations may not be equal for upside and downside bets. Investors may not be rational on upside and downside risk expectations. They occasionally get greedy for upside or get petrified on the downside and then act accordingly. Thus, the true risk may not be measured. This then leads to adjusting the CAPM for behavioral issues

Then we have other issues, usually copycat ones. For example, if everyone used technical analysis, or say, price to book in fundamental analysis, then all would come to the same price. In some sense this is true, with certain approaches losing their effectiveness if they get a broad following. For example, the January effect of buying distressed tax-loss stocks in December and then flipping them out on the rebound in January has been well exploited.

This will likely not happen in the case of just using technical analysis. First, there are relatively fewer numbers of technical users relative to fundamentalists, who mainly rely on financial data analysis. Even then, there are many different technical approaches, from sentiment to charts to momentum. Not all technicians can agree on the "correct" approach. Even if they do, there is also some subjectivity on the technical measure: Should one use a 200-day MA or a 50-day?

Fundamentalists also have their issues. Some use discounted cash flows, while others use comparable analysis. Even then, some use GAAP data but others use a different type of analysis special sauce to adjust the data.

Fundamental analysis has a longer and more accepted pedigree than technical analysis and behavioral finance. Even though some technical approaches have been known for over 100 years, such as the Dow Theory, most focus has been on the pioneering fundamental work of Graham and Dodd of the 1930s. This is not to say that practitioners did not accept factors such as technical analysis and behavioral analysis around that time, only that their prime approach to evaluating stocks was based on fundamental approaches.

Thus, business schools and financial publications focused on fundamentals. It is the study of financial statements, like income and cash flows, to make proper price valuations. However, some of the financial data may need to be properly interpreted and cannot be taken at face value.

Gradually, technical and behavioral analysis grew in importance (much to the chagrin of some economists who feel that efficient markets don't reward chart gazing or emotions). A few years ago, the Nobel Prize in economics was awarded for work in behavioral finance and the study of investment bubbles. Technicians knew about this for a long time, with references to manias published in the mid-ninetieth century in *Extraordinary Popular Delusions and the Madness of Crowds* by Charles MacKay. The Market Technicians Association has its own exam series for technical analysis. Upon passing, one can earn the Chartered Market Technician designations (CMT). It covers various technical approaches from chart patterns to sentiment, as well as the more exotic approaches of Japanese Candlesticks, Elliott Wave, and Point and Figure charts. We will further discuss the CMT as well as the CFA later in the book. Gradually, technical analysis and behavioral analysis has grown in visibility.

2

BIG QUESTION: WHERE IS THE MARKET GOING?

At this stage, we should do some fusion analysis on a popular topic: market timing. "Where is the market going?" is one of the most discussed questions by investors. Generally, absolute returns are tied to the correct asset allocation. It is felt that this decision accounts for 75 percent, if not all, of the absolute return picture. The explanation is very simple.

For example, if the market rallies sharply and enters a bull market for several years, the investor will do well by being fully invested in a broad stock index. The returns will naturally be better than being invested in traditional, lower-yielding cash returns, such as money market securities. Conversely, in a broad market decline (or a bear market), the investor will do better in cash returns. Selling stocks at the peak and going into cash will obviously produce much better returns than having all assets in stocks and riding them down to lower price levels. This is the "buy low and sell high" theory that any novice can appreciate. But how does one become savvy and able to take advantage of a market turning point?

Similar to some people looking for the fountain of youth, there is no shortage of those attempting the market timing exercise, including thousands of economists and market strategists at mutual funds, brokerage firms, and government offices. In general, they have a collective record that is not good, but still they peck away and get good money for doing it. For example, mutual funds have lots of cash at market bottoms, being hurt by lower yields when stocks rise, and low cash at market tops that could cushion a decline. Economists constantly redo forecasts and miss turning points. They may stay with a broad asset allocation strategy that rebalances strong sectors into weaker sectors in order to maintain some balance of cash and securities. Still others use a bottom-up approach and analyze choice companies with good growth opportunities or special investment situations that are not as dependant on the health of the economy as top-down analysis requires. So they may seek out the company that has a cure for some disease or one that can ride out economic storms with its good growth at a junior stage, such as was the case of McDonald's and Coca-Cola. Of course, the risk is that the economy does better and the company turns into a prune rather than a peach, or worse, a fraud like Enron.

There are many popular approaches to market timing, but in general, positive trends in profits favor the decision to buy stocks with some proper valuation method to ensure that one does not overpay. We shall now return to our Fed model, which can be popular among both fundamentalists and technicians.

Fed Valuation Model Examples

The Fed model (see upcoming figures) attempts to show whether the stock market is over- or undervalued. A major way of making stock market decisions based on competing interest rates is by calculating the forward earnings yield of the S&P 500 Index (expected earnings per share, or EPS, of the S&P 500 Index divided by the S&P 500 Index Price). So, if EPS are $40 and the index is 1000, we get an earnings yield of 4 percent. The Fed model then divides this by the 10-year U.S. government bond yield. Assuming the 10-year yield is 4.5 percent, then the result is 0.04/0.045 = 0.89. Users of the Fed model may then create buy and sell bands that would then indicate cheap or expensive zones for the market.

Though it does have some academic support,[1] not all investors love the Fed model. One objection to the model is that you may see some sort of inflation illusion[2] in the bond yield, so you should use Treasury inflation-protected securities (TIPS) and not a 10-year U.S. government bond to better capture the inflation effect. There are also those who question the forecasted earnings because earnings can be accounting-biased or include many one-time wonders that can distort the true picture. Then we have the bean counters who will adjust and tweak the earnings based on various factors like factory utilization. To overcome fluctuations in the earnings, some may use trailing earnings. Some, like Yale economist Robert Schiller, even take the S&P 500 Index price and compare it to a historical 10-year average of S&P earnings.

In any case, there are various ways to tackle the subject. Note the Fed model in Figure 2.1.

If we concentrate on the period 1999 to 2003, we can see a divergence between forward P/E (dashed line) and bond yield, risk free (black line). Recall the 1999 Internet bubble that showed stocks topping out in early 2000. Yield on bonds was way above the earnings yield as investors continued to buy in anticipation of strong earnings growth. So even though P/Es were

FIGURE 2.1 Earnings Yields (Forward and Trailing), Dividend Yields, and 10-Year Risk-Free Rates for U.S. (1/1976 to 3/2007)

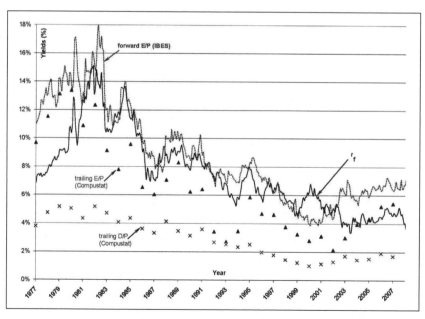

Source: Used by permission of "Don't Fight the Fed Model," Jacob Thomas, Frank Zhang, April, 2008 version, http://www.som.yale.edu/Faculty/jkt7/papers/fedmodel.pdf

FIGURE 2.2 S&P 500 Index, 1997 to 2003

Source: Used by permission of Stockcharts.com

high (or earnings yields rather low), investors kept buying. Once the market
sold off, P/Es went down and the earnings yield went up. We then see more
pessimism on that growth because investors did not want to pay as much
for the earnings when they perceived lower growth prospects. We then see
earnings yields way above bond yields, indicating a good buying opportunity
—the reverse of 2000.

Note in Figure 2.2 the rise and fall of the S&P 500 Index during this
period.

Now note Figure 2.3, which combines the graphs shown in Figures
2.1 and 2.2. With this action, we can fuse the fundamentals and technicals.

A good use of this analysis is by Richard Shaffer, who shows the
range for the period of 1988 to October 2002. So, historically, this
number is more toward the pessimistic end. It is evidenced in the
figure by the red line, which is a threshold for the pessimistic zone, based
on a one-standard deviation range. Of interest are the market extremes
evidenced by the top in 2000 and then the plunge to a low in the fall
of 2002. During this period, the stock market averages plunged where

FIGURE 2.3 Earnings Yields (1/1976 to 3/2007) and S&P 500 (1997 to 2003)

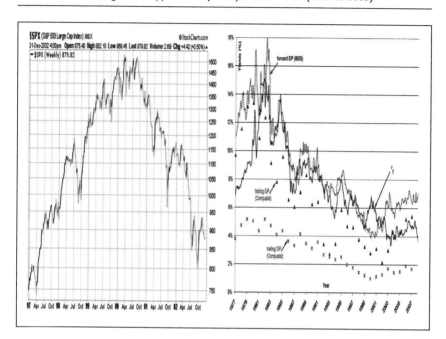

the Dow Jones went from 11,600 in March of 2000 to around 7500 in October 2002.

Notice that the market was showing irrational exuberance around the 2000 top, with the line hitting 0.60. Then at the bottom, it showed irrational pessimism, with a reading of nearly 1.60 in October 2002.

Thus, we have buy and sell signals based on the Fed model. During this period, economists and strategists were rather optimistic at the market top and of course very pessimistic at the bottom. A measure of investor sentiment is from Investors Intelligence, which showed bears over 60 percent near the bottom of 2002, indicating very high pessimism. Technicians would use this as a contrary indicator to buy the market. This then would have been the correct decision.

Compounding the Fed problem is the measure of true economic earnings. The S&P 500 earnings may need to be normalized due to non-recurring events that may distort the picture. For example, large writeoffs may artificially depress earnings and sharply rising oil prices may give

FIGURE 2.4 S&P Earnings Yield vs. 10-Year Treasury Yield (1988–2002)

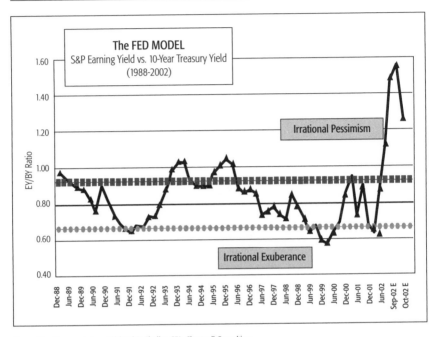

Source: Used by permission of Richard D. Shaffer, CFA, Chartwell Consulting

temporary oil inventory profits. In refining the earnings, Dr. Edward Yardeni may substitute the Moody's A-rated corporate bond to show a better trade-off on fixed income yields versus corporate earnings.[3] Additionally, earnings may be adjusted for capacity issues.

In the recent economic recession of 2008, one also has to consider these issues to get the real earnings. Note the S&P 500 earnings are adjusted for things like AIG's writeoffs on its credit default swaps. When forecasting earnings, one must realize that fundamentally, analysts may reverse prior charge-offs and may even make adjustments for inventory profits of oil companies, once one estimates oil prices. These are only estimates, which means there could be behavioral bias, with those who are optimistic seeing the earnings "glass" as half full and pessimistic forecasters seeing it as half empty. Thus, "half-full" analysts may fill the glass with more earnings than pessimistic ones.

Looking back at Figure 2.4, note that at the market bottom of 2002, when the DOW was around 7500, the Fed model indicated very high market pessimism. As stated, this proved to be an attractive time to buy, as compared to December 1999, when there was high bullishness, with the Dow nearing its high of about 11,600.

Review the detailed explanation of S&P in Table 2.1. (Welcome to half-full glass analysis.) Note the differences between reported and adjusted earnings.

TABLE 2.1 S&Ps Index Services; S&P 500 Earnings and Estimate Report

Source: http://www2.standardandpoors.com/spf/xls/index/SP500EPSEST.XLS

STANDARD & POOR'S INDEX SERVICES

S&P 500 EARNINGS AND ESTIMATE REPORT

As Reported	AIGs record setting Q4,'08 As Reported loss of $-61.7B; -$22.95 per AIG share, $-7.10 index impact (first negative quarter for index ever) 28%, 138 of the 486 As Reported EPS are negative; **index lost more this quarter than it ever made 49 issues with mega-$billon losses**
Operating	AIG Operating loss of $-28.2B (record); $-10.49 per AIG share, $-3.24 index impact (first negative quarter for index ever) 20%, 99 of 494 Operating EPS are negative; 18 issues with mega-$billon losses $-5.2B loss for the quarter, with $-101.3B from the Financials; Non-Financials therefore positive
Sales	**Sales (based on reported current membership) are down -8.78%; 42% higher Y/Y (avg +6.64%), 58% lower (avg -18.12%)**
P/E	Massive charges warp P/Es (field H33), forward numbers more important - but many investors have a lack of trust in the estimates
Commentary	Cash flow now high priority, dividend cuts to 'preserve cash', ride out the storm-> companies are worried No major shift in estimates yet as stimulus/TARP/housing/budget details come out Howard Silverblatt, S&P Senior Index Analyst

Data as of the close of:	03/25/09
S&P 500 close of:	813.88
Dividend yield (last 12 months: Feb,'08)	3.43%
Dividend yield (indicated rate)	2.70%

QUARTER END ESTIMATES	PRICE	OPERATING EARNINGS PER SHR (ests are bottom up)	AS REPORTED EARNINGS PER SHR (ests are top down)	OPERATING EARNINGS PER SHR (ests are top down)	OPERATING EARNINGS P/E (ests are bottom up)	AS REPORTED EARNINGS P/E (ests are top down)	OPERATING EARNINGS P/E (ests are top down)
						(estimated P/Es use current price)	
12/31/2010			$8.77	$11.79		19.62	16.80
09/30/2010			$9.79	$11.50		19.78	16.66
06/30/2010			$11.63	$12.88		20.26	16.32
03/30/2010			$11.30	$12.27		21.83	16.42
12/31/2009		$17.61	$8.43	$12.19	13.05	23.43	16.60
09/31/2009		$16.79	$8.81	$12.54	18.23	258.37	22.16
06/31/2009		$14.96	$8.75	$12.57	18.58	199.97	20.28
03/31/2009		$13.00	$8.75	$11.72	17.74	99.50	18.25
12/31/2008 (99%)	903.25	−$0.11	−$23.16	−$0.11	16.45	54.37	16.45
					18.25	60.34	18.25
						(12/08 P/E if based on 12/08 price)	

Source: Standard and Poor's 500 Earnings and Estimate Report

Also note the differences between top-down and bottom-up approaches. For example, 12/31/09 operating earnings shows a large spread between reported ($8.43) and presumed analyst earnings ($12.19) per share, not to mention differences between top-down and bottom-up forecasts for 2009. Then we have the huge P/E ratios of 258.37 for 9/30/09 and 199.97 for 6/30/09, which reflect Q4 2008 AIG losses. The analysts smoothed these out to get a P/E of 22.16 for 9/30/09 and 20.2 for 6/30/09.

Realize that others will fine-tune these earnings, and so when we do our Fed model ratios, we have potential "spin city" on the earnings, the P/E, and the valuation. As mentioned, some economists (such as Schiller of Yale) use a 10-year average of trailing earnings to get a market P/E for valuation, while others use cash flows, EBITADA, and so forth. So what you see in earnings may not be real!

Once we make reasonable earnings estimates, we can use the Fed model. We will now bring in the other factors as we fuse the technical and fundamental approaches.

Moving Average Convergence-Divergence

The moving average convergence-divergence, or MACD (see Figure 2.5), shows buy points for the S&P 500 Index (top chart) as it approaches deeply oversold conditions in late September 2001 and mid-July 2002. Note the positive divergence of the MACD, as the market low in October 2002 was not confirmed by the MACD that made a higher low. Here you can also use the S&P 500 Index as the market proxy. Note that the October 11, 2002, low in the market had a positive divergence in the MACD. So the attractive fundamental valuation of the Fed model was confirmed by technical indicators, such as the MACD. Note the positive divergence of the MACD. The market is bottoming in October 2002, but the MACD makes a higher high. During this time, sentiment figures from Investors Intelligence surveys also reported a very high level of bears.

We can also use a quant model on absolute P/E ratios. For example, the market has trended in a range of 10 to 20 times earnings, where 10 times is cheap and 20 gets to be expensive, as Figure 3.1 will show. During this period (1997-2003) the market P/E went way over 20 at the top.

Another use is the T. Rowe small-cap valuation model, where the P/E of small-cap stocks relative to large cap shows a good buying opportunity

FIGURE 2.5 S&P 500, July 2000 to December 2002

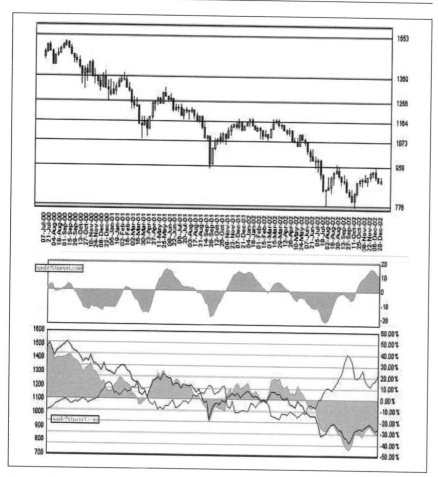

Source: Used by permission of Mr. Greg Campbell, tradeNtravel.com

near one time and overvaluation near two times. (As discussed, all of this supposes correct earnings measurement.)

The next question is whether or not fundamentals can conflict with technical and behavioral in terms of signals. Note that the fundamentals may indicate good or bad earnings and technicals may indicate the opposite. For example, in the 2002 bottom, earnings were downgraded by the fundamentalists and dire outlooks emerged. Yet the technicals showed positive signals, such as the low bull sentiment, the non-confirmation of the MACD, and so on. The bottom chart shows the undervaluation (shaded area in the

FIGURE 2.6 S&P 500, July 2000 to December 2002–MACD Positive Divergence

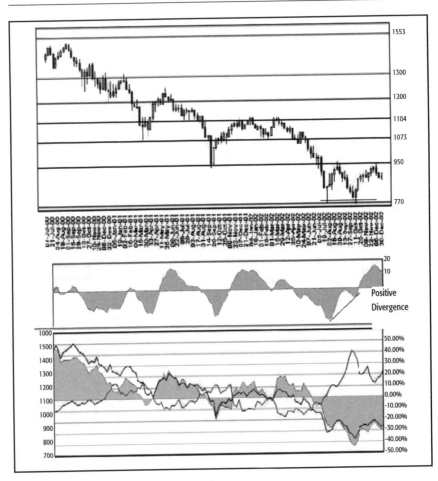

Source: Used by permission of Mr. Greg Campbell, tradeNtravel.com

readings) with potential gain (lower line with left scale) of the S&P 500 Index (upper line with left scale). So in the fall of 2002, the shaded area was large and the line (lower line with left scale) showed positive returns as high as 40 percent when the S&P 500 Index approached the bottom of 800. This compares to overvaluation in the period July 2000 to October 2000, when the lower line (with left scale) indicated negative returns. Soon after, the market that topped out near 1500 started its slide to the bottom.

Herd, Trends, and Contrary Opinion

Since many funds run a top-down approach, they usually require setting a consensus opinion by committee or chain of command. For example, there may be a strategist, economist, portfolio manager, and other professionals on an investment committee to determine the market outlook. The questions about this committee are many: Are they groupthink? Do they act independently or are they yes-men to a leader who controls their future career opportunities? Can junior officers tell a senior officer (or boss) that they disagree with her opinion? Is it easier to cave in to groupthink and not rock the boat? Also, what if the client feels one way and the manager another? What if the client feels this is not a good time to invest and wants to be in cash? Do you antagonize a client or do you say something like "Yes, let's watch the market and get in when times are better"? As the group starts to think the same way, we see signs of herd thinking introducing a possible trend development.

Groupthink

Groupthink has been examined in various studies, including the popular work of Solomon Asch dealing with a line measuring experiment.

FIGURE 2.7 Line Measuring Experiment

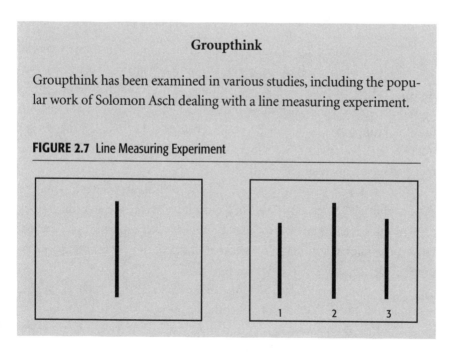

Suppose you have to decide among the lines in the right box of Figure 2.7. Which one best matches the height of the line in the left box? By eyeballing the lines, one can only come to the conclusion that line 2 is the correct one, though the others are rather close.

Now suppose one subject was in a room with some people who were told ahead of time, without the subject's knowledge, to choose an incorrect line the majority of the time (say, 12 out of 18). The unknowing subject has been told that this experiment tested some sort of visual accuracy, but the actual purpose is to see if the person caves to the group or stands his ground, considering the others delusional. Surprisingly, the subject did conform to the misleading groupthink solution 36.8 percent of the time. If one disagreed with one individual, there was a tendency to hold one's ground, but if one was alone and the number of differing opinions increased, then one conformed more to the view of the majority, caving in to a herd mentality.

There are some key reasons for conforming in the investment world. You wish to be correct, even if you do not know the answer. So, if the group thought is that oil prices will go down, then your stating that oil prices will indeed go down will garner some respect, especially if you use the reasons that the group does. Additionally, you may wish to be accepted (or at least not rejected). You may not wish to make waves. Having a groupthink opinion means that you are easily accepted.

So, it is not surprising to see record attendance at companies or themes that play to groupthink. For example, one may see a popular stock presentation reach maximum capacity in a hotel meeting room or a real estate professional command overflow attendance to hear pointers on flipping properties quickly to make money.

This groupthink may spill into broad food chains, such as private equity funds. Let's say investors feel commercial real estate is a bargain. The groupthink at the private equity fund may insist on buying more properties and even stretching the valuations a bit. Now, the clients may ask you to take more money, as some clients like endowments and Public Employment

Retirement System (PERS) accounts have already received groupthink green lights from their advisers and boards. The bankers who will lend to complete the deals will also beg you to consider larger deals with larger loans, because they too have the groupthink green light. More loans mean more bonus monies; more assets under management mean more fees. Also, we get "winners" wanting to associate with "winners." Bragging at a cocktail party that a certain hedge fund manages your money may elicit peer praise for your cunning, since "all" know that is the correct way to invest.

This eventually can lead to bubbles that behaviorists are familiar with and that technicians already know as prominent market tops. Thus, technicians would use contrary opinion (the "masses are asses" it is sometimes said). While you can be more of an individual, market action seems to indicate that collectively we actually act like sheep when it comes to sentiment data and chasing the next hot investment idea.

Stock market forecasting has been shown to fool the experts, and even popular sites caution that picking the market move could be the equivalent of flipping a coin.[4] While some forecasters are good, some are bad—so they tend to cancel each other out. Some forecasters change their opinions as the market moves up or down, thus creating the same effect as holding on to the tail of a galloping horse. Strategists on Wall Street tend to be biased on bullishness in order to comfort investors who place their trust in the firm's sales forces or brokers. Academic studies follow measures of beta and cash ownership as proxy for bullishness or bearishness. Technicians also use the cash as a proxy for bullishness and bearishness.

Sentiment in 2008

It is interesting to see that just before the great market meltdown of 2008, strategists were highly bullish. *Barron's* surveyed about a dozen analysts who expected higher stock prices in 2008, though their estimated gains varied widely, from 3 percent to 18 percent. On average, the group "saw" the S&P 500 at 1640 by the end of next year, or about 10 percent higher than the recent 1486. The bulls' argument was based on global growth and lower interest rates.

"We expect the U.S. economy to show the strains of the deflating housing market and credit-market disruptions in early 2008," said Goldman Sachs strategist Abby Joseph Cohen. But "recession likely will be avoided, due to strength in exports and capital spending by corporations and government."

Credit Suisse equity strategist Jonathan Morton said, "Conditions for a hard economic landing—like slack in the labor market and weak balance sheets—are still largely absent."

Barron's suggested that overseas investment valuations were too high. Richard Bernstein, chief investment strategist at Merrill Lynch, also thought the overseas exodus was overdone.[5]

The S&P 500 Index actually did not go up, but fell sharply to close 2008 below 1000, far from the 1640 that had been forecast.

Going into the 2002 market decline, some key strategists surveyed by Barron's magazine got it all wrong. As one analyst writes, "At the 2001 Barron's Roundtable, two of the 12 forecasters were close to the actual market year-end close. In 2002, two of 11 Barron's Roundtable participants were close. In the 2000 issue of BusinessWeek, 52 of the 55 experts (95 percent) who forecast the year-end level of the S&P 500 were wrong. At the beginning of 2002, BusinessWeek again held their survey of 'the smartest players on Wall Street.' The consensus forecast of the 54 participants for the S&P 500 was 1292. The actual close was 32 percent lower at 880. Not a single esteemed participant came close to the actual close."[6]

By the fall of 2002, the economy was hurting and the stock averages were continuing to decline from the prior year closing. (This was after the decline in 2001.) In December of 2001, Daniel L. Thornton, vice president and economic advisor of the Federal Reserve Bank of St. Louis, indicated that prior consensus of economic growth was marked down considerably. He mentioned that, for example, "the September Blue Chip consensus forecast of economic growth for the third and fourth quarters of 2001 were 1.6 and 2.6 percent, respectively—not a hint of a recession." Of course, 9/11 caused a blow to the economy and the economic mood of the country. Then, as Thornton stated, "the October Blue Chip Consensus forecast for the third and fourth quarters of 2001 were revised sharply down to –0.6 percent and –1.3 percent, respectively. This single event appears to have caused the Blue Chip forecasters to revise their outlook for economic growth in the last half of the year by more than 3 percentage points—from 2.1 percent to –1.0 percent."[7] The pessimistic downgrade of outlooks was definitely sparked by 9/11, and this mood put wind into the downtrend.

The situation worsened, as Thornton stated, "Whether preemptive or not, the relatively large and aggressive cuts in the target for the funds rate appear to have had only a modest effect on economic activity. Despite reducing the funds rate target by 275 basis points by the end of June 2001, the economy continued to slip deeper into the recession—and things appear to have gotten worse, not better. Just last week the estimate of real GDP growth in the third quarter was revised down from –0.3 percent to –1.1 percent. Moreover, most analysts believe that the fourth quarter growth will be slower still."

This must have pressed upon the market bottom in the fall of 2002. While Thornton forecast an economic rebound for 2003, he was more guarded on its strength, saying, "Overall, I believe the economic outlook is rather good. Spurred by technology, I anticipate that during the next economic expansion, which will likely begin in the first half of 2002, economic growth will average close to 3.5 percent. This is historically rapid growth, but much slower than the 4.25 percent output growth during the latter part of the 1990s. I expect the economy will get a boost from monetary and fiscal policy in 2002, but not beyond. However, the boost may be largely or completely offset by the fact that economic growth in the rest of the world appears to be slowing."

So we have slightly optimistic economic outlooks at the top and relatively pessimistic ones near the bottom, yet technically we see something else. Remember, this is the bottom of the market after the Internet bubble burst in 2000. We went from great bullishness to bearishness where fundamental outlooks were downgraded considerably. Many who bought Internet companies bought companies with little, if any, sales and earnings. They were called "dream" stocks.

FIGURE 2.8 S&P 500 SPDRs (SPY), August 2002 to July 2003

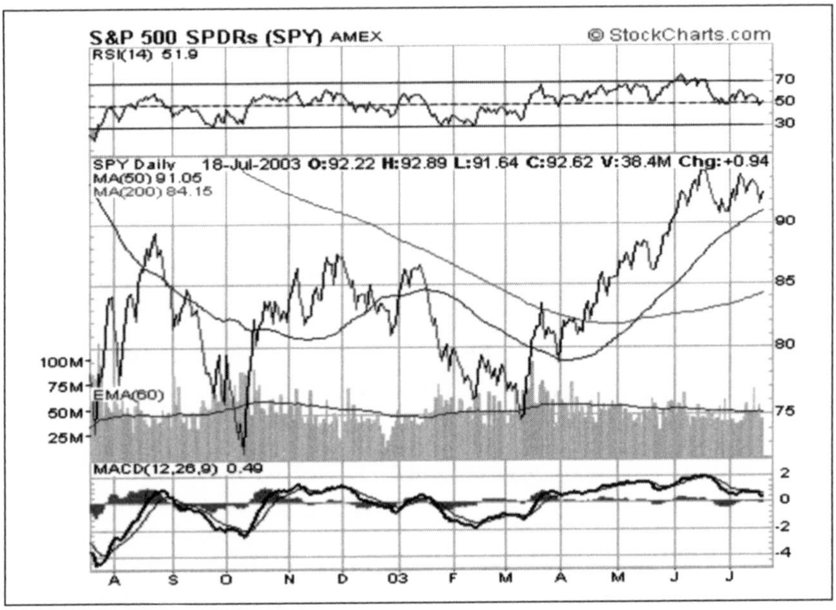

Source: Used by permission of Stockcharts.com

Notice in Figure 2.8 that the S&P 500 Index made a bottom in October 2002. We then had another bottom, but not a new low, in March 2003. If we connect the bottoms, the MACD was actually trending up. There is also a positive divergence, where the low in March exceeded the low in February 2003, but note that the lows in the MACD were higher. This, as we mentioned, is called a divergence, and it was positive as the lower lows of the index were not confirmed by the index.

If we look at the Bear and Bull indicators of the Investor's intelligence surveys in Figure 2.9, we see that the Bulls were very low at the bottom. Note that the difference between the Bulls and Bears was at a very low level of over –10. This extreme pessimism would also lead technicians to use contrary opinion to buy stocks and not sell stocks.

As mentioned, sentiment is not an exact timing tool as technicians will smooth the data. It may indicate that soon the market will go in the opposite direction, but not necessarily the next day or next week.

FIGURE 2.9 S&P 500 Index, 2001 to 2004

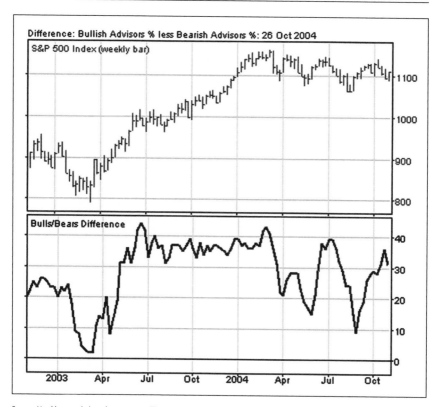

Source: Used by permission of Investors Intelligence as advertised on their website: www.investorsintelligence.com

During this period of pessimism there were already positive factors indicating a market turn to the upside. Later in April, we see another buy signal when the index went over the 200-day moving average. In May 2003, we get another buy signal as the 50-day moving average crossed above the 200-day line. Technicians call this the moving average approach double crossover method (Murphy, 2003).

3

TECHNICAL AND FUNDAMENTAL DECISION

At this stage, the key questions are these: Which method should lead and be used first—technicals or fundamentals, and why? In other words, at the bottom or top, are you more likely to follow a fundamental outlook or a technical outlook? At the bottom or top, investors are still cautious and are skeptical of the market rally that is common in the beginning stages of a bull market. Technicians call this "climbing a Wall of Worry," which is bullish for rising stock prices.

Does it take time to change opinions on a fundamental basis? Would fundamentalists gradually see the glass as half full the higher the market rose? James Montier, author and global equity strategist (previously at Dresdner Kleinwort Wasserstein in London), indicates in his behavioral comments that analysts tend to move their cash flow estimates with the market direction. They may anchor a stock's valuation to the existing market price.[1] Does this mean they come to the same investment solution at the time the market direction changes? Is there a possibility that the fundamental data doesn't support the technicals that may lead market moves? It would seem that you would buy in anticipation of a market move; however, at this point a portfolio manager may wonder whether her analyst is really adding value or is just reporting what she's read in the newspaper or seen on TV. Imagine if the technician is pounding on the table regarding positive indicators of non-confirmation or sentiment, while the fundamentalist is parroting statistics in relation to the slow economy, such as unemployment levels and weak production. To answer these questions, we have to review the concepts of fundamentals, technicals, behavioral, and quant, recalling their various approaches and uncertainties.

Although picking the market direction may look easy based on ads we see regarding the sound judgment of various strategists, it most likely is a reflection of groupthink. I am often asked, "If all traders see this way, why don't they buy at the bottom?" First, not all analysts or portfolio managers use the same valuation model. One may look at earnings, some variation of earnings, or even cash flow. But even with these different types of valuation, the fundamental model may show overvaluation or undervaluation. However, here comes the rub. While the model shows one thing, it can always be second-guessed with the comment, "It's different this time." It is possible that emotions will cause investors to look the other way. If this is the case, and the model shows a sell, it is likely they would keep buying or at least not sell. This was the rationale in both 1929 and 1999, as we entered new eras, thinking that the old rules no longer held. The same rationale was used to buy Japanese stocks near the top of Nikea, 30,000 in 1990. While P/E multiple were much greater than that of the United States, investors chased the Japanese stocks as if the old valuation rules didn't apply anymore. This was because many funds missed the boat on the Japanese stock rise in the late 1980s.

On a longer-term basis we can see the buy and sell signals of a 52-week moving average. Usually, technicians will grapple with the best moving average for a time period, as too short a period will result in whipsaws and excess transaction costs. They will stay with the decision until the moving averages give a contrary signal. So, if the stocks fall below the 200-day moving average, then a sell signal occurs. The technicals recommend to stay with the trend, as tops and bottoms are usually overdone. Things that are cheap may get cheaper, and things that are expensive may get even more expensive.

During a period of a sharply rising and then falling market, can investors behaviorally buck the trend or will they get sucked into it? Sometimes the knowledge that seems to indicate similarities to past market volatilities does not accurately identify a turning point. This was seen in Alan Greenspan's famous speech on irrational exuberance (the wording was borrowed from Professor Schiller) on December 6, 1996, when he warned of a top in the stock market that was fundamentally overvalued. Although stocks immediately fell, they later recovered and went much higher over the next few years.

Investors can't believe the market is going up with bad news out there, and there is disbelief that the market is going down while the economy is still sound. We hear that it is only a healthy correction; bargains are back again, and so forth. Some technicians call this the "Slope of Hope," as the market keeps the investors in as it continues to erode. The opposite of keeping investors out on the way up with the Wall of Worry. This cycle of fear and greed hurts investors through their purchases at tops and sales at bottoms.

For a few years after the peak, there was disbelief of the market decline after the 1929 top. Government officials and brokerage firms felt that it was only a correction and the economy was sound. Irving Fisher's "Permanently High Plateau" call just before the 1929 crash claimed that the market was on the brink of a long-term upward movement. Unfortunately, a few days later the market crashed and started its long journey to the 1932 low. The same occurred for the 1972, 2002, and 2007 tops. Consider the housing bubble, which surprised many by showing declining housing prices. The flippers certainly felt like they put their finger in the electric socket. Behaviorally, sellers of homes felt they could not part with their houses at declining prices and held on, only to see further price erosion. Thus, they fell into the Disposition Effect—that is, the experience of selling winners too soon and holding losers too long.[2]

Traders and Investors

Generally, trading is for professionals, as the transaction costs often kill the hope of any profit for the amateur. More professional traders use sophisticated trading systems that may include technical indicators such as Stochastics, Elliott Wave, and other more exotic methods.

In the late 1990s, we saw the entrance of day traders who started to account for a significant (over 10 percent) portion of exchange and NASDAQ trading. Many were amateurs who absorbed high transaction costs on the belief that they knew what they were doing. Some agreed to a certain number of trades per day at specified commission rates. Some took a discount brokerage firm's one- or two-hour technical analysis course that supposedly gave the trader all the secrets of making money. As can be expected, many exited the business with heavy losses.

The North American Securities Administrators Association reported, "70% of public traders will not only lose, but will almost certainly lose everything they invest. ... only 11.5% of the accounts reviewed evidenced the ability to conduct profitable short-term trading."[3] Commercials showed how easy it was to make money in trading. Online brokerage opportunities removed the human broker who could hold an enthusiastic trader more in check. Later we saw similar themes in FX trading and real estate flipping.

In 2010, it was reported by the *New York Times* that day trading had somewhat returned.[4] Quoting brokerage firm Charles Schwab, the *New York Times* reported trades at one-half of the levels of 2000. (Schwab was a pioneer in cutting trading commissions, but today offers a broad array of financial services.) Citing a pending study of tens of millions of trades in Taiwan over the years 1992 to 2006, Brad M. Barber, a finance professor at the University of California, Davis, said that "only 1% of the traders were profitable."

Trading should not be confused with the trading desks of major brokerage firms. Some of these trades are proprietary ones where gains and losses can be earned on specialized trading strategies. There are also agency trades where firms can make good money just by matching orders and getting some spread. On May12, 2010, the *New York Times* reported that four big banks scored a perfect 61-day run of making money: Bank of America, Citibank, Goldman Sachs, and JP Morgan. Each finished this time period without a single day's loss. While this is hard to constantly do, in theory, one can continue this by making trades at one's bid and ask. For example, a customer would buy near the ask of 10 and sell near the bid of 9.75. The market maker (or the banks) would make a 0.25 profit. One can easily see that amateur traders can be the food for the better-placed banks who just want their cut.

The poor, amatuer traders cannot make a market, as they are too small and have little capital (not to mention the regulatory requirements). They must actually buy low and sell high on speculation of future price changes. This is generally not a successful result for the amateur trader.

If we use monthly moving averages, being in the market at the bottom in the early nineties gave us a nice profit when prices fell below the monthly moving average in early 2001. Usually, more volatile prices are better shown in log scale, as a 5-point move on a base of 50 is less as a percentage (10 percent) than 5 points on a base of 25 (20 percent). Once again, we need a trending market to benefit from moving average analysis, and we certainly see the rise and fall of the SPDR S&P 500 ETF (SPY), as it more than doubled off the bottom and then fell by over one-third from its 2000 peak.

We did see trending markets in history such as in 1929, 1970, and 2000, but during those periods, market analysis of valuation used various tools to determine cheapness. Certainly, one measure is the P/E ratio of the market itself, where 20 times earnings is the borderline for expensive and 10 times is the borderline for cheapness (see Figure 3.1). Extremeness of the valuations tend to be near the crossover of long-term moving averages.

FIGURE 3.1 P/E of S&P 500: Price Dividend by 10-Year Real Earnings, 1880–2004

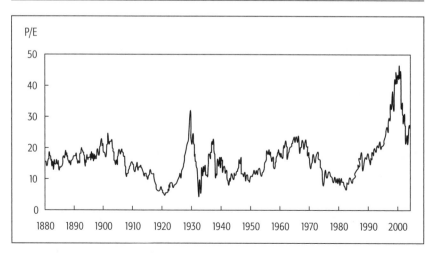

Source: Used by permission of Clifford S. Asness, "The Future Role of Hedge Funds," *CFA Institute*, June 2006, p 2

TABLE 3.1 P/E Range in Relation to the Real Stock Market Return in the Next 10 Years, January 1927–February 2004

P/E Range	Real Stock Market Return in the Next 10 Years	
	Median (annual)	Worst (total)
5.2–10.1	10.9%	46.1%
10.1–11.9	10.7	32.0
11.9–14.6	10.0	4.0
14.6–17.2	7.6	−20.9
17.2–19.9	5.3	−32.0
19.9–31.7	−0.1	−35.5

Note: P/Es are based on current price divided by the average of the past 10 years' earnings adjusted for inflation.

Source: Clifford S. Asness, "The Future Role of Hedge Funds," *CFA Institute*, June 2006, p. 2

Historically, when the S&P 500 P/E exceeds 20, as it did in 2000 by a great margin, subsequent stock market returns in the next 10 years tend to be poor.[5] See Table 3.1.

In using a monthly moving average, a buy and sell decision is easy to ascertain. One is long in 1994 and only sells in early 2001 as the index drops below the 36-month moving average. Once again, here it works because we have a major trend. If there was a lesser trend or even flat price movement, then the monthly would not be that useful. While technicians may constantly experiment with shorter moving averages, they run the risk of getting too many transaction costs with whipsaws, or longer ones that become less useful if trends don't materialize. It appears that the 200-day trend line is a major one used by technical market analysts, but some others that are close to the 200 days are used as well.

Going back to a daily, they would also use a 50-day moving average. When it crosses the 200-day line (at a later time period where the black line goes over the grey in March 2003), it further confirms the buy signal and is called a Golden Cross. When it goes below, it confirms a sell signal and is called a Black Cross. Some technicians will use only the crossing of the 200-day line as a buy and sell signal, as this tends to be the most significant. Others will wait for the cross effect to get more confirmation, but then suffer the risk of paying higher prices. Still others will wait to see the 200 trend line in an upward direction—also for a better confirmation. The direction of the 200-day line is not important, as a downward line that is upwardly crossed by stock prices still gives a buy signal.

> You can use exponential moving averages where more recent data is weighted more than distant data. They turn up or down sooner than an ordinary moving average where all data is equally weighted. You can set boundaries for various moving average lengths that give further buy or sell signals. These are called envelopes. These can lead to more exotic measures such as Bollinger Bands that incorporate statistical standard deviation analysis. For traders, you can use triple cross averages with much shorter 4–9–18 days. A technical analysis book will cover these strategies in detail.

Moving averages have been tested many different ways, but simple analysis of crossing the 200-day line to get a buy or sell decisions gives some useful confirmation.

The moving average challenges the Weak Form of the Efficient Markets model. In college texts, one can review information indicating the 200-day moving average is effective in generating buy and sell signals. Nobel Prize winner William F. Sharpe presents this information in his finance textbook.[6] Using a 200-day average, there was statistical significance based on 25,000 trading days, using the DJIA, where the difference between buy and sell decisions was 16.8 percent—statistically significant from zero. Buy is where price exceeds the 200-day average price; sell is where price is less than the 200-day average price.

As stated, there is never 100 percent certainty with any technical measure, as it is based on tendencies or probabilities. Hence, technicians will most likely blend more than one indicator. Also, given various uses of the moving average, one may see various forms of confirmation or even non-confirmation in academic journals. No matter, it is a foundation tool of technicians, and it is often used as a talking point on the business programs.

In looking at this exercise, we can see a possible conflict between technicals and fundamentals. Technically we get buy signals, yet fundamentally we have grave outlooks from the strategists. In addition, traders and longer-term investors may also view markets differently.

The Head and Shoulder Pattern

Technicians have various tools like the Head and Shoulders (HS) indicator for determining market turning points. Fundamentally, market P/E ratios of 20 or higher indicate excess valuations and turning points. This happened in late 1999 when the S&P P/E went way above 20 and the NASDAQ topped 40. One can also do relative P/E ratios of small versus large cap stocks. This analysis has been done for years by T. Rowe Price. When small-cap P/E ratios approach twice the P/E of large cap, they tend to be overvalued and subsequently underperform large caps stocks. Near 10, they tend to do well and are very attractive.

Figure 3.2 examines the Dow Theory. It is one of the earliest technical theories that attempts to measure market turning points via confirmations and the use of volume. While not used by all technicians, it still has a good following.

Note that as the Dow and Rails (now known as Transportation) Index rise, there is confirmation of an uptrend (see Figure 3.2). Then we see that the Dow makes new highs, but the Rails do not confirm. This is a caution signal that the uptrend may be reversing. The Dow is the first to signal a bear trend at point A, as a prior low is violated. However, this bear trend is not confirmed until the Rails also make a subsequent low at point B. Note that at point B, the Dow is already well off its high. It does not get the exact tops and bottoms. However, even with those limitations it has done well in its performance.

Looking at Figures 3.3 and 3.4, you see that the Dow (using the ETF for the Dow, DIA. The DIA ETF is 1/100th of the index) peaked in early 2000, but its high was not confirmed by new highs in the Dow Jones Transports. The Transports were near 3500 in August 1999, but when the Dow made a high in early 2000, the Transports were only at the 3000 level. A sell signal was created when the Transportation Index confirmed

FIGURE 3.2 Dow Theory Stresses General Market Trends

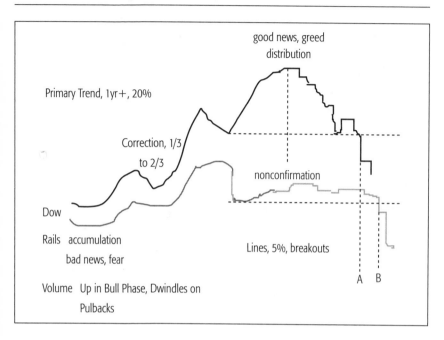

FIGURE 3.3 Diamonds (DIA), June 23, 2000

Source: Used by permission of Stockcharts.com

FIGURE 3.4 Dow Jones Transportation Average, June 23, 2000

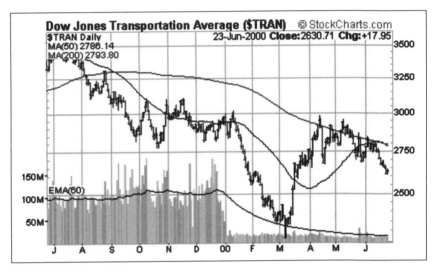

Source: Used by permission of Stockcharts.com

the subsequent low in the Dow in March 2001. (Thereafter, the market made a broad and severe decline from the Dow of around 11,000 in early 2000 to the mid–7000s by late 2002.)

While many technicians still use the Dow Theory, some do not use it as their primary approach. Still others have modified the Dow Theory and substituted the S&P 500 Index and the Russell 2000 Index to reflect the largest companies with the smaller company growth prospects.

More recently, bullish outlooks at the end of 2007 surprised analysts with a crushing market drop. They had fundamental reasons, but were those reasons in conflict with technicals? Technicians say, "Things that are cheap, can get cheaper, and things that are expensive, can get more expensive." In December 2007, *Barron's* surveyed leading analysts who were fundamentally bullish on the market. However, what ominous chart pattern was developing? Did it give a measurement rule for the downside?

From Figure 3.5, we can see a HS pattern, with the left shoulder around July 2007, the head in September and the right shoulder in November. Technically, this is a sell signal. (While this has been well supported in research, it does not happen that often.)

FIGURE 3.5 Dow Jones Industrial Average, August 25, 2008

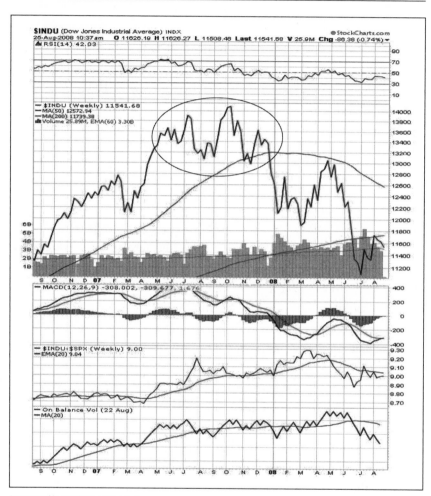

Source: Used by permission of Stockcharts.com

There are various reasons why the HS pattern demonstrates a sell signal. The uptrend is broken as we enter the right shoulder. Then it comes after an up move. (Inverse HS would be opposite and come after a down move.) As investors miss the rise by climbing a Wall of Worry, they finally get their feet wet in the left shoulder. Once they see the peak exceeded by the head, they get giddy. In order to make up for lost ground, they pile in—usually with margin purchases. Finally, the right shoulder is the last bastion of hope but disappoints as the new high is not met.

A quick look at the HS pattern in Figure 3.5 shows the head is 14,200 minus the 12,900 neckline, leaving 1300. Subtract 1300 from December's 12,900 and we get the price objective of 11,600, which was hit by June 2008. Of course, the market went even lower and there is nothing to say it can't continue to move in that direction. It can also base and then rally, but this measurement tool gives a realistic, immediate price goal. That means long-term investors may be scaling down or moving out and traders should start covering their shorts.

For example, a trader may short around 12,900 by using the Dow Diamonds (DIA) ETF and then cover at 11,600. Since there is no 100 percent certainty, you may short, but hedge with calls at about the 13,000 strike. My rule of thumb is that the calls should be near term with little Theta or time value, since HS patterns tend to create quick, near-term drops. I would also buy close to strike prices at the neckline, as this may be the key resistance level. Finally, a 3:1 ratio is desired, or the downside should at least give three times the reward as the cost of the call. So if one translates to ETFs, if the drop is 13 points, a call cost of 1.3 would be attractive for strike only one or two months out, as this is 10:1. For example, if the analyst is using an option valuator and assuming a strike of 130, the current price is 129, with two months expiry and a standard deviation of 20 percent for the Dow, 3 percent interest rates, and 2 percent dividend yield, then the cost of the call is calculated as $3.81. So the ratio is 13 to 3.81, or over 3.4 times. Of course, one would have to make a probability analysis to see how many times this works and how many times it does not. Since HS is considered fairly predictable, it would be a good play in this situation. (Readers may be interested in reviewing the 1929 stock chart which shows an HS with a downward-sloping neckline along with subsequent, sharply lower prices.)

Fundamentals or Technicals and the NASDAQ Market

Once again, which method would market timers be more comfortable with: fundamentals or technicals? So far, we have used the S&P 500 Index for our analysis. We will now do the same for the NASDAQ and then later, make our next level of analysis by combining both.

Why would an investor be interested in the NASDAQ as compared to the S&P 500 Index? The answer to this question introduces style strategies and the concepts for investing that go along with those strategies. Some investors favor growth stocks and others favor value. Still others wish to exploit their differences, as they may get close together or far apart in terms of price performance.

The NASDAQ is more growth oriented, as it tends to have more technology and growth service stocks. Growth stocks are noted for higher P/E ratios and p/book ratios, as well as growth rates. Value stocks tend to be lower than growth stocks in growth, P/B, and P/E ratios.

Generally, when the S&P 500 Index is compared to the NASDAQ, professionals most often use common index construction methods to compare growth versus value. Some may use the various Russell indices: the Russell 2000 Index, the Russell 2000 Growth, and also a Value Index. Others may lean toward the FT (Financial Times) or the S&P indices.

The Russell indices can be used as a common base for evaluating large and small companies and value and growth. The Russell indices are also used by funds who wish to passively invest in a specific index. On their Web site in 2010, Russell indicated that over $4.3 trillion are indexed against the Russell indices. This means that this money is invested in a manner to replicate certain indices. This is usually done with very low fees and offers a better result for investors who find they most likely will underperform in the indices when paying higher fees for active management.

The largest universe is the Russell 3000 Index that tracks the 3000 largest companies by market cap. This covers 98 percent of the investable U.S. equity. The Russell 2000 Index is the smallest 2000 companies and the primary measure for the U.S. small-cap index, which accounts for 8 percent of the Russell 3000 Index.[7]

As to value and growth indices, on its Web site, Russell categorizes "higher price-to-book ratios and higher forecasted growth values (growth companies) and lower price-to-book ratios and lower forecasted growth values (value companies). When company stock characteristics don't allow for absolute style distinction, Russell's indices represent them as both growth and value stocks."

Usually there are more specifics on cutoff points by the various index providers on growth and value. One criticism of these categories is the judgment on what is growth and value beyond the P/B and growth ratios. Also, in bull markets, the index may get "too growth" and in bear markets "too value," as the ratios tend to expand or contract. Thus, some managers may see Microsoft as a large-cap growth stock, while others view it as a large-cap value stock. Then we get into spin accounting.

Jumping into various strategy styles and market sizes can enhance a portfolio; this is called "performance drift." At this point, the correlation to the benchmark index decline and agencies like Morningstar may start to label the fund as mid-cap or even large-cap as compared to the fund's own classification of small-cap. Sophisticated institutional investors may see through this smoke, but the average retail investor may not, especially if the fund just bends a little. The extra performance pick up could be the difference between being in the top half of one's competitors or the bottom half.

Let's review the Russell 2000 Index in Table 3.2.

When comparing small-cap indices such as the Russell 2000 Index, we see Value has a price/book of 1.22, which is less than the Growth's 2.74. The P/E 19.2 for Growth is greater than 15.8 for Value. Also, the forecasted growth from IBES is 16.48 for Growth versus 9.17 for Value. We can make the same comparison for large cap. In this comparison, note that negative earnings are excluded from P/E.

Some would use NASDAQ as more of a proxy for growth with companies such as Apple. But of course there is always controversy over which companies truly have above-average growth rates in earnings. The Russell indices show the difference in performance on a year-by-year basis from the style performance.[8] In 2009, for example, the Russell 2000 Value Index

TABLE 3.2 Style Indexes, Russell 2000, Small Cap

Broad Market	P/B	Dividend Yield	P/E (X-neg Earnings)	IBES LT Growth	Largest Sector
Russell 2000 Value	1.22	1.9	15.8	9.17	Financial Services
Russell 2000 Growth	2.74	0.5	19.2	16.48	Health Care

Source: Russell Investments, January 31, 2010

returned 20.58 percent. However, it would have been nice to have dipped a toe in the Russell 2000 Growth Index of 34.47.

Assume your manager exactly matched the Value Index with the same risk within the stated benchmark. Obviously he cannot justify a management fee for a job well done, because there was no job done. Just matching the index can be replicated with the ETF called IWN. Now, if the manager puts 10 percent of the portfolio into the growth category, (IWO) you can pick up an extra 1.39 percent (10 percent of 34.47–20.58). Hey, why stop there? Why not do 15 percent, 20 percent, and so on? The reason is that some funds are guided by outside regulatory authorities, plus their own mandates. Institutions ask for regular data to see evidence of performance drift, but the manager still has wiggle room with accounting spin.

Of course, a skeptic may question whether or not the manager acts after the fact or during the process. Actually, managers act gradually, as they see the width of the performance widening, rather than just waiting until the year is over. Basically, they look in the rearview mirror. (This is also true of selecting funds by retail and institutional investors.)[9]

Of course, the managers don't know when the width may collapse. Consider the years 2006 and 2007. The Russell 2000 Value Fund did better than the Growth Fund in the first year. Value did 23.48 versus 13.35 for growth in 2007. Value did well in the prior years on a cumulative basis, so a manager could feel comfortable beefing up the value component of the growth portfolio. Then in 2007—BAM! To our horror, we saw value drop 9.78, while growth went up 7.05 percent. Hey, that's not supposed to happen, but we better beef up growth while value is hurting our portfolio returns. In 2008, another BAM! Value dropped only 28.92 percent, but growth dropped to –38.54 percent. Here is the rub—we get whipsawed in doing performance drift. It's like having your face slapped many times. It is not unusual to see funds change their stripes only to result in dire consequences.[10]

The NASDAQ has the same technical picture as that of the S&P 500 Index. In Figure 3.6, it also breaks its 200-day line on the upside, and has a Golden Cross around April 2003. The NASDAQ correlates high with the S&P 500, so there should not be too many surprises. However, one index can do better than the other. So if you feel the market will rebound, you may

FIGURE 3.6 NASDAQ Composite, August 2002 to July 2003

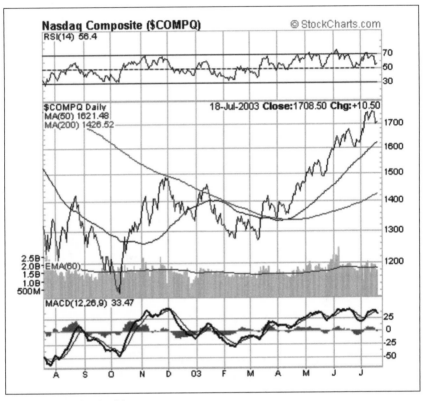

Source: Used by permission of Stockcharts.com

speculate that NASDAQ will outperform on the upside. NASDAQ also has a higher beta, which indicates more volatility to the beta of 1 for the SP 500. One can use the ETFs to play this with QQQQ for NASDAQ and SPY for the S&P 500 Index. One can also play ETFs on the Russell indices as well.

You could also pose the same question in comparing small stocks to large-cap stocks, such as the Russell 2000 Index to the S&P 500 Index. As mentioned, it is better to compare categories within the same index in order to keep the analysis clean.

Figure 3.7 shows similar technical signs to what we saw in the S&P 500 Index. This is not surprising for indices that correlate (or move together). Again, recall the fundamental optimism at the 2000 top and the angst at the bottom. Note how the favorable technical picture develops during the

FIGURE 3.7 NASDAQ Composite, September 2002 to November 2003

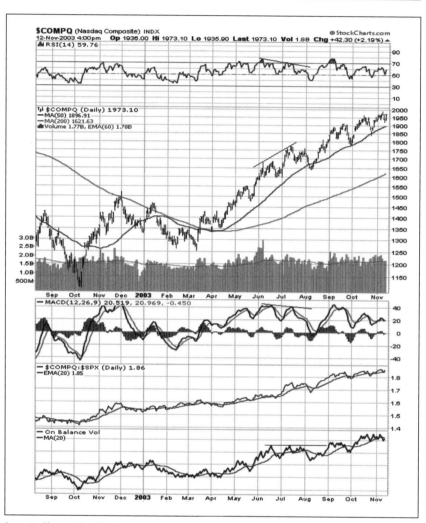

Source: Used by permission of Stockcharts.com

angst period as the NASDAQ Composite Index crosses the 200-day moving average for the first time since its peak. This crossing briefly occurs in January 2003 but quickly fails, giving a decisive buy and then sell signal. However, in March 2003, we see a buy signal that holds. Note also that usually, the 200-day moving average (as well as other moving averages) can be used as support and resistance lines by technicians.

Note that in November 2002, the NASDAQ bumped against the 200-day line as it met resistance. However, in late March 2003, it successfully found support at the 200-day line and then stayed in buying territory for the months shown after that date in the chart. Sharp eyes see that by July 2003, the NASDAQ made higher highs, but the Relative Strength Index (RSI) had lower peaks. This would imply a pullback is on the way and would be of interest to traders. This is a divergence, and in this case, a negative divergence.

So what happened? Yes, the market temporarily sold down, giving traders a good, short opportunity. Note that the peaks of the NASDAQ are rising. (While we usually draw an uptrend by connecting the bottoms and not the tops, here we are showing the rising peaks in order to identify confirmations or non-confirmations.) Now focus on the RSI, which has a declining trend and non-confirmation. While the NASDAQ is making higher highs in June and July, the RSI is not. Technicians would also see that the OBV or volume measure (as shown by the flat line) is not confirming the rise and so is raising a sell caution. Also note the divergence of the MACD and the actual sell signal of the MACD in July 2003, where it moves below its own nine-day moving average.

The result was from early July to early August 2003, the market stalled and actually went down, creating profits for shorts as the index went from 1775 to 1650. Thus, we have a small trading lesson within the context of looking at the big, longer-term picture. Along the way to the decline to 1650, there was a brief rally from 1680 to 1755 that tested the nerves of shorter traders. At the low of 1650, we had a buy signal again in the MACD as the OBV moved above its own moving average. The RSI was no longer in a sell signal mode and showed neutral, as it was not above 70.

Going back to the big picture, we see the NASDAQ going up with the S&P 500 Index (see Figure 3.8). We see the NASDAQ Composite Index using the weekly moving average, and once again, we see that very few decisions need to be made to capture the upside and avoid the downside. One starts with a buy as the index is above the 52-week moving average, then does the sell and buy in late 1998. This occurs again in 2000, followed by a sell in the third quarter of 2000. There is no buy strategy until the start

FIGURE 3.8 NASDAQ Composite, 1998 to 2003

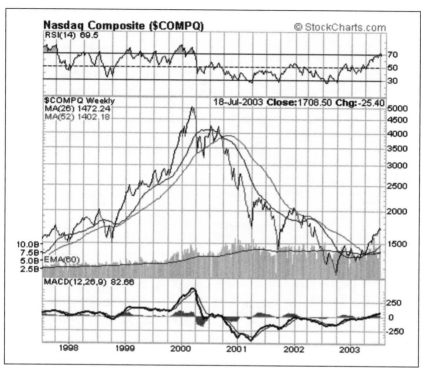

of the second quarter of 2003. Note the buy is basically from well under 1500 to the sell near 3800, and then a buy under 1500. This is about six decisions in five years.

Also note that the NASDAQ Composite Index surged from 3000 to the 5000 level, a gain of two-thirds in a bit less than six months. How was this possible? The Federal Reserve Bank of San Francisco stated:[11]

> *Although almost 6,000 stocks are traded on the NASDAQ, that market is dominated by technology companies. At the peak on March 10, 2000, the 20 largest domestic companies in the NASDAQ were in the technology sector, and together they accounted for over one-third of the total capitalization of that market. Quite amazingly, 6 of these top 20 firms were losing money as of the fourth quarter of 1999.*

FIGURE 3.9 NASDAQ Composite, 1994 to 2003

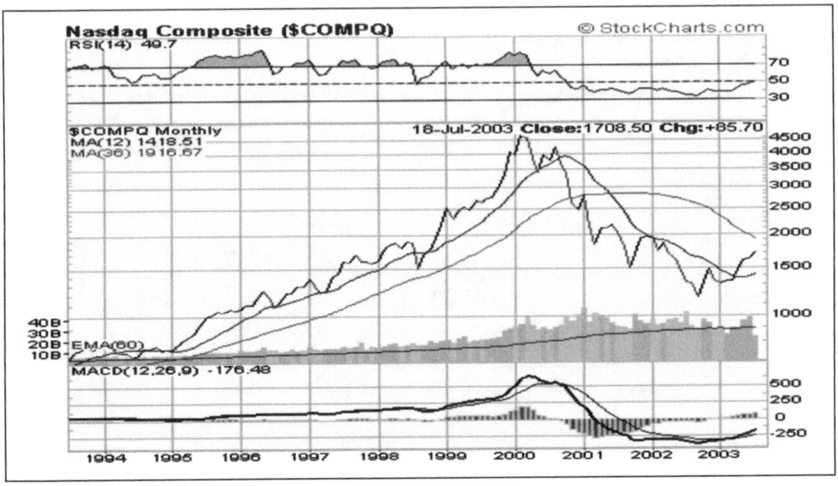

Source: Used by permission of Stockcharts.com

As the market rose sharply in the fall of 1999, some of the hot money, like hedge funds, fell behind as they got caught by surprise on the way up. They then began to play catch up, jumping on the bandwagon and pushing the index even higher. Then they got whacked on the way down, as they didn't expect such a steep drop.

Consider the woes of Soros funds, which have an excellent long-term reputation but got a black eye on the technology craze in 2000. In a *New York Times* article by William A. Galston, Stanley Druckenmiller, then the portfolio manager for Soros Funds, was reported with woes as follows:[12]

> *Stanley Druckenmiller knew technology stocks were overvalued, but he didn't think the party was going to end so rapidly. "We thought it was the eighth inning, and it was the ninth," he said, explaining how the $8.2 billion Quantum Fund, that he managed for Soros Fund Management, wound up down 22 percent this year before he announced yesterday that he was calling it quits after a phenomenal record at Soros over the last 12 years. "I overplayed my hand." ... But, he added, he expected that it would continue longer than it did, because the public was putting so*

much money into the stocks. He said he began to sell in February, but only
at a slow rate. When the fall started after the peak was reached March 10,
he believed it would be more gradual and be marked by rebounds after
drops of 15 percent or so. "I did not think it would go down 33 percent
in 15 days," he said. That is what did happen to the NASDAQ composite
during the three weeks, or 15 trading days, after March 24.

Soros was not the only fund caught in this bind. It stretched from
institutions to the amateur day traders. Unfortunately, it would seem some
of these day traders did not have the income and wealth of Druckenmiller,
who earned it with his many good calls during his career.

In general, portfolio managers will always have their bases-loaded
strikeout. The point is that there is a batting average and they stay in the
game and not get completely blown out. The unfortunate day traders and
later condo flippers bet the bank and lost. They did not have the record and
the means to get back into the investment game.

Pair Trades

In pair trading, investors short the index that they feel is going to do worse
than another index, while simultaneously going long in the second index.
Pair traders are numerous in the market and they pair trade all kinds of
indices, stocks, commodities, and so forth. One can short gold and go long
platinum, short long bonds and go long short-term bonds, long bonds,
short stocks, and so on.

In a pair trade, you no longer make a market bet of an asset going
up or down. You only care if it will do better than, say, the S&P 500 Index.
The key point in a pair trade is that you use some method to determine
if one asset is priced too rich in relation to another. You then assume that
richness will evaporate and return to some normal state. That is the key.
The problem may arise if the two come back to their normal relationship.
For example, the old GM and Ford pair trade was warped once the auto
industry, especially GM, had credit problems. Or consider the good old

days of pairing Citibank and JP Morgan, then trying the same as Citibank went below 3 due to credit issues while JP Morgan Bank still had a decent price of 40.

Also, past correlations must hold. In the old days, emerging markets correlated low with the S&P 500 Index, but now they correlate much closer. As some commentators say, "There are bulls, there are bears, and there are 'I don't cares.'" The "I don't cares" don't care about market direction. They only care about relative performance of one measure to another.

You may feel the S&P 500 will underperform on the upside, so you short the SPY and buy the NASDAQ ETF QQQQ. You only care about the spread increasing in this case. This assumes that correlations will hold and that NASDAQ will do better than SPY. Using the fundamental approach, you may come to this conclusion by comparing the P/E ratios or using some other metric to determine if value is too expensive in relation to growth or vice versa. Now this would be a fundamental approach. It may not incorporate the emotional approach that we saw with the Soros situation.

If one uses more of a Fama/French approach, is value eventually corrupted by too many growth features in an index? This may happen at market bottoms. Conversely, at market tops you may see growth stocks being too influential on an index. This was the case in 1999 when Cisco and a few other technology stocks were over 20 percent of the NASDAQ and the S&P 500 Index had a large weight in technology stocks. This leads to fundamental spin, as the indices themselves may be too value or too growth in nature. At this point, traders may use equally weighted indices or fundamentally weighted indices to help offset the phenomena.

The fundamental index solution of academics like Jeremy Siegel of Wharton proposes to weight the index by fundamental factors like dividends or cash flows. Not all traders feel this is theoretically correct, as who is to say that cash flow or dividends are the correct measure? In fact, some may say that this criteria would bias the index toward more value stocks and away from growth stocks. Consequently, opponents of fundamentally weighted indices feel that way. If you test fundamental indices against a broad market cap index, you may get higher returns, but that may be because value stocks did better than growth stocks to begin with. Even with fundamentally weighted indices, you hear critics saying they may be value indices in drag. After all, what is likely to have higher dividend payouts or cash flows but value stocks? Technology stocks may have less incentive to pay dividends, as they would be more likely to reinvest given their better growth opportunities and desire to keep capital costs as low as possible. When growth is king, how long can a value player survive the "torture" of underperformance. Didn't people at one time say that Warren Buffet was out-of-date; then when value came back, he was OK again? Can technical analysis help fundamental forecasts in terms of determining which style is better?

Figure 3.10 is a comparison over a year period, mostly 2004. It can be viewed in the form of a ratio chart with the value of the S&P 500 as

FIGURE 3.10 S&P 500 SPDRs/NASDAQ 100, May 2004 to April 2005

Source: Used by permission of Stockcharts.com

the numerator and the value of the NASDAQ as the denominator. The actual number is not that important. The significance is that these can create support and resistance points. In August 2004, a top is made after a bottom in July 2004, so a trader could use that as resistance and support, reversing positions at this point. The trader may be long on the S&P 500 and short the NASDAQ. Note in the figure that in early September 2004, a resistance is being tested. You can speculate that it may fail and short the S&P 500 and buy NASDAQ until late October, when you would reverse that because the July support is being tested. So you would buy the S&P 500 Index and short the NASDAQ, then reverse in August 2005 as a resistance is met.

The use of fundamentals to time the market and pick sectors has not been rewarding. We have seen growth/value opportunities, yet the question remains how to exploit them. Unfortunately, fundamental outlooks are enhanced as the asset increases in value and diminished upon declines. This invites painful whipsaws.

Technical use of contrary opinion may offer more promise; however, this is not a popular strategy in boardrooms and the lone wolf usually gets behavioral pressure to conform to the crowd. Bottom line: Which felt more comfortable in forecasting the market: Fundamentals or technicals? Levels or spreads?

The difficulty in market timing has led to a greater emphasis on non-directional decisions such as pairs trading, seeking anomaly investing, and other more non-traditional investment strategies. Since some are complex and perhaps even unproven. This can cause a challenge to obtaining alpha.

Conclusion

In this part, we saw that the universal question of where the market is going is not always easy to answer and tackle. Fundamentals can conflict and lead to emotions that make one get greedy or fearful. Technical analysis can help overcome this problem, but it may not be used or, if used, may not be believed. Investors may feel that it is different this time, which again is a trap that technical analysis exploits. Finally, the investor may wish to play in pair trades and avoid market direction decisions. The investor may still then have to decide how to determine whether the comparison of two assets can be determined fundamentally or technically. This too may run into the same issues and problems of market timing.

Part 2

THE FLUCTUATING MOVES

Whether you use a top-down or bottom-up approach, you still are naturally interested in knowing what to buy or sell as it relates to individual securities.

So, how do you evaluate the intrinsic price of a security? In addition to fundamental approaches, you can also use a Fusion approach by incorporating technical, behavioral, and quant approaches. For now, let's tackle the issue of using fundamental analysis and its particular challenges.

4

VALUATION AND
BROAD APPROACHES IN
FUNDAMENTAL ANALYSIS

There tend to be two major approaches to valuing stocks on a fundamental basis. Similar to seeing two large rivers, they have many variations or smaller rivers flowing into them. They can actually converge, just like two rivers meeting at a common point. One approach involves reviewing balance sheets, while the other approach focuses on cash flows that are supposed to be generated by the balance sheet. There are other methods that can be used such as option pricing and even eyeball clicks in Internet companies, but they eventually have some dependence on these two major approaches.

Asset Approach

The first approach is Graham and Dodd's value approach, where we look at a stock price and compare it to the value of the company's assets. From this we can estimate the value against more specific measures like book value and working capital. In using an asset approach, you may view all of the assets of a manufacturing company and then subtract all of its liabilities to get an equity or a book value. So, for example, if the assets are $100 and liabilities are $30, the book value is $70. If the stock trades below $70, you can acquire the net assets (upon paying all liabilities) cheaply.

Of course, this assumes that the assets are worth something economically, as compared to just an accounting estimate. By this we mean the assets can generate profits and cash flows. Under accounting procedures, the assets would eventually be written down once the profits and cash flow are diminished from the asset use.

You can also seek more conservative values by looking at net working capital—current assets minus current liabilities. These are more liquid assets and liabilities which would be expected to turn to cash within a year. Fixed assets are long term in nature and are not expected to be quickly liquidated for cash, as they are required to manufacture products of the business. Suppose working capital is $50 and you subtract a long-term debt of $10. You can get the fixed assets for free and still have net working capital at a discount if you buy the company for under $40. Again, you assume the resulting company will still be able to generate profits and cash flow. In a troubled company, you may get these kinds of discounts because the investors have serious doubts about the firm's outlook. Also, stock prices may be beaten down as investors view the market more pessimistically. You still can get something in the middle, where the assets are offered at bargains because the investment outlook is lowered. At this stage, it's possible that it may be cheaper to buy a company for its assets rather than building them to add to your own company.

You can also borrow money when the cost of the debt will still keep the cost of capital low enough to capture higher returns based on the resulting synergies. This process helped spark takeovers with junk debt in the 1980s, when it was thought that it was cheaper to buy out companies and use their assets rather than perhaps incurring capital expenditures (CAPX). This is done in times when you try to gain market share that would likely take too long to grow organically or when you did not have the capital to grow and so sold out. Acquisition of regional banks is another example where their inability to raise capital in the 1990s led to them being acquired by larger banks who could then quickly gain deposits from the newly acquired banks' branches.

Today, many banks are needing more capital by regulators. Also, investors are suspicious of book values as banks may not be showing their true liabilities as regards to some of their foreign obligations. Also, are the assets that good? Have the real estate loans really been marked down, and are earnings real, given reserve reversals and a cushy zero deposit cost from the Fed?

When Graham and Dodd's book came out in the 1930s, the asset approach had appeal, as manufacturing firms or companies with physical assets were the dominant types of organizations. While we still believe that brand images for food and beverage firms are still solid assets, you can run into a problem when you start dealing with a service organization. Imagine going to a lawyer's office and saying that she is worth only the price of the desks, law books, and computers minus the debt of the firm. (This analysis is similar to the asset minus liabilities equal equity or book value approach we discussed earlier.) Once you get the bill for $600 an hour, however, you'll realize that the net assets or book value is not the major consideration involved.

The same analysis can be used with the rock band U2. The band is worth far more than their guitars, touring bus, speakers, and so forth. The pricy tickets tied to their musical performance skills and merchandise sales with their names add greatly to their value. A T-shirt is worth maybe a few dollars, but with the name of a prominent rock band, you can increase the profit margin by selling the T-shirt for a premium price. This concept of merchandising has worked for various designer apparel; you pay more for the markup of the labor and material costs in order to garner the mystique or status of a name or symbol on the clothing item.

So, the asset approach leaves some void in the analysis. It appears that some assets have relatively low costs in themselves but actually generate formidable cash flows.

Discount Dividend or Cash Flow Model

We now turn to the second major approach, John Burr William's discounted cash flow approach. It looks at the value of a firm as the sum of the present value of all of its net cash flows. The cash flows can be dividends or various types of free cash flows from which dividends are supposed to come. They are discounted because the inflows of cash may come in the future. Money received now does not equal the same amount in the future, as there is some discount mechanism required to compensate for the risks involved.

The Discount Dividend or Cash Flow model (DCF) requires the discounting of future dividends or cash flows. It can be a few months out, to many years out. The value of a security is the present value (PV) of the expected dividends. So if we have a discount rate of 10 percent and we shall get $100 in one year and no more thereafter, the value of the stock is $90.91. Thus, if the stock is trading at $70, we should buy it, but if it is trading at $110, we should avoid it or even short it. Of course, this is a very simple illustration, as you should expect to see at least some investments along the way in order to get the future cash flows. Suppose in the previous example the stock is trading at $95; we would not buy the stock, as it is overpriced. However, this assumes rational investors because if one feels that the overpriced stock may go higher in price and get more overpriced, perhaps one then buys on the expectation that there will be a greater fool who is willing to pay more. Thus, we can buy high and sell even higher, until the perception changes on the value of the stock. At this point we may start to see an investment bubble.

Deviating from a simple DCF, we have entered a new playing field—that of the greater fool who will pay more, even if one perceives something to be overpriced. Or, more importantly, the asset may seem expensive, but it is expected to appreciate even more and thus it would not make sense to sell it at this time. We can also flip this argument to discuss prices that are cheap and going lower. So, when discussing one direction, realize it may apply to both directions of up and down, cheap or expensive.

This opens the door to technical analysis and behavioral issues which may state that the market is not always rational.

Taxi Cab Illustration

Going back to fundamentals, we can look at both the asset approach and the cash flow approach by examining a simple business decision on whether or not to buy a taxi cab. We have seen that fundamentals can give one answer, but the inclusion of emotion can warp the process.

To illustrate, consider there is value in a taxi cab in New York City. On the one hand, you can buy the car and see what it sells for as scrap value or as a yellow used car. The car may be worth, say, $15,000 after some wear and tear; however, the real value will be the license that is required to operate the car as a taxi. In 2007, that was reported to be $600,000 (or nearly a one-bedroom apartment in Manhattan).[1] In NYT, it was reported last week of October 2011 that the medallions went for $1 million, a new record.

The prices have gone up over the years, as the number of licenses is limited by the New York Taxi and Limousine Commission. So obviously, this piece of metal is overpriced; after all, you can buy a Ferrari for less. So why pay this ridiculous price? Under Graham and Dodd, you might be reluctant to do this for just some piece of metal. However, the obvious reason you would pay over $600,000 for a taxi is that you expect to use it to collect fares and generate a net cash flow. Net cash flow would be after all cash expenses were deducted and discounted by some required return to make it worthwhile. You may decide not to drive the taxi, but outsource it to others who will get compensated with a share of the fare. You may also share the cab with family members who are part owners and who would drive at various shift times. The hours of operation could be close to 24 hours, operating several shifts. Also, to lock in a cash flow, you may require the hired taxi drivers who are not owners to pay cash up front to you, the owner, before they collect a portion of the fare. Without getting into all the nuances of taxi cab valuation, we can see that the expected cash flow is more important than the scrap metal value of the car.

Companies tend to be seen as having long lives, not just an entity that has a one-year life span. As a result, we can discount cash flows into the future. However, if we sell the company to someone who is looking into the future dividends at this point, the model then would look like the following equation:

Equation 4.1: Dividend Discount Model

$$P_0 = \frac{D_1}{(1+K_e)} + \frac{D_2}{(1+K_e)^2} + \frac{D_3}{(1+K_e)^3} + \frac{D_4}{(1+K_e)^4} + \frac{D_5}{(1+K_e)^5} + \frac{P_5}{(1+K_e)^5}$$

We determine the price of the security (taxi cab) by discounting a cash flow. The cash flow is the dividend that is cash.

So D is the dividend and K_e is cost of equity that we want in order to compensate us for the risk of doing the business. So what return would you want on each $100 invested in operating a taxi cab? Would $1.00 be good? Obviously not, as you can get better returns in less risky situations like T-bills, which on average over many years has yielded about $3. The average wage of a New York taxi cab driver in 2004 was about $49,532: gross revenue was $90,717, with operating expenses of approximately $ 41,215. More recent data for 2010 shows that those in the 25th to 75th percentile earn about $30,500 to

$44,800 per year.[2] So this would place them somewhat near a normal wage of $50,000 in the United States (though "normal" seems hard to pinpoint with the recession and rate of unemployment since 2008).

How about getting $50 return for $100 invested? Be realistic! This high return of 50 percent would invite a flood of both skilled and unskilled labor. The price of the license would be bid up and the returns would fall dramatically, as people riding in the cab would be unwilling to pay $100 for $10 trip to bail out the taxi cab's investments. However, there has to be some balance for the risk and reward of the business.

So, would one spend $1,000,000 to earn $50,000 a year? One will see that this depends on forecasts of future growth rates of a taxi cash flow, and the costs of capital as some of the purchase may be done with borrowed money. Is there a bubble when one sees the medallion cost jump from $600,00 to $1,000,000 in only 4 years? Even the taxi cab business can open the door to a fusion analysis.

Going back to the cash flow model, we need to discuss the selling price. We must ascertain a selling price in the fifth year. This is the P5 symbol in Equation 4.1. So how do we ascertain a selling price? Well, there again we have many methods but can use the two main approaches. You can just sell the cab for scrap and license rights or sell to another operator. This operator may also adjust the paid price by the expected increased maintenance costs, but also perhaps the higher taxi fares that are forecasted. The price of the license would be expected to go up if one expects higher cash flows down the road.

We can assume that the eventual cash flow will be constant. In this case, we will use a perpetual dividend assumption where the dividends don't grow but stay the same forever. The formula would then be D/K_e as the selling price (or it could be called a terminal price). So if we want 10 percent (K_e) and the perpetual dividend or cash flow is $100, we get a selling price of $1000. The estimated dividend is a forecast, so no guarantees, and the required return is the discount that investors want in order to accept the risk of the investment.

Using the Gordon Growth Model

Of course, on a more realistic model, we can assume that there is some growth in the dividends, even if it is only the effects of inflation. Using the formula developed by Professor Myron Gordon in the late 1950s, we see the following equation:

Equation 4.2: The Gordon Growth Model

$$PV = Do(1 + g) / (k - g)$$

Do$(1 + g)$ is the expected dividend one year out, and Do is the current dividend. So, if the current dividend (Do) is \$100, expected return (k) = 10 percent, and growth (g) = 5 percent. The PV = \$100(1.05) / (.1 − .05) = \$2,100.

As we can see, a company that is growing is worth more than a company that is not. This makes intuitive sense, as the net cash flows increasing the company's value is worth more than if it does not—all things being equal. Technicians may say that as the prices rise, the trend is created and investors jump on the bandwagon; again, the selling prices are just moved up to justify the current price. Behaviorists describe this process as anchoring the price. Still, achieving cash flows seems more reasonable because we may have a promising asset. But, again, if it does not generate sufficient cash, it will not be worth as much as original expectations. So, a taxi once paid for is not worth as much sitting in the garage as it is cruising for fares. We can easily apply the taxi example to other areas of industry, such as service industries, software companies, and entertainment firms.

Other firms may also have valuations with small amount of assets, such as service industries and software companies. These are rather creative businesses and don't need much in terms of hard assets. So do we look at assets or cash flows? Are they really one and the same? Eventually, as mentioned, there is no disagreement between both approaches, as cash flow valuations can be converted mathematically to P/B valuations. One can also convert these cash flows to P/E approaches that are more popular. Here the P/E ratio looks more at the current situation of a company, the current price, and the recent earnings per share.

For example, by dividing both sides by E (or earnings), we can get an expected P/E ratio for a firm:

Equation 4.3: Expected P/E Ratio

$$PV/E = Do(1 + g)/E / (k - g)$$

So, if we keep all things equal, the higher the growth rate, the higher the P/E ratio of the company. (This assumes that the required return of K is higher than the growth rate of G, and that the payout ratio of the company's dividends from its earnings [Do(1 + g)/E] is constant.)

The time horizon is what really changes when we are analyzing these two approaches to stock evaluation. An asset approach looks more at values now or in the near future, whereas cash flows are projections of the future. This can lead to behavioral implications, as investors may start dreaming of the future cash flows, similar to the 1999 dot-com bubble era.

PEG Ratio

In fundamentals, when you make a trade-off between the growth of future cash flows and what you pay for those cash flows, you may start to use something like the PEG ratio.

The PEG ratio is the P/E of a stock divided by the estimated growth rate. So if the P/E is 10 and the growth rate forecast is 10 percent, we get a PEG of 1.0. A PEG of 1.0 tends to be a reasonable norm for most seasoned companies. Small-growth companies may have little in earnings. So with little earnings, they would have a high P/E ratio, let's say 30. Then, if the growth is only 10 percent, we get a high PEG ratio of 3.0. Still, we expect a high PEG for a company that is growing rapidly, definitely more than our stated 10 percent. Thus, managers may actually disagree with a 10 percent growth rate and decide to use a forecast of 30 percent growth, getting a normal PEG of 1. (At this point, we can start to justify high P/E ratios with higher estimates of growth. Who's to say our growth rate is wrong?)

What if the growth rate is not really 30 percent? Also, what if the earnings are not real and actually worse on an economic basis? At this point, the PEG becomes deceptive. In theory, there is no problem with the PEG method; in actual use, there can be a great problem. Once again no problem with academic theory in a rational market and good earnings estimates. However, behavioral bias on the estimates, as well as non-symmetrical returns (upside does not carry the same deviation as the downside) can cause this model to give bad results. So two forces tug at investors from different directions:

1. Growth investors may be willing to pay high P/E ratios due to PEG analysis.
2. Value investors may seek companies with low P/B, P/E, and P/S (profit-to-sales) ratios.

In addition, behavioral bias may warp the analysis. Behaviorally, individual traders are different from professional traders, and so are results. There is much academic evidence that says P/Es matter. High P/Es seem to perform worse than low P/E stocks. Again, it does not have to be this way if the growth is for real and materializes. It doesn't happen this way when emotions bias the growth rates and make crazy speculators buy stocks at high P/Es in their pursuit of dreams.

In a roaring bull market, value investors may sell too soon. Likewise, in bear market massacres, they may buy too soon. In bull markets, growth investors may keep justifying paying higher prices because of perceived higher growth. In bear markets, growth investors may buy too late because perceived growth is not easily apparent. So both approaches have vulnerabilities.

This then brings up other behavioral topics of the Prospect Theory, which states, "People behave as if extremely unlikely events are impossible and extremely likely events are certain") and the Disposition Effect, which states that people are likely to hold on to losers longer than winners.[3] You may hear that a particular stock's P/E only looks expensive, given the great growth prospects; that there is little chance that it can go lower, as it is already at a nice discount to book. In general, we may expect that technicals are already hidden in the P/E and P/B ratios, as these measures reflect more expectations and thus sentiment, rather than a true estimation of growth or value.

Real or Padded Earnings?

Fundamental analysis can initiate more problems than just deciding on a valuation approach. In dealing with financial numbers, how seriously is one to take them? Sure, one may say that they are audited, but that does not mean that they have economic value.

Should the given numbers for cash flows or asset amounts taken from balance sheets be believed, or should they be adjusted? It is possible that the numbers are properly accounted for under GAAP (Generally Accepted Accounting Principles) but may still be deceptive. We tend to do this in our everyday lives when we shop. We see a shirt marked $20 and that price is below the normal cost of $40. We clearly see that the shirt costs less, financially. However, economically, a savvy shopper might not be so sure. For example, while cheaper, it may not last as long because the material is poor. It may wash poorly and shrink, thus lowering the number of times it can be worn. Using our experience with shopping, we begin to make some assumptions and conclude that the lower price is not a bargain at all. This does not even include the hassle of going through this process, which we can label our transaction costs.

So, in looking at financial statements, does one use the financial data coming from GAAP, non-GAAP, or economic non-GAAP? (For now, we will lump International Financial Reporting Standards, or IFRS, as a GAAP category.) GAAP are numbers that are properly reported; non-GAPP are those that tend to give analysts more information on non-normal transactions, such as selling land to bolster earnings. Non-GAPP is not required to be reported by companies, but because many analysts have had the shirt problem after washing it, they tend to demand such information and so many companies provide that information along with GAAP. Economic non-GAAP goes further; this is the cost that is difficult for analysts to adjust for. These are financial numbers that should be reported instead of the ones that are actually reported. For example, you might question the proper amount of a company's CAPX. By doing this, you may get a different free cash flow number than what is determined by using company data.

In valuing a company, one must decide if one should approach it from a specific source. Should it be earnings? Should it be dividends? Should it be cash flow? And if cash flow, what kind? Also, since DCF methods use terminal values, what should they be and how valued? Should it be Gordon, EBITDA (earnings before interest, taxes, d*epreciation,* and a*mortization*), which is more likely, or perpetual?

As you can see, there are many challenges in using financial data for a company's valuation. You may come to erroneous conclusions about valuation models like the Fed model if you use one number versus another that is more economic in nature. It may be tricky to accurately use a set of historical financial numbers like P/E ratios and then attempt to make some conclusion on whether the stock or market index is cheap or expensive. Using reported numbers may give a different conclusion than using economic numbers. Thus, technical analysis may already capture the true economic interpretation of the real financial numbers as compared to a blind use of reported numbers. The market participants already influence the stock price based on their perceptions, which may differ from the obvious reported ones.

Growth Estimates and Challenges

The estimation of growth is key to proper valuation with tools such as the P/E ratio. We have seen, all things being equal, that the higher the growth rate, the higher the expected P/E ratio. Growth is a challenge in and of itself, and several techniques can be employed to estimate it. They range from accounting methods, to linear regressions methods, to life cycle analysis, and sadly, to seat-of-the-pants emotional estimates.

The accounting method would be an estimate of the return on equity (ROE) times the retention rate. If the ROE is 20 percent and the company retains 75 percent of its earnings, assuming all stays the same, its expected growth would be 15 percent. This assumes that the ROE will continue at the 20 percent rate, along with payout rate—forever. Most likely that would be hard to assume, but in the short to medium term, it is a reasonable compromise.

With linear regression, we get $Y = a + bx$, where we can regress past changes in, say, earnings with that of the GDP in order to get future projections. Of course, projections are linear and may not hold for a dying company. In other words, the past growth of the company may not continue as there are changes to the business model.

Then we can do a life cycle company approach, shown in Figure 4.1, where we add the PV of the cash flows in each stage of the company's projected existence. This assumes that analysts can make an accurate assessment of when the company blooms and when it dies. So for each stage, you can add the cash flows, venture, high growth, and so on. You would also estimate the number of years the company would exist in each stage. This is naturally tricky, as getting the number of years may seem to be difficult as compared to just picking a stage a company is in. Yet identifying a particular stage is challenging to analysts. Companies that seem to be in one period may soon move into another. In 2001, Apple was considered dead near 10, only to surprise analysts by blossoming to over 200 a few years later when it developed new products like the iPod. Dell, which was considered a growth company, and HP, a dying company, reversed roles as Dell started to decline and HP started to grow again.

FIGURE 4.1 Company Life Cycle

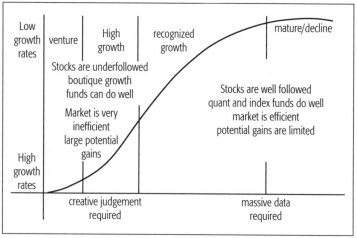

Another good method for estimating growth is to break the growth into various factors. This helps identify changes to the business model that would eventually lead to the company's growth rate. Most challenging is forecasting sales, and then eventual cash flows. The process includes an analysis of GDP, since, as we have discussed, most companies correlate their growth with economic conditions. So:

- Continue with growth estimates of company markets by product line, then,
- Growth of the market and the growth of the company's market share, then,
- Operational efficiencies, and finally,
- Financial efficiencies.

Even if the GDP grows only a small amount, a company can grow faster than the GDP by expanding its market to more users. You can also see that if the economy does not grow, the market does not grow, and the market share does not grow, a company can still grow its earnings and cash flows from operational and financial efficiencies. This would entail changing the level of its fixed costs to get operating leverage. For example, the company may outsource some production to lower its break-even costs. It could also finance itself with cheaper costs of capital. Instead of financing all with costly equity, it could borrow some funds to finance itself with cheaper cost of debt. This breakout of growth factors tends to be commonly used by analysts and appears to be a more accurate way of forecasting growth. But it too is challenging for analysts. Getting all the reasonable growth estimates of each factor is not always that simple; however, upon getting them, you may then produce a growth rate that is the sum of its parts. So, you could estimate GDP growth of 3 percent, market growth of 4 percent, market share growth of 5 percent, and efficiencies of 2 percent and get an estimated growth of 14 percent for the company.

While we can use fancier multi-growth models, a behavioral bias can influence expected growth rates g, as well as k, the required discount rate. Growth rates tend to be increased as stocks rise, and vice versa. K, itself, may be changed based on the perceived market outlook and trading liquidity.

The terminal value tends to be the largest component of the present value of cash flows. You might place a terminal value many years out in order to make it a small component, but then you must assume the company's finances so far out that few would find it credible. It would be like buying the company on the "promise" of its prosperity. However, when the terminal value is only a few years out, it becomes the dominant part of the valuation, so the early cash flows are not that important. So distant or far we have challenges. Sometimes this leads to "fantasy" valuations. The 1999 dot-com stocks are a memorable example, as many assumed very high growth rates which would lead to some terminal value such as a sale. Of course, many did not achieve the valuations and even went out of business.

To compound valuation and growth estimates problems further, you must assume that there is always a range of possibilities in the growth factors. Thus, there can be a high estimate if they all work out, or a low estimate if they do not. Cash flows should also be done under scenario analysis. For example, a good economy would lead to better business conditions and hence higher sales, profits, and cash flow. A weak economy would naturally result in lower sales, earning, and cash flow. You may already be thinking ahead and see that bullishness may lead to higher probabilities on the high scenarios, and lower probabilities on the low scenario. Again, behaviorists would see this as the Prospect Theory.

Skewness in scenario analysis can also bias results upward in bull markets and downward in bear markets. The following example demonstrates this.

Assume a simple three-part outlook (bullish, neutral, bearish) on investment returns where each scenario has the same 1/3 probability. The bullish scenario is forecasted to return 10 percent; the neutral, 0 percent; and the bearish scenario, –10 percent.

The expected return would be 0 percent, as $(.33 \times 0.1) + (.33 \times 0) + (.33 \times -0.1) = 0$, or 0 percent. So, if you were forecasting sales growth, the expected return for sales would be 0 percent growth. There would be 1/3 chance of growth of 10 percent, but this would be offset by a 1/3 chance of negative growth of 10 percent.

If the bullish scenario is enthusiastically raised (as the bull market continues to rise) to 50 percent, and the other scenarios are split to 25 percent apiece, the expected return would be 2.5 percent, as $(.5 \times 0.1) + (.25 \times 0) + (.25 \times -0.1) = 0.025$, or 2.5 percent. So now sales would increase by 2.5 percent.

Of course, compounding the issue is the more realistic assumption that increasing bullish attitudes would also increase the bullish forecasted return to a greater amount than 10 percent. So instead of forecasting just a 10 percent increase in sales, you may now assume a higher amount. Why not 15 percent? Well there should be some rational for this increase, but if its mostly emotional, then you can easily make a higher forecast that is accepted by others who are also more bullish. This increase would then further increase the expected value.

Technicians sometimes call this whole process of changing more bullish or bearish the "herd instinct." (We saw this in an earlier example.) This can feed upon itself, as rosier projections are made by funds in order not to fall behind the increasing returns of competitors. The upward spiral eventually ends in a correction. In bubbles, there is evidence that near the top, the rosier projections are made by less knowledgeable investors.

Another problem is that instead of building a DCF from bottoms up in order to get intrinsic value, some analysts "anchor" to the current stock price and keep their valuations close to it. So the old chant of analysts saying, "You want earnings; I'll give you earnings" is not surprising when it comes to justifying stock prices at lofty levels. This problem is exacerbated when many DCF models have large terminal values that dwarf the contributions of the prior yearly cash flow analysis.

Curved Universes of Emotion

An emotional market can distort cash flow projections. Analysts tend to bias their DCFs based on market action by anchoring.[4] As a result, we are not always sure of what to make of DCFs in an emotional market. Can we get a clearer picture? We can make an adjustment by considering the investment universe in its various stages of either greedy, normal, or fearful. We can perhaps then say the universe of investment warps the cash flows.

One could make an adjustment by considering the investment universe in its various stages of either greedy, normal, or fearful. One can perhaps then say this universe of investment warps the cash flows.

In Figure 4.2, the most bottom graph shows the investment universe as flat and devoid of any emotion. Borrowing from physics, the energy indication or Lambda equals 1 and so going back to our simple DCF equation:

$$PV = FV/(1 + k)$$

FIGURE 4.2 Universe of Investment

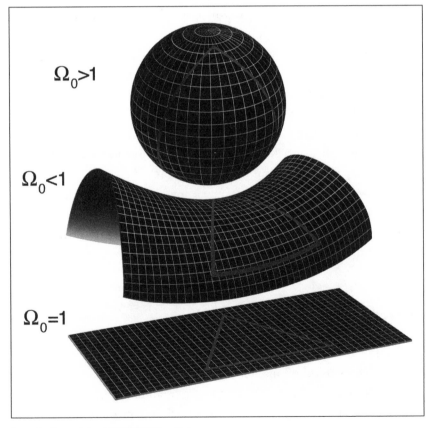

$\Omega_0 > 1$

$\Omega_0 < 1$

$\Omega_0 = 1$

Source: Used by permission of NASA/WMAP Science Team

If the FV is 120 and the discount rate is 10 percent, then the PV would be 109.09.

If the market is pessimistic in the middle graph, expected cash flows would be depressed. If the market is euphoric in the top graph, then the expected cash flows would be inflated. We can view this as a universe that is inflated or depressed at times from the norm.

So how can cash flows be adjusted from distorted emotional ones to ones that may better reflect reality? You could divide the cash flow formula by the energy or "hype" constant in the market. If the market is rational, we would get:

$$PV = FV/(1 + k) \text{ divided by } 1.0 \text{ or, in our case, } 109.09$$
$$\text{Or } 109.9 \text{ divided by } 1.0 = 109.09$$

If the market is euphoric, we should divide 109.9 by 2.0 to get 54.55. All things being equal, the stock would not be as attractive. Likewise, if the market is pessimistic, we can divide by 0.5 to get 218.18. The cash flows would then be more attractive than they appeared to be.

In reality, some of the cash flows may be bumped up or down, but discount rates would change as well. There may be some dynamic interaction. For example, the cash flow of 120 may be bumped up. That would result in a higher PV. But if the market is getting euphoric, you would expect the stock volatility to increase and so its market beta. Thus, the discount rate may also increase, thereby lowering the PV. Most likely the changes in cash flows would be the dominant factor raising the valuation, rather than changes in the discount rate. Since it is the P/E that dominates market attractiveness, you can conclude that it reflects higher sales earnings, and so cash flows and thus growth rates. The higher growth rates would tend to move the P/E up or down. In the discount rates, the cost of capital, as evidenced by the cost of equity, would not see as much change in the excess return or the risk-free rate, although there would be some small adjustment.

So, we adjusted the DCF by some factor, and it appeared to be rather arbitrary, 2.0 for euphoric, 1.0 for normal, and 0.5 for pessimistic. But how do we decide the adjustment is 2.0, 1.0, or 0.5 or some other factor? How do we know if the market is pessimistic or euphoric? Here, both fundamentals and technicals can help. Let's examine a situation in deciding whether small-cap stocks are more attractive than large-cap stocks. Small-cap stock valuation is of particular interest, as small-cap stocks are more prone to emotion than are large-cap stocks. They are often viewed as a quick way to get rich, but also as ones to jettison in declining markets where investors seek the safety and liquidity of large companies.

To analyze small-cap stocks, we can fall back on the T. Rowe Price P/E model, which shows that over many years, when small-cap stocks trade at 2 times the P/E of the S&P 500, they tend to be overpriced and should be sold; whereas, if they trade at 1.0 times, they tend to be good buys. So at 2 times the P/E, we use a factor of 2, and at 1 times the P/E, we can use the factor of 0.5. As discussed, others use similar measures, such as Russell 2000 P/E (adjusted for negative values) compared to the S&P 500 P/E, the Russell 3000 stocks to Russell 2000 stocks, and so on. This gives us at least a fundamental starting point. Now, let's add a technical tool: sentiment.

We can add the sentiment measure such as Investors Intelligence's ratio of bullish readings. High bullish readings nearing 60 percent tend to be tops, thus we would say the market is euphoric. Let's divide the cash flows by the factor of 2.0. (Sentiment may have to be smoothed out, as we have already discussed.) Other technical measures like the MACD line can be used to get a handle on confirmations and non-confirmations to determine if the small stocks are a good buy or sell. Note that we can start to create a package of technical tools to tell us if the market is overpriced or underpriced on a technical basis. No matter what our package of tools, we can say that when overpriced, we adjust the discounted cash flows by 2.0 and when underpriced, we use 0.5. In effect, we are taking seemingly accurate consensus earnings projections of analysts and stating that their emotions are probably bending the universe of valuation. These factors would then tend to "unbend" the universe into a more reasonable range, as it is adjusted for emotion.

We have been using rather simple (and extreme) factors in a range of 2.0 to 0.5. This was done for illustrative reasons to show how consensus estimates can be better adjusted. This implies that estimates are in reality twice overestimated or estimated by one-half, while, in fact, estimates can be overestimated by less than twice and understated by less than a half. In this case, one would use a more narrow range, perhaps 1.5 to 0.75. Further research could fine-tune each industry. It would seem that the most volatility around the actual range would be in speculative or even cyclical companies. For a market index, we can get a weighted average of all the industries. Since a market P/E was shown to have extremes of about 10 to 20 times earnings, we could say a base case is 15 times earnings. We could then make a range of about 0.65 where (10/.65 = 15.4) and 1.3 where (20/1.3 equals about 15). This assumes the earnings are economic to begin with. Assuming they are then theoretically we adjust the curvature of the estimates caused by emotions. You may wonder why we adjust the market multiple and not just use a range of 10 to buy and say 20 to sell in terms of P/E. In fact, this is a common use of the P/E factor where low amounts contribute to a buy signal and high ones contribute to a sell signal. You would still be vulnerable to the concept of 20 still being cheap if the real growth rate was higher. Perhaps past growth rates will no longer be the norm on the upper end, but be exceeded. Of course, technicians may then add that "Here we go again" and have the beginnings of the phrase "It's different this time," which open the emotional trap. Thus, confirmation with technical tools indicate the ranges seem extreme, and so you can make the case to adjust the consensus estimates. Upon adjustment, you can see that the market is not actually that cheap or that expensive.

You can also do fundamental checks by using other benchmarks such as P/B ratios, dividend yields, and so on. As we discussed, these are both fundamental and technical indicators at the same time. While there are many things to consider, the most likely blend would be the P/E ratio, sentiment, MACD, and even a moving average, but this is just my opinion from years of observation. One can then blend this quantitatively based on a type of back testing.

Illusory Cash Flows

We still have another problem in that we assume the cash flows are real—not overstated or understated. This implies that earnings can be viewed the same way.

We can call this P/E expansion or contraction, as we go through some sort of chicken-or-egg problem. Are the earnings overstated and thus the P/E is also overstated? We can surmise that in booms the earnings are overstated and investors gladly pay higher P/Es to adjust for this overestimation. If not, why carry overestimated earnings to begin with? Likewise, depressed earnings would seem to carry depressed P/E ratios. We always wrestle with the concept of how much will the market go up because of just earnings or cash flow increasing, and how much will it go up via P/E expansion; or even using both—higher earnings and a higher P/E expansion. It does not matter if the cash flows are padded with optimism or plucked because of fear; the actual cash flows may not be the economic ones. In other words, we may take them as is from GAAP and suffer two errors, padding, and misleading actual numbers. This pumping up of earnings seem to invite pumping up the P/E and vice versa.

This is what can ruin a DCF analysis and even value models. For example, the earnings can be an illusion due to accounting gimmicks and cash flows can also be deceptive because they don't reflect true expenditures and expenses. When we do real free cash flows, we must decide which cash flow to use. Also, should we use cash flows or earnings to get an economic value? (Some have indicated that earnings are better than cash flow for valuation purposes, which tends to be contrary to conventional thought.)[5]

My contention is that not only will analysts pad earnings, but they may also look the other way and not dig deep into their true values. Why not? They want the story they can believe in. It's little wonder investors bought subprime paper and Internet stocks in great haste, only to repent when the real numbers came out.

Another issue to consider is the type of cash flow to use. One may assume that there is only one. The most primitive is usually shown as net income plus depreciation. While this is a quick and easy way to cash flows, it has some serious shortcomings that other cash flows better address.

Free cash flows are true cash flows that a company has after it has met all of its obligations. The free cash flows are broken into two types:

1. Free cash flow for the firm (FCFF), which is discounted by WACC (Weighted Average Cost of Capital)
2. Free cash flow for equity (FCFE), which is discounted by the cost of equity

The Weighted Average Cost of Capital

The weighted average cost of capital (WACC) is composed of:

- Cost of debt
- Cost of preferred shares
- Cost of equity (ordinary or common shares)
- Other forms of capital (including leases, convertible bonds)

While the formula for WACC is rather easy to do, estimating the cost of equity is challenging. You can use CAPM, Gordon Growth formula (restated), or even option pricing models; however, each method may give a different cost of equity.

Equation 4.4: Weighted Average Cost of Capital

$$WACC = K_d \left(1 - t\right)\frac{D}{T} + K_e \frac{E}{T}$$

K_d = Cost of debt

t = Tax rate

D = Total debt (market value, if available)

E = Total equity (market value)

T = Debt + equity (market values)

K_e = Cost of equity

The following example indicates specific values for WACC:

Outstanding debt	$2 m
Book value of equity	$1.5 m
Market value of equity	1,000,000 shares © $3.00
Cost of debt	8%
Cost of equity	15%
Tax rate	35%

With these values, the actual WACC calculation looks like the following:

$$\text{WACC} = [0.08*(1-0.35)]*[2/(2+3)] + [0.15*(3/(2+3))]$$
$$\text{WACC} = [0.08*(1-0.35)]*0.40 + [0.15*0.60]$$
$$\text{WACC} = 0.0208 + 0.09$$
$$\text{WACC} = 0.1108$$
$$\text{WACC} = 11.08\%$$

(Note: In order to get the current state of a company, we tend to use market values of capital and not accounting book values.)

FCFF

The general formula for free cash flow for the firm is as follows, using a start with:

Net income + Noncash charges + Interest expense (1 – Tax rate) – Net investment in fixed capital – Net investment in working capital (excluding cash and ST loans).

Note that we add back interest after tax, because even though it is cash, we would double count its cost, and the cost of debt is already in WACC.

Firms will tweak this formula, but the basic formula is fairly standard. You can also start with other measures such as CFO and EBITDA to get FCFF. Some might adjust CFO and only use items that affect the income statement such as account receivables, account payables, inventory, and prepaid expenses. Even though a change in short-term borrowings is a current liability, it would not be included in the CFO method.

The result is a forecasted cash flow stream, and then you discount it by WACC to get enterprise value. From this we can further make adjustments, mostly subtracting debt to get equity value. If you divide the equity value by the number of outstanding shares, you get a value per share, giving you the opportunity to then compare it to the actual stock price.

DCF and Free Cash Flow Valuation Example: Ajax Corporation

Table 4.1 shows an example of free cash flow using a mythical company, Ajax.

TABLE 4.1 Ajax Corporation

	AJAX CORP ($ Millions)	
	2001	**2002**
SALES	1000	1150
CGS	500	510
GROSS PROFIT	500	640
R&D	100	102
SGA	150	155
ADVERTISING	25	20
OPERATING INCOME	225	363
INTEREST	0	0
OTHER INCOME	5	100
EBT	230	463
Tax 35%	81	162
NET INCOME	150	301
Plus		
DEPR&AMORT	50	55
WC	−10	−12
CAPX	−100	−102
FINANCING	0	0
FREE CASH FLOW	**90**	**242**
EPS (100S)	1.50	3.01

To keep it simple, we will assume no interest or financing. However, if there were financing, we would add back the interest on an after-tax basis. So, if interest was 10 and the tax rate was stated at 35 percent, we would add back 10 times $(1 - .35)$ or 6.5 to the free cash flow (which in this case would be for the firm).

This cash flow would be discounted by WACC, and it would have to be calculated each year as it may change in future years. This would result in an enterprise value, from which we can subtract debt to get equity value. To make matters simple, we will also assume no excess cash or other operating entities, which are adjustments to enterprise values. (Note that we did not include a terminal value or a WACC to get an enterprise value and eventual equity value.)

DCF and Free Cash Flow Valuation Example: Newbie Company

Let's now look at a more detailed model of another hypothetical company, the Newbie Company. We will add other factors that have been alluded to in previous discussions.

Assume the market for the Newbie Company's new clothing item, THERMO-CONTROL, is expected to be $100 million in sales—a year from today. THERMO-CONTROL clothing automatically controls body temperature within a comfort zone. It can be worn on the ski slopes and in the tropics. Using a breakthrough in technology, small sensors sewn into the fabric automatically adjust the temperature.

Determining the market may include predicting a product's various uses, dating, and so on. It may also include demographics, income levels, competing products, price points, product appeal, and regulatory issues.

Next, let's estimate Newbie's market share. If it is the leader with 30 percent market share, its sales would be $30 million a year from today. Then estimate its same-store sales (SSS) growth. SSS reflects more seasoned sales generated by stores opened for at least a year. Will Newbie grow by opening new stores, licensing, being carried by specialty chains—or all of the above? In other words, will it use operational efficiencies to own and operate its own stores or just sell in department or specialty stores? This also involves making a decision of whether or not this would affect the company's brand image and the nature of its advertising. Sometimes, selling to chain stores will lower profit margins but enable a company to gain quick market share. At the same time, selling to chain stores may lower its brand image if it is considered a premium product. Some brands can do both, like Armani, which sells certain items in upscale department stores like Bloomingdale's but also sells the same items in its own stores.

Here SSS should be broken out by units, price increases, and product lines. Let's say in a year the company will have 10 stores (all SSS), and each store will have estimated $3 million in sales. Based on this, we forecast $30 million in total revenue. We then estimate normalized sales of $3.5 million per store (16.7 percent growth) for 20 stores, 2 years in the future, and thus get an estimate of $70 million in sales. How did we get this estimate? We can study demographics and lifestyles and compare Newbie to those markets. Of course, we could be very bullish and pad the earnings on a firm belief that may not be supported. At this point, Newbie is a concept stock and very vulnerable to emotional investing. Most analysts are wrong on the prospects of a new product, as early as one year out. We saw this investment challenge in the innovative Crocs shoes where some hedge funds took short postions that turned to losses as the stock rose substantially. Later, it plunged on weaker fundamentals. Adding to sales growth would be geographic and product expansion estimates. Will Newbie go nationwide? Overseas? How? Will Newbie capitalize on its brand image and offer accessories such as sunglasses? Will it develop these items or license them? How will it market them and what is the marketing budget? In 1999, many of the new Internet companies were expected to grow 50 percent+ for many years—or so the Excel models showed. In fact, within a few years many were out of business.

It takes years to get a feel for an industry.

With this in mind, we can make some sales estimates which will eventually lead to free cash flow forecasts; however, along the way, we can make certain profit margin assumptions. We assume a slow rate of growth going forward but add an accessory line that will add to earnings. We also forecast a terminal value, based on specialty retail price/cash flow ratios. This is usually the largest (80 to 90 percent) portion of the PV of future cash flows. (This is an easy place to make big bets that go wrong.)

We calculate a WACC of 18 percent and assume the company debt is $8.0 million. We also agree that 18 percent is the appropriate discount rate calculated with a realistic cost of equity method for this company. When determining if we should buy it or not. This WACC of 18 percent implies a high cost of equity because most of the capital comes from equity. Still, it is not unreasonable, as it will start to rival returns that venture capitalists require.

Determining the actual cost of equity involve different methods such as CAPM, option pricing and reengineering Gordon Growth. You may also want to forecast the costs of capital in each year. For example, in later years, Newbie may wish to take advantage of borrowing funds at a lower cost of capital as its business gets more established. Initially, banks may consider this company too risky to lend to initially; however, as the company gets a solid track record, the banks may reconsider. The company could do a bond raise at lower costs than 18 percent for equity. In fact, the costs of equity may start to come down as the stock may become less volatile relative to the ups and downs of the market. This would lower its beta and so lower the company's cost of equity. Table 4.2 is an example of a worksheet for the Newbie Company.

If the stock is trading at $100, we would recommend a buy decision. Newbie's cash flow analysis indicates a value of $132.46; that exceeds the current price of $100. However, this may be disturbing to an outsider; professionals will reexamine the results. Are we right or is the market right? Are our estimates too high, or are factors such as beta incorrect? Also, we need to see if the universe needs to be adjusted for emotional curvature. If there are negative technical signals, we would be prone to do this.

While the spreadsheet creates numbers that lead to a buy decision, judgment factors are also important. Will the clothing line be in style? Will accessories be in demand? The answers to these questions require experiences in fields besides finance. These questions also allow for the behavioral excuse to skip the numbers. (So if one were to get the stock as being unattractive after looking at the cash flows, we already saw the anchoring way to get a buy by pumping up the cash flows.) You can decide to live with the numbers, but state that the clothing line is so hot that it is hard to quantify. In other words, buy on concept or buy based on a preconceived decision. Another fundamental trap is taking numbers at face value. We have alluded to this point before, and while all numbers are not fictitious, enough are that we need to be on guard.

TABLE 4.2 Newbie Company Worksheet

	NEWBIE COMPANY					
	YR1	YR2	YR3	YR4	YR5	YR6
Stores	10	20	30	42	47	50
SSS ($MM)	3	3.5	4	4.2	4.5	4.6
Total Sales ($MM)	30.0	70.0	120.0	176.4	211.5	230.0
Net Margin	0.25	0.2	0.18	0.15	0.12	0.1
Clothing Income ($MM)	7.5	14	21.6	26.46	25.38	23
Accessory Income	0	0	0	5	7	15
Total Net Income	7.5	14	21.6	31.46	32.38	38
Non-cash Charges	2	2.8	4	5	5.5	6
Working Capital	−1	−1.8	−3	−4	−4.5	−4.75
Interest	0.5	1	1.5	1.8	2	2.2
CAPX	−10	−11	−12	−15	−7	−5
FCFF	**−1**	**5**	**12.1**	**19.26**	**28.38**	**36.45**
Plus Terminal Value based on 7 times Year 6 FCFF of $36.45 =						255.15
Total FCFF	**−1.00**	**5.00**	**12.10**	**19.26**	**28.38**	**291.60**
NPV at 18% (Assuming 1 MM shares outstanding)						
This assumes you feel that 18% is the appropriate discount rate.				Less assumed debt		8.00
					Equity Value	132.46

Assume stock is trading at $100, then you would buy the stock as you calculated the value at $132.46
Therefore, BUY Newbie Company.

Upon generating sales forecasts, we must realistically forecast costs.

The costs should be "normalized" for valuation purposes. Junior analysts fail to take this into account, often carrying forward unusual costs or revenues. Finally, while we can calculate earnings and free cash flows, we must assume that competitors will take action to take away market share from Newbie, as this is the nature of a competitive market.

We now select a peer group to see how Newbie compares in specific financial measures. We would expect divergences if the cash flows are out of whack with comparable analysis. At this stage, we could assume that technical indicators will show signs of this. For example, the DCFs may indicate a buy, but at the same time the P/E and P/B ratios are stretched to high levels based on historical ranges. This may indicate the midst of a buying frenzy. We may see that technically, there may be overbought indicators such as steep trend lines which are not expected to be held, a plethora of bullish recommendations which indicate over optimism, and perhaps even non-confirmations from momentum measures. At this point, the Fusion analyst will begin to balance the fundamentals and technicals.

Peer Group Analysis

Peer group analysis has special challenges, especially picking a realistic peer group (company) with similar businesses, clients, and product lines. Analysts may disagree on the list and even not use private companies. (Imagine analyzing Hershey, a public company, and not using Mars, private company—big mistake.) In addition, some of the companies may truly have few comparable competitors and thus real comparisons are less meaningful. This may necessitate comparing not the product lines but the risks inherent in comparable types of product lines. For example, for Newbie there may be few or no competitors, so we may have to compare Newbie with an apparel company that also has a new product, say, shoes, even though it is not the exact same clothing item.

We also may need to adjust the accounting methods, so we are comparing apples to apples. While one company may use FIFO (first in, first out), another company may use LIFO (last in, first out) as its inventory methods. We must also "normalize" revenues and costs.

Many services provide peer group analysis like Value Line and Standard & Poor's. Most likely you will second-guess their peer group selection and adjustments for accounting; however, they are a good place to start for someone unfamiliar with an industry.

TABLE 4.3 Peer Group Analysis versus XYZ Company

PEER GROUP ANALYSIS VERSUS XYZ CO				
Select Company Ratios	XYZ Ratio as Reported	PEER GROUP (SIC Codes)	XYZ Ratio Adjusted	PEER GROUP (Select)
Price/Book	3.5	5.0	3.3	3.0
Price/Sales	2	3	2	1.5
Next 4QP/E	220	30	27	20
LT Growth	20	15	20	20
PEG	1.1	2	1.35	1
Price/FCF	12	20	15	12
Price/Enterprise	1.5	2	2	1.2
XYZ Appears	Undervalued		Overvalued	

Peer Analysis can be tricky. Taking numbers at face value my lead to the wrong conclusion.

XYZ appears cheap relative to the peer group of companies utilizing SIC codes.

However, when we adjust XYZs accounting for a more realistic peer group, it appears expensive.

Adjustments for XYZs accounting is conversion from FIFO Straight Line Depreciation to the Peer's LIFO and Accelerated Depreciation Naturally, there can be other accounting issues.

Adjustments for the Peer Group include using the top 5 companies which reflected 75% of the industry as a more realistic measure. Also, key private companies are included and outliers are excluded.

Other qualitative adjustments may have to be made such as adjustments for client types (government versus private), geographic concentrations, similar product lines.

Another challenge is to do trade-offs on which measures are more important in cases of conflicting results. For example, price/book may seen cheap, but PEG any seem expensive.

Professionals will make necessary adjustments, but that requires experience and patience. An example is shown in Table 4.3.

Originally, the peer group analysis looks quite good for XYZ Company. The P/B ratio is 3.5 for XYZ versus the peer group's 5.0. So, on this measure, XYZ is better looking or cheaper. The same is true on price/sales as XYZ trades at twice sales, whereas the peer group trades at three times. So again, XYZ looks cheaper. The same applies to higher growth, the lower PEG, plus the lower price to free cash flows and price-to-enterprise value. On all these factors, XYZ Company looks cheaper—on the surface. At this point we make adjustments to compare the quality of the financials, as a company may seem cheaper in price but prove to be a worse value.

Now we can compare accounting methods for inventory and depreciation. Note that XYZ Company uses FIFO, giving it more profits in a period of rising prices as compared to LIFO, which is a better reflection of true profits. Also, accelerated depreciation tends to be more conservative than straight line that XYZ uses. In order not to distort results, we can use the main companies that reflect the bulk of the industry, in this case 75 percent.

Deciding on what to do with outliers is a delicate task, as the analyst can include or exclude them to make any case. In a bull market where prices are rising and you have already decided to buy the stock, it may be more tempting to adjust the outliers to make your case. So if the P/E is high compared to the industry, you may include more outliers that have little earnings and thus high P/E ratios. This process will increase the average and perhaps the median P/E of the industry. This will make it easier to justify buying what originally had a P/E higher than the peer group, but now has a P/E lower than the peer group. (Of course, there is some judgment on this, but we need to see a fair representation without weird outlier events.)

Notice that the adjustments are accounting in nature. The real challenge begins when we start to compare companies on the quality of brand image or management. At that point, we may see that these factors are worth paying more for if they are good. If not, then things like poor brand image would eventually downgrade the company's value. The same could be said of the quality of a company's management. Are investors willing to pay more for Apple with Steve Jobs at the helm? Does the Apple image make you willing to pay more for your iPod as compared to the Microsoft Zune that also handles MP3s but sells fewer units?

In review we can see that there is an art that goes into valuation, and this may lead to different conclusions from different analysts using different assumptions. This is not physics, so valuation could be in the eye of the beholder and therefore technical analysis would offer a more objective and thus superior approach.

Tables 4.4 and 4.5 present key benchmark data of clothing industry leader Polo Ralph Lauren Corp. The benchmark numbers, found on Reuters Web site, compare the company to the Industry, Sector, and S&P 500 Indices. This is a good place to begin the process of making comparisons with similar

TABLE 4.4 Polo Ralph Lauren Corp. Growth Rates

Growth Rates (%)	Company	Industry	Sector	S&P 500
Sales (MRQ) vs. Qtr. 1 Yr. Ago	26.83	15.54	8.26	16.94
Sales (TTM) vs. TTM 1 Yr. Ago	NA	13.22	9.68	17.46
Sales-5-Yr. Growth Rate	10.98	16.82	7.67	9.44
EPS (MRQ) vs. Qtr. 1 Yr. Ago	54.26	15.88	34.05	16.03
EPS (TTM) vs. TTM 1 Yr. Ago	NA	14.34	23.13	22.60
EPS-5-Yr. Growth Rate	36.42	25.75	11.86	13.71
Capital Spending-5-Yr. Growth Rate	8.56	14.47	3.02	6.29

Source: Yahoo!

TABLE 4.5 Polo Ralph Laruen Corp. Valuation Ratios and Ratio Comparison

Valuation Ratios	Company	Industry	Sector	S&P 500
P/E Ratio (TTM)	20.13	22.69	17.19	19.95
P/E High - Last 5 Yrs.	NA	33.31	32.74	36.83
P/E Low - Last 5 Yrs.	NA	13.68	12.92	14.37
Beta	1.31	1.17	1.23	1.00
Price to Sales (TTM)	1.73	2.55	1.23	2.79
Price to Book (MRQ)	3.16	4.81	3.15	3.79
Price to Tangible Book (MRQ)	5.83	9.32	6.24	7.23
Price to Cash Flow (TTM)	14.38	17.31	11.28	14.08
Price to Free Cash Flow (TTM)	22.06	22.79	22.43	30.68
% Owned Institutions	55.06	54.05	55.32	68.30

Source: Yahoo!

companies. Realize again, some companies may be further removed from Polo in terms of product line and some may be more close.

Notice that the 5-year growth rate of Polo at 36.42 percent is higher than all other categories. The P/E on the trailing twelve months (TTM) is cheaper or close to the categories, with only the Sector being much cheaper. Using PEG, we can see that the company is a good deal. Polo is cheaper on price-to-free cash flows. Its 22.06 ratio on TTM is less than the other categories.

Key Challenges for Analysts

While I selected some key data for discussion, we could run into problems if I cherry-picked only the factors that supported my decision. Supposedly we stay with an investment discipline to keep consistency; however, that is not always the case. Analysts may start making exceptions on the excuse of buying something that doesn't meet their investment discipline, at this point, we have to suspect behavioral bias is influencing our decision via anchoring.

Going back to our hypothetical clothing company, Newbie, we can make some further comments. Newbie's product, while a clothing item, is not similar to the classic clothes of Polo. Should Newbie be compared more to tech companies? If Newbie is introducing a radically new clothing item that is tech based, perhaps that may be a valid point. Some analysts might not make that kind of connection and thus misjudge financial results.

The real trap is that we are using GAAP earnings. There could be flukes in revenues and expenses that should be considered as "one-time wonders" and thus may not add to long-term value. This could be a fire in a factory that temporarily shuts down a line, or the sale of unneeded land that can pad earnings. Companies today increasingly report GAAP and non-GAAP earnings to give analysts a better picture of recurring business. Also, sales may not be high quality, as some are probable in their repeat, while others may be more of a one-time event.

Let's look at some other major categories that challenge analysts.

Management

Expect to see proven experience in the field of work, professional designations, and a clean, ethical background. Thus, a retail company should be managed by experienced apparel executives, rather than a lawyer or investment banker who has no experience in the industry. A biotech firm should have an academically trained professional as head of R&D and an objective scientific advisory panel. Finally, expect to see a clean, ethical background by checking with Kroll or doing a Lexis/Nexus search. Expect to see similar features from the broad management team. Management scandals or their potential are hard to quantify initially but will eventually lower sales, earnings, and cash flows.

Marketing

Financial analysts who did not take marketing classes are at a great disadvantage in forecasting a company's future. Remember when Dell sold only directly to the customer, but then started putting its computers in retail distribution centers like as Best Buy? How should a cosmetics firm market itself? Does it have a good brand image? How much should the marketing budget be? Putting numbers in Excel boxes can only be numbers, and rather useless unless you can make proper decisions on marketing.

So again, if proper marketing is 10 percent of sales, and a company does 5 percent, then we can initially see higher profits and solid cash flow. The question is whether the company will start to lose market share because it has underfunded its marketing budget.

Marketing is rather tricky because one can't make the assumption that more marketing automatically leads to more sales and that less marketing leads to lower sales, both in a linear manner. Moreover, spending more on marketing may not help sales beyond a certain point but cutting back can quickly lead to detrimental sales results. (This makes advertising a punching bag for some economists.)

Product Niche

Many analysts seek product niche as a basis for their selection of attractive investments. Some will seek a "prime mover," or the company being the first and dominant player in the market. They would pay as "me too" followers would be expected to eventually drop out of the market. This was the analysts' rationale for recommending Internet companies in the late 1990s. While they did seem to be very expensive on traditional valuation measures, the argument was that if they could be the first and grew fast, the sales and earnings would later follow. Being dominant or having a major market share in a more established industry can change overnight (recall Beta and VHS). In my investing experience, I emphasize only one of a kind companies or dominant players, rather than "me too's." My feeling is that these companies will eventually get premium valuations for their niches either in the current market or in eventual takeovers. This will then increase the company's terminal value in a DCF.

R&D

This is usually a current expense that will not bear fruit until sometime in the future. The possibility to fudge this number to boost earnings in the short run is tempting to companies that must meet analysts' earnings estimates. As a rough rule of thumb when considering a growth company is that R&D should be 10 percent of sales. There is good R&D and bad R&D, so you need to peek into the quality and the amount of this expenditure. You can easily shortchange this category in order to beef up earnings and cash flow, but like marketing, there may be a price to pay down the road as the products become less competitive and start to lose market share. This loss then translates to lower sales, profits, and cash flow. (Once again, professionalism of management and an analysis of the acquired company are required.)

CAPX

This concept is similar to R&D in that you can easily question future prospects if proper machines are not being acquired to make the company's goods. Eventually, quality may suffer and this can result in the loss of market share. You may get a cheap company on paper, but if it is not certified on ISO 9000 manufacturing standards, you will eventually pay the price of losing contracts to competitors who do meet the criteria. More difficult to ascertain is the correct level of CAPX. It should exceed the amount of depreciation, especially if you are using straight-line depreciation. Failing to exceed depreciation means that the company is not even meeting inflation replacement needs.

You can also compare CAPX and depreciation to the average useful life of the plant and equipment with the peer group. However, it is more difficult to forecast future CAPX needs when trying to address the company's future competitive position. There could be quantum jumps in CAPX based on how the industry is changes. For example, new environmental regulations or breakthroughs in technology may allow only larger companies to have the capital sufficient to fund future needs. CAPX is a large portion of free cash flows but can easily be fudged in the short term by cutting back. Free cash flows would be higher, but again, what is the price to be paid down the road? So, you could actually confront management, and while $10 million seems to be adequate for now, $25 million should be the norm. In addition, you may second-guess management's expectations on environmental regulations, production methods, and other areas.

5

VALUATION IS JUST
THE BEGINNING

Determining stock prices with valuation models is a good beginning to the investment process. However, professionals will know that it is a beginning and not a complete process. In fact, being myopic with valuation models may mean that one sees the trees but not the forest. Data has to be adjusted for qualitative and accounting issues. More importantly, correct judgments must be made on the company's outlook. This also clouds back-testing issues. You may hear some organizations who state "we correlated earnings with such and such indicator and there is no correlation." Again, which earnings? GAAP, non-GAAP, or economic non-GAAP? Were the earnings adjusted to meet the required needs, and were they time-delayed to show these effects? Not doing this means you can only make assumptions based on data that may no longer be valid. Stock prices would already anticipate some of these issues, and the technical charts may start to show the ensuing trends.

Analysts and shareholders are at times frustrated when the fundamentals look good but the stock seems not to be reflecting it. Was General Electric an example of this? Analysts complained that GE stock price was languishing to the S&P 500 Index, even when the market was rising post-2002. See (Figure 5.1.)

After 2000, GE eroded relative to the S&P 500 Index, yet earnings were supposed to have been good—why? In hindsight, the answer would seem

FIGURE 5.1 General Electric Company, NYSE, 1996 to 2010

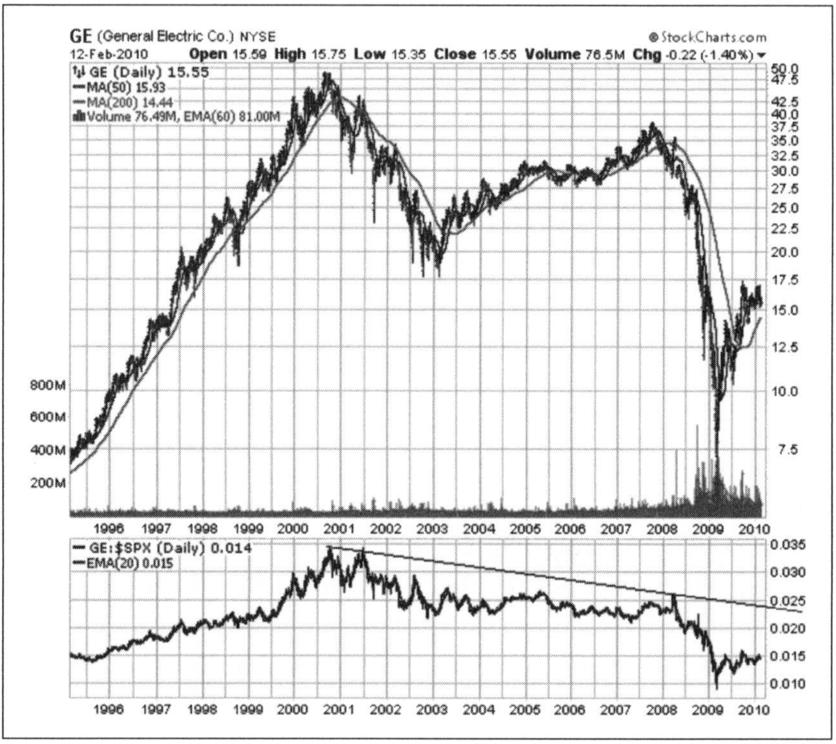

Source: Used by permission of Stockcharts.com

to include some liberal accounting measures that GE used to pad its earnings. This point was brought up in business publications like *Forbes*, which indicated that GE had an assortment of accounting issues, including underreserving its receivables and thereby artificially boosting its earnings.

"The company has been wringing earnings out of its loan book by taking loss reserves in the other direction, to 1.1 percent of receivables from 2.9 percent in 2003. RiskMetrics Group, a financial consulting firm, reckons bringing that ratio back up to 2 percent would cost $4 billion after taxes. GE says it has been increasing reserves on consumer loans to keep them in line with defaults."[1]

The purpose of this short discussion of GE is that a major U.S. company has had issues with its accounting. Somehow the reported data may not have been as useful to investors than if the subsequently known accounting issues were shown. Which numbers do you believe when one back-tests? Are the technicals already telling you that there is smoke?

The Analyst's Learning Curve

Notice that fundamental research can be exhausting as the analyst must look at much data from industry and the company, and then adjust it to give realistic economic results. In addition, much of the grunt work is often given to newbies or freshly minted MBAs who may be good at processing data but still too green to get savvy about the true numbers. We often call this a learning curve, and for analysts there may be a process of several years before they become more seasoned. Some catch on very quickly, and some need time. Some catch on and know the answer their boss and clients want to hear and thus lay the groundwork toward anchoring and making the numbers work out. Sometimes a portfolio manager may decide that training newbies is not worth the effort. The newbies may go to some lunch presentation of a company and come back with stars in their eyes, as the fundamentals look great, but so is the stock price. The more seasoned portfolio manager may have to bring the analyst back to earth and discuss the reasons why this may not be the time to buy the stock because it is fully priced or even overpriced.

So some firms may have extensive training programs for newly minted business majors. Hopefully, with their prior education they can start to form some good judgments. They will be given assignments and cases and then evaluated by more seasoned professionals who would try to get to the fast-track analysts. The rest would eventually be shunned or even let go. Therefore, some funds may have a policy of only hiring someone with at least five years of experience—the assumption being that they have gone through some wars and are savvier. The training costs may not be worth it.

Certain technical tools can assist in making potentially better investment decisions. They can help cut down on fantasy valuations by assigning buy/sell points in seemingly perpetually improving/deteriorating financial conditions. These technical tools include measures such as:

1. Momentum analysis with the use of oscillators
2. Reliance on moving average rules
3. Gann angles
4. Doji reversals
5. Climax reversals

These and other tools will be discussed further later on, but I would like to illustrate the possible uses of technical analysis with regards to one example of an investment situation, the Falling Knife.

Falling Knife

Dealing with sharply falling stock prices is a challenge to fundamental analysis. Fundamental outlooks can change radically overnight, and panic sets in. The bubbly analyst who only a few weeks ago went to a nice lunch and was pumped up to buy more stock is now shell-shocked and ready to sell.

Technicians call a sharply falling stock price a Falling Knife. Highly popular stocks are prone to the Falling Knife when bad news hits.

Falling Knife with Gann Analysis

Fundamentals and technicals can be applied to a Falling Knife situation where a popular stock becomes unloved very quickly. Let's review a real example in VimpelCom (VIP).

VIP was an early mobile phone operator in Russia in the 1990s. It listed on the New York Stock Exchange in 1996. It attracted investment interest for good reasons. The general investing mood was positive toward emerging markets. On a company level, the land lines of Eastern Europe required long wait times and were not as efficient as wireless for communication in the post-Communist era. Finally, higher incomes would lead to more phone users.

Russia defaulted on its debt in the summer of 1998, when emerging markets sold down. VimpelCom's stock price plunged sharply as its subscriber base decreased in the fourth quarter of 1998. The company reported in its year-end report:[2]

Despite the Russian economic crisis, VimpelCom's total year-to-year subscriber growth was approximately 13 percent. As of December 31, 1998, the number of subscribers on the company's Moscow networks was 124,037, as compared to 110,140 subscribers reported in 1997. The number of subscribers on VimpelCom's Moscow networks decreased in the fourth quarter by approximately 12 percent, as compared to the 141,600 subscribers reported as of September 30, 1998.

Of concern to analysts was a high churn rate with VimpelCom disconnecting customers because of non-payment. Again, from the company's 1998 year-end report:

VimpelCom also recorded an extraordinarily high churn rate in 1998, estimated at 54% for the year, most of which occurred subsequent to the Russian economic crisis. The company has continued its strict policy of disconnecting non-paying customers, which accounted for almost two-thirds of all disconnects during 1998.

All of a sudden, investors went from a very bullish opinion to a pessimistic opinion, causing the stock to plunge like a Falling Knife. While there was initially a need for more wireless communication, the mood shifted to a "so what?" attitude. While there was a need, no one was paying their phone bills, so the company would have no profits.

Another dagger in the heart of VimpelCom related to more specific fundamentals of the company. VimpelCom had outdated technology as per the wording of Joe Lunder, CEO:[3]

The company also suffered, as its DAMPS technology could not successfully compete against GSM used by its main competitor. Initially the company had to take DAMPS because the regulator would not issue more than one GSM license per region due to the shortage of frequencies.

So VimpelCom became a Falling Knife upon Russia's economic problems in 1998. Fundamental projections were scaled down, but technicals gave a good entry point on November 23, 1998, and VimpelCom later rebounded.

Contributing to the recovery of the company and its stock price was the rebuilding of the company by attracting two strategic partners of Telenor from Norway and the Alfa Group of Russia.[4] VimpelCom changed to GSM and became more national in scope. In 1999, it took only six months to build a network of GSM stations in Moscow and its neighborhoods.[5] (It also enhanced a good brand image under its Beeline name.[6])

In a Falling Knife situation, you must decide whether to buy or not, and if so, when. The plunging prices indicate some sort of terminal doom and a possible implosion of any remaining value. In other words, the sky is falling. Either the stock is going to zero or you have a reasonable expectation that the fundamentals are still strong enough to give the company some value. With fundamentals being so cloudy, you may want to resort to technical analysis in order to determine an entry point for a possible purchase.

Figure 5.2 presents Tulips and Bears' excellent analysis of the use of technicals to bottom-fish with purchases. Points to watch are identified in the circle in the bottom right-hand corner of the first part of the chart.

Stock broke decisively out of the downtrend with the crossing of the GANN 45-degree line. So while originally the stock was popular at a price of well over 50, it plunged to under 10 on the chart. The buy point was around 15 as the 45 degree line (1 × 1) was breeched. Below the line was a sell signal; above it, a buy signal. VimpelCom closed above GANN 1 × 1 resistance angle (at 15.43) for first time since August. The stock also broke out above its 50-day moving average. The daily MACD line moved above 0, giving a buy signal. The volume measure (OBV) was in a strong uptrend since hitting bottom in early October. The rising highs of the OBV confirmed the rebounding prices, as there was no negative divergence. There were additional technical indicators that gave confirming buy signals. These included the momentum indicators of the uptrending RSI and Stochastics. The fund successfully blended various technical disciplines to give a buy confirmation that later proved to benefit from higher prices.

FIGURE 5.2 VimpelCom, December 1996 to November 1998

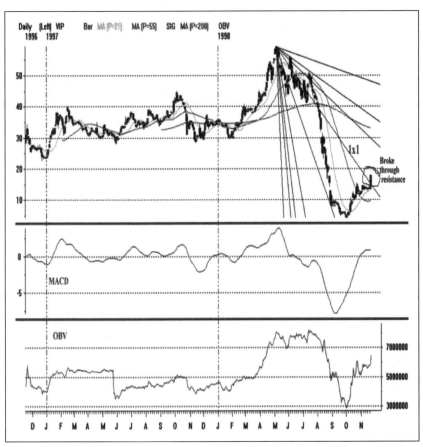

Source: Used by permission of Tulips and Bears LLC

VimpelCom later recovered with splits from its low of under $0.10 in 1998 to nearly $45 by 2007 year end. With the global market selloff in 2008, it went as low as $5 in early 2009 and then quadrupled to $20 a year later as global stock markets rebounded. (I would add to this chart analysis that most likely investment sentiment was negative at the bottom of well under 10, contrary to the euphoria at the 50-plus top. This was reflected in changing brokerage and investor decisions.)

Because GANN has subangles for various trading considerations, one of the challenges is to smooth the trends that create the degree lines.

We usually take the peak and draw a 45-degree line down to give a sell signal below the line and a buy signal above the line. Likewise, once we get a decision, we take the low (here it would be the low under 10) and draw an upward 45-degree line that gives a buy signal above the 45-degree line, but a sell signal if it drops below the line. As you can imagine, if you do this for every small change, it will result in many trades, which means additional transaction costs that could wipe out profits and even cause losses. (See Figure 5.2.) GANN users may use proprietary methods to choose broader price trends, such as the move from 30 to the 50-plus top price. Notice that in 1997 there were several reversals between 30 and 40, and so other technical factors may help the analyst make buy and sell decisions.

One may add that in emotional markets, fundamental valuations usually follow price trends, thus missing turning points.

The Selling Climax

The Selling Climax is similar to the Falling Knife where prices drop sharply; however, the time period may be rather brief, perhaps only one or a few days.[7] While prices drop sharply, they may soon recover just as sharply. Traders may speculate on this possibility, especially if it is perceived as only a one-day or few day's drop at most.

In general, a climax whether buying or selling may entail both technical and fundamental considerations:

1. Technically, these climaxes mark turning points, evidenced by high relative trading volume and indicating extremes of fear and greed.
2. With Fama-French (as well as other valuation criteria), these stocks may exhibit good/poor valuations. The sharp price movements in selling climaxes tilt the stocks into good valuation measures based on P/B and size, compared to their positions prior to the climax, as prices tend to move significantly in one direction.

Based on the definition of leading technical analyst John J. Murphy, a Selling Climax is a significant reversal occurring at chart bottom. It is "usually a dramatic turnaround at the bottom of a down move where all the discouraged longs have finally been forced out of the market on heavy volume. The subsequent absence of selling pressures creates a vacuum over the market, which prices quickly rally to fill. ... [W]hile it may not mark the final bottom of a falling market, it usually signals that a significant low has been seen."[8]

Selling Climaxes may result from fundamental information such as earnings outlook disappointments based on corporate announcements. Optimistic PEG and DCF models are then scaled back substantially. Upon selloff, a stock may reach valuation levels that offer the opportunity to generate future risk-adjusted excess returns (Alpha).

A Selling Climax challenges the Semi-Strong Form of the Efficient Market Hypothesis. Under this form, historical financial information would not be useful to generating an alpha. We could also assume it say it would challenge the weak form, as a Selling Climax makes a plunging price pattern. However, a Selling Climax based on the long-time observations of leading technicians appears to provide good return opportunities. Technical stock analysts Robert D. Edwards and John Magee, in their book *Technical Analysis of Stock Trends* (8th edition, pg 171) state, "It is a harvest time for traders who, having avoided the Bullish inflection at the top of the market, have funds in reserve to pick up stocks available at panic prices."[9]

These levels would show more attractive valuation factors that offer alpha opportunities. The attractive fundamental factors show relatively lower P/B value and smaller market cap size, based on the work of Fama and French.[10] Some would also claim that the lower P/E ratio of the stock would enable it to show future risk-adjusted returns. This is based on the belief that over long periods, low P/E stocks perform better than high P/E stocks. We can also add that as the P/E goes from high to low, there is an element of sentiment changing from optimism to pessimism.

Fama explained the validity of these factors by pointing out there is a convergence between extremes of valuation that can be explained rationally because they are expected by certain investors (of the Fama and French camp), or irrationally, as investors get surprised on deteriorating fundamentals after a stock has moved to a growth category.[11] So, initially, investors get carried away with their expectations by being too optimistic, accepting more expensive ratios such as P/B. It would seem that Fama's work is a proxy for recognizing the influence of behavioral finance.

James Montier, a leading observer of behavioral finance on Wall Street, has commented, "if a stock price drops, then in theory if the analysts were correct in their initial price target, it should become even more attractive to buy. However, in practice, analysts actually reduce their target prices in response to a drop in the current market price."[12] One behavioral influence on analyst forecasts is Representativeness. Montier defines it as a "tendency to evaluate how likely something is with reference to how closely it resembles something rather than using probabilities. Representativeness generates excessively extreme forecasts ..."[13]

This could partially account for the willingness to trade the stock at much lower levels. Other behavioral factors could also come into play. The risk of a loss may not be equal to the risk of a gain even if both sides produce the same percentage. A loss of 25 percent will be more painful than the benefit of the gain of 25 percent. With Representativeness in a Selling Climax, we may associate a company's problems that seem similar to that of another which had dire results. Some might quickly say "It's another Lehman," even though the problems may not turn out to be so dire. (Evidence the rebound of many financial institutions from their deep lows of March 2009.)

Figure 5.3 highlights Impath, a clinical lab that experienced a selling climax in April 2001. This instance was tied to earnings disappointments but soon proved profitable for traders upon subsequent rallies. (A few years later, a massive corporate fraud caused Impath to enter bankruptcy and liquidation, initiating another profitable opportunity with a selling climax.)

Note the sharp price plunge from around 46 to around 30. Also note the daily volume reached over 3 million shares traded, considerably more than the normal past volume of under 500,000. The fundamentals entered the Fama-French territory for potential risk-adjusted outperformance. Wall Street and the leading fund holders became despondent with earnings downgrades and large selling.

FIGURE 5.3 IMPATH, Inc., 2001

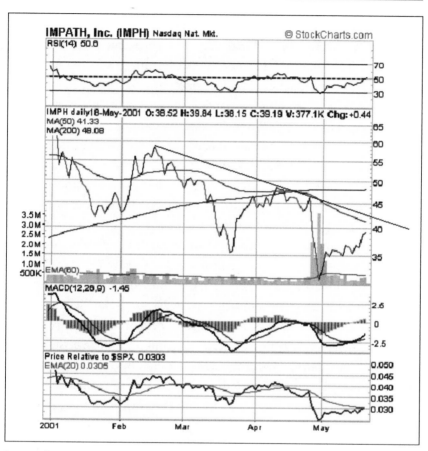

Source: Used by permission of Stockcharts.com

Why would a short-term trader buy IMPH stock when it went below 30 at the end of April? The stock's P/E and P/B relative to the market was markedly more attractive at the approximate 30 selling climax low and appealed more to value investors and technical analysts. The expected P/E was 26 (1.2 × the S&P 500), the trailing P/E was 33 (1.3 × the S&P 500) and the P/B was 3.3 (about 60 percent of the S&P 500).

Just a few months before the selling climax, IMPH traded at 60 with much higher absolute and relative valuations. After the selling cllimax, the stock then rallied nicely and profits were realized. IMPH showed a technical opportunity with a selling climax. Fundamentally, valuations were more attractive and behavioral opportunities could be exploited. (Ironically, later, in 2003's selling climax, due to a management imbroglio, the stock went from about 20 to under $1.00! Impath was forced to file for bankruptcy and eventually sold off its assets. It repaid its debt, and there was about $5 a share left over for shareholders as the stock was then trading on the Bulletin Board as DIP, or debtor in possession.)

Impath's three largest funds were handled by active managers, a possible indication of quick selling. If the funds were all index funds, we would assume that a quick sale may not be as likely. If the funds were more growth-oriented rather than value-oriented, that would indicate more probability of a sale. (See Figure 5.3.) By using a technical measure of establishing a downward trend line resistance (by connecting 58 in February and 48 in April), a near-term price objective of 40 would be realistic.

Selling climaxes are becoming more common, especially with the increased use of momentum strategies by hedge funds. In a selling climax, it as possible to attempt to buy the stock at the low and hedge risks with derivatives—namely, buying a protective put option with an elasticity that is a close as possible to −1.0. If the stock does not have options, synthetic options from other securities could be created or the trader can put a mental stop into place. Behaviorally, will the trader stay with the stop, as he succumbs to the Disposition Effect of holding on to losers too long? So, even though the trader places a stop to sell if he is wrong and the stock declines a certain amount, with the Disposition Effect, he may not do it or override it at the last minute. The trader may hate to admit that he was wrong. A trader may also buy puts. Because the rally is expected to be rather soon, the trader would tend to look at low theta or time and buy a near-term strike price (to get Delta close to 1.0) and also a nearby time expiry.

In the Impath example (Figure 5.3), if we bought near 30–31 for rebound trade, upon seeing the Selling Climax, we would be better off to do a technical decision on when to take possible profits. New fundamentals may not be apparent for quite some time on financial measures. Technically, one sees a resistance at 35, as this was the support in March. So we would then take profits of $4 to $5 before transaction costs. Now, we may also be wrong, so I would recommend putting a stop 2 points under the buy price and then walking away with a small loss if wrong. This would protect us against a further plunge in the stock. If we could buy a put, then a 3:1 trade-off should be made. If the gain is 5 and the put costs $1.50, that is over a 3:1 ratio and the derivative should be used. If the put were to cost $2.50, then we would have only a 2:1 ratio, which would indicate the risk to reward is not that attractive. In that case, we would use a stop to cut losses.

From my observation, a selling climax is a profitable opportunity for traders, but still there are no guarantees. The stock may not rebound that day; however, I would enter a buy about one hour after the stock opens. Here we would expect the maximum selling to start easing, as there is now enough time to better match orders. Of course, the stock may just bounce around a rally a few days later, and this could challenge profits as your stop may be hit just before the stock rallies. In my opinion, the first selling climax is the best to play, as it is then likely to create that disgusted feeling that was not there earlier. If another selling climax happens, say, within a year, I would back away, as investors saw a rally last time and this time around may not be as eager to sell in distress. One should not be surprised to see further bad news down the road, as selling climaxes often invite an investment concept that is sometimes called the Cockroach Theory: when you see one (disappointment), you will soon see another.

Trading on Economic Events

Traders like to play events. Pending economic releases, such as the job numbers on the first Friday of each month, often cause wide fluctuations in stock futures, bonds, and commodities just before the 8:30 a.m. release and just after it. Traders also play events such as Fed meeting notes releases, CPI, and so on. Behaviorally, traders feel they can correctly anticipate these events and profit from them.

One method of anticipating earnings releases is called Standardized Unexpected Earnings (SUE) trading. Here, short-term traders sometimes speculate on a company's earnings releases and their impact on the stock price. If earnings are good, the stock may rise sharply, and if they disappoint, then the stock should plunge. For traders, these swings can bring nice profits in a very short period of time. Can one still make economic returns after earnings are released? How about events in general?

There is some evidence that one can do this because the news does not always adjust to the news as quickly as it should. Some news may not affect the stock price such as accounting changes. Technicians would say that the stocks then make trends as more and more investors realize the correct nature of the news. This trend can be exploited, as the news does not instantly adjust. Behaviorally, some are pushed into actions to maybe save face. One who has been too high on earnings and then sees lower actual earnings may perhaps show clients that they are doing something to save capital by selling some or all of a position. Likewise, good news and not having a position indicates that you missed the boat. Thus, you may have to at least aggressively nibble to show that you are "with the program" as much as other smart managers who have this good-looking stock.

Standardized Unexpected Earnings

Earnings events have been studied for many years and there is some evidence that traders can get returns after news is released.[14] However, there are those who feel these returns are actually a function of other things such as the P/E effect. While some traders are good at predicting the earnings before they are released, others feel the Standardized Unexpected Earnings (SUE) method is important, in that both analysts' estimates and surprise earnings are captured, which is better than just using some linear extrapolation of past earnings. However, using both methods is better than using one method alone.[15]

Traders can use the fundamentals of SUE with technical tools. The exploitation of SUE[16] can be optimized via momentum indicators.

$$SUE = FE_t \text{ / Standard deviation of } FE_t$$
$$FE_t = \text{Forecasted error of a time period (t)}$$
$$= \text{Actual earnings reported} - \text{Estimate of expected earnings}$$

So if ABC Company has estimated earnings of $3 and reports $5, its forecasted error is $5 − $3 = $2.

Investors are positively surprised by $2. If the standard deviation of past errors is $0.80, this surprise is notable because SUE = $2/0.80 = 2.5. (If the standard deviation was $4, then the SUE is 0.50, a minor surprise.)

Traders cannot take advantage of SUE before earnings are made public, as this can be construed as trading on material, nonpublic information and is illegal. However, evidence shows that there is a "direct relationship between the size of unexpected earnings and abnormal stock return"[17] Thus, a large SUE tends to push stock prices up, while a negative SUE tends to push stock prices down.

Technically, short-term traders can scan for high SUEs via IBES and "ride the stock" till the oscillator (such as the Relative Strength Index, or RSI, or Fast Stochastic) reaches extreme overbought/oversold conditions and the short-term relative strength no longer confirms the ensuing flow of high/lows of the stock. Behaviorally, some institutions may try to avoid the risks of peer pressure for short-term forecasting based on events by taking a longer-term approach to valuation, such as picking stocks with a low P/B ratio. While this may not always be popular in the short term, this method helps to avoid the behavioral pressure and gets good long-term results.[18]

As an example, we can review NCI, Inc. (NCIT).

Table 5.1 shows released earnings of NCIT on the Business Wire on February 17, 2010 at 4:05 p.m. They appeared good, as management guided the improved earnings forecast from $1.74 to $1.82.

Table 5.2 shows the 2010 estimates were in line with consensus as shown on Yahoo's financial page and had earnings projections of analysts of $1.78. So far so good. However, the first quarter was below projections, as analysts had $0.39 and management guided a bit lower at $0.37 to $0.39.

Note in Table 5.3 that analysts were already downgrading quarterly estimates from 7 days and even 90 days prior to $0.41. Also, one may question

TABLE 5.1 NCI, Inc., First Quarter and Full Year, 2010

	1st Quarter 2010	**Full Year 2010**
Revenue	$115 million–$120 million	$530 million–$550 million
Diluted earnings per share	$0.37–$0.39	$1.74–$1.82

TABLE 5.2 NCI, Inc., Earnings Estimates, 2010

Earnings Estimate	Current Quarter Mar-10	Next Quarter Jun-10	Current Year Dec-10	Next Year Dec-11
Average estimate	0.39	0.43	1.78	2.00
Number of analysts	11	11	12	8
Low estimate	0.38	0.41	1.71	1.89
High estimate	0.42	0.45	1.88	2.13
Year ago EPS	0.34	0.37	1.55	

TABLE 5.3 NCI, Inc., EPS Trends, 2010

EPS Trends	Current Quarter Mar-10	Next Quarter Jun-10	Current Year Dec-10	Next Year Dec-11
Current estimate	0.39	0.43	1.78	2.00
7 Days Ago	0.41	0.43	1.78	2.03
30 Days Ago	0.41	0.43	1.78	1.99
60 Days Ago	0.41	0.43	1.78	1.99
90 Days Ago	0.41	0.43	1.78	1.99

whether analysts really show their true earnings versus their core belief earnings sometimes called "whisper" earnings.

The next day, the stock opened higher (see circle on price chart in Figure 5.4; shown in minutes). For half an hour, the stock traded above the prior day's close of near $28, the stock actually went over $28.80. (So some saw the earnings as good, but they were most likely looking at the whole year.)

The traders saw the quarterly earnings as weak and sold or had the opportunity to sell short. By 11:30 a.m., the stock dropped to near $25.60. So did the stock adjust immediately? Also, could one have traded that quickly—perhaps algorithmically as well as humanly. This is a small-cap stock of a market cap of $350 million and trades 68,000 shares a day with a float of 6.1 million. The stock traded only about 1000 shares per the one-minute periods. Hence, an elephant fund may not have been able to visibly trade; however, the SUE studies indicate that small-cap stocks benefit more.[19]

FIGURE 5.4 NCI, Inc., February 2010

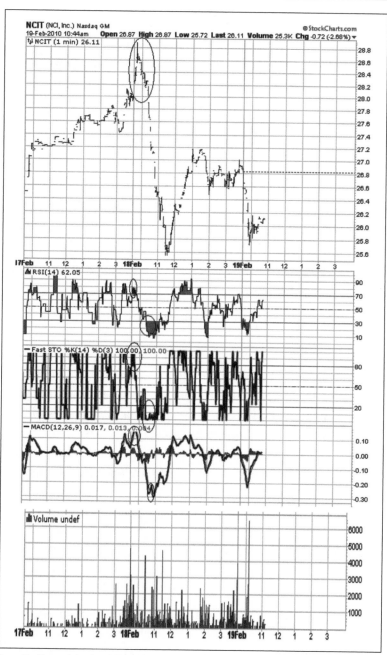

Note the peak price has sell signals on the RSI which is over 70 (circle); the buy or short cover could be under the 30 level (circle). These are supported by the Fast Stochastics and the MACD, which are adjusted for the minute intervals. One can then reverse and buy at the bottom and get sell signals near 27 with the RSI at 70 again, with Fast Stochastics and the peak of the MACD also helping to confirm.

So we can summarize some key points. Which earnings do we look at and are they economically presented? Are the estimates published or whisper? Should we do only certain SUE trades, such as small-cap stocks? Are the behavioral pressures more pronounced in such areas? Are we better off doing algorithmic trades which can do this electronically very quickly or have humans do this? (We discuss algorithmic trading later in the book.) And should we even do trading versus investing? There are always human traders who feel they have the magic touch, and that in itself makes technical analysis work as they succumb to follies and emotions.

Case-Group Rotation Permutations

Changes in economic trends naturally lead to emphasizing some industries or sectors more than others. Another strategy involves the exploitation of a popular group that would seem to have investment opportunities based on changing economic data. The group may be acting one way now, but based on this new data, they are expected to turn directions. The turn may be due to a change in basic economic data such as interest rates. This change may be dangerous, as estimates tend to be raised as stock prices go higher and vice versa. It would be too late for traders to exploit. By the time fundamentals change and the changes are apparent, stock prices have already changed direction.

Technical analysis can help the trader to better time the fundamental decision, as technically, there are multiple ways of exploiting a perceived change in economic data.

During June and July 2003, we saw the bond prices fall sharply, and so interest rates rose (see Figure 5.5). In hindsight, this was caused by a recovering economy from the 2002 bottom. It was summarized by Mutual of America Capital Management Corporation on August 20, 2003, as follows:[20]

The fixed-income markets have seen much turbulence lately, with some of the most dramatic yield swings in history. Yields rose as bond prices were pushed lower on news of improved economic forecasts (with the possibility of consequent inflation and higher interest rates) and the Fed's unwillingness to purchase Treasury securities with longer maturities as a means to lower interest rates. These high yields are a turnabout from 45-year lows reached in the spring. Yields in the short end of the yield curve have risen more slowly than securities of longer maturities, which reflects expectations for low interest rates to stay that way for the foreseeable future. The spread (or difference in yield) between notes of two and 10 years to maturity, reached highs that haven't been seen in over 20 years.

FIGURE 5.5 T-Bond 20+ Yr iS, April 2002 to July 2003

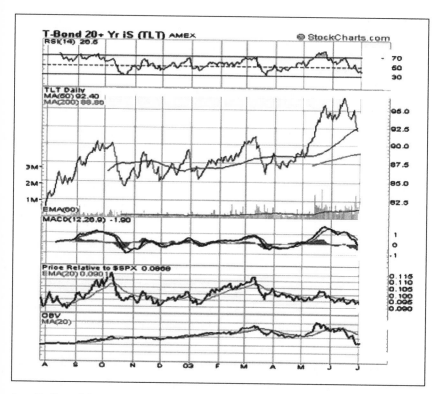

Ben Bernanke, then a Federal Reserve governor, prepped for the rise in interest rates with his speech "An Unwelcome Fall in Inflation?" on July 23, 2003. This must have put angst on the bond market that was already sniffing rising interest rates, as Bernanke warned that further deflation could harm the economy.

"Today I would like to share my own thoughts on the prospect of an 'unwelcome substantial fall in inflation'—in particular, why a substantial fall in inflation going forward would indeed be unwelcome; why some risk of further disinflation, though 'minor,' should not be ignored; and what such a fall would imply for the conduct of monetary policy." Later in the speech, Bernanke hinted, "At some point in the future, if all goes well, inflation will stabilize, and interest rates will begin to rise."[21] So did bond managers shoot first and ask questions later? Consider such a situation for a trader who believes that interest rates are now ready to move up, perhaps being stoked by fears of more inflation.

Shorting the Bond

Maybe a trader using technical analysis sees this (see Figure 5.6). A downward-sloping Head and Shoulder (HS) pattern indicates a fall in bond prices is coming and, thus, rising interest rates. Take the head to the neckline and subtract where it breaks the neckline—roughly, 97 minus 93.5, or 3.5 points. Then 93 minus 3.5 points gives us 89.5 as a price objective on the bond.

We can also use a technical analysis tool of using round numbers. Some traders trade with round numbers as a guide, so let's call it 90. Note the bond hit and briefly bounced off this level before going even lower. So shorting at 93 gives us 3.5 points or 3.76 percent, or about 3.8 percent before transaction costs.

We could have made more, as the HS was confirmed by other measures which were very negative, thus giving us the incentive to go for lower prices than 93. RSI has a negative divergence, as the rising peak of the TLT in June was not confirmed by the RSI, which had lower peaks. MACD was still in a sell signal mode at 93, as the MACD did not cross its moving average. (See Figure 5.7.)

Still, there is no guarantee that the bond price will keep falling, so one can buy calls on the short or do a simple mental stop, ala our prior analysis. We could have kept a short to about 85.0 because that is where we see

FIGURE 5.6 T-Bond 20+ Yr iS Head and Shoulder Pattern, April 2002 to July 2003

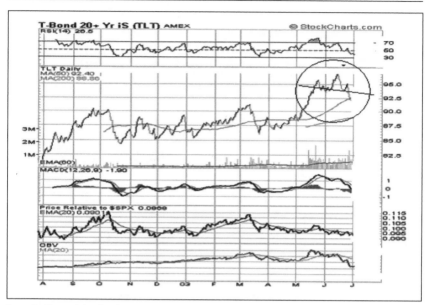

Source: Used by permission of Stockcharts.com

FIGURE 5.7 T-Bond 20+ Yr iS, April 2002 to July 2003

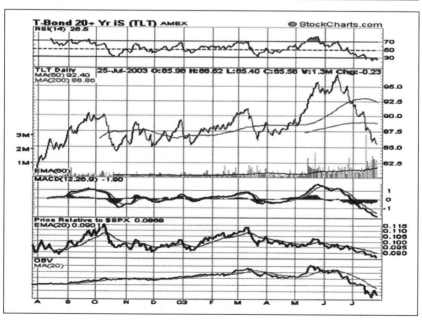

Source: Used by permission of Stockcharts.com

FIGURE 5.8 T-Bond 20+ Yr iS, April 2002 to July 2003 (annotated)

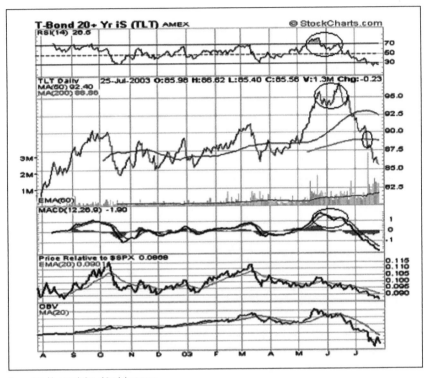

Source: Used by permission of Stockcharts.com

support from April levels. We may try to cover earlier at 87 because there is some near-term support from April. (See Figure 5.8.)

So far so good. There is a profit on the short of at least 3.8 percent and maybe more like 6.5 percent, if we cover around 87. So an expected value play could be mid-point of 5.1 percent—before transaction costs. Being liquid, TLT could be assumed to have a round-trip costs of 1 percent. What else could we do? How about a pairs trade with the stock market?

Pairs Trade

Bonds lead stocks for broad moves but not always in the short term. Actually, a rebounding economy can be bullish for stocks even if infla-

FIGURE 5.9 PerfChart–Interactive Performance Comparison Chart

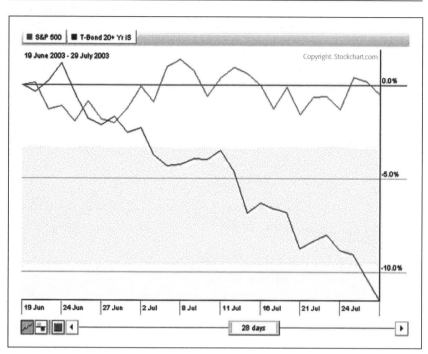

Source: Used by permission of Stockcharts.com

tion picks up because it implies more pricing power of companies and more profits. It is only later when the economy hits full employment and full production that price increases lead to inflation and the Fed raises interest rates. While interest rates go higher, a trader may speculate that stocks would rise or do better. So a pairs trade can be done by going long on the S&P 500 and shorting the TLT (see Figure 5.9). Note that, in about a week, one makes 10 percent before transaction costs, so subtract 1 percent to get 9 percent.

Shorting Housing Stocks

Instead of prior actions, the weak bond outlook may have led a trader to short the housing stocks, as the reflex action would initially hurt home-builder prospects. Again, a recovering economy may increase mortgage rates, but the number of job holders would increase and rising incomes may allow for more people to buy houses. Still, there is a tendency to see rising interest rates in the short term as being negative for homebuilders. As one can surmise, assumptions on short term correlations can be a challenge.

Looking at Figure 5.10 for TOL, a homebuilder, what trade would you do at the end of June? Would your decision be only for a short-term trade, or for a longer-term change in strategy? Why?

We also see a HS and a short around 14. Let's say you seek a point where you would not reach 13 in this chart. Now what? Wait?

FIGURE 5.10 Toll Brothers, Inc., April 7, 2003 to July 28, 2003

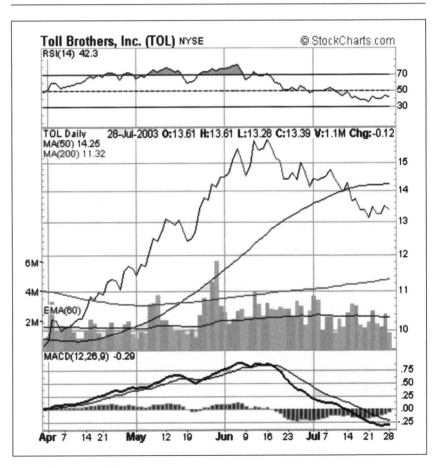

Source: Used by permission of Stockcharts.com

What about taking a smaller profit of 1/2 a point on 14 or 3.5 percent before transaction costs? That is a dangerous wait, as trading can be volatile. I would take the small gain and go on to another situation. Still, one may hang on to the short, as the RSI gave a negative divergence and the MACD has a negative reading and is still negative, with the MACD below the moving average. (See Figure 5.11.)

It's unlikely fundamentals will give any meaningful input so quickly. Investors obviously may smell the higher interest rates and start the process of selling, but giving exact fundamental valuation levels would be difficult in such a short period. One would have to have a longer-term outlook.

FIGURE 5.11 Toll Brothers, Inc., April 7, 2003 to July 28, 2003 (annotated)

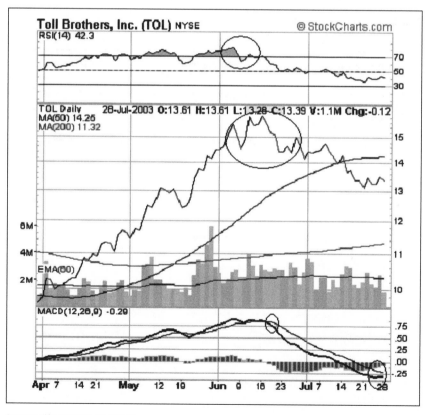

Source: Used by permission of Stockcharts.com

It would seem that in this case a trader would be at a disadvantage in using fundamentals versus technical indicators.

Let's try something else then. How about the cyclicals?

Buy Cyclicals

If inflation is picking up, commodities should do well and we can play the Cyclicals Index, or the ETF CYC (see Figure 5.12). Note the breakout on the resistance and the buy on the MACD. Go long on the CYC. Can you see why?

The weakness of the bond market also led to the chart presented in Figure 5.13. A short-term trader with an investment horizon of one week

FIGURE 5.12 Cyclicals Index

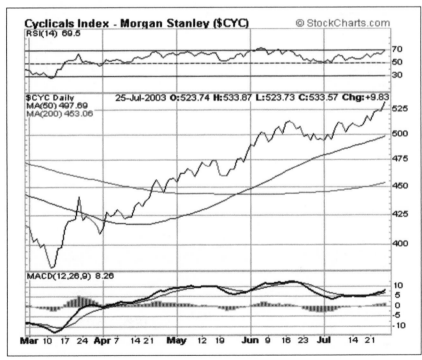

FIGURE 5.13 Cyclicals Index (annotated)

Source: Used by permission of Stockcharts.com

must decide whether to buy or short the cyclicals based on the five-month chart. Note the buy signals with the breakout on July 21 and the confirmation with the MACD.

What about an investor with a horizon of one year? Would it make sense to seek cyclicals as the "other side of a two-way trade" with housing? Inter-market analysis may require more focus on technicals first, rather than fundamentals first.[22]

Longer term, one may hold on to the cyclicals to the resistance of 575. So one buys CYC at 515 and may hold on to 575, or a gain of 11.7 percent. (See Figure 5.14.) However, that is a bit of a stretch for a trader. While the resistance looks reasonable, it may take too long for some traders. Of course, one can hedge with puts and so forth, but to keep our analysis simple, we shall assume that the end trade is a sale. But where?

FIGURE 5.14 Morgan Stanley, 1999 to 2003

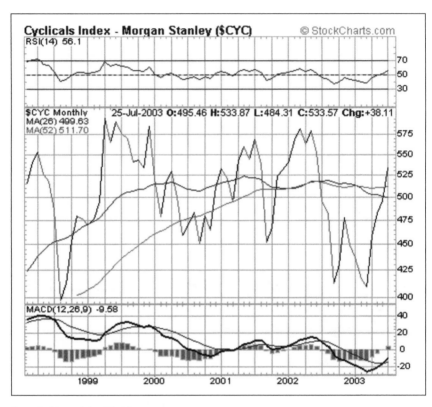

Source: Used by permission of Stockcharts.com

Most likely a sell would be done around 530, as the RSI is getting near a sell signal. Also, the MACD histogram indicates a nearing resistance, evidenced by the June 9 (see histogram at bottom in Figure 5.14). OK, so let's say we sell at 530 on a 515 buy or gain of 2.9 percent before transaction costs.

How about call options on the CYC? We will keep this simple by leaving out derivative strategies, as we can also do swaps and eliminate transaction costs of doing the actual trades. For example, we can do a swap to exchange returns of, say, stock versus bonds or versus cyclicals and so on. This would be the providence more of hedge funds and other institutions rather than retail traders.

Decision Tree Time

So, which action should a trader do? Should she pick one branch of the decision tree, all them, or just some of them? Short the bond? Pairs trade? Short a housing stock—and if so, which one? Enter the inter-market and buy the CYC or do a call option on the CYC?

Do all of the above or only some?

At this point we can also start to use algorithmic trading systems that can perform this action a hundred times per second in many markets and many situations. Maybe we can hire PhDs in math and get rid of the human traders. This has been the trend over the past few years, since a large amount of trades are now done algorithmically. Still, as the saying goes, garbage in, garbage out, and programming the right decision is key.

Let's recap the choices and the expected returns of our examples:

Short TLT	3.8%
Pairs trade	10.0%
Short TOL	3.5%
Buy CYC	2.9%

The pairs trade looks like the best deal, but it carries a high risk of the correlations between bond and stock returns. CYC carries the lowest return but is more liquid than TOL and is easier to hedge via derivatives. (TOL is also more prone to specific risk.) Shorting TLT is also good, but it means that yield curve assumptions hold. What if we play a package of these types of trades over time? Assume we get an average return of 5.0 percent minus 1 percent for transaction costs; we get a return of 4 percent for one to two weeks' work. Let's round this time period to two weeks, and without compounding, we get 4 percent times 26, or 104 percent return a year. From this we must subtract potential losses.

Many traders believe fundamental research but are often disappointed by the uncertainty of the data and the brevity in timing. Also, the fundamentals may not help in short-term trading positions. Technical tools can make specific actions for potential profits in trading and even asset allocation. These may contradict fundamentals, as many traders may not be willing to admit early on that rates are really an issue to begin with.

Completing our example, we can start to incorporate other factors such as liquidity portfolio constraints. We can take a weighted average to get an expected value of 5.05 percent, if all are weighted equally. We can also use Bayesian inference to update outcomes and their probabilities. Probabilities may no longer be the same because of new information, but we would adjust to new probabilities. This can result in a better decision going forward, but we have to assume that the new probabilities take hold. If not, then the benefit is naturally lost.

6

INVESTING, TRADING, AND GOLD

Individual traders often cannot make a good record in trading, and so are at a disadvantage to institutional traders.[1]

Some key differences are behavioral. Well documented is the Disposition Effect where winners are sold too soon and losers are held too long. Amateurs hate to admit they are wrong and will more likely hold on to losing positions on the hope they bounce back. Usually, new traders exhibit overconfidence. They also trade too much and generate excessive transaction costs.

There are other traits that can challenge amateur traders. There tends to be limited attention to stocks in general, while stocks that received recommendations from news or finance programs gained volume and new highs. This ultimately leads to chasing stocks. The stock may not necessarily go down right away at this point, but it will start to churn. This can trap traders into whipsaw situations. Quantitatively, purchases and sales may be highly correlated, as all traders tend to jump in at the same time, and so don't take advantage of Contrary Opinion. In addition, there are other characteristics of traders, such as getting more aggressive when making money and getting more pessimistic when losing money. This tends to cloud opportunities and leads to chasing prices, rather than anticipating them.

This usually is not a good way to trade, as past winners are not a good predictor of future results. Later, we shall examine this concept also for picking mutual funds.

Individual U.S. trader folly of the late 1990s was repeated with similar players in the Saudi market of early 2006 and China in the fall of 2007. They also took heavy loans to buy stocks and thus compounded losses when these markets crashed.

In the late 1990s, some U.S. day traders agree to do 25 trades per day at $10 per trade at some trading brokerage firms. Also, a one- or two-hour "technical analysis course" for several thousand dollars fed on their overconfidence. In the end they lost most of their money within a year, as one would have to double initial capital just to break even! In fact, some define a long-term investor as a day trader who is losing money.

While we discussed a rather complex trade with decision branches in an example in the previous chapter, trading can be much simpler. It is unlikely that amateur traders can identify complex alternatives on their own. Therefore, much trading is seeking temporary pricing inefficiencies where the trader is speculating that either a stock is overpriced and will soon drop or it is underpriced and will soon rise. Thus, we have two issues at stake: pricing and timing. The pricing decision may be based on perceptions of fundamentals or the use of some technical analysis. The timing part is different for various traders, as day traders tend to move their positions into cash by the end of the trading day, while swing traders seek time periods of a few days or a few weeks to capture an expected price move and so may carry a position longer than overnight.

Following is a simple trading decision that I experienced. It will illustrate some specific issues.

Case Study: Emaar Properties

Emaar Properties is a real estate developer in Dubai that is described on its Web site as a company that aspires to be a global provider of premier lifestyles. The stock is listed on the Dubai Financial Market. Since its inception in 1997, Emaar has had six business segments and more than 60 active companies. It has a collective presence in several markets spanning the Middle East, North Africa, Pan-Asia, Europe, and North America. Among its notable properties, Emaar built the Burj Khalifa, the tallest building in the world.

Dubai had a boom and then a bust in its real estate prices as it became a victim of the global recession in 2008. Emaar had been popular with many investors who rode the stock price up during the good times in Dubai. HSBC Bank estimated that property prices declined 23 percent in the fourth quarter of 2008 and that vacancies were expected to rise considerably in light of the oversupply of property that was created in the boom years.[2] In actuality, vacancies rose and prices declined even more, dropping over 50 percent. Dubai entered into a financial crisis that required a $25 billion bailout from nearby Abu Dhabi in early 2010. (Emaar stock hit near 20 dirhams in early 2006 and went to under 2 in early 2009; as of March 2011, 1 dirham = 0.1236 USD).

In a conference in Dubai that I gave on May 30, 2006, the Emaar stock closed at $12.40. While this was before the crises period, there was a clue that the real estate market was ready to drop. The shopping malls had kiosks of future real estate apartment projects that strolling individuals could quickly sign up for with minimal money down. Of course, the properties were designed for foreigners who would come to Dubai on weeklong junkets. These people may have eventually bought some property with loans from foreign countries, maybe Switzerland in a carry trade (Borrow at cheap rates to invest in seemingly high returning assets.) In other words, like with the 1929 stock market, there was hype, easy credit, and buying assets with liberal margins. The foreigners bought not necessarily to live in the residences but to use them as investments. This would include renting them out or even quickly flipping them once some gain was realized. (As prices began rising, this was a reasonable exit strategy.)

On the day of the conference, May 30, traders with a horizon of a few weeks thought that the stock bottomed out because of a major selloff in the UAE stocks. I was asked if this was the time to bottom-fish in Emaar. (See Figure 6.1.)

FIGURE 6.1 EMAAR Properties–Arab Stock Market Tech Analysis–30-May-2006

Source: Used by permission of Orient Consulting Center

Using Japanese Candlesticks, the technicals did not support their assessment for buy opportunities. We shall discuss Japanese Candlesticks later in the book. Note the recent Dojis and Spinning Tops in early May. These chart patterns looked like either a cross or a fatter crossbar in the cross. Generally, these may have indicated a lack of expected direction from that of the prior trend in the short term. While the prices are rising from 11 in mid-May, they soon seemed to be stalling. After a sharp decline from 20 to 11, I could only ask: Is this all the firepower that the bulls have? If so, this was not enough fuel for a near-term rebound.

The stock peaked intra-day at around $13.40 in early June and then fell to $11.20 by June 21, 2006 (see Figure 6.2). This confirmed my prior expectation that the stock was not poised to rebound. Maybe a day trader

FIGURE 6.2 Emaar 21-Jun-2006

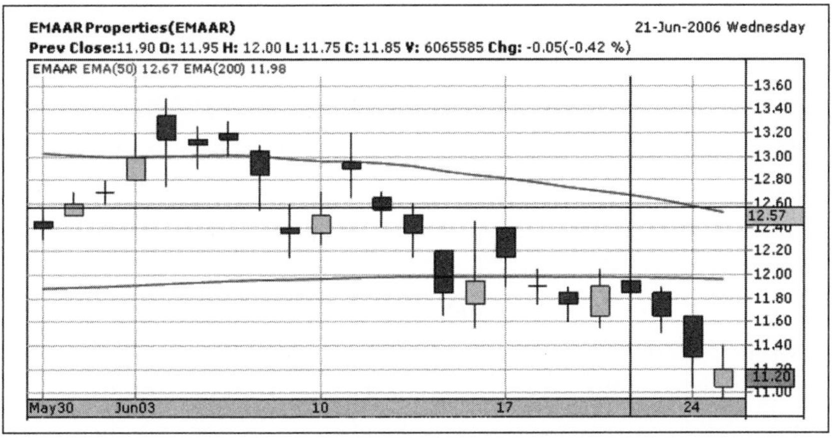
EMAAR Properties(EMAAR)
21-Jun-2006 Wednesday
Prev Close:11.90 O: 11.95 H: 12.00 L: 11.75 C: 11.85 V: 6065585 Chg: -0.05(-0.42 %)
EMAAR EMA(50) 12.67 EMA(200) 11.98
13.60
13.40
13.20
13.00
12.80
12.57
12.20
12.00
11.80
11.60
11.40
11.20
May30
Jun03
10
17
24

Source: Used by permission of Orient Consulting Center

could have squeaked in a trade, but in the Middle East with daily trade limits and a lack of algorithm scalping on the spreads, this was not a doable strategy.

Commodities and FX

Commodity and FX trading is a popular area, and seasoned traders know they are linked to other markets like interest rates, economic news, and the dollar. While trading seems simple in terms of buying oil at 50 and selling at 52, in reality, the oil move may not be due to an actual energy factor such as falling inventory levels. In fact, while inventory levels may rise, oil prices may rise as a result of the U.S. dollar getting weak. A weak dollar could be hedged with the oil commodity, as it would likely hold its value better than paper money. Again, we see the statistical challenges of short-term correlations that we experienced earlier.

When trading commodities and currencies, traders want to capture meaningful turning points or bottom-fish upon pullbacks from a trend. Naturally, there can be many strategies to decide how to do this, from simple to complex. Using fundamental analysis in trading currencies like the U.S. dollar versus the euro, a trader could include factors such as the real growth prospects of both areas, interest rates, the ability to buy the same good in one country as compared to another, and capital flows. An assessment could then be made on the expected exchange rate.

Originally, traders who use purchasing power parity buy the same goods in each country. So, a beer in the United States must be the same price in the United Kingdom, and the exchange rate should reflect it. If beer costs a dollar and a pound each, respectively, there should be an exchange rate of $1.00 to 1 pound. However, if the beer costs 2 pounds in the United Kingdom because of inflation, but exchange rates stay 1:1, you can then take one pound and exchange it for a dollar and buy a beer in the United States. You can bring it back to the United Kingdom and sell it for 2 pounds and make a pound profit. Thus, should beer prices rise in the United Kingdom you should get more pounds for your dollar.

We can also relate this concept to interest rates. In general, "the expected movement in the exchange rate should offset the interest rate differential."[3] This hypothesis is based on the work of Irving Fisher and follows the idea that interest rates follow inflation rates. However, the economic data is at times lagging, making future exchange rate forecasting uncertain. The expected inflation rates may also be affected by different consumption patterns of goods and services among countries. Then, arbitraging the same goods from one country to another is not always instantaneous, and there are transaction costs, such as import taxes. So we have a theory of how things should work, and this is called the Uncovered Interest Rate Parity Relation, as one cannot automatically arbitrage to an FX rate. So, "if the interest rate differential does not reflect the anticipated and certain exchange rate movements exactly, an arbitrageur would simply borrow in one currency, transfer the amount to the other currency, and lend it at that currency rate."[4]

The product of the forward rate and one plus the domestic risk-free rate *equals* the product of the spot rate multiplied by one plus the foreign risk-free rate:

Forward rate $\times$ (1 + rDC) = Spot rate $\times$ (1 + rFC)

or

Forward rate/Spot rate = (1 + rFC) / (1 + rDC)

where

- rDC is the interest rate of domestic currency (DC)
- rFC is the interest rate of foreign currency (FC)
- Exchange rates are *indirect quotes* as number of units of foreign currency (FC) for one unit of domestic currency (DC)

Assume you must determine the expected spot rate one year hence, or the forward rate of the U.S. currency and a mythical Zapland:

Problem (Indirect):

$$\text{U.S.: Rate} = 4\%; \text{Spot FX} = 9.5238 \text{ Zaps/\$}$$
$$\text{Zapland: Rate} = 7\%; \text{Forward FX} = ???? \text{ Zaps/\$}$$

The solution would be:

$$\text{Forward rate} \div 9.5238 = 1.07 \div 1.04, \text{ so Forward rate} = 9.79853 \text{ Zaps}$$

(Again, this assumes that we are correctly estimating the true interest rate that is guided by the correct [versus a manipulated] inflation rate.)

Thus, you can see that relying on economic data is fraught with risk in determining FX rates. The data may be stale, it may not be accurate, or it may be manipulated, among other possible factors. For example, there can wide disagreements on the true inflation levels in a country. So, traders may rely on technical analysis to guide them on entry points for key buy and sell decisions. The implication is that moods and perceptions of various economic data (no matter how it is massaged) may create FX rates. These can result in trends, support, and resistance levels.

Figure 6.3 shows that the dollar's appreciation against the euro ended in late 2000 at about \$0.82 = 1 euro. In early 2002 the dollar started a trend of depreciating against the strong euro. This depreciation ended in late 2004, when \$1.35 = 1 euro, showing the dollar beginning to rally.

Using the three-year trend from 2002, we could have applied a 38.2 percent Fibonacci retracement. (This is a favorite technical tool of some traders because it gives mathematical support and resistance levels.) This would have caught the profitable euro bounce in late 2005. Further confirming this retracement area is the nearly identical support seen in early 2004,

FIGURE 6.3 $XEU (Euro Index) INDX 2-Aug-2006

Source: Used by permission of Stockcharts.com

at $1.17 = 1 euro. While we can apply the Fibonacci ratio to a short-term trading period, it is a challenge, as some traders look at the bigger picture for more comfort. In the short term, there may be disagreements on where a trend started, thus influencing the eventual Fibonacci price levels.

At this point we may move on to examine a popular and controversial commodity of gold and blend some fundamentals and technical tools for both long-term investing and trading.

Gold Trading

Gold has been cherished, used as a store of value, and maintained its purchasing power for hundreds of years. This conclusion is demonstrated in the book *The Golden Constant* by Roy Jastram.[5] While fluctuating at times, gold has moved in a broadly constant, long-term level. It therefore has created a level of confidence and comfort for gold holders. However, as the printing presses went to work and flooded economies with paper money, prices began to escalate in a gradual inflationary spiral. Since 1930, the dollar has lost over 95 percent of its purchasing power. Even with reinvestments in Treasury bills, there is still a loss of purchasing power after taxation.

Gold, as a commodity, is very controversial today. It performed well in the 2000 period, at a time when the S&P 500 had low returns. And, it hit new highs in 2011. The collapsing dollar and other currency worries caused a renewed love affair with gold.

Portfolio Considerations

As shown in Table 6.1, gold returned a surprisingly strong 15.9 percent per annum at the same time period that the S&P 500 Index returned a low total return of 0.3 percent. The S&P 500 Index return would not have been predicted by asset allocators at the beginning of the decade, as the two prior decades were much kinder to the stock market with solid double-digit returns, sometimes approaching 15 percent per annum.

The table also shows that global small-cap stocks did better than the S&P 500 Index, with a 7.8 percent return. So, during the somewhat dark period of the S&P, there was hope as smaller companies with new products and services contributed to better investment returns. As expected, competitors with similar strategies in the Lipper universe showed much lower returns of 3.8 percent per annum. They (not surprisingly) underperformed the index, based on what we already discussed about market efficiency. If we were to update these numbers to late Fall 2011, we would see similar results in terms of gold having better returns, and global small cap stocks doing better than the S&P 500 index and Lipper competitors.

Investors looking for action may swing into emerging markets, commodities, and other glamour areas that show better returns than the large cap U.S. stocks. As a matter of fact, they often dip their toes into hot areas in order to pick up some performance against their S&P 500 benchmark. (This is called "performance drift", as discussed earlier in the book.) The usual naive retail investors may not see this until something goes wrong; the investments get on a bad streak and drag down performance.

TABLE 6.1 Gold Return Comparisons, 2000–2010

YEAR	GOLD	GOLD NET	LIPPER GLOBAL SMALL/MID CAP	S&P/GLOBAL SML CAP INDEX	SP500
2000	−4.1	−5.1	−7.8	−2.3	−9.1
2001	1.6	0.6	−15.5	−6.8	−11.9
2002	20.3	19.1	−18.9	−12.5	−22.1
2003	22.4	21.1	46.1	47.5	28.7
2004	10.2	9.1	19.7	23.5	10.9
2005	15.4	14.2	12.8	15.5	4.9
2006	23.4	22.2	20.1	23.6	15.8
2007	28.7	27.4	2.4	9.1	5.5
2008	2.3	1.3	−45.4	−45.6	−37.0
2009	32.6	31.3	43.6	48.3	25.2
2010	29.6	28.3	25.0	24.7	15.1
TOTAL RETURN	409.3	356.4	50.1	127.4	3.5
GROWTH OF $1.00	5.09	4.56	1.50	2.27	1.04
PER ANNUM	**15.9**	**14.8**	**3.8**	**7.8**	**0.3**

Performance must be adjusted for risk. We call good performance as risk-adjusted excess returns to the benchmark. Sophisticated investors usually have some ways to measure a manager's effectiveness on this matter. Absolute returns without regard to risk is a dangerous game. For example, let's say you want to improve your $10 per hour clerical job. A friend offers a new job that pays $100 per hour; however, the job is to jump off the roof of a 10-story building into a bathtub of water and let tourists take pictures of the grand event. Of course, this happens once an hour. To spice matters up, you can make $1000 an hour if the owner can shrink the bathtub a bit. You agree as long as the bathtub is actually a swimming pool and you only have to dive one story. Now there is a flood of applicants. So, the market is efficient, as higher returns require more risk. Also, it is unlikely that any tourist will pay to take pictures of someone diving one story into a swimming pool; hence, no business. As you can see, we can sleep well with T-bills or eat well with more risky investments, but it is not likely we will be able to do both.

In investing, it is obviously necessary to adjust the return to the risk. One way to address this is through the Reward to Variability ratio, where we take the excess return of an asset to the risk-free rate and divide it by the standard deviation of the returns of the asset. This is also called the Sharpe ratio. While gold had very good returns against the S&P 500 Index, it also produced desirable excess returns by taking on less risk. You can measure this risk by taking its volatility or standard deviation and then doing a Sharpe ratio. The higher the excess return per unit of risk, the better the result. This then adds good diversification features to a portfolio.

For the 11 years ended 2010, gold provided good diversification features under Modern Portfolio Theory (MPT). Compared to the S&P 500 Index, gold has shown:[6]

- Annual returns of 15.9 percent vs. 0.3 percent
- Quarterly correlation to the S&P 500 Index of 0.05 and low coefficient determination
- Beta of 0.06 vs. 1.0
- Sharpe of 1.17 vs. negative for the S&P
- Treynor of 3.96 vs. negative for the S&P
- Jensen Alpha of 12.3

Annual returns of 15.9 percent vs. 0.3 percent. So far so good. Quarterly correlation to the S&P 500 Index of 0.05 and low coefficient of determination means that the S&P 500 Index did not influence the movement in gold that much. Other assets found in the NASDAQ and emerging markets move together in market selloffs, offering less diversification features. A beta of 0.06 means that gold is not that volatile to the market. It seems to follow its own drummer; big up and down days in the stock market don't translate to gold. Gold has a Sharpe ratio of about 1.2 versus a negative amount for the S&P. We can also start adding more risk measures such as the Treynor ratio, which substitutes beta for the standard deviation in the Sharpe calculation. Treynor of about 4.0 versus negative for the S&P again shows positive excess return comparisons for gold.

Using the CAPM expected return and then subtracting it from the return of gold, we get a Jensen alpha of over 12. We can start the risk adjustment engines purring with more measures, such as gold being very liquid, having a high Information ratio (the difference between its return and the S&P 500 Index on a period basis), and dividing it by the standard deviation of that difference over the entire time period. Gold has an information ratio of over 1.0 calculated on a quarterly basis—very good. Gold is also positively skewed on a quarterly basis, meaning that there is more chance of an upside.

Investors should have had gold in their portfolios to offset the low stock returns and dampen the volatility. However, this has not been the case for individuals and even institutions which had low or no holdings in the precious metal. Why? Behaviorally, investors saw a low probability of gold going up and a high probability of stocks rising with other assets not going down and even showing good returns.

For a portfolio, gold is a reasonable holding. We can optimize the portfolio with the following equations that get weighted average for a two asset class portfolio return and the portfolio standard deviation. (For multi assets, you would use matrix algebra in Excel.)

Equation 6.1: Portfolio Return and Standard Deviation

$$E\left(R_{port}\right) = w_1\, E\left(R_1\right) + w_2\, E\left(R_2\right)$$

$$\sigma_{port} = \sqrt{w_1^2 \sigma_1^2 + w_2^2 \sigma_2^2 + 2\, w_1 w_2\, \mathrm{cov}_{12}}$$

$$\sigma_{port} = \sqrt{w_1^2 \sigma_1^2 + w_2^2 \sigma_2^2 + 2\, w_1 w_2\, r_{12} \sigma_1 \sigma_2}$$

The top equation in Equation 6.1 is the weighted average of returns of two assets. The next two formulas show the weighted averages of the standard deviations, with adjustments to covariance in the middle formula and the substituted correlation in the bottom formula.

Let's apply these equations to the gold scenario:

$E(R_1), E(R_2)$	=	Expected rate of return of assets 1 and 2
w_1, w_2	=	Portfolio weight of assets 1 and 2
σ_1, σ_2	=	Standard deviation of assets 1 and 2
Cov_{12}	=	Covariance between assets 1 and 2
r_{12}	=	Correlation between assets 1 and 2

Assuming the S&P 500 will not continue to show negative returns going forward, we can assume a more normal, but low return for stocks of 5 percent. For gold, we can temper its return to an assumed 14.65 percent return.

Of course, various assumptions may make gold have different weights in a portfolio. Assuming the economic crises end and stocks return to their more attractive 1980 to 1990 decade returns, you can almost switch the categories and have gold become 10 percent of a portfolio. At this point, gold is more of an insurance policy for future economic accidents than a doom asset. Your assumptions drive the conclusions, but the assumptions must be correct before you do the investing.

Assuming the S&P 500 ends its negative returns and shows a more normal 5.0 percent yearly return in a low-growth environment, gold should be 90 percent of a portfolio mix of gold/stocks. Should stocks continue a decade of negative returns, then gold should be 100 percent of the portfolio. Assuming risks are constant, if gold returns 4 percent, stocks return 10 percent, and T-bills yield 3 percent, gold should then be 28 percent of a portfolio. These returns would be more realistic for an economy that has reasonable real growth. As one can see, assumptions on returns and risks determine the eventual weight of gold in a portfolio.

Cases could be made for investing in non-stock areas like fixed income or into alternative investments, such as real estate, private equity, and even other commodities. Even in stocks, some investors will favor emerging markets over developed markets. However, the problem with this analysis is that you must assume their correlations will not be high with the S&P 500 Index. Also, the conditions that favor these investments are not the conditions that affect developed country stocks.

FIGURE 6.4 Gold and S&P Opportunity Set

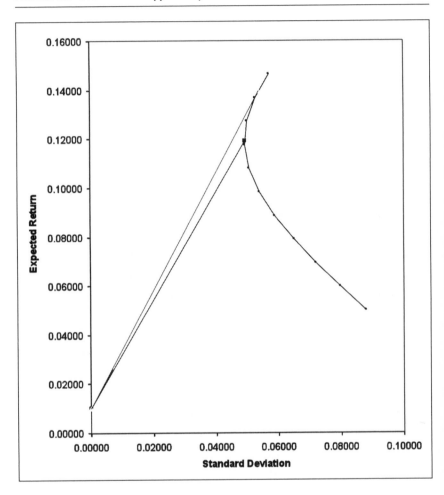

Gold may then be the only unique investment in that case. Note in Figure 6.4, we see the creation of an efficient frontier by mixing gold with the market index. From this one see the optimal mix of gold and the index. Using even other assumptions than discussed above, such as a risk free rate of under 2 percent (see bottom left of chart) one can see that gold should be about 10 percent of the portfolio (see top left dot near 14 percent). Diametrically opposed viewpoints have led to a major showdown between Gold Bulls and Bears; still, volatility appeals to traders.

The Big Bang

At the end of World War II each of the 44 allied countries which signed the Bretton Woods Agreement agreed to maintain the exchange rate of its currency within a fixed value—plus or minus 1 percent—in terms of gold. On August 15, 1971, the United States unilaterally terminated convertibility of the dollar to gold. For purposes of this discussion, this is what we will consider the "Big Bang." This action created the situation whereby the U.S. dollar became the sole backing of currencies and a reserve currency for the member countries. Having the dollar as a reserve currency was an acceptable alternative, assuming the fiscal house of the United States stayed strong and solvent.

President Richard Nixon ended the U.S. gold standard in 1971 and allowed gold to trade above its $35 per ounce fixed rate. Gold hit $850 per ounce in 1980 in response to inflationary pressures. Since 2001, gold has climbed each year, and in November of 2009, gold topped at $1225 per ounce. In August, 2011 gold topped $1900 an ounce and its absolute returns looked favorable against stock and bond returns. During this period, other economies developed rapidly and other currencies became more desirable, such as the euro. Later, when the euro started to falter with the Greek or PIGS credit crises, gold took a luster again and again reached new highs. As the dollar's value eroded, a black hole of uncertainty was created. Thus, the stage was set for gold's future price rise to be even higher.

Gold has risen sharply over the past decade, continuing to outperform the S&P 500 Index. Gold has also made new highs against leading currencies such as the euro, the pound, and the yen.

Gold reached new highs in 2009. Figure 6.5 shows breaching of a top that had four resistance points around $1000 per ounce. This gave an important technical buy signal, as the breaching of a major resistance extended for almost two years.

In addition, there was also a Golden Cross in February 2009. The 50-day exponential moving average (black line) crossed above the 200-day exponential moving average (grey line), thus confirming a buy signal. It was successfully tested with support in April 2009. This break above resistance also invited short-term trading moves.

FIGURE 6.5 $GOLD – Continuous Contract (EOD), INDX 6-Jan-2010

Source: Used by permission of Stockcharts.com

On October 1, 2009, a trader may have bought when the MACD gave a buy signal and/or it (bottom graph, black line) moved above the nine-day moving average of the MACD (grey line in bottom chart). (See Figure 6.6.) A sell signal was given when the MACD fell below the average on October 20. Then another buy signal occurred in early November, and a sell signal was given at the peak price of over $1200 per ounce in early December. (Note RSI also confirmed the sell signal by going over 70 and showing a negative divergence, as the second RSI peak was lower despite the price of gold being higher.)

In late December 2009, the MACD gave a buy signal, as gold looked to be ready for another move up. As a result, we may ask how high can gold go? Several technical methods can be used when entering the uncharted territory of breakouts to new highs. These may include point and figure charts, round numbers, Fibonacci projections, and pattern analysis, among others.

Figure 6.7 shows how a horizontal count of point and figure charts simplifies markings to only meaningful moves and gives traders the opportunity to forecast price objectives once a buy/sell signal has been made.

FIGURE 6.6 Gold–Continuous Contract (EOD), August 2009 to January 2010

Note the GLD pattern is above the black 45 degree buy line. Count the columns between the consolidation that takes place between the two walls. The left wall just happens to coincide with the beginning of the grey line pointing downward in 2009. The right wall is 19 columns going in the right direction to where prices break out of trading range. (Sometimes technicians disagree on exact wall locations.)

The reversal is three boxes, and each box is $1.00. Actually, above 100 each box becomes $2, as point and figure can scale boxes depending on price. The rule is then to multiply the columns (19) by the reversal (3) by the dollar value per box (1) to get 57. Note the boxes are mostly $1.00, but

FIGURE 6.7 Traditional, 3 Box Reversal Chart Bullish – Price Obj. (rev.): Met (105.0)

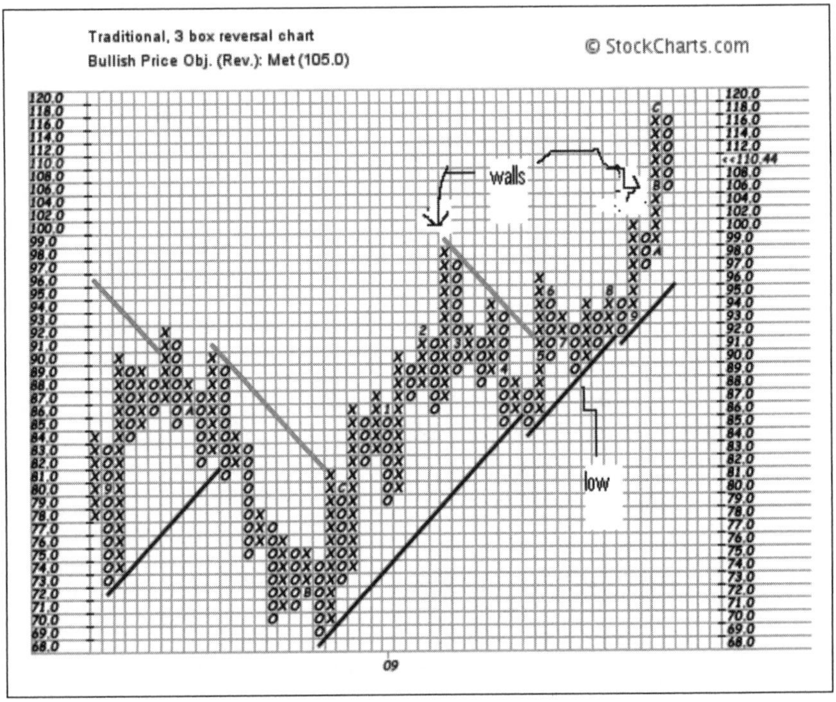

Source: Used by permission of Stockcharts.com

then scale up to $2.00 a box over the price of $100. Point and figure scaling is commonly done to adjust for price levels. The assumption is the more the consolidation, the higher the price if it breaks out on the upside. This amount of 57 is then added to the lowest point in the consolidation pattern between the walls (85) to get a price objective of 142. Since the ETF is 1/10th of an ounce of gold, this implies a price of over $1400 per ounce. Of course, this assumes that the buy signal stays in place.

For traders, a Fibonacci projection method may also be employed. Figure 6.8 demonstrates this method. We need three points: a trend with a low point (#1) and a high point (#2), plus a point to start the projection (#3).

The Fibonacci projections are 61.8%, 100%, and 161.8%.

So, trend is 200 points long. (#2) 1225 − (#1) 1025 = 200

FIGURE 6.8 $GOLD – Gold – Continuous Contract (EOD), INDX 8-Jan-2010

Source: Used by permission of Stockcharts.com

Add to (#3) 1075 : 200 × .618 = 123.6 + 1075 = 1198.6
200 × 1.00 = 200.0 + 1075 = 1275.0
200 × 1.618 = 323.6 + 1075 = 1398.6

Using Fibonacci projections, a trader may use the price levels of 1198.6, 1275.0, and 1398.6 to take profits. This assumes that prices will hold at point #3 and that an upward direction takes place.

Swing Trading

Swing trading may involve playing price moves that last several days or weeks. The frequency of trading is always challenging, as trading involves transaction costs that lower returns. Usually, sophisticated back-testing of trading strategies will help determine optimal frequency of trading. It should be a response to opportunities that provide risk-adjusted excess returns, and that involve probabilities associated with investment outcomes that include upside and downside possibilities. Of course, results are only as good as the assumptions in the trading model.

Triple Cross and Gold

Using a triple cross method for swing trading creates an interesting profit picture in gold. In Figure 6.9, you can see a triple EMA average of 4, 9, and 18 days to show good profits. When the 4-day (black line) and 9-day (grey line) moving averages go above the 18-day (broken black line) average, we get

FIGURE 6.9 $GOLD – Gold – Continuous Contract (EOD), INDX 6-Jan-2010

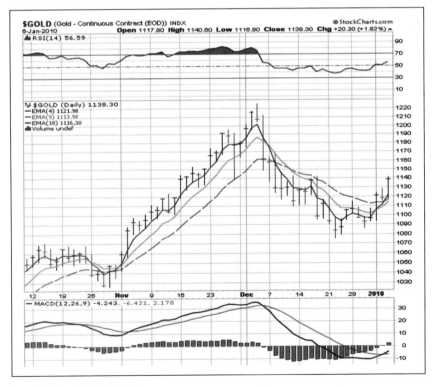

Source: Used by permission of Stockcharts.com

an indication for an uptrend or a buy signal; below, then a sell signal. We would like to see the 4-day go above the 9-day and then have confirmation of the 9-day going above the 18-day moving average. However, some traders place different degrees of selling or buying (depending on the movement above or below) when the 4-day crosses the 9-day, and not necessarily wait for the confirmation.

In early November 2009, there was a buy signal around 1045 and then a sell signal near December 7 at 1180 as the 4-day moving average went below the 9-day. A confirmation was reached a few days later on December 12 at 1150, as the 9-day moving average went below the 18-day. Then, in early January, the 4-day crossed the 18-day, as the 9-day also appeared ready to cross the 18-day. So we have a partial buy signal, but the clincher may be incorporating a technical tool like the MACD, which gave a buy signal as it crosses above its moving average.

Some technicians would also add the buy signal in the MACD (bottom chart) as confirming the triple cross buy in early November, and then the MACD sell signal in early December. So traders may use that to make a trading decision along with or even ahead of the 9-day confirming with the 18-day cross of the moving average. We already mentioned the RSI (top chart) divergence function, as it showed a negative divergence sell signal in early December. Even with the lower peaks of the RSI, the higher peaks of the gold price in the middle chart confirm the sell in early November.

Here, again, we have hints that by combining more than one indicator, we may get better results. We can also see that there is opportunity to create even more complex trading systems by incorporating other technical factors. Once again, one must determine if they are flukes or reasonable (having appropriate confidence intervals) predictors of future price moves in many types of markets. Therefore, as more technical tools are employed, the approaches can be quite numerous and complex. This leads to a learning curve and cost for the user. Some technicians will follow certain schools of thought: Japanese Candlesticks, Gann, patterns, momentum, and sentiment. Of course, one wants a consistent approach because cherry-picking one approach may not carry forward into similar situations. Once again, this is done by back-testing or the law of the jungle. If traders get poor results, they eventually drop the approach. So, if technical tools seem to indicate good results, they will stand the test of time and be used again and again. Therefore, we still see use of some popular methods, such as the MACD, RSI, and the moving averages. The key issue will be to find some way of tweaking technical indicators to make them better. Is there something missing to add and make it even more indicative?

Patterns and Gold

We shall look at a pattern method, using the Triangle Measurement rule. Patterns are not supposed to happen in technical analysis, as all stock price movements are random. However, we see similar ones and they can be fractal (same pattern but different size). Patterns offer measurement estimates—that is, they provide the trader or investor guides as to where the price may go.

In looking at Figure 6.10, we see the pattern formed a triangle that is bounded by the diagonal lines for the top and bottom portion. Take the height of the triangle in early April 2006 and add it to the breakout near October 2007 to get a price objective. Looking at the height in early April 2006—$725 − $550 = $175. Add this to the breakout price of $700 (between July and October 2007), and we get $875 as a price objective for gold.

Another feature is that the steepness of the trend going into the triangle should be the steepness going out of the triangle. Note the rather steep move into the triangle from July 2005 to April 2006; thus, we can expect a similar steepness on the breakout. This is exactly what happened, when the $875 price objective was reached and even exceeded. This data helps swing traders, and even long-term players gauge the possible gain, as well as the speed of the gain.

Stochastics and Candles—Gold

Traders use traditional technical tools like Stochastics to indicate momentum. Some may also rely more on exotic tools like Japanese Candlesticks. Let's see what happens when we blend the two.

Figure 6.11 shows gold's top was already warned with a Hanging Man in late November (black candle with long shadow in left circle). A subsequent rally by two white candles was squashed by a black body

FIGURE 6.10 Gold–Continuous Contract, 2006 to 2010

Source: Used by permission of Stockcharts.com

candle in early December. On December 22, the bottom was cushioned by Spinning Tops that gave hints of price stability (right circle). We could also blend traditional RSI and MACD considerations to make a trading decision. In early December, the RSI showed a negative divergence sell signal and the MACD gave a sell signal.

Dollar Decline

Since 2001, the weakening of the U.S. dollar has resulted in gold's upward movement. The dollar decline has been due to a blend of many factors: weaker U.S. economic growth compared to emerging markets, increased levels of debt, and speculation that the inflation of the late 1970s will

FIGURE 6.11 Gold–Continuous Contract (EOD), November 2009 to January 2010

Source: Used by permission of Stockcharts.com

return. Therefore, the solid downward dollar price trend of the past several years supports even higher gold prices in the coming years.

Therefore, the solid downward dollar price trend of the past several years has supported "gold bug" forecasts for even higher gold prices in the coming years.

Fundamentals: Car and Gas Prices

One can make a case that if productivity increases, more gold is needed to purchase an item. But if productivity is not improved (relative just to price increases), then less gold is necessary. For example, productivity enabled more affordability in cars and gas prior to 1970 (see Table 6.2).

TABLE 6.2 Average Car Prices and 10,000 Gallons of Gas (in Ounces of Gold)

Year	Car Price ($)	Gas ($)	Closing Gold Price ($)	Ounces/Car	Ounces/Gas
1930	600	1000	21	28.6	47.6
1950	1510	1800	40	37.8	45.0
1970	3450	3600	38	90.8	94.7
1990	16,950	35,500	424	40.0	83.7
2008	27,958	20,510	860	32.5	23.8

Sources: Calculated from Kitco, wiki.answers.com; thepeoplehistory.com. Gold prices are either NYSE closing prices or Kitco

After 1970, with paper money creation, more of the prices were a reflection of inflation. Hence, one needed more gold to buy cars and gas before 1970. In 1950 one needed 37.8 ounces of gold to buy a car; then just before inflationary prices really got to the spring board stage, 90.8 ounces of gold in 1970. But in 1990 we dropped to only 40 ounces, and in 2008 32.5 ounces. Of course, cars also got better, offering A/C and, later, satellite, and many options along the way. Thus, the customer got a better car in the post-1970 era for less gold as the years went by.

The same could be said for gasoline at the pump. All one needed was 23.8 ounces of gold to buy 10,000 gallons in 2008, down from 94.7 ounces in 1970. We could also note that many different kinds of gas, with different octanes, are available today. An additional consideration is that gold may have been held down from its true level in 1970 by political policy in the United States. This was changed a year later, as we shall see.

7

GOLD AND PAPER MONEY

Throughout history, transitioning from gold to paper money has often been a precursor to higher inflation. In the late 1700s, France's currency, the *mandat*, flooded the economy and fell to 3 percent of its face value. It actually replaced the previously worthless French currency, the *assignat*, in a currency exchange where 30 old assignats equaled one new mandat. The assignats were supposed to be backed by Church properties that were later confiscated. Unfortunately, too many assignats were printed and thus created hyperinflation. While there were legitimate spending needs, back then printing money was not the answer.

Other famous inflationary incidents include Germany in the 1920s and, more recently, Zimbabwe. You have probably seen the zeros on banknotes that were required to buy basic goods. In Germany, you needed a suitcase to transport the currency. In general, however, gold has maintained its purchasing power, hence being referred to as the "golden constant." When German citizens needed these briefcases of paper money simply to buy essentials, gold would have kept its purchasing power.[1]

Later, other currencies tacked on one or more zeros to increase the denomination's value. Brazil found itself in a credit mess a few decades ago due to printing more zeros and then scrapping the currency, replacing it with a new one and giving it a new name.

So why is it so easy to print money? Well, it is estimated that there are 163,000 tons of gold supplies above ground, with 18 percent being held as official country reserves and jewelry being 51 percent.[2] Of some 3800 tons demanded in 2009, jewelry accounted for 58 percent and electronics 8 percent. However, investment demand has escalated rapidly in the past few years, and it now accounts for about one-third of the demand.[3] Gold supply peeked in the late 1990s and since then has been relatively flat.

Worldwide government reserves as of December 2009 were 30,100 tons of gold.[4] The United States is legally required to maintain gold reserves and has the largest reserve of 8100 tons (approximately 259 million ounces).[5] Gold represents 69 percent of its reserves.

Other larger holders include Germany with 3400 tons, the IMF with 3000 tons, Italy with 2500 tons, and France with 2400 tons. These countries also have about 65 percent of their reserves in gold. This invites the possibility of monetizing country debts with gold.

While the United States' reserves have been constant for years, many countries like the U.K. sold much of their gold in 2000, when prices were low. However, other countries in emerging markets have been accumulating gold. China now ranks number 6 with 1,100 tons, but that is only 1.5 percent of reserves. Russia and India rank numbers 10 and 11 with 600 tons. They too have a small portion of their reserves in gold (5 percent). These countries have diversified their reserves more into gold as compared to paper currencies. This may mean further purchases in the future.

Money Supply

Money supply changes eventually lead to higher prices. Money follows the Fisher equation of MV = PQ, where Money (M) × Velocity (V) = Price (P) × Quantity (Q). Assuming velocity is constant, excess printing of money without gains in production leads to inflation. In general terms, M0 refers to outstanding currency (banknotes and coins) in circulation excluding vault cash. M1 is currency plus overnight (demand) deposits plus vault cash. M2 includes the sum of M1 and savings deposits (agreed maturity of up to two years or deposits redeemable at notice of up to three months). M3 is the sum of M2 and repurchase agreements, money market fund shares/units, and debt securities up to two years.[6]

The global money supply of M3, which has grown nearly 10 percent a year for a few years, has been estimated to be around $50 trillion.[7] Dividing $50 trillion into 163,000 above-ground tons of gold would equal a price of over $9500 an ounce!

For some countries, M2 is fairly close to M3, and for others, such as the United States, M2 is estimated to be about 60 percent. So, conservatively, if M2 is 50 percent, then gold would be $4,750 an ounce. This is also an amount much higher than the current prices that are under $2000 an ounce.

So why is it so easy to print money? In my opinion and that of others, it is perhaps the fastest way to tackle the misery index. The misery index is the sum of inflation and the more important political concern—unemployment.[8]

More realistic solutions for long-term, real growth would be to have nations raise educational levels, which leads to greater economic productivity. Then, foster the innovation of new products with amounts of investments that exceed their costs of capital. While these are long-term solutions as compared to quick money printing, such actions would lead to sustainable growth that creates new companies and, in turn, creates new jobs. Money printing just creates more banknotes that buy less and less and punish the unfortunate who cannot earn more banknotes or do not have assets that are hedged against the inflation. While pump priming requires some money to stimulate the economy, often the initial intentions soon give way to the uncontrollable monster of inflation.

Business Cycles

We have shown that money printing is often a response to the misery index or a way to alleviate economic stress when unemployment is high. Economic stress has been caused by the cyclical nature of capitalism that is reflected by booms and busts, and these are only aggravated by investment bubbles.

Nikolai Kondratieff, an early economist, pointed out a recurring pattern in economic boom and busts in his Kondratieff Wave (KW). This theory is based on a study of nineteenth-century price behavior that included wages, interest rates, raw material prices, foreign trade, bank deposits, and other data. Kondratieff was convinced that his studies of economic, social, and cultural life proved that a long-term order of economic behavior existed, and it could be used to anticipate future economic developments.

Basic economics show that when there is an economic upturn, the result is more jobs and increased production. Later, production reaches the maximum, as it cannot be expanded due to capacity constraints and prices rise as demand exceeds supply. As prices rise, speculators borrow money from banks to buy assets at inflated prices. Later, the prices cannot be sustained, at which point asset values provide less cushion against the borrowings. Soon, speculators default to the banks, and eventually the banks write down the loans and may even go bust as problem loans erase their capital with large losses. Bottom fishers who are liquid then take advantage of low prices to invest in cheap assets—and the process begins again.

Technicians don't necessarily use the KW today as a main technical tool, given its broad time range. Fundamentalists are also skeptical of its importance due to today's monetary and fiscal policies. Still we cannot dismiss the implications of KW, as human nature has always exhibited fear and greed.

In 2002, the Nobel Prize in Economics was jointly awarded for behavioral analysis to Vernon Smith and Daniel Kahneman. Smith showed how investment bubbles may develop, and Kahneman helped develop the Prospect Theory, which states that investors do not value upside risks and downside risks equally. Investors tend to overreact to small-probability events but underreact to medium and large probabilities.

In more recent times, investment bubbles include the dot.com bubble and, of course, the global real estate bubble. They reflect similar patterns. While the levels of stock prices are influenced by economic cycles, others show peaks and valleys of different time periods. Interested readers should see the work of strategist Francois Trahan of Bear Stearns, whose work indicates similar patterns from prior bubbles in the Nikkei, gold, oil, and the 1920s Dow. Given the various fundamental tools used to estimate values in each market, the similarities can be haunting. While the fundamental models say it will be different this time, the chart patterns are almost identical.

"Real estate prices never go down," or so goes the tale. Naive investors learned the hard way that this is not true. Many investors and their backers (banks) who loaded up on debt to play real estate investing games took large losses. Given the vast amount of economic data available, it would seem the Federal Reserve would have anticipated the recent real estate bubble—but it did not. While housing started to deteriorate in 2005, it was expected that commercial real estate would hold its value because it was more institutional and institutions in commercial real estate were expected to make more rational decisions. However, this expectation burst in 2007 when commercial real estate prices started to collapse. Fundamentally, commercial real estate was bought at inflated prices with very low yields. A growing recession eventually caused vacancy rates to climb, lease rates to fall, and property values to decline.

In speculating on a real estate top, you can apply the EW to the $RMZ, the REIT ETF. Is the RMZ near the top at 960? (See Figure 7.1.) Using EW analysis for an extended 5th wave, the rule (per Murphy's Technical Analysis[9]) is as follows:

> If Wave 1 and Wave 3 are about equal, and Wave 5 is expected to extend, then the bottom of Wave 1 to the top of Wave 3 is multiplied by 1.618. The result is added to the bottom of Wave 4 to get a price objective. Thus, Wave 1's bottom is about 250 (late 1999) and Wave 3's top is 650 (early 2004). Thus, $(650 - 250) \times 1.618 = 647$ points. Added to the bottom of Wave 4's 525 (near mid-2004), we get 1172, which turned out to be pretty near a major top of 1225 in early 2007.

The RMZ declined by 80 percent from its peak. Fundamentals were greatly stretched on cash flow measures, yet the bank lent with gusto.

FIGURE 7.1 RMZ (MSCI US REIT Index) INDX 2-Aug-2006

Source: Used by permission of Stockcharts.com

Servicing the Debt

While the real estate bubble resulted in a massive decline in values, the debt still had to be serviced. Those that could not be serviced would be written off. Many parts of the world had deep pocketed "white knights" who attempted to restore fiscal sanity. In the United States, the U.S. Treasury and the federal government borrowed massive amounts of money to help bail out the distressed institutions—many of them large banks.

The size of the current global debt crisis is unprecedented in history. The pain associated with deleveraging has required major government stimulus programs worldwide to bail out economies.

Debt is expected to be serviced from a nation's GDP. However, in addition to government debt, consumer debt also has claims on the GDP.

In the fourth quarter of 2009, U.S. federal debt was estimated to be near $12 trillion, or about 75 percent of the GDP. This is the highest level since WWII, and the U.S. government expects it to increase to over 100 percent in a few years.[10] The G-20 nations have a similar picture.

Of the debt, $2.5 trillion is due in one year and may have to be refinanced at higher interest rates. Interest payments are expected to exceed $700 billion, up from a year ago of only $202 billion. So while the federal government has a zero interest policy, servicing the debt may be considerably understated.

Actual measurement of the government debt is difficult, especially when we add other types of like entitlement programs. In addition, many of the states in the United States are running deficits.

Euro currency zone members have large amounts of pension obligations, relative to their GDP. Based on analysis of the Cato Institute, it was reported that debt-burdened Greece has a current debt of 113 percent of its GDP, but current and future pension obligations of over 876 percent. On the same basis, the EU-25 has 72 percent and 434 percent, and the United States has 83 percent and 500 percent, respectively.[11] Naturally, these ratios have gotten worse and Greece subsequently entered a precarious state.

This increasing debt will create trillion-dollar deficits that may require further quantitative easing. This will invite the printing of more money. For example, the federal government bought long-term government debt, as did the United Kingdom This caused a reflex drop in the pound and an increase in U.K. long-term interest rates. In addition, forcible currency devaluations will increase the money supply. (Some say that currency devaluations are the new "tariff" wars.)

Large creditors of the United State may begin to balk at accepting more U.S. government debt. (China has already hinted there may be limits to their appetite for U.S. debt.) Long-term rates would then climb, as the bond vigilantes are fearing an inflationary exit strategy.

Exit Strategies

Overcoming the increased levels of debt requires high levels of real growth with interest rates tied to that growth. Barsky and Summers use the analysis that gold should be inversely related to long-term interest rates.[12] Once we take out massive consumer borrowing to maintain consumptive lifestyles, we see this growth has not existed in the United States since 2000. Decoupling of the BRICs also cast doubt on future worldwide growth.

Another exit strategy is to increase taxes to pay for the debt servicing. This process has already begun, as increased tax rates on capital gains and income levels are being proposed in the United States and elsewhere. However, this will increase capital costs and provide less incentive to create needed investments. Since much new job creation in the United States comes from small businesses, this is considered a challenge.

Another solution may be to let the "good times roll." Print money, print more money, and let the prices rise. A $4.00 cup of coffee could become $40.00, then $400.00! But your assets, especially gold, would also rise. Since the 1930s this has been done in creeping fashion; however, an overnight burst could trigger social unrest and even more speculation leading to larger busts. Those whose incomes and assets (if any) don't keep pace would become poor overnight. We already have seen that in recent demonstrations.

Another method would be for governments to monetize much of the debt, in effect, devaluing it against gold. President Franklin Delano Roosevelt did in the 1930s by raising gold from $22 per ounce to $35 percent.

So if we took the $12 trillion in debt and divided it by the U.S. reserves of 8,100 tons of gold, we get $46,296 per ounce! Not all the debt would be monetized, but a few thousand dollars an ounce would be more realistic. Growth appears to be the most promising outlook, but it requires innovation and education, and at best is a long-term strategy.

The World Bank recently estimated the global GDP to be about $61 trillion, while the U.S. GDP is $14.2 trillion.[13] It was mentioned that estimates of M3 were about $50 trillion, which equals $9500 per ounce of gold. A distrust of currency would then equate the $61 trillion of GDP into a value of approximately $11,600 per ounce. While some currencies may be considered stronger than others, a case could be made to still have gold worth a few thousand dollars an ounce.

Technically, the S&P 500 Index has created massive twin peaks in the years 2000 and 2007 (see Figure 7.2). Major support levels have been broken, inviting the dismal implications of the "lost generation." This implies that the most recent recession does not resemble a typical recession. Perhaps the

FIGURE 7.2 SPX (S&P 500 Large Cap) INDX 5-Jan-2010

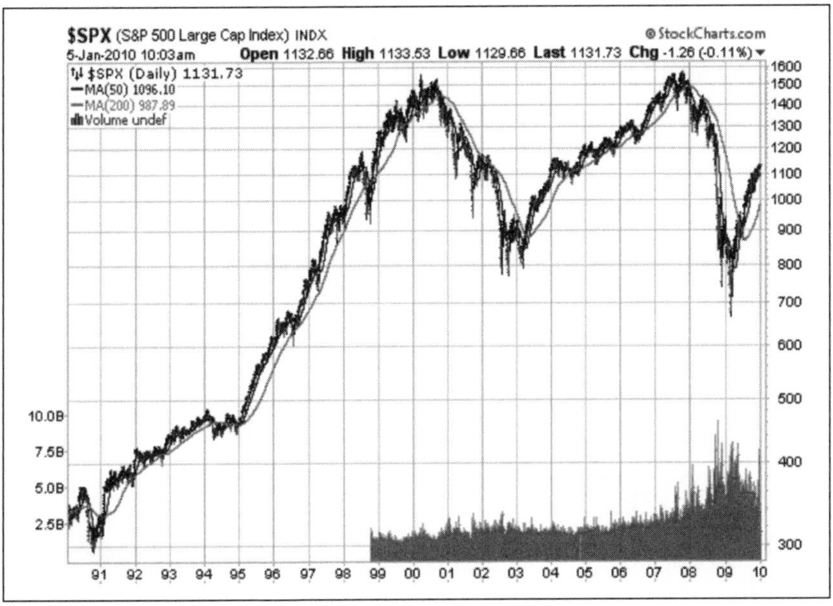

Source: Used by permission of Stockcharts.com

real growth was less than economists recorded, especially as consumers used inflated home price loans and credit card loans to finance much of their purchases.

The twin peaks indicate heavy overhead resistance to a stock price rally. It supports the notion that since 2000, there has been little real economic growth. In real terms, breaking the support levels of 2002 indicate that stock prices may labor for a considerable period of time.

Going forward, one can have rising stock prices, but they could be an illusion if the purchasing power is not maintained. They could represent a monetizing effect, rather than real economic growth. As you can see in Figure 7.3, the S&P is going down.

Consequently, growing budget deficits may increase the risk of default. The CDS swaps (in euros) on U.S. government debt have touched at times 50 basis points (BPs). Geopolitically, this may not be acceptable for the United States, and reflation may be an outcome. (This followed the severe recession of the mid-1970s.)

FIGURE 7.3 SPX GOLD–S&P 500 Large Cap–Continuous Contract (EOD) 4-Jan-2010

Source: Used by permission of Stockcharts.com

We have seen portfolio diversification features for gold. These features reflect many investment scenarios; however, putting aside industrial and jewelry demands, gold reflects concerns about inflation and deflation. As mentioned, there could be a monetization of gold, similar to FDR's action in the 1930s when he increased the price of gold.

Homestake Mining's stock price did very well in the 1930s. It more than quadrupled as the price of gold was increased by Roosevelt. They went from approximately $75 at the beginning of 1928 to over $450 by the end of 1953.[14]

Exploring Gold Further as an Investment Opportunity

Gold is an inflation hedge, as it protects against a currency devaluation. It has recently correlated a negative 0.81 with the dollar.[15] As mentioned, gold has hit a high against virtually all currencies in the world.

Fear

Gold offers an insurance premium against fear, as prices can rise in a period of deflation, similar to recent times and the 1930s. While gold is used in industry (12 percent) and thus has some fundamental economic support, more than half of it is used in jewelry as a proxy for elegance and a store of value.[16]

Commodities have outperformed the S&P 500 Index since 2000. More importantly, gold has tracked a basket of commodities, then broke on the upside after 2008, as it captured the fear factor. Until recently, gold has tracked Reuters CRB Index when it broke out to capture the fear factor. Commodities have outperformed the U.S. stock market. More importantly, gold has outperformed commodities.

Financial Engineering Opportunities

Adding gold to a fixed-income portfolio can help hedge currency and inflation risk. Gold is also attractive for traders in such a situation, given its recent increases in volatility, such as Average True Range (ATR). As ATR gets larger, there are more extremes in a price from the high to low of a period. The bigger the ATR, the more likely traders would be attracted to this trading, as it gives them more opportunities to capitalize on price swings. Non-believers in gold can benefit by shorting or buying puts on the ETF or GLD, or by doing fixed interest rate swaps against gold.

Ways to Invest in Gold

The physical holding of gold bullion is one method of investing. While it requires storage, it has clear possession visibility. Buying gold bullion may require a cost premium of 4 percent, and even more for some popular gold coins. Investors' bullion holdings are more traceable. ETFs like GLD, store gold on behalf of investors. However, uncertain future actions of various governments may somehow confiscate gold holdings. ETFs provide better liquidity but carry a small administrative fee of usually less than 1 percent.

Mining Company Stocks

Gold mining stocks offer the potential to do better than gold through their operating leverage and ability to discover new deposits. Discovery could make a small gold mining company's share price soar. They also may pay dividends and provide good liquidity for purchases and sales. The downside may be high break-even costs that retard profits, an inability to maximize gold production, and the risk that companies may sell much of their production forward. This would cap upside potential as gold prices rise. This is what many gold mining companies did around 2000, as gold prices were low and they wanted to capture some sure revenue.

One way to compare gold mining stocks and gold bullion is to compare BUGS (Basket of Unhedged Gold Stocks; index symbol is HUI) with gold. HUI is composed of 15 of the largest gold mining companies in the world. As of January 2010, the top three included Hecla Mining Company (HL), Compania de Minas Buenaventura (BVN), and Couer d'alene Mines Corporation (CDE). Sentiment was very bullish in the late 1990s when gold prices were low as companies hedged much of their output. However, when gold prices increase, HUI is expected to do better on the upside and vice versa. Rising gold prices not supported by a rising HUI signify a divergence and contribute to a sell signal on gold.

Technicians use other tools to make a sell decision. For example, the peak of gold happened during a major event: the anticipated release of the unemployment numbers in the United States. Smart traders bought puts (perhaps the ETF GLD) near the gold highs, especially as HUI indicated caution. While they did not know the actual results until the data was released at 8:30 EST, they speculated there would be a big downside move on gold. When the actual unemployment numbers were better than expected, gold dropped sharply, as it was assumed that rising interest rates (which soon occurred) would compete with gold returns.

As gold prices rose (see Figure 7.4), the trend showed an upward direction of HUI as compared to gold in Figure 7.5, until September.

At that point in September, there was a divergence where rising gold prices were not supported by rising gold mining prices, indicating a caution and giving a possible sell signal. As gold peaked in late December 2009 and then proceeded to sell off sharply, HUI started to underperform.

FIGURE 7.4 GOLD–Continuous Contract EOD) 5-Jan-2010

Source: Used by permission of Stockcharts.com

FIGURE 7.5 HUI: Gold–Bugs Index-AMEX/Gold–Continuous Contract (EOD)

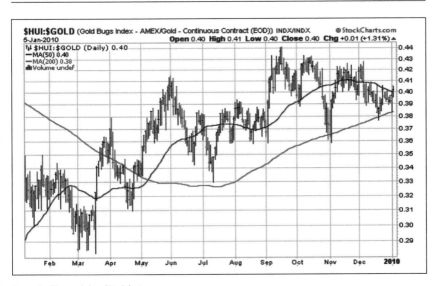

Source: Used by permission of Stockcharts.com

Pair Trades

As mentioned earlier, traders can also do pair trades, shorting one asset and going long on another. In this case, if the trader feels that HUI will do better than gold, the trader can buy HUI and short gold. At this point, the trader is only speculating on their divergence and not direction. The risk in pair trading is twofold: There may not be enough of a spread to cover trans-action costs, and correlations may temporarily break down and not hold.

With the gold peak in late 2009, traders speculated on when to buy in anticipation of a rebound.

One method was to combine the technical methods of support/resis-tance and Fibonacci ratios. These would indicate a good area to buy at the 61.8 percent retracement area (see Figure 7.6). Traders started a trend at the 1000 resistance/support line of the Fibonacci retracement. Savvy traders sidestepped the 38.2 percent and 50 percent levels, as there was

FIGURE 7.6 Gold–Continuous Contract (EOD), 5-Jan-2010

Source: Used by permission of Stockcharts.com

little support confirmation. However, at 61.8 percent, traders were near a 1075 support line (prior resistance). A trader may buy here in order to sell at the 50-day resistance line (straight, horizontal lines) to capture about 40 points. You can also make a pair trade with platinum. Platinum moves closely with economic strength, as it is used in building catalytic converters for the auto industry.

A trader can speculate on the divergence of gold and platinum. A declining trend means platinum is doing better. By early 2010, it appeared that while gold has lagged platinum's performance, it could be a good time to buy gold and short platinum on the hopes that gold would now outperform platinum.

Supporting this notion is gold/platinum being near a support level as shown in Figure 7.7 by the parallel line near 0.72. Note the Fast Stochastics

FIGURE 7.7 GOLD: PLAT (Gold–Continuous Contract [EOD]/Platinum Futures [EOD]), 6-Jan-2010

Source: Used by permission of Stockcharts.com

is also oversold and below 20. Finally, you may decide to wait for the GANN 45-degree line (slanted line on right-hand side of chart) to be broken before establishing positions. Traders can also play subangles of GANN to get more trading strategies.

Intermarket Analysis Using Gold

Traders can speculate on short-term correlations with gold. For example, gold normally trades inversely with the dollar. Also, it can be affected in the short term by trading inversely with interest rates. When rates rise, the dollar tends to firm and gold prices drop in the short term. This follows the interest rate parity concept.

However, in the short term, gold can correlate highly with the dollar, but at the same time, trade inversely with the stock market. This happened in March 2009. The dollar firmed and gold prices went up, but the stock market declined. Again, we see the challenges of correlations not acting as they should in the short-term.

We already illustrated the potential for intermarket trading. Let's bring in gold with an examination of the rising interest rates in the summer of 2003. Traders had many chances to exploit this situation. Another opportunity could be in buying gold. While rising rates may initially firm the dollar, they can also mean that the economy is getting stronger and that inflation is picking up.

A trigger for the intermarket analysis could again be the viewing of a Head and Shoulders pattern in the TLT, an ETF for the 20-year U.S. government bond. Determining a trigger event is challenging in itself. In early April to June of 2009, while we saw a falling dollar, gold was rising (see Figure 7.8).

After July the dollar and gold moved in sync. This indicated better economic conditions, but with more inflation. How can we be sure? No guarantee, but it seems that cyclicals are in an uptrend, and Figure 7.9 supports this notion.

While rising interest rates indicate better economic conditions but may be with more inflation. We made the decision to buy gold, as higher inflation would favor rising gold prices. Figure 7.10 shows MACD confirming gold support at the 200-day trend line.

FIGURE 7.8 US Dollar Index, 20-Aug-2003

Source: Used by permission of Stockcharts.com

FIGURE 7.9 Gold – Continuous contract (EOD) 29-Aug-2003

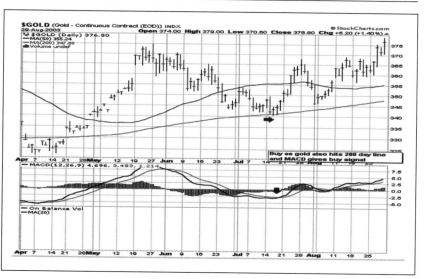

Source: Used by permission of Stockcharts.com

FIGURE 7.10 Gold–Continuous Contract (EOD), Buy Signal, 29-Aug-2003

Source: Used by permission of Stockcharts.com

On July 21, MACD gave a buy signal near 340 (note the horizontal arrow on the MACD portion of Figure 7.10). In early August, we get a quick sell signal at 346, where we give up great gain but still have a small amount. Soon there is another buy at 355. MACD still shows a buy signal and prices go over 375, thus capturing a good gain.

Gold Trading Summary

Attitudes on holding gold are gradually changing. For some cultures, such as India, it has been closely tied to lifestyle events such as weddings. "Pocket wealth" also supports the notion that one should have physical gold. In countries such as those in Eastern Europe, gold has been hoarded as a measure of portable wealth. Recent weakness in some currencies has led to purchases in gold and jewelry.

Still, buying gold on a regular basis is not in the psyche of the amateur investor. While the investor may occasionally dabble in the metal based on the current events presented in the news, a longer strategy of diversifying wealth using gold is still behaviorally unaccepted.

Let's recap and raise some questions that may come up during gold trading (most of which apply to trading in general as well):

- What is the trigger point?
- Which factors and markets do we look at to confirm our decision?
- How do we handle the possibility that correlations may break down?
- How often do we want to trade like this?
- How long will it take to do these trades, and should we be looking at alternative trades in other areas that are unrelated to the ones we have discussed?
- Should this trade analysis be done by human traders staring at a Bloomberg or a programmed computer?

After considering these questions, ask which action is the best route for the gold trader:

- Short the bond?
- Pair trade?
- Short a housing stock, and which one?
- Enter the intermarket and do a call option on the cyclicals?
- Buy gold?
- Do all of the above?

Considering this, can the trader make probability assumptions and payoffs on a decision tree quickly? Furthermore, should the trader be replaced algorithmically by a computerized trade? (We shall evaluate the likely outcome of this case but in slow motion.)

Summary Questions

Fundamental valuation models can have behavioral bias. Technicals can help overcome the bias. Now consider these questions:

- Realistically, will technicals carry weight in a conference room discussion?
- What are the conflicts between basic trends and short-term trading as it relates to fundamental and technical analysis?
- What are the challenges if one accepts shorter and shorter trading time horizons?
- What are the benefits and risks of using intermarket technical analysis?
- Should an investor's effort be spent more on investing with a long-term horizon, as compared to trading with a very short-term horizon?
- Do fundamentals matter for short-term traders?
- To make relatively short-term profitable trades, is it likely that risk will increase with the need to use margin?
- Are we really able to invest or trade profitably, or are the cards already dealt and we just look at them?

These considerations open the door to Part 3 of the book.

Part 3

THE TICKING CLOCK: GROWTH OF CONCENTRIC CIRCLES

Attempting to forecast economic outlooks inevitably leads to a discussion of the business cycle. A pure linear expansion, while desired, is often met with business cycles that have periods of upward growth followed by contractions. While prosperity represents good times, feeling well, and having a sense of wealth creation, then times are often followed by recessions and even depressions exhibiting wealth destruction.

Governments know that these kinds of cycles can upset voters, and voters can change governments, especially with the downside of the business cycle. We certainly saw this development in several countries, such as those in the Middle East and Greece. So, governments attempt to tame the business cycle with fiscal and monetary policy. There are bright minds in government institutions that study the economy, and surely they will not let it get out of hand. With their skilled staff, they can analyze economic data and then propose policy that will best stabilize the economy for real long-term growth. Yes, this is the supposed dream. "We have learned, and it will be different this time"… until the next downturn.

The meticulous analysis of economic data is combed and filtered to provide econometric models, the food for forecasting economic trends needed to determine governmental policy. These trends can be in such diverse areas as real GDP growth, interest rate levels, and demographic trends to predict consumer demand for housing.

One well-known governmental institution is the Federal Reserve System, or the Fed. It was created in 1913 to seek maximum employment and to stabilize prices. It oversees the nation's monetary supply, which includes the creation of money and regulation of banks. It is estimated that the Fed employs or contracts with "easily 500 economists at any time," the Federal Reserve spent $389.2 million in 2008 on "monetary and economic policy," money spent on analysis, research, data gathering, and studies on market structure; $433 million is budgeted for 2009."[1] OK, there we have money and brains addressing the issues of the economy.

Then add the Congressmen and Senators with their army of aides, the strategists and their analysts on Wall Street, plus other government agencies and—you get the idea. We have many people at the cost of vast sums of money analyzing data to hopefully eliminate the business cycle, if not significantly ameliorate it, yet we continue to have booms and busts in the twentieth-first century. It makes you wonder if we would be better off with a free market economy that had no governmental or institutional intervention.

Milton Freidman, the Nobel prize winner for monetary policy advocated replacing the Fed with a computer. While he felt the Fed did good research, he felt it created poor policy. He said, "Surely a computer would have produced far better results during the 1930s and during both world wars."[2] We can speculate that while laissez-faire made economic outlooks uncertain due to the unexpected free flow of supply and demand, surely a firm hand from governmental intervention could have eliminated or at least greatly mitigated this uncertainty.

8

DETERMINISM, INVESTING, AND TRADING

Fundamentalists cast doubt on the idea of the potential role and outcome of government intervention. While the economic policy of institutions seems to be the main ingredient for taming the business cycle, it is still based on data and the perceptions of that data. Thus, not only investors but also government officials look at data to make decisions. Some have better data than others, and some make better interpretations of that data. If you know there are obstacles to using specific data because of a governmental organization, you may actually skirt it or game the system. So, for example, if you know the government will give you a stimulus check because the economy is weak, you may decide that instead of spending it and stimulating the economy (as the government hoped), you actually either pay off debt or save it. Likewise, if there are rules as to how much debt a bank can carry in order to curb lending, a bank can go off the balance sheet with credit derivative strategies.

Cynically, since we know from past observation that economic cycles have existed in the twentieth century, we probably will take a grain of salt with any government words of reassurance. Perhaps, one would have been better off letting market forces dictate economic policy, because the cost of all this policy makes things even worse in the long term. This is the counter argument to the stimulus program in the late 1990s that bailed out companies like Lehman, Bear Stearns, GM, and other firms that ran into financial problems. Government set the stage for the misery that came about 10 years later, by covering their failed financial strategies, and allowed others to take on leverage under the concept that some institutions are "too big to fail." Hence, the government poured billions into AIG, Citibank, and other institutions and ran up the Fed's balance sheet and the U.S. government debt into the trillions of dollars, as we discussed earlier.

Like investors, government institutions can also draw the wrong conclusions. Part of this reason is that while they look at the same data, albeit at earlier times, they may eventually interpret it the same and make some of the same decisions. Going back to the Efficient Market Hypothesis, while it is unlikely that the government will set long-term policy based on historical information, knowing information in advance can help the government to trade effectively before the news is actually made public.

It is also possible to recognize that the data somehow seems to flow from prior data which flows from prior data, which flows from even earlier data. So, in looking at a chain of data, one is almost programmed or destined to perhaps follow a beaten path. This concept, as we shall see, is not lost upon those who look philosophically at the actions of humankind.

While behaviorists also acknowledge the flow of data and the need for making decisions, they also add the point that not all decisions are rational and calculating, as some can be quite emotional. These actions can range from playing casino games to flipping condos. In addition, they are not symmetrical, as for some, losing $10,000 in a casino is much more charged with emotion than winning $10,000.

Technicians are also somewhat skeptical, as they, too, doubt that periods of great fear and greed can be tamed. Investors make trends, as smart money buys first. Next come the imitators. Finally the dumb money buys from the smart money at the top or sells to the smart money at the bottom. Hence, the business cycle continues. Technicians also believe that certain patterns and chains of events lead to predictable human behavior—but they are not the only group. In addition, philosophers have extensively studied the concept that behavior is predictable and destined. While technicians may adapt the philosophical concepts to financial markets with the study of cycles and waves, philosophers apply this concept to all human behavior, including religion.

Actions Lead to Actions Lead to More Actions ... Deterministically

If actions lead to actions, how predictable are they? Must we follow them?

Are we perhaps programmed to act in a certain manner? Do we really have free will? Is the universe a series of causes and effect? Is there a major system, math formula, or mechanism that really runs the universe in a more or less predictable pattern?

Consider the chilling opening of *The Trial* by Franz Kafka: "Someone must have slandered Joseph K., for one morning, without having done anything wrong, he was arrested."[1]

The plot of *The Trial* is about the prosecution of a man for an unknown crime by some bureaucratic authority. The prosecution is seemingly capricious, as one gets the feeling that one day all is good and the next day, for some reason, all is bad. Consequently, existence is absurd and you can't fight the system. Sounds like some form of business cycle. Somehow the wheels were set in motion and you just happen to have gotten caught in the spokes.

So perhaps this is not too far-fetched from today. One day you have a house, a job, a spouse. Now a short time later, it is all gone. What happened? We can wonder about this a lot as we see the high unemployment rate, the debt delinquencies, and the tide of foreclosures. (Perhaps the Great Recession should be called the Great Trial?)

Though determinism is a key philosophical concept, it is also the basis for technical analysis: "Determinism is the idea that every event or state of affairs, including every human decision and action, is the inevitable and necessary consequence of antecedent states of affairs."[2] This was elucidated by Laplace's Demon, which was a proposition by Pierre-Simon Laplace in 1814. The experiment supposed that if one knew the exact location and momentum of every atom in the universe, then one could use deterministic principles to predict all future and past actions. While one may suppose that human free will could break the chain of events, some philosophers say that free will is not really a factor. One may have free will, but, here is the rub, one may only *seem* to have it. What if all events have been planned *and* one is only a cog in a great machine? So, you think you can keep your job if you work hard and study, but you get laid off because the entire department is being shut down or the company goes out of business due to some action at corporate headquarters or some bank overseas or whatever. Yes, you had free will, but was it only an illusion?

In finance, we can call free will specific risk, which can easily be trumped by systematic risk. We can see where a financial firm can be mired in specific and systematic risk. If the banking industry is having problems like in 2008 (systematic risk) and our little corner bank is accused of being among the problem banks, the head of the bank may reply that it was not us that made the subprime loans. We may be in good shape regarding the specific risk. Yet the systematic risk will crush its stock price along with the group in a market selloff of the banks. The assumption would be that this corner bank is just as guilty—it is another one of "them."

This determinism can happen naturalistically or theistically. Naturalistically, there are events that have cause and effect. Atheists feel all events came from the Big Bang or maybe endless Big Bangs. Some of these events could relate to Skinner's idea that genetic or environmental events control human behavior.[3] Thus, good genes and an educationally positive environment could lead you to better study habits and eventually getting a better job. But while you may choose college, you are already oriented that way given above-average intelligence and coaching from your parents.

Theists imply a deity, or as some call it, God, who sets all of this in motion. God creates the universe, but lets it run forward and knows the results. Some religions have a deterministic belief—that is, they do not dismiss the notion, even though there may be various levels of acceptance of the idea.

This has lead to various forms of determinism, one of which is predestination. Obviously, this has caused much controversial discussion over time and has even caused religious splits. However, while we plod through the nuances, the bottom line is there is some form of acknowledgment and response to predestination and, more broadly, to determinism in all religions.

Universe Expansion

Determinism also collides with physics. While events may lead to other events, there are some roadblocks that have stumped deterministic followers.

Specifically, one is the Heisenberg Uncertainty Principle, which states that one can observe the location of a particle but not its momentum, or one can observe its momentum but not its location. Einstein, who believed in God, was not comfortable with this uncertainty, as he made the famous quote, "God does not play dice."

Another problem is that of entropy. This involves the Second Law of Thermodynamics, which states that one cannot go from cold to hot; one only can go from hot to cold. So when one boils water and leaves it on the stove with the flame off, the pot gradually gets cool and eventually assumes room temperature. If the room temperature is very cold, one cannot exist. So eventually, the universe gets cold and dies; there is a predictable end. One theory that opposes this idea is that of Peter Lynds, who proposes that the Second Law can be overcome.[4]

One can go from the cold to the hot by having the universe go from the Big Bang to the Big Crunch and then back to the Big Bang. So, just as we get really cold, the universe explodes again into another beginning. Then many years later, it gets near death in a big crunch, and—BAM—the whole process starts again. This would lead to some sort of repeating loop as an explanation of existence.

With all this controversy, it would seem that the current mainstream thought of physicists based on current evidence supports a growing universe and perhaps even at an accelerating pace.[5] This is similar to a growth curve for companies, or some S curve, minus the decay part. Hence, the big crunch is nowhere in sight, yet. However, this may change as we further unravel the mysteries of the universe. In general, this notion of the universe expanding would influence one's notion of determinism. One could then say that the previously discussed monetary inflation that we have seen post-WW11 is in good hands in such an inflationary universe.

Faith, Determinism, and Investments . . . and an Introduction to Time Travel

Some physicists do not rule out the possibility of time travel. There are many permutations on the type of time travel, but the most famous is the Grandfather Paradox. (Suppose a man traveled back in time and killed his grandfather before the grandfather met the time traveler's grandmother. Then, of course, the time traveler's parents wouldn't exist to conceive him, so the person couldn't have existed to go back in time. So the grandfather would have to have survived in order to allow the traveler to go back in time to kill him. The time traveler's existence negates the possibility of his changing the past.) If we could time travel, then we might be able to change past events and break the notion of cause and effect in determinism. More obvious, we could change our past of losing trades, as we now know the winners. So can time travel change determinism and thus make investing a sure thing?

As we have discussed, determinism and religion seem to coincide, but we can get on dangerous ground if we approach these matters from another direction—that of a type of religious faith. Even scientists cannot prove some religious concepts, but they still take things on faith. All of these actions then lead to one, important conclusion: the acceptance of a deity and the concept of eternal reward. For Christians, it is the belief in Jesus Christ and that the eventual happiness with Him in eternity is all that matters, while other religions have variations on this theme. At various times, religions may have not seen eye-to-eye with some scientific discoveries, as they may have repudiated some religious beliefs. We can take an existential point of view and assume life is absurd and devoid of any meaning. Atheists would most likely believe some sort of endless lack of meaning but might say this is still better than believing in a religion. Conversely, some might accept Voltaire's proposition that if God didn't exist, man would have to invent him (as a psychological crutch that enables one to cope with this life). At any rate, we cannot deny that scientific evidence can lead to rethinking determinism and, as such, can influence religious thought.

Investing can follow this discussion. We can analyze data that leads to other data, which leads to some valuation model, which in turn leads to an investment decision to either buy, sell, or hold. We can buy stocks strictly on faith; however, unlike true religious faith, which is supposed to be firm and unshakable, investing on faith may only be a by-product of bullishness or bearishness.

Regardless of beliefs, both religious and physical, determinism leads to speculation on human actions and continues to mesmerize us.

Illusions in Economic Data

The reality we understand may only be a sliver or speck of something more complex. Consider our three dimensions of length, width, and depth. These three dimensions are on three different planes. To this we can add a fourth dimension: time. But what if we existed in only two dimensions? How much more primitive would our perception of reality be? For example, suppose we lived in a two-dimensional universe of width and length, like a sheet of paper. In 1884, Edwin A. Abbott wrote *Flatland*, a book about a two-dimensional universe. It is a satire on Victorian lifestyles where inhabitants of Flatland gain more status as they gain two dimensional sides. (So a square has more status than a triangle; the highest status is a circle, which has many sides [kind of a calculus idea]). When a three-dimensional person visits Flatland, the two-dimensional inhabitants cannot comprehend the shape, as they see it as a series of growing circles. They cannot explain depth, and if a character attempts to do so, there is total disbelief and the character is eventually jailed for his views. So one would know nothing about depth. Thus, extra dimension gives richness to our experience. But what if there were more dimensions? What would be the perception of reality? In physics, there is a theory that has had various swings of popularity with physicists called String Theory. It requires not one, two, or three dimensions, but nine dimensions, plus one time dimension—to make ten dimensions. (Some even propose 11 dimensions.)[6]

This discussion might seem esoteric, but these issues of determinism, faith, and the nature of the universe have not gone unnoticed in the financial arena. In fact, they have led to the creation of special investment models. Both the issues and the models influence various parts of the Fusion process.

Regular cycles in human behavior and in investment decisions are a controversial point. They challenge linear thinking and support the business cycle. Behavioral and technical analysis accepts the concept and rejects the notion "It is different this time." It doesn't matter if there is a Fed, stabilization fund, or a new tax policy, investors will find a way to get around these to speculate and so contribute to the business cycle.

Fundamental economists do not reject the business cycle, as they actually helped to lay its foundation. On the other hand, technicians will eventually apply their own analytical methods. But if deterministic action is not accepted, then we can easily dismiss the value of their techniques.

Efficient Markets and Determinism

In finance, the Efficient Markets Hypothesis (EMH) acknowledges determinism. We have the free will to choose investments: to buy IBM, GE, or some other stock or asset. We can create all types of portfolios. However, in the end, the EMH system is against this type of active decision making. The EMH acts in a deterministic manner—economic data is translated to investment data in a series of cause-and-effect actions. In the end, the market generates a return for the collective risks that are assumed. No matter how much free will we use in picking various types of stocks, we are predestined to underperform the market. We may do better with returns, but we will assume more risk, or with the same or less risk, we will generate lower returns. The market is efficient; it makes the best trade-off on risk and return.

Thus, we avoid active management. So while we feel they are analyzing data and making some type of value-added decision, it is all an illusion. It is unlikely that we can benefit from their data. While it can be fundamental, like financial statements, or even technical, like stock charts, the market already knows the data and reflects it in the pricing of its assets.

Active management is a nice illusion. However, most fund returns research recommendations and corporate finance deals don't outperform the market. Their managers run around visiting companies, reading research of brokerage firms, and crunching numbers in Excel, but they don't beat the market. There are greater forces that will crush the active manager in a deterministic manner. Some call these forces the result of the mysterious Elliott Wave or non-mysterious economic cycles such as Kitchin and the Kondratieff.

But is there a savior or deity that can save the investor? We have them in various religions; however, in investing there is only one: indexing.

Predestination in relation to investing can only be ameliorated by indexing, yet who wants to index and just match the market? Surely there are exceptions to indexing. Yes, there is hope, as the market is not always that rational and efficient. This may be the only reason to do Fusion and take advantage of the loopholes offered by technical, behavioral, and quant systems.

Infinities

Dealing with cause and effect and determinism in various formats, we run into the concept of infinities. In other words, as cause and effect happen, where does it lead? Certainly, eternal happiness or eternal damnation are infinity concepts, and serve as the basis for many religions. Also, if we presuppose the universe always existed, then it must always be—and so, another infinity concept.

The purpose of discussing infinites is not necessarily to analyze them as something abstract. It is to analyze the implication of actions that can gain or lose something in a seemingly infinite situation. The most common situation comes from religion, where there is some infinite reward or infinite punishment. Not all believe this type of range, as some assume the universe is what it is. One exists, then dies and no longer exists. There is no payoff. Still, as evidenced by the numbers who follow religions, one would say that this is not the dominant view of humankind. One can make a case that there is the feeling that some type of material reward on earth is desired. We may desire more pay, more goods, a better lifestyle. While deity considerations may be numerous, this type of spiritual desire appears to be even greater.

Let's extrapolate the concept of infinities to more real actions in the marketplace. Suppose you read a brokerage report that recommends Apple stock. Apple is trading at $200 a share. The analyst may have an upside price target, but must also show the risk of where the price may go under general economic conditions or those specific to Apple. So, if the economy slows down, it is possible Apple may sell fewer iPhones; the cash flows will be less and thus command a lower price. If Google upstages Apple with a better phone, it may take away market share from Apple and lower its cash flow projections. The opposite could happen as well. There could be a strong economy and the Google phone does not become a mainstream competitor. Thus, Apple would then be valued at a higher price. Let's assume that Apple is worth $100 if things don't go well, but $300 if they do in a year's time. Now we have an upside, and a return/reward range for investors.

Imagine if another analyst recommended a stock. Now the deal is as follows: If you buy the stock (no derivatives are allowed), it can go to infinity on the upside or stay at a $200 on the downside. But if you do not buy the stock, you get only $200 on the upside but suffer a complete loss of everything you own and forever roast in Hell. Hmm. Seems like some weird stock, but just to play safe, there is no doubt you would buy it.

In 1670, Pascal's Wager was proposed by mathematician Blaise Pascal in his book *Pensees*. Studied by many philosophers, theologians, and mathematicians, it was not intended as an investment proposition, although implications exist. Instead, it dealt with the infinities that related to God—specifically, the infinities of reward and punishment. Rather than trying to generate a rational proof for the most desired infinity, God, Pascal basically stated that one would be foolish to bet against the existence of God. His argument follows:

> *"God is or He is not." But to which side shall we incline? Reason can decide nothing here...A game is being played at the extremity of this infinite distance where heads or tails will turn up...Let us weigh the gain and the loss in wagering that God [exists]...If you gain, you gain all; if you lose, you lose nothing. Wager, then, without hesitation that He is.*[7]

We could make a box where we would multiply a payoff by the probability to see if one should play a game. For example, flipping a coin (50 percent chance of heads) where one earns $4 on heads but loses $1 on tails (50 percent chance on tails) would show a return of $1.50 as follows:

$$(0.5) \times \$4.00 + (0.5) \times -\$1.00 = \$1.50$$

So, if one pays $1.00 (over and above the $1 one can lose) to play this game, statistically one is ahead, as the expected gain of $1.50 minus the $1.00 fee to play the game results in a profit of $0.50. Now, if the fee was $1.50 to play the game, one would not play, as the resulting profit would be breakeven.

We can now substitute Pascal's payoff box as seen in Table 8.1.

TABLE 8.1 Pascal's Payoff Box

	God Exists	**God Does Not Exist**
Wager for God	Gain all	Status quo
Wager Against God	Misery	Status quo

Wagering *for* God:
(Some probability) $\times \infty$ + (1 – Some probability) $\times$ Status quo = ∞

Wagering *against* God:
(Some probability) $\times$ Misery + (1 – Some probability) $\times$ Status quo =
Either $-\infty$ or a non-∞.

Note: Misery is not defined but can be $-\infty$ or some value that is a non-∞.

Pascal implied a 50/50 probability, but the exact probability is not required, as any probability times infinity is infinity. One can immediately see that wagering *for* God results in an infinite payoff. Wagering *against* God either generates a negative infinity (worst-state of Hell) or some finite return. So, one would risk very little in accepting on faith that God exists.

This simple solution has provided a good appeal to believe in God among some churches. The Catholic Church, through Papal spokesman Monsignor Francisco Pompino, stated the following: [8]

The argument provided by Blaise Pascal has weathered over three centuries of theological debate. It has been one of the strongest intellectual weapons in the church's armory for over three hundred years, convincing countless individuals that the interests of their immortal soul lies not

with abandoning belief but with accepting His existence. As Pascal wrote,
treating the belief in God as if a wager, belief is the more logically ben-
eficial option, for "if you gain, you gain all; if you lose, you lose nothing.
Wager, then, without hesitation that He is."

So, as one of the "strongest intellectual weapons" of the Church, it is no wonder that Pascal's Wager is considered as perhaps among the most famous arguments in the philosophy of religion.[9]

Among the religious objections, one may question which God is the true one? What if one believes in the wrong God? Also, if one gets to Heaven by this wager, what kind of God would be fooled by this trickery? Isn't there supposed to be something like true belief, called faith? Also, if God is truly merciful, would he automatically condemn non-believers to misery?

Then there are statistical issues. This is supposed to be a costless trans-action, but if there is no God, then think of all that time that was squan-dered by going to places of worship and studying religious texts. Also, the payoffs may not be infinities. Sure, Heaven is an infinity, but only God can appreciate that, whereas man can only ponder finite matters. Does man then become God? Even so, is the misery of Pascal's Wager truly Hell, or some other state?

While Pascal's Wager is a theological concept, it opens the door to decision theory. It also leads to our discussion of taking the arguments of the Wager and honing them down to a specific financial situation.

The simple appeal of Pascal's Wager could be warped into financial returns that also seem quite simple and appealing where one can gain a lot or lose very little. This appeal may then be used to behaviorally prey upon investors. Investors will be very gullible, and the fear and greed nature of their psyche will perhaps make them vulnerable to unpleasant losses.

As a first application of Pascal's Wager, consider substituting a lottery payoff. Here we know the probabilities and the payoff, as well as the cost. We seem to have a situation of a large reward for a transaction where a per-son loses little. By doing nothing, one stays in one state—presumably low income and low happiness. Let's assume that the lottery is Pick 6 of New York City, where if you pick 6 numbers out of 59 (order does not matter), you win $5,000,000 (before tax in a lump sum). So should you play this game?

The odds of winning are 1 out of 45,057,474 to gain the $5,000,000. The cost of the lottery ticket is $1.00. You can see that unless you were very lucky, you would need to spend over $45 million to win $5 million. Not a good deal.

Now if the chances were 1 out of a hundred, you could easily spend $100 and be assured of a bonanza of $5 million. But you may question why the payout would be so high if the odds were that good. More likely is the situation of spending $45 million, but now only if the prize is much larger, say, $70 million. Assuming you could quickly get all the numbers before the closing, you would have a sure thing unless, of course, prizes would have to be shared among the same winning-number holders. So if there are two winners, you get $35 million and again lose out to the probabilities. If there are 10 winners, you would really lose out. So what we see is a very remote chance to win a great reward. Would wealthy people play this? Probably not, as they already have money and the remote odds are not worth going to the candy store and rubbing shoulders with the masses.

However, the poor or wealth aspirers would certainly be interested in the lottery, as they don't have much money (relative to a sum needed for a great lifestyle) and they would only spend $1.00. So you could make the case, you either win the lottery (or somebody does) or you don't. But what do you have to lose? Well, it depends on one's financial situation. For a rich person, there is virtual zero cost (assuming the process of buying a lottery ticket is painless and quick). For a poor person, however, this is not the case. The loss of a dollar to the poor person is much more costly than the loss of a dollar to the rich person. This resembles a behavioral concept of gains and losses that may not be equal for all, even if they involve the same sum of money. In other words, their utility curves are not identical.

Index Fund Investing

Now, let's move on to a similar example—placing money with asset managers. Suppose for only a 1.5 percent fee per year, you earn good returns in the stock market. Once again, you must ascertain the cost and the reward. The real cost is is the extra cost you would pay over the costs of an index fund. The reward is the alpha, or the risk-adjusted excess returns of the fund. (Generally, these are measured several ways with measures, such as the Sharpe, Treynor, and Jensen alpha, as we shall further discuss later on. Specialized managers in hedge funds may have more specific measures.)

So, if the fund mimics the S&P 500 Index, you can buy an index fund and pay 0.25 percent per annum. That means the real cost is 1.5 minus 0.25 percent or 1.25 percent per annum. The return is not the absolute return but is the risk-adjusted excess return of the fund over the index. While you could say that jumping in and out of stocks is a skill that preserves capital and enhances gains, you also need asset allocation strategies to measure this skill.

If you assume that in one year, 70 percent of the managers do not generate an alpha, then you can see that paying a fee is not an automatic way of gaining alpha. (Of course, we rigged the analysis by stating that 70 percent do not, but this is not objectionable as most do not in reality.) Let's assume these managers only match the index. They start with $1.00, and at the end the year, they have a $1.00—before fees. (Note: We assume that there are no taxes or transaction costs to keep things simple.) Thirty percent of the managers generate a true alpha of 2 percent. Since we can assume the fund has the same risks as the index, we can assume that they start with $1.00, but at the end of the year, they generate $1.02 before fees. Then compare the outcome of hiring an active manager with that of just plain indexing at lower fees. The index fund would start at $1.00 and end at $1.00, before fees.

So which approach is better? Looking at the expected value of the payoffs after fees for active management, we get $0.7 \times (\$1.00 - \text{Fees of} \$0.015) = \$0.6895$ as a payoff for those who did not exceed the index. To this you must add the benefits from those who did. Thus, $0.3 \times (\$1.00 + \text{Difference of alpha of} \$0.02 - \text{Fees of} \$0.015) = \$0.3015$. Together the payoff is $\$0.6895 + \$0.3015 = \$0.991$. An index approach shows $1.00 \times (\$1.00 - \text{Fees of} \$0.0025) = \$0.9975$. Note that indexing gives higher expected returns than selecting active managers of $\$0.9975 - \$0.991 = \$0.0065$. So one would need active managers to achieve even higher alphas than the 2 percent, or have a greater portion of them beat the market, or have them lower their fees. Thus, it is not surprising that in choosing active managers, one should choose fund whose fees are not on the high end. Fees can easily be controlled but the other factors are much harder to realize.

Among the first to recommend index investing was the academic scholar Burton Malkiel. In 1973, he wrote *A Random Walk Down Wall Street*, which recommended that investors pick index funds. At that time, there was no such opportunity, but his book helped the growth of indexing with major funds like Vanguard. Today we also have ETFs which copy various indices and sub-indices. In a 2009 interview with Barron's, Malkiel indicated that he still felt the same as he did in the early 1970s. His research shows that two-thirds of asset managers are beaten by the indexes and that winners in one year are not necessarily the winning managers the following year.[10]

Matters can get worse if you buy into a fund that may have been hot in the prior year, as the odds increase that it will turn cold the following year. Since most managers don't have an alpha and investors use the rearview mirror to invest, the odds of getting one's money's worth for the fees diminishes. Thus, like Pascal's Wager, you must be willing, continuously, to be *for* God *or for* the fund. Getting in and out is a recipe for getting whipsawed and missing the possibility of an alpha. Malkiel also did a study of hedge funds and concluded the same. Yet technicians would not be surprised to see large sums of money come into an asset class or funds near the top and then exit near the bottom. They can't beat the index once some performance tricks such as survivorship bias are stripped out. Say we use a reporting service that shows a group of hedge funds against benchmarks, We might only be comparing the good ones that are left. If we included those that dropped out (mostly bad performers, but it could be that some good ones closed their doors and did not desire to report), results could be skewed upward. We might also speculate that they are around because they took less risk.

Malkiel did, however, leave the door open, indicating that when you adjust the hedge fund underperformance against the risks, they perhaps did offer an acceptable Sharpe ratio.[11] Others questioned how the databases are constructed on hedge funds, as this may also bias returns upwards.[12] We could then conclude that hedge funds are really lottery tickets for the rich. They seemingly offer large gains with acceptable risks, but like the lottery ticket system, in general, they do not pay off. Similar to lottery tickets, just pick the winners. Still, some academic evidence does support hedge fund skill, even though there are thousands of them. Thus, there is hope, just like the hope in a lottery ticket for the poor.

A Sure Thing?

OK, how about something that seems like a sure thing. Suppose I say that if you give me $100, in 5 years you would get $100, guaranteed, and the fee is 1 percent per annum. There would be resistance if you realize that the return is 0 percent per annum before fees and about −1.0 percent per annum after fees. A more savvy investor would say she could get a return of 5.0 percent on 5-year government bonds and a fee of 1 percent per annum is a rip-off since she could buy directly from the government in an auction or pay a small commission to a discount house.

That's not fair, as she would be charged a fee for doing nothing. How about you agree to invest the money in the stock market and if the market goes down over the next 5 years, you still get the $100 (minus the 1 percent per annum fees), but if it goes up, you and the investor split the gain? Since the stock market in this country has returned 15 percent a year for the past 10 years (hypothetically speaking in this example), anything over 10 percent will be shared equally. So unlike buying into the market now, you can lose money in five years and end up with losses. This offer ensures that you at least get all of your money back and still have a chance to split some profits.

The key here is to price the investments with a zero-coupon government bond having a maturity of five years. You also can strip it from a bond that has coupons and then invest the money into a call option.

First, you can buy a zero coupon with a 5-year maturity at a rate of 5 percent per annum for $78.35 and use the remaining $21.65 to buy a call option on the market. Assume the stock market index is 100, the volatility is 20 percent with no dividends, and a risk-free rate of 5 percent. The cost of the 5-year call option on a 120 strike price is $20.58, using an option price model, like the B-S model. So, your out-of-pocket costs are $98.93, with the rest going to the brokerage house.

Note that I picked 120 on the index. This implies a reasonable growth of 3.7 percent per annum for the stock index. After all, rearview investors would see 15 percent, and thus, 3.7 percent would seem an easy hurdle to beat. Also, they would get one-half of the gain over 120, so if the index returned its 15 percent, it would double to over 201 in 5 years. If I picked 100 for the strike price in 5 years, that would make it more attractive; however, there would not be enough money to do this, as the option would now cost \$29.19. So your total cost is then \$107.54. We can assume the seller of the product is not putting that in, as he would be at risk of losing money. The other way one would be to use OPM (Other People's Money).

The seller of this product would get 1 percent per annum for 5 years, plus the chance to get 50 percent of the gains over the 120 strike price, without putting up any money. The customer would get the certainty of her money back, minus 1 percent per annum, minus possible taxes on the 5 percent zero-coupon return per annum (zero-coupon bonds are taxable each year for individuals, though some such as IRAs or pension accounts are not taxed), plus the chance to get the one-half gains on the investment—virtually risk free. I could sell this to behaviorally risk-averse clients, as more savvy ones would want to know the chances of the index going up versus down. If stock returns are negative, then the opportunity to capture gains are eliminated. In the decade of 2000, the S&P in the United States returned –1 percent per annum, so the possibility of getting positive stock returns was not possible.

Obviously, in the rearview mirror of the 1980s and 1980s when the stock market did rather well, the customer would have missed some extra gains. But this result would have made the sale of the investment easier, as investors may have felt that the past would continue. One could play upon the upside of the investor, but at the same time show a controlled downside. So a little Pascal wagering enters here again.

I could sell this as: Either the market stays the same or goes up or it stays the same or goes down. If it goes up, you gain a reward at no risk, or your money back if it stays the same. If it goes down, you get no reward but lose only a small amount. So this loss is relatively small, so you must play. Depending on the option costs, the interest rates, the volatilities, the risk profile of the customer, and the various financial instruments, we can start to make a business out of this and perhaps call the instrument a Liquid Yield Option Note (LYON). A LYON is a type of zero-coupon bond instrument that can be converted into equity. The product allows corporations to raise cash by issuing debt, paying lower interest rates than they would with ordinary debt, and earning a tax break. The holder of the bond just puts the bond to the company in exchange for stock at a certain price. LYONs were invented by Merrill Lynch executive Thomas H. Patrick in the mid-1980s. Other Wall Street firms have their own brand of liquid-yield option notes.[13]

Bloomberg reported that the average yearly dollar amount in global equity-linked notes between 2008 and 2009 was about $100 million.[14]

This concept has led to many variations, one of which is auction rate securities. These securities are a form of zero-coupon notes sweetened by tying the return, in part, to the performance of an equity index. Now to make things interesting, you may have the notes be the credit of a firm, rather than that of the U.S. government, and the stock returns tied to a range of returns of an index. That is, you can have the IOU of a brokerage firm and the notes can generate stock returns only if an index performs within a range, say, plus or minus 20 percent. Beyond this range, there is no stock payoff. (Note: We are taking the upside here, as the downside would not have a penalty.) At maturity, the securities promise to return an investor's principal, typically at the end of 18 months, with the added gain from the index's performance, if that index trades within a certain range.

The *New York Times* reported the unhappy experience of an investor who bought one of the ARS and then lost about all because it was the credit of Lehman Bros., which went bankrupt.[15] In this case the product was described as "an investor in one of these notes [that was supposed] to earn the return of the index as well as get the principal back [and] the index cannot fall 25.5 percent or more from its level at the date of issuance. Neither can it rise more than 27.5 percent above that level. If the index exceeds those levels during the holding period, the investor receives only the principle back." The article implies that these notes tend to be sold to conservative investors who may not have been fully aware of the structure or risks. Quoting the Securities Litigation and Consulting Group, a financial economics consulting firm, the *Times* further reported that this group analyzed 14 issues of these principal-protected notes and found that more than half of them carried a yield of less than 2 percent. More than half the time, the analysis concluded, "Investors would be better off investing in Treasury Securities." Once again, the concept of Pascal's Wager enters the picture where one can seemingly earn much with little risk. As one can also see, Lehman is no God when it comes to reward.

Another form of this security is a traditional convertible debt issue that can be exchanged for equity in the future at a certain price. By shorting the stock and buying the bond, you can profit if the stock becomes worthless, but there are still sufficient assets to cover all debt holders, including those of the convertible issue. A hedge is created by participating in future gains of the equity with the convertible issue, thus mitigating the losses on the stock short. Ideally, you would expect the gain on the short exceeds the loss on the convertible bond. In general, these types of instruments are for sophisticated investors or trained advisors who know and can explain the risks and trade-offs. On the surface, they may seem too good to be true.

9

TIME TRAVEL REVISITED

So, can time travel be possible, and if so, under what circumstances? One can accept time travel into the future as explained by the work of Einstein. Imagine stepping into a spaceship that travels near light speed for 30 years to a distant planet. Finding it barren, the ship immediately turns around and returns with the same speed back to earth. About 10 years have passed on the ship, but on earth 80 years have gone by. This is called the Twin Paradox. According to people on earth, the clock on the spaceship runs slower than an identical, stationary clock; this is called time dilation. This theory was confirmed with experiments observing decaying muons (similar to electrons) and analyzing atomic clocks in jet flights.[1]

However, traveling into the past is more controversial, as Einstein's equation left this possibility open. One would have to travel faster than light, but the energy to do this would not be possible. Others feel that entropy prevents backward time travel. Entropy is a "measure of a disorder of a physical system. It is the number of rearrangements of a system's fundamental constituents that leave its gross, overall appearance unchanged." Entropy follows the Second Law of Thermodynamics, which states that "on average, the entropy of a physical system will tend to rise from a given moment."[2]

For a simple explanation, consider opening a Coke bottle and somehow being able to observe the millions of molecules that scatter into the room. It would be very difficult to put them back into the bottle, and if possible, would take a very long time. This would be high entropy. Now if the Coke bottle contained only two molecules, it would be more reasonable to assume they could find their way back into the bottle. This would take only a few seconds.

With three molecules, it would take a few days; four a few years. Billions and billions would require more than the time of the universe. We can continue this analysis by dropping an egg from a counter and seeing it splatter in many directions. The events needed to restore the egg intact on the counter would be great indeed. In both cases, it is easy to get into a high state of entropy.

What about going into the past? Shouldn't it be easier, as if there is more entropy going forward, there should be less going back? Actually, some physicists feel entropy also increases going into the past. Consider seeing 100 pennies on the floor, all of which have landed on heads. If they are tossed again, it is highly unlikely they will all land on heads. You may need a lot of time and many tosses to get this same arrangement of all heads again. What about going into the past? It is likely that when you first saw all 100 pennies heads up, it was only after many coin tosses in the past; hence, high entropy. Perhaps it is entropy that prevents us from traveling into the past, as it would be far too difficult.

Time travel can certainly be exploited under determinism by knowing what led to what and then intervening. But then there would be something leading to something else. This is the concept of Chaos Theory, whereby unknowingly changing one small thing in the past changes the future, as that past event affects many events that feed upon themselves. Imagine if you went back in time and bought Apple. Perhaps some smart trader would discern that Apple is now a good bet even though he was originally looking at purchasing Dell. Given your reputation as a solid trader, he changes his mind. Others begin to jump on the bandwagon because this new trader also has a good record and a solid following. Next thing you know, Apple soars. Apple management scratches its head in puzzlement but decides to offer more shares to raise capital. They use the new capital to buy Netscape and even borrow a huge amount of money against it. Netscape eventually collapses as Microsoft issues Internet Explorer. The previous actions cripple Apple, which then puts a hold its plans for new products, the MP3 player and the early drafts of an iPhone. Apple gradually erodes into bankruptcy. If only the stock did not rise, thus causing this change of fate. In corporate finance, we often see companies get giddy when stock prices soar and they then make questionable acquisitions, that are also partly financed by all too giddy bankers.

Some physicists claim that time travel is not possible because there is a cosmic censorship that prevents absurd examples like the Grandfather Paradox discussed in the previous chapter. However, there are theories on how to overcome this issue. Some feel that time travel is possible, but one cannot change the past. So, if you went back in time to kill your grandfather, the gun would jam or someone would push him out of the way and thus the past continues into the future. Other solutions of the Grandfather Paradox involve the acceptance of parallel universes. You travel back in time and actually kill your grandfather, but he is alive in another universe and so more than one universe exists. Still others make the case that someone was trying to kill your grandfather, but you actually saved him from a potential killer. Were it not for your time travel, you would not exist, but since you went back in time, you preserved a timeline. Recall the String Theory which states a broader universe than we can imagine. In this other universe, you do not exist, as there is no grandfather.

The Relationship to the Stock Market

What could be the effect of possible time travel as it relates to the stock market? Consider the CAPM model of $K_e = R_f + B(EMR)$, where the required return of Ke is a function of the risk-free rate (Rf) plus the beta (B) of an asset times the Excess Market Return (EMR). Beta would be the volatility of the asset relative to that of the market. It is shown statistically as the covariance of the asset with the market, with the covariance being divided by the variance of the market.

With time travel to the future as an added component, the ending price would be known. So one travels into the future and then returns to the present, buying the highest returning assets under the CAPM. Keeping things simple, if all stocks had a beta of 1.0, there would be the same required return for all stocks, say, 10 percent. Thus, pick the stock that has the highest return. Let's say it is a gold mining company in Vancouver that went up 600 percent. Why stop there? You can borrow some money and max out your purchases. Since you may end up owning too much in one stock, you decide to spread the money around. You can invest in highly leveraged stocks, only constrained by the amount you can borrow (or margin). Within a few years, you can become the richest person in the world!

However, you may or may not reach that state. There would be uncertainty if chaos created a fly in the ointment. As you start to gather quick wealth, word gets out and investors begin to imitate your successful investing.

Prices would start to go up, causing shorts to borrow heavily, as they cannot understand why prices are going up. Their losses would send shock waves into the financial system, causing a possible meltdown. In addition, beta becomes unresponsive to the market and K_e starts to represent the R_f rate. Thus, you don't get real wealth—just a risk-free rate that is taxed and trails inflation.

If you can travel in time, the parallel universe seems more probable. So, considering this possibility, you start to buy discreetly, and control your behavioral urges of overconfidence. But what if there is a parallel universe? Perhaps when you borrow all this money, there are different outcomes in the stock prices than what you had seen. Now what?

At this point there is uncertainty, and your utility curve says don't borrow all this money to invest, as there is no certainty that the future you saw will happen. There could be parallel universes. The whole system of time travel is so uncertain that the original CAPM takes over and there are no easy paths to richness.

What I have tried to show is that under the possibilities of physics, you cannot earn a risk-adjusted excess return strictly on time travel. Therefore, the CAPM would hold, as would other financial tools. Technical analysis and behavioral considerations would also hold. The uncertainties would, therefore, create bullish and bearish attitudes on eventual outcomes, or sentiment.

Financial Time Travel—Legal and Illegal

By far the most practical application of financial time travel is getting future price information and then acting upon it. In this way, you can lock in a gain, assuming the future price will be higher (assume that it is a risk-adjusted return). But how can you get this type of information? There are several means, but some are legal and others are illegal.

Arbitrage

Legally, you can do arbitrage. The same asset should have the same price no matter where it is traded. Assume Apple trades at $200 in New York and is also trading at $210 in London. You could short the London shares and simultaneously buy the New York shares. You can then deliver the New York shares, covering your short and pocketing a difference of $10 ($210 minus $200). The market would be crazy to allow this kind of price differential, as there would be two types of universes: New York and London. These would be subsets of a universe that is well known and defined: the global market. With high-speed trading, if there is a difference of a few milliseconds, you could exploit the differential within the global market.

In the days of the Soviet Union, some adventurers did some arbitrage by buying several pairs of jeans in New York and then selling them (for perhaps double the price) to jean-craved consumers behind the Iron Curtain. In this way, one could finance the airfare transaction cost. Of course, additional transaction costs would be considered such as obtaining hard-to-get travel visas, bribes to officials, and even confiscation of the jeans at the border. As you can see, there were risks and transaction costs associated with this transaction, which had originally on the surface seemed to be very simple.

You could also get into more complex arbitrage, if you want. For example, there could be good news on a competitor, but that good news could also affect other competitors in a positive way. Let's say homebuilder A has just surprised Wall Street with strong orders for its homes. Its shares jump 10 percent, but a competitor, homebuilder B, is still flat. You surmise, with all being equal, that homebuilder B's shares will move up as well. At this time, you could then do a pair trade by shorting A and buying B. Remember that in pair trading, the direction of the stock movement is not important; the only important thing is that B does better than A. If this occurs, then you make a profit. If the opposite happens and A continues to do better than B, then you lose money.

Insider Information

A form of illegal time travel is trading on insider information. For example, let's assume you get information from an investment banker who is working on the deal, that Company ABC will be taken over in a few weeks at a 30 percent premium to the current stock price. Trading on nonpublic and material information is illegal. In this case, both the trader and the banker would be guilty of inside trading.

If you would set up an account with a relative in another country who traded under their names, the result would be the same—trading on inside information. However, trading on *speculative* takeovers is legal.

So what you want is to get a future indication from seemingly parallel universes that are in reality, parts of one. Arbitrage and derivatives are such examples. Can we exploit technical analysis in a similar manner? Imagine if one traveled to another planet and discovered life. Not only is there life, but there are intelligent beings which trade stocks using technical analysis. Wouldn't one be curious about the technical methods on the planet and then compare the similarities and differences?

Parallel Type Universes: Traditional and Candles

One way to do this "parallel universe" investing is to use perhaps two different technical analysis approaches. Use the one "on the planet" and then use the one "on earth" and compare results.

Let's compare two technical methods that may use two different approaches. If the principles of technical analysis hold, the result should be some common buy and sell decisions. We can use Japanese Candlesticks and then compare the results with traditional technical analysis. These approaches are very different in that candles don't incorporate volume, which is extremely important under traditional technical analysis. However, there are some similarities such as a Head and Shoulder pattern, which Candlestick users call a "three Buddha top" and represent the same topping process. Steve Nison, a leading expert on candles, writes, "The Japanese three Buddha pattern was used over a hundred years before the head and shoulders was known in America."[3] Candles require confirmation and make use of traditional technical measures of support and resistance.

Candlesticks have simple charting techniques and are used for short-term trading strategies. The candles or chart marks have only the trading period's (usually a day) high, low, open, and close. If the close is above the open, then the candle is white and shows bullish power. If not, it is dark and shows bearish power. Candles have various shapes and can only be read clearly when the analyst is looking at the types of candles that come before the current one and perhaps those that come after. From this, the analyst can decide if the price is going up or down in either a bullish or bearish direction.

In October 2009, Goldman Sachs (GS) had a price top of $192. Within a month, the stock dropped (after its fraud allegation imbroglio) to $162. Are there clues in the Western charts indicating a possible top? What about clues in some parallel type of universe using Japanese Candlesticks?

Figure 9.1 is a Western chart that shows two large ellipses. The top ellipse is the RSI that shows a negative divergence, as the rising stock price of GS is not confirmed by the rising highs in the RSI. The large bottom ellipse is the MACD, and that is also negative for the same reason. The small circle near October 19 shows a sell signal on the MACD as the MACD moves below the grey (line) moving average. So for traders, we get two strong sell signals near the top price of $192.

Figure 9.2 is a chart made of Candlesticks. Once again, Candlesticks are created simply by showing the closing price compared to the opening price. If the close is above the open, the candle is white and bullish since the bulls pushed the close above the open. The opposite is a dark candle. Highs and lows relative to the open and close are called shadows and indicate lurking strength of either bulls or bears. Various candles have Japanese names and must be

FIGURE 9.1 Western Chart—Two Large Ellipses

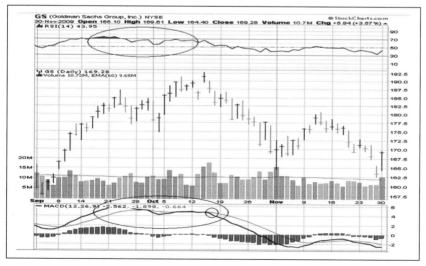

Source: Used by permission of Stockcharts.com

FIGURE 9.2 Candlestick Chart

Source: Used by permission of Stockcharts.com

analyzed within the context of what just happened before a particular candle and even what happened after. Candles thus show an immediate investment outlook. For example, a solid white candle, called a Marubozu show great bullish power, like a truck speeding on a highway. To then see a neutral candle like a Doji (a cross design) would indicate that the bulls must have lost much power, similar to the truck hitting a wall. Thus, the trend would appear to changing to perhaps favoring the bears. Going back to Figure 9.2, we can see negatives. The left circle is a negative pattern called a bearish engulfing pattern. When one blends the white candle in the circle on the left with the higher dark one on the right it creates a synthetic candle called a Shooting Star. Shooting Stars are considered a potential reversal of the stock price trend into a bearish direction. Usually, one may look for confirmation by looking at the candles to the right to see if this trend may perhaps be reversing to an up move. No luck here as they indicate either a hanging man (black candle, just before the right circled candle) or Spinning Tops which are more neutral (candles just after the black one and the one right after which is circled). So this too indicates that the up move has been most likely ended.

So in comparing both approaches, which one would a trader use? Some would prefer one over the other, but showing both would give a method of comparing and perhaps doing the trade only when both show a bullish pattern or a bearish pattern. It is not surprising to see that candles and traditional technical analysis tend to give the same results, as they have the same basic underpinnings in the assumptions of their discipline. For example, both traditional technical analysis and candles feel that prices are determined by fear and greed.

Derivatives

In looking at parallel types of universes, we can come back to derivatives. As the name implies, they derive their pricing from the actual financial instrument in the real world. We can call the real world the cash market, where you transact in an actual asset, such as a stock. So, for example, if you have the right to buy a stock at $100 in 6 months, the value of this call option would increase as the price approaches $100, but before the expiration of the option. In fact, once the stock exceeds $100, the call option would increase point for point with the stock.

The question then arises as to whether traders will first make their intentions known in one universe as compared to another. If they are bullish, will they buy the stock in the cash market or buy the calls in the derivatives market? Traders today feel that clues happen in both markets; looking at only one will not provide the best trading solution. If a company is expected to release news that could significantly move the stock, traders may keep an eye on the ratio of calls to puts. (Note: The opposite of a call is a put, where one has the right to sell the stock at a specific price.) Rising calls may indicate trader expectations that the news will be good rather than bad. Of course, informed traders would make the best decision, but we do not know if all increases in the calls are informed or just herd mentality. It could be that call buying will soon be shattered with the opposite—bad news. Also, the calls could be a hedge for short positions. These derivative strategies can get complex, as we may buy both calls and puts to either hedge our bets or speculate on price objectives. Recall the earlier example of a other companies in an industry, where one trader may feel good news will spill over to the industry, while another trader may prefer to buy call options in competitors, assuming the news is positive. At this point, complex pricing decisions would be calculated to see which company was the better deal and which would company would have the least amount of transaction costs.

Determinism and Technical Analysis

While we went into the deep areas of philosophy and physics on cause and effect, we can actually make projections in an economic manner. Estimates are also cause and effect, and can follow determinism. Technical analysis will almost certainly say it must. Some will accept certain deterministic technical models, while others will casually look at them but not really use them as a prime method of technical analysis. To some extent, all technical analysis is deterministic, as it looks at past market statistics, such as, stock data and volume data to make future projection of prices. There are both economically based models and mathematically based models.

Estimation of earnings can be a predestined or determined process, as one event leads to another. Fundamentally, forecasting earnings per share (EPS) usually starts with an economic outlook from a tops-down basis. For most companies, a key component of EPS is to forecasted sales. While other factors such as industry characteristics, same store sales growth, market share gains, and so on also influence sales estimates, a weakened GDP forecast sends shudders through the stock market, as it translates to a weak outlook for earnings growth. (Note the chain reaction of cause and effect.) Some models assume the cause-and-effect process, and the only way to exploit it is to ride the wave and don't try to change it.

Once sales are forecasted, profit margins and tax rates are more easily projected, as they are more predictable. So, economic cycles eventually affect the rise and fall of stock prices. But if the prime mover of the economic cycle is already in motion, then our estimates of the sales and margins are inconsequential.

Kondratieff Wave

There are many economic cycles/waves considered by economists. Some are short term and others are long term. The Kondratieff Wave (K-Wave) shows a boom and bust wave over a long period. This long view is about 50 to 60 years, or may also assume to take place over two generations. It was developed by Nikolai Kondratieff in his 1925 book *The Major Economic Cycles*.

His view of the wave is an economic one. His theory is based on a study of nineteenth-century price behavior that included wages, interest rates, raw material prices, foreign trade, bank deposits, and other data. It can be analyzed in phases or seasons. "The Kondratieff wave cycle goes through four distinct phases: beneficial inflation (spring), stagflation (summer), beneficial deflation (autumn), and deflation (winter)."[4] Spring is the accumulation of goods and the creation of wealth. Savings foster capital expansion and prices start to rise. Jobs are created, but there is social concern regarding new production methods.

The spring lasts 25 years. Economists such as Joseph Schumpeter, an Austrian economist from the first half of the twentieth century who popularized the term "creative destruction" with regard to economics, foster the notion that key to economic growth is the necessary innovation done by the entrepreneur. The innovation could be intense for some. Consider the typesetter in the printing industry being replaced by word processing used by a reporter; the horseshoe-maker being replaced by the tire manufacturing system, or the agency trader being replaced by algorithmic systems. One could then conclude that education and training is a sound investment.

We then enter summer, where production is maxed out, inefficiencies occur, and work moods change. (Maybe it is easier to raise prices in order to get more profits, rather than to create more efficient production methods?) We also tend to have wars that create strains on production capacity and put additional upward pressure on prices. We then see a drop in output followed by the beginning of recessionary forces. Summer lasts 20 to 25 years.

Then comes autumn, which is deflationary. The change in price structure, along with the mood of a population used to consumption accompanied by the vast accumulation of wealth from the past 30 years, causes the economy to enter a period of relatively flat growth and mild prosperity. The economy becomes consumption-oriented accompanied by rapid increases in debt levels. We get a plateau of prosperity, creating greed and overconfidence, combined with a sense that the debt is manageable. Technicians who use sentiment measures would certainly see something like a high percentage of bulls versus bears.

The inflated price structure from the primary recession, along with the desire for consumption and the rapid increase in debt, sets the recipe for a severe and protracted depression. Autumn lasts 7 to 10 years.

Finally comes winter. For a three-year period, prices collapse and debts lose their collateral. This is then followed by deflation where interest rates and wages decline; this lasts for 15 years and eventually sets the stage for a cleansing process. Firms are restructured and innovations improve production. This gives the springboard to an eventual rebound, where we may see either new companies forming or old ones growing rapidly. For example, FedEx Corporation was started in 1971 and grew rapidly after the mid–1970s recession, with it being listed on the NYSE in 1978. In 2009, it had over $35 billion in revenue and a workforce of over 275,000 workers.[5] Microsoft was founded in 1975, went public in 1986, and also created many jobs and billions in revenues. As of 2009, it had 93,000 employees and revenues in excess of $58 billion. But more interesting is the fact that Microsoft created 4 billionaires (with Bill Gates being the richest man in the world) and 12,000 millionaires!

This sounds like our recent economy. Shop till you drop pervaded the economy for many years, and if you ran out of money, the 2000 decade offered more support from home equity loans and the rising stock market, not to mention the usual standby of generous credit card lines. Then came the eventual unpopular Iraq War, followed by the financial crisis that crushed borrowers and leading financial institutions, and for some, the big depression or perhaps at least the "New Normal." The New Normal is described as an economy "with lower household debt, higher personal savings, and less consumption as a share of Gross Domestic Product. The effects of this transition will ripple through both the domestic and the international economy. At home, some of our bloated retail infrastructure will disappear as businesses shift their focus to producing more for export. Abroad, countries that have depended on exports to fuel economic growth will have to shift toward domestic consumption, which means lower savings rates and a diminished appetite for U.S. government debt, putting pressure on U.S. fiscal policy."[6]

Consider the following debt analysis:[7]

> *Between the mid–1960s and the mid–1980s, household debt was remarkably stable, varying between 44 and 50% of GDP. From 1985 until 2008, that figure rose almost without interruption, topping out at 102% in the first quarter of 2008. This seemed sustainable because household net worth relative to GDP also rose sharply, boosted by higher prices for stocks and housing. When both of these markets collapsed, households were left with debt burdens much higher than they could sustain, making debt reduction a matter of immediate urgency.*

Kondratieff was convinced that his studies of economic, social, and cultural life proved that a long-term order of economic behavior existed and could be used to anticipate future economic developments. The K-Wave has been criticized as a reflection of laissez-faire economics (pre-twentieth century) that is conducive to cycles. Free market forces make volatile swings in the economy with booms and busts. With government intervention and monetary policy, we can help stabilize these swings. However, cynics would say that the Fed missed it in the Great Depression by tightening money instead of easing it. Criticism of fiscal policy is that it comes too late and from the wrong areas and may represent politician pork handouts. No matter what the views, we must realize that the markets have fluctuated in prices and employment levels over the past 100 years. Some have also said the prior peak should have come at a time when prices in the stock market were still rising and for years thereafter, so the K-Wave lost it. Not so fast, the K-Wavers may say. If you use the two-generations concept, you expand the time line, as the life expectancy increased after WWII and with this the peak came on time.

The fact that the K-Wave covers two generations is appealing as an analytical tool. The idea is that the first generation makes the money, the second loses it, and then the third must rebuild. This has been observed by both historians and economists. In family-run businesses, it is estimated that the average life expectancy of a successful business owned by one family is 50 to 60 years."[8] So why does family wealth cease at the end of the second generation or at the beginning of the third? It may that the entrepreneurial juices cease as the second generation becomes fat and lazy.

Technicians also use generations as an analytical tool. Technicians would say the current generation invests in a rearview mirror that becomes faulty. Thus, after the Great Depression ended, many investors lost money in the stock market and so began to avoid purchasing stocks. As a result, they missed the powerful gain of stocks of the 1950s and 1960s. Instead, they bought bonds that netted lower returns and then were crushed by ensuing inflation. For many years, Merrill Lynch's technical analysis included the concentration of investments in an asset. High levels indicated the asset would be scheduled to underperform in the coming years. So if households had record high allocations of their assets to stocks, we concluded that soon the stock market would decline, as there was no one left to buy.

This was the case in the 1990s with stocks based on an analysis by the Federal Reserve Bank of New York.[9] During this time, all asset classes were about equal except stocks, which became double the household allocation. For example, in 1989, real estate was 44.6 percent of household assets versus 1998's 41.6 percent. Bonds, cars, and other assets were relatively even. However, stocks in 1989 were 5.0 percent and went to 11.6 percent in 1998. The analysis stated that the rise was due to increases in the stock prices and not necessarily a result of more individual buying. By the late 1990s, we had the growth of day traders and speculators in Internet stocks. It seems stocks were desired again, but unfortunately near the top. Technically, we can make the case that perhaps greed got in the way of asset allocation. This doubling in stocks was later lowered and punished by a severe stock market correction.

Record home ownership in the 2000s preceded the decline in home prices. Homeownership rates, which have been tracked since 1965, hit a record high of 69.2 percent in the second and fourth quarters of 2004.[10] Soon thereafter, housing prices began to stall and then to fall within a short period of time, causing the housing crash. So, the K-Wave is a repeating, deterministic event. Trying to second-guess this under its deterministic influence would appear to be useless. Technicians would take advantage by surfing the wave rather than getting wiped out.

10

OTHER ECONOMIC CYCLES

There are many cycles to analyze. Some are economic, such as that of French economist Clement Juglar, the already discussed K-Wave, and the Kitchin Cycle, which is discussed in this chapter. In their 1946 book *Measuring Business Cycles,* Arthur Burns and Wesley Mitchell described an economic cycle as an expansion and contraction of economic activity of one to 10 to 12 years.[1] The National Bureau of Economic Research also developed a cycle. Unfortunately, by the time it labeled the recession as ending, it was after the fact and the stock market has already moved up in price, considerably.

Some cycles are caused by changes in the money supply, investments, credit, and in the case of Kitchin, inventory. Again, some feel that a deterministic cause of a cycle is impossible, as the cycle can adapt and make changes, while others say it is the same old, same old.

Technicians also look at the Four-Year or Presidential Cycle. Based on the work of economics professor Wesley C. Mitchell and Yale Hirsch, editor of the Stock Trader's Almanac, a leading technician, Charles Kirkpatrick, claims the four-year cycle is the "most widely accepted and most easily recognized cycle in the stock market."[2] In the work of Hirsch, the strongest part of the Presidential Cycle is the latter two years. He muses that perhaps in running for office in the last two years, a candidate promises much (sounds familiar) and helps enact programs to stimulate the economy. After all, in politics, some feel that people vote with their pocketbooks. Then once elected, reality sets in and the screws have to be placed on the economy.

Anomalies and Trading Patterns

There are other event cycles called anomalies. An example is the January Effect that involves buying in December and then selling in January. The rationale is that investors dump their stocks at the end of the year in order to take tax losses, and of course the market makers behave as conditioned sellers by marking down the prices. Then, once the year ends, stocks bounce back as the distressed selling is over. Much research has been done on the January Effect, showing in more recent years that hedge funds have arbitraged the opportunity, or that it only works on small-cap stocks that are not as liquid and less likely to be held in tax-free ERISA accounts.

There are also anomalies and other cycle observations such as trading patterns. One that has been extensively studied by researchers is the "turn of the month" effect. This period is defined by John J. McConnell and Wei Xu in their "Equity Returns at the Turn of the Month" article as starting on "the last trading day of the month and ending on the third trading day of the following month."[3]

McConnell and Xu state that all positive returns in the market happen in the four-day trading period. So investing on the other days is not profitable, as you get little or no return on the assumed market risk. This situation involving the four-day trade period held true in the United States from 1926 to 2005 and spilled over to foreign markets during that time. However, the positive returns in this four-day period cannot be explained by other various effects in the market, including those dealing with small-cap stocks, low priced stocks, or calendar events, such as quarter-end trading patterns. The authors conclude, "The turn-of-the-month effect in equity returns continues to be a puzzle in search of a solution."[4]

Another observation is made by seasoned traders: The first hour and last hour provide the bulk of the volume on a general trading day. For example, traders see an event that triggers either a strong up or down opening. Then they wait till 10:30 a.m. (one hour after a New York opening) and take a contrary position at the lunch hour. So if a stock opens sharply lower (recall our Selling Climax) at 10:30 or so, the selling may reach a temporary low as the panic sellers have their orders mostly filled. Then the traders buy the stock and see it rally a bit toward noon, when it then becomes listless. Later in the day, it starts to tank again. So the trader will flip the stock around noon and then perhaps short later in the day.

Other observations include Fridays and Mondays. Why do investors wait till the end of the day, especially Friday, to buy in an uptrend or sell in a down trend? Is it because on Monday there can be a slight reversal of the closing price? Is it that they want the trade to occur as close to the market close as possible, so there can be no negative contradiction? Institutions may also buy late in order to "paint the tape" and show better results for clients who may seek short-term performance results.

We also had a "Blue Monday" effect where Mondays tended to be the weakest returning day of the month. This was for the period 1928 to 1982, but by the 1990s, Monday became the strongest day of the week and Thursday was the weakest. Martin Pring notes that there does not appear to be any acceptable rationale for this effect.[5] My guess would be that in the 1990s we had a rising market and thus over the weekend investors read the papers and went to cocktail parties to boost their bullish opinions, which then led to Monday purchases. The prior period had many severe bear markets, which then acted in the reverse and offset any positive Mondays.

You can study daily stock price moves and the weather conditions. Some feel the Sunspot Cycle affects commodities and wars, while others study sunny/cloudy days. If it is cloudy, does the stock market go down? Seems not. Obviously, snowstorms lower volume, as traders may not be able to get to their posts. The same may hold true for religious holidays.[6] The moon phase cycle and stock price trends are also studied, and here there appears to be some relationship. Although some might view such predictions as ludicrous. There may be some evidence that moon phases affect behavior and stock price trends.[7]

The work of Arch Crawford discusses planetary alignments and their effects on stocks. The publisher of Crawford Perspectives feels that "astronomic cycles and harmonic events have a profound impact on the stock and commodity markets." For example, he may surmise that the gravity caused by planetary alignments resulted in investors' mood swings and thus helped to create bull/bear markets. His call of the 1987 crash was identified in his August 8, 1987, newsletter as a warning of "an imminent 'horrendous' stock market crash." He advised his subscribers that his "long-term sell signal is set in stone" and to "be out of everything by August the 24th," indicating that unusual "geocentric planetary arrangements" would put an end to the long-enduring bull market of that time.[8] Crawford has some peer acceptance, as in 1992, he was voted the best, long-term market timer by *Timer Digest*. However, he should not be confused with paranormal astrologers like Madam Zoran. He deals "exclusively with what has always been the first premise of natural astrology that celestial (planetary) events correlate with terrestrial events. Since the correlations can be statistically demonstrated and are cyclic in nature, knowledge of the correlations serves as the basis for predicting what kind of events will occur and recur 'in time' (so to speak) with specific planetary arrangements."[9]

With that said, we must also realize that superstition is seen on Wall Street, as some traders will consult their astrologers and may not even trade if the astrological signs are not positive. Is this caused by economic reasons? No, it is behavioral. So, whether one procrastinates selling a loser for tax reasons, or is hot to trot to transact in the opening hour of trading, emotions seem to play a good role.

So, if you believe in cycles, you must accept determinism in some manner and reject the random walk of stock prices. Besides you can make easy decisions using a cycle. Instead of doing cash flows and complicated momentum analysis, you only have to know how long the cycle is and when it began, and then act at the midpoint. So if the length of the cycle or wave is four years and it just started, then you buy. Two years from today, you sell and wait till the cycle falls to its low—two years later.

Technicians and Cycles

Technicians would also look at features of cycles. The longer the cycle, the more important it is. So a bottoming of a 10-year cycle indicates a much more serious buying opportunity than some cycle that has only a one-month wave. Cycles can be added together to get summation principles and that create patterns and so give a better sell signal such as the Head and Shoulders pattern.

Once you decide on a cycle, you can then blend other technical criteria to make even better buy and sell decisions. For example, consider Figure 10.1.

FIGURE 10.1 Dow Jones Industrial Average, 1997 to 2002

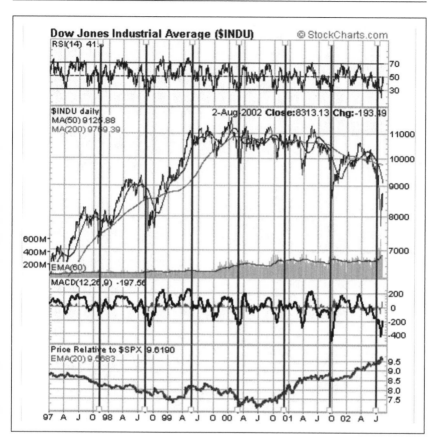

Source: Used by permission of Stockcharts.com

We could make a buy decision at the beginning of a cycle and sell in the middle. So, October 1997 looks good and we sell around May 1998, and then buy at the drop near August 1998. However, selling in mid–1999 was not that good, as the market went higher. Near July 1999, we should be buying but near the top? (Not so good.)

Now if we overlay RSI to confirm our earlier decision in 1998, we see it was sound as RSI gives a buy on the grey line, a sell in mid-cycle and then another buy on the grey line (see Figure 10.2). While we sell in mid–1999 and prices go higher, we are saved from buying at the top of the grey line as the RSI gives a sell signal. We don't buy again until March 2000, when both

FIGURE 10.2 Dow Jones Industrial Average, 1997 to 2002, Buy and Sell Points

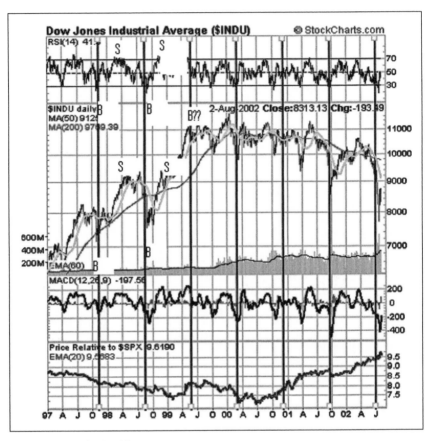

Source: Used by permission of Stockcharts.com

the grey line and the RSI give buy signals. After that, we get better signals when using RSI with our cycles.

What about using other indicators? The Price Relative appears not to have any use, as its downtrend happens in an uptrend of price and then vice versa. Again, the Dow is compared to the S&P 500, so it may not be that useful. MACD appears to cross the zero line a bit earlier than the cycle turn, so it may not be that useful. So we would decide to either use only the cycle or to use overlays as indicators. (This would require back testing.)

Traditional Business Cycle and the Stock Market

We must realize that the market anticipates economic scenarios and so certain groups may lead the actual economic performance.

We shall focus on the cycle in Figure 10.3 picture to point out its various features. It is an idealized business cycle chart from Martin J. Pring's excellent book on technical analysis, *Technical Analysis Explained*.[10] Murphy also provides some good commentary on the business cycle and its effect on the investing cycle which we shall also include.[11] Realize that the market anticipates economic scenarios and hence certain groups may lead the actual economic performance. This may confuse investors who just read the newspaper, as they continue to make comments like "how can this market go up when the news is so lousy?"

The business cycle is divided into six stages. Stage 1 begins with the economy falling into a recession, and Stage 6 ends with economic expansion ending and a recovery on the horizon. Each stage is marked by a turn in one of three asset classes: bonds, stocks, or commodities. We will see that particular industry sectors or market groups are expected to be favored in

FIGURE 10.3 Idealized Business Cycle

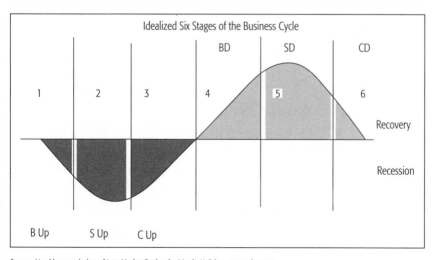

Source: Used by permission of InterMarket Review by Martin K. Pring. www.pring.com

certain parts of the market cycle. (Remember: The market cycle anticipates the economic cycle.)

- *Stage 1.* Bonds turn up (meaning interest rates decline) as the economy weakens into a looming recession and loan demand decreases. Usually bonds lead the stock market by several months. Stocks and commodities are falling as investors expect lower corporate profits and pricing pressure due to less demand.
- *Stage 2.* Stocks turn up as smart investors anticipate a recovery. Banks tend to lead the market, as rising stock prices and poor bank stock trends make the recovery suspect. Banks are expected to see more loans coming and better interest spreads. Consumer discretionary stocks start to rise along with technology stocks. Small-cap stocks tend to lead the performance of large-cap stocks, as they are expected to be in a better position of benefiting from an economic rebound due to their operating leverage and market share growth potentials. However, newspapers still have much bad news on the front page. Most investors are still scared out of the market. Bond and commodity prices are falling during the recession. Loan demand is still weak, and price discounting with sales prevalent in the market.
- *Stage 3.* Commodities turn up as recession forces are being spent. All three markets are rising. More borrowers come on stream as they need to beef up inventories in anticipation of demand. Commodity prices start to firm in anticipation of growing demand, and some production has been shut down, making supply increases more difficult in the short term. Cyclicals start to do well in the market. Investors are still careful regarding the market, as the news is bad and most economists and strategists are cautious.
- *Stage 4.* Bonds turn down, as loan demand causes increased interest rates. Stocks and commodities are rising. Cyclicals, including energy stocks and basic industry stocks, get more attention in the market from investors who probably are underweighted in the group and start to play catch-up. Prices are increased for

commodities as capacity constraints are being factored into pricing. Fear that the Fed may start to tighten the money supply and raise interest rates may initiate speculative purchase of assets and inventories to beat further price increases. Initially investors have a Wall of Worry and wait till the economic news gets better. They are reassured once they see economists and strategists get more positive.

- *Stage 5.* Stocks turn down as inflationary fears cause interest rates and commodities to rise. Capital goods stocks are positive, as corporations are finally bullish and expand CAPX; in addition, they get into the acquisition mood. It is also expected that profit outlooks are priced for perfection with high P/E ratios for valuation of the market and stocks. Sales peak (with mostly price increases) and assets may be acquired with heavily borrowed money. (In 2007, we saw this in private equity and real estate.) Bond prices continue to drop, as fears of rising interest rates are tied to upcoming inflation. Then sales start to get soft, and attention turns to consumer staples, utilities, and defensive stocks such as service companies. Newspaper stories show rather good economic data. Investors who missed the boat make up for the rise in the market as they start to make short cuts into more speculative stocks that offer big upside promise. Later, investors wonder why the market is weakening with such good news. The Slope of Hope psychologically makes investors nonchalant, and this leads to melting gains and even growing losses. Denial in the marketplace leads to the Disposition Affect as losing positions are not sold on the hope that they will rebound.
- *Stage 6.* The peak was reached in Stage 5, and the economic slowdown begins. Higher prices and weaker fundamentals cool off demand, and as a result, lower profits are expected by investors. Commodities turn down as business demand for materials slows. All three markets are declining. Assets purchased with heavy leverage start to show massive defaults and collapses. The foundations of financial institutions are rattled, and government intervention

in providing stability is likely. Disgusted investors see the scary headline news and dump stocks and swear off investing again ... until the next time.

In general, the cycle is just a guide to timing.

Market Timing

Market timing is prone to disappoint the experts. Is the market on its way up when you start to make trading decisions? Which group, technicians or fundamentals, will lead? Decisions will no doubt be influenced by sentiment and behavioral biases. If I am reluctant to invest in the market, then I will avoid early stage outperformers like banks and small-cap stocks. So I may have high levels of cash and then defensive stocks, compounding the problem. For this reason, indexing may be the best compromise, as we get the entire market and don't suffer by having too much in the dragging sectors. If we are always indexed to stocks, we don't get whipsawed by buying high and then selling low. So is all this business cycle analysis, even for the experts, just another way to generate underperformance in portfolios, or can the economists, strategists, and individuals rely on their "magic touch"?

Looking at Figure 10.4, we superimpose a rough stock market cycle. The stock market anticipates the economic cycle and so moves before economic indicators get better on the upside or worse on the downside. Naturally, this provides the fertile ground for technicians who can anticipate the market turns, before the economic news hits. Hence, you will see many reading the newspaper and wondering why the stock market is doing one thing when the economic data is doing something else. Realize that within the stock market, certain groups will do better or worse in each stage, just as we discussed. These groups may be more influenced by their association with interest rates and commodities. So cyclicals would follow commodity movements.

FIGURE 10.4 Rough Stock Market Cycle

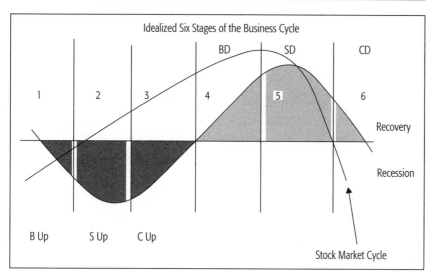

Source: Used by permission of InterMarket Review by Martin K. Pring. www.pring.com

Kitchin Cycle

The Kitchin Cycle, developed by Joseph Kitchin in 1923, is an economic cycle of three to five years that is caused by changes in inventories. Its forecast and description more recently appeared in *Barron's* magazine in July 2001. At that time, I was teaching a technical analysis class, and so I asked the students their thoughts on the article that stated the market would plunge much lower than where it was at the time. You must understand that we were coming off the 2000 high, and so a good number felt that the market was oversold, and also indicated that the worst was perhaps behind us, especially as we had been consolidating for about 1½ years. The article, authored by P. Q. Wall, publisher of P.Q. Wall forecast and user of Kitchin analysis, showed a scary chart.[12]

If past cycles follow suit, such as the 1970 to 1975 cycle that had a peak in 1973 of around 1000 and then a market collapse two years later under 600, then in 2001 (see Figure 10.5), we were heading for danger and the market should bottom around 7500 in late 2002—much lower than the current 10,600! While there was the probability of a blow off at 13,900

FIGURE 10.5 INDU (Dow Jones Industrial Average) INDX: 23-Jul-2001

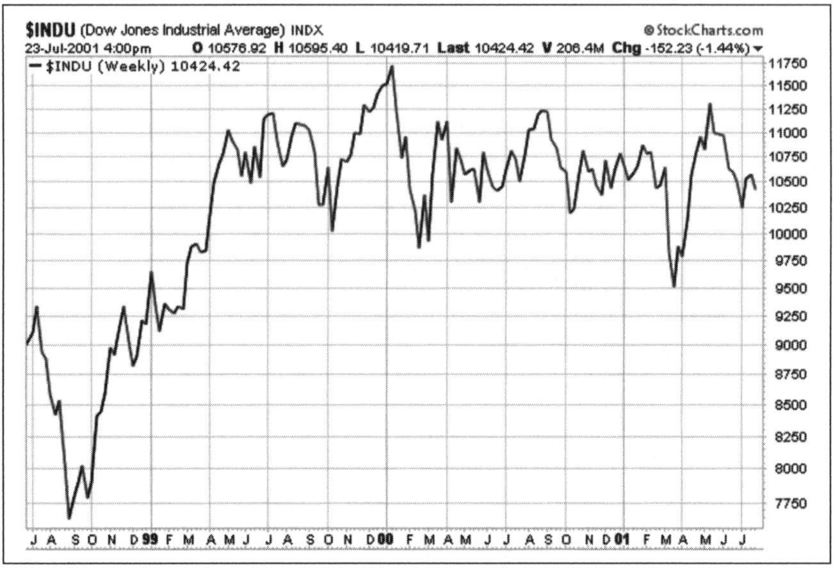

$INDU (Dow Jones Industrial Average) INDX   © StockCharts.com
23-Jul-2001 4:00pm   O 10576.92 H 10595.40 L 10419.71 Last 10424.42 V 206.4M Chg -152.23 (-1.44%) ▼
— $INDU (Weekly) 10424.42

Source: Used by permission of Stockcharts.com

in January 2002, the odds favored a "whimper," reminiscent of the 1970 to 1975 market.

Figure 10.6 shows a cycle pattern ending on the right at around 7500 in 2002. In 2000, after meandering for about 1½ years, we were around 10,500. Investors felt the market corrected enough and we were ready to rally back to the previous highs. After all, we were marking time for almost 1½ years. That should certainly be enough time to consolidate and regroup for a try at the highs again, right?

Wall used the Kitchin overlay to show a likely landing spot for the Dow *at much lower levels*. The actual comparison charts from *Barron's* article is shown in Figure 10.7.

David Chapman of Union Securities LTD. describes the Kitchin cycle as "a primary technical cycle that fundamentally follows the business cycle, but whose application is generally applied to the stock market."[13] A subset of the Kondratieff cycle, it has a shorter length of

FIGURE 10.6 INDU (Dow Jones Industrial Average) INDX 23-Dec-2002

Source: Used by permission of Stockcharts.com

42 to 54 months depending on the monetary and fiscal policy of a government. It is divided into parts—first into thirds, called Kitchin Thirds, with each third lasting roughly 12 to 18 months. These thirds are divided into thirds again and are called Wall Days, lasting roughly four to six months. Of interest to traders is the continued subdividing. Note the Wall notation in the *Barron's* article. According to Chapman, we can see where a wall occurs, identify the depth and height of the next third, and then start to make conclusions whether it is going higher or lower, sooner or later.

So cycles/waves can be explained economically as well as mathematically. The use of cycles by technicians assumes the repeating pattern that they create, even though, as we have seen, they cannot always be explained. Once again, we go back to deterministic issues that have perplexed many philosophers and theologians. Technicians, therefore, can join the club.

FIGURE 10.7 *Barrron's* Two of a Kind Chart

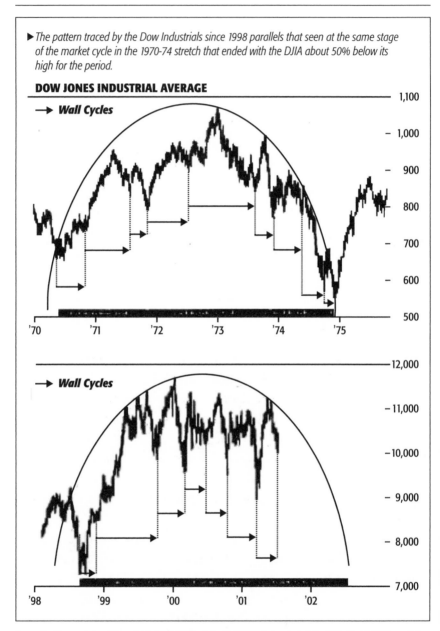

▶ The pattern traced by the Dow Industrials since 1998 parallels that seen at the same stage of the market cycle in the 1970-74 stretch that ended with the DJIA about 50% below its high for the period.

Source: Used by permission of *Barron's* July 23, 2001 ("Fire Or Ice," by P.Q. Wall); two charts first published in P.Q. Wall's newsletter, July 3, 2011.

Bubbles and Scams

A corollary to the cycle and anomaly phenomena is the bubble. Now when we think of a bubble, we are reminded of our childhood when we created bubbles out of a liquid by placing the liquid in some device. When we ran with the device, we created a bubble or a series of bubbles. We saw the bubbles floating in the air, popping, and finally disappearing into the sky. The point here is that we have devices in the marketplace that can create investment bubbles or even a series of bubbles.

Let's look at bubbles and deterministic investing. These are not as readily predictable economically, but they can be measured as fallout from behavioral folly. They create the illusion of wealth and attract many investors, but in a short time they pop. Usually there are heavy losses for investors, except for those who foresaw the bubble and got out in time.

Even completely crooked and illegal activities like the Ponzi schemes used by Bernie Madoff are prone to bubbles. He promised rather high returns and then gave returns to early investors from the proceeds of more recent investors. This appealed to those who wished to get in on the good life. In financial terms we call this a large alpha. Some managers do this legally by buying into the next Microsoft. These are offset by managers who try this and fail. So there is risk in earning high, legitimate returns. However, Bernie's road ended when the market collapsed in 2008 and investors wanted some cash—which was not available.

There are other scams like the famous Nigerian letters that offer vast fortunes if only we give them our financial data. For a relatively small fee to cover expenses and some government duties, we can then participate in a multimillion dollar bonanza. (Why are we so lucky to be picked out of a crowd of billions to receive this honor?)

Another scheme, reminiscent of the movie *Boiler Room*, is the Pump and Dump. A con broker contacts a patsy and promises a large return on a speculative company. The con claims to have the inside scoop (which is illegal insider trading if true) on the results of major clinical trial that will produce a drug to cure some type of cancer. Meanwhile, the price has been going up (other patsies are buying an illiquid stock that can be easily marked up) and is already rather high. The patsy buys many shares as the con brokers dump their shares at the top. Soon the company is found to be pure hype and is eventually delisted. The patsy has lost his money and maybe when he goes to the broker's office to investigate, he finds no such address or a dirty basement with a dripping overhead pipe instead.

We can also find scams in real estate. For example, one con involves the unsuspecting investor placing cash deposits to get in line for buying hot condos, with the idea of flipping them for a quick profit. My friends in Dubai related one such scam where a person was told that a new project was hot and prices were already being increased. He had to get a lottery number to see if he could get in line to make the tiny deposit that could earn him the right to win this property (and, of course, to soon flip it for big profits). Once again, either the property did not exist or if it did exist, a "licensed" broker could take his cash deposit. Please meet the broker (perhaps an empty condo that masquerades for an office) with the cash. The broker quickly files the registration papers, and gets the bank deposit receipt in order to meet the "deadline." The next day the office is empty and—you guessed it—the broker is out of the country.

We can get into more sophisticated cons that are legal but are not ethical or good business practice. Most managers underperform the index, but they can still get a high rating if they look good against competitors. Suppose a manger decides to closet the index by buying many larger stocks in the index with close to actual weights. One could then come very close to the index return. Index tilt funds are those that actually do come close to the index return and are advertised as such (they basically mirror the index fund). Managers then charge much lower fees that are closer to index fees as compared to active manager fees.

The client may actually like this strategy, as she may come close to index returns and even beat them with a slight tweaking of the stock and weight selection by the manager. But if the manager charges full active fees and does so without disclosure, the client gets fleeced because she is basically paying active fees for indexing. When they charge the regular fee and fail to inform the clients, a line has been crossed. The clients think that they are receiving active management, but in fact they get little, if any.

This is a more subtle scam, but sophisticated investors can discover this by running an R² or Coefficient of Determination on the fund. Something like over 90 percent starts to create suspicions, as 100 percent is an index. Also, investors may demand weekly portfolio holding that can be compared to the index and see how they trace out. But if the investor is not professional, he may not be aware of these precautions.

Now that I have your attention, I'll re-create some schemes that have been used by others. One is the old incubator fund trick.

Incubator Fund Trick

During a hot IPO market where only a few shares can be bought, I start a new fund to place these shares because I want to separate it from my big funds in which I do a lot of business. Here, I place this small amount of shares in an incubator tiny fund, so if the stock pops on the opening, it would have no impact on my large, say, billion-dollar, fund.

Since the incubation fund is small, I flip out for a quick profit. Nearer the end of the year, I have a great performance that beats 90 percent of the managers. So in December I create a diversified portfolio with seasoned companies that create the illusion that I have broad investment skills and— voila! I am in hot demand and money pours in from the retail segment. I can do variations on this when I hire 10 managers who take big risks: one in energy, another in technology. By the end of the year, one manager looks great, as usually one sector shines. I then fire or lay off (budget cuts) the others. Then I sell this record to unsuspecting investors who think this manager is the next Soros. Naturally we change the name from something like XYZ Fund to Global New Frontiers, quickly expanding the portfolio to create the illusion that the fund was diversified all along.

If I am a hedge fund manager, I need to have a great first-year record if I want to quickly attract lots of money. So I bet the bank on buying oil and hide the true leverage with swaps. Once again, if I win, I get my 20 percent incentive and investors want to put money into my fund. If I lose, I shut down the fund, but like a restaurant, I reintroduce myself with a new name and new strategy. (Eventually a woodpecker can become a carpenter.) Could these scams exist if investors are rational and educated?

It is less likely if both occur; however, it is not impossible that well-educated and rational investors will fall for scams. Greedy investors are prone to these traps; greedy and uneducated investors are the food for sophisticated scam artists. Combining greed with the Pascal's Wager implies that, deterministically, scams will never disappear.

Financial Bubbles

As we discussed, economic cycles are expected to repeat and hence influence asset prices in a predictable manner. We have seen that prices can rise and then fall in a repeating cyclical pattern. However, there can be a rise and fall in prices that are more isolated, as patterns are not necessarily related to each other. There can be events and influences that make the price fluctuate, but each time they may crop up in different economic forums. This leads to the discussion of financial bubbles. Financial bubbles have also shown a rise and fall in prices. However, there is a major difference in financial bubbles and economic or anomaly cycles. Bubbles create a rise and fall in prices that are at great variance to the expected price and with a great amount of volume and investor participation. Also, they tend to be one-shot wonders in brief periods of time. This means they may repeat, but many years later and perhaps in different formats.

Take the price of a banana that costs $0.25 at the fruit stand. Occasionally, it may cost $0.30 or $0.20, depending on its ripeness and the vendor's estimation of its marketable value. Now imagine if all of sudden there was a great move up in price from norms, with a rise to, say, $1.00 one week, then $5.00 the next week, and $100 within a month. Banana experts may start to suggest buying the fruit before prices get even higher. Consumers would clamor to buy bananas, perhaps not even to eat them; some may be buying because they think that they can sell them to someone who will pay even more.

In fact, buyers may borrow money from the bank to start purchasing bananas in bunches or by the truckload. Banks may start to increase the interest rates on the loans and borrowers gladly pay them, since the profits of flipping the bananas are so lucrative. In fact, if bank lenders see they can exceed their loan quota, and therefore qualify for a bigger bonus, more "banana loans" will be given out.

Now the government knows that eating bananas is good for your health, so they also give tax credits to investing in banana ventures. Overseas banks who don't grow bananas, such as a country in the Nordic region, start to pay depositors twice the interest rate. They then take the deposits and also invest in banana ventures. By now, within a year, bananas have hit $200 apiece. People no longer eat them but just buy them because the prices keep going higher. Did I also mention that planned construction in plantations that overlook banana trees are now accepting deposits? Did you get your lottery number to wait in line so that you can make the deposit by the deadline date?

Soon, however, everything starts to turn down. The bananas begin to rot and the stench and spoil is too great to be contained by government-provided plastic bags. Some bananas are left in the open, and by now every banana-producing country has scoured the jungles and plantations to scoop up all the bananas and ship them to the market. The stench and the supply eventually crack the prices, and they start to go down; $175 ... $150 ... $125 ... Experts state that the price correction is overdone and that the prices should rally soon; in fact, now is a good time to get in at bargain levels.

Prices soon start to plunge even more rapidly and hit $10 ... then $5 ... then $1 ... and then $0.10. As a matter of fact, one can get four for $0.10. The banks lending on the banana loans start to have delinquencies and face capital squeezes as they write off the loans. The government launches an inquiry into speculation and wants new regulations to govern the banana industry. It starts to help banana eaters buy more bananas or avoid paying debt servicing. It prints enough money to cover this. The Nordic bank is in shock as it defaults and asks it citizens to make good by working on banana plantations for free for 10 years in servitude to pay off the country's debt. New studies crop up that bananas are overrated. The real beneficial fruit is the apple, but for a few extra dollars, one should have tulips in one's house, as they provide a healthy scent (also detracting from the rotting bananas). Soon investors start to buy tulips, and they rise from $1 to $ 5 to $10. ...

At this point you might be thinking, "What idiot would buy these bananas in the first place?" But we can easily replace bananas with something that makes more sense, such as real estate. How about those tulips? Well, funny you should ask.

Tulips and CDS

Well known is the controversial Tulip Bulb Mania in Holland in 1637. This mania was examined in 1841 by Charles Mackay in his book *Extraordinary Popular Delusions and the Madness of Crowds*. He labels this mania under the heading "The Tulipomania." He stated that in 1634 "the rage among the Dutch to possess them [tulips] was so great that the ordinary industry of the country was neglected, and the population, even to its lowest dregs, embarked in the tulip trade."[14] Prices rose rapidly; one speculator even offered 12 acres of land for a tulip. Everybody sold his or her property to raise funds for bulb purchases. Foreigners also poured money into tulips. A large supply eventually came to the market from gardens of the rich who wanted to cash in; prices collapsed and many buyers were ruined. The government then rescinded all contracts before November 1636. Purchases after that date could be cancelled by having the buyer pay 10 percent of the contract to the vendor, or treating this as an option that expired. Tulips, which were at one time worth 6000 florins, crashed to 500.

Some have disputed the exact price moves and the extent of the average person participation. As mentioned, it would appear that the tulip contracts would be more of an option rather than a future, so the damage was not as pronounced.

Figure 10.8 presents the view held by economist and UCLA professor Earl A. Thompson.[15] This figure represents a bubble if we assume these are future contract prices.

However, Thompson maintains that the real chart in terms of spot is a flat line on the bottom and that these are option contracts, as shown in Figure 10.9.

Therefore, there was no real bubble and prices followed mostly option contract pricing. This is a controversy about flat-line pricing, as tulip bulbs were observed to fall rather sharply.

While some may feel that the Tulip Bubble was perhaps overstated in impact, there is a curious door that is opened by Thompson. We could reverse-engineer the above charts by stating that while spot prices may not show much change or only some gradual change, what if there are hidden derivative contracts and hidden spot contracts that were made with leverage? Wouldn't a decline in prices, even if only 10 to 20 percent, set off a massive collapse?

FIGURE 10.8 An Index of Prices Recorded in Dutch Tulip Contracts

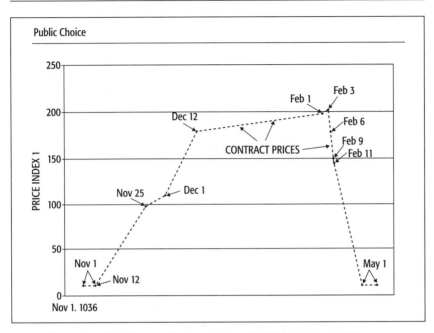

Source: Used by permission of Earl A. Thpmpson, "The tulipmania: Fact or artifact," *Public Choice*, June 26, 2006

FIGURE 10.9 Commonly Expected, Realized, and Unexercised Strike Prices

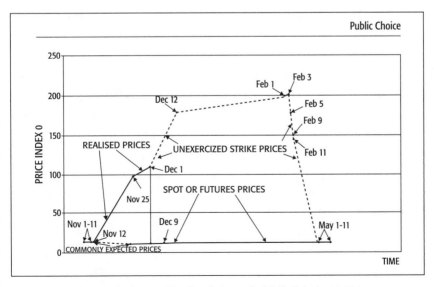

Source: Used by permission of Earl A. Thpmpson, "The tulipmania: Fact or artifact," *Public Choice*, June 26, 2006

This is what seems to have rocked the real estate bubble a few years ago. The Credit Default Swap (CDS) paper related to the subprime paper, which related to real estate prices, escalated where the subprime paper ended up amounting to well over a trillion dollars. Real estate prices declined as a result of rising defaults and job loss due to the recession, and so paper lost value. Certainly the real estate bubble did not have condo prices going up like the large percentage that happened with the tulips. And so, they would not fall as dramatically, although 50 percent drops in some markets were bad enough. However, declining prices with all the hidden debt sure made investors feel that way. Out it this way, if one pays all cash and the property declines 10 percent, then it is not too bad;but, if one puts up 10%, one is wiped out.

As we shall see, a small price decline can be magnified with the use of leverage. Other bubbles such as the Internet and 1929 saw more pronounced spikes in prices and then in declines. So, with high leverage, even a small decline can wipe out equity. Also, recalling the tulip option argument, if one is then trading CDSs, this elimination of equity could move the CDSs from $.01 on a dollar (when there is little credit risk) to, say, $0.50, where half of the asset becomes worthless. Some of the CDSs were leveraged and so magnified gains or losses, depending on who took what side of the trade.

Bubbles are a curious study. There are some good theories to explain why they develop; these include the "drunken sailor effect." If a drunken sailor is given a short leave and a month's pay, that amount will soon be blown in the bar and the next day there will be little remaining in the pocket of the sailor. In economic terms, this can be called a liquidity effect. If one prints too much money and spends it in a short period of time, soon prices rise and then collapse when the sums are exhausted.

Technicians say a bubble happens when the "bandwagon" gets going on a trend. Called the herd instinct, perceptions of rising prices can create manias, especially if there is a feeling that greater fools will buy at higher prices. There must also be confidence the investment is sound. Behaviorists would say the key ingredient is overconfidence, and it is part of investing that eventually gets out of hand.[16] Also, valuations are hard to estimate, one can buy with margin, and there are lottery profiles where there is a chance of a very large gain (however small), and the ratio of inexperienced to experienced investors abounds in bubbles.[17] So, again, this is Pascal, trends ending with idiots,greed … same old, same old would say technicians.

Recall the Internet bubble where stocks rose with great valuations but devoid of earnings and sales? (Some called them not Internet stocks but dream stocks.) You couldn't value those stocks by using P/E and P/B ratios. These were special cases that used special valuations based on the new techniques of first movers and eyeball clicks. So, while good in theory, the fantasy of seeing many of these eyeballs and making the assumption that the first company was the chosen one led to many disappointments. Of course, day traders, many of whom were homebodies and newbies, gave tips and hints to this road to riches. So much for the ratio of inexperienced to experienced theory.

Fast forward a few years later to real estate. Newbie perceptions may have been that post-WWII, real estate had only gone up. After being burnt on dream stocks, the newbies determine they will now only buy sound investments they can touch and feel

With all the bubbles in history, there seem to be some common price patterns. Recall the tulip bulb discussion; whether it was prices or call options, there appeared to be a pattern. It took place over a rather short period of time—say, one to two years with the spiky nature taking place in a much shorter time of only a few months.

Look at the 2000 NASDAQ Chart in Figure 10.10. While it rose substantially in the 1990s, it made a very sharp move up in a short period of time—about doubled from October 1999 to March 2000.

The same happened with gold in 1980. (See Figure 10.11.)

Also note the Japan Nikkei 225 Index in Figure 10.12.

In the more recent, past one can see the oil chart bubbles of 1980 and 2008, as shown in Figure 10.13.

The monthly average of the oil $38 top peak in December 1979 was identical at $107.35 in January 2010 dollars; the 2008 monthly average of $125.10 was a bit higher. Oil actually went higher in both periods in intraday prices. In 2008, oil went over $140 a barrel at the same time that Goldman Sachs predicted that $200 was coming. The eventual recession killed commodity prices as oil dropped to near $30 in early 2009 when Citibank made a prediction that $20 oil was coming soon. Once again, note the sharp spikes in oil and the subsequent steep correction, especially in the 2008 period. By

FIGURE 10.10 NASDAQ, April 1999 to July 2002

Source: Used by permission of Stockcharts.com

that time, there were hedge funds and ETFs that enabled the speculative juices to be better satisfied than in the earlier period of 1979.

In fundamental analysis you must keep in mind that a loan portfolio may go bad and so there could be eventual write-offs. However, it takes a while for a loan to go bad. Hence, a clue to follow is to see how quickly some loan category is increased. A sharp increase in loans in a short period of time may indicate that credit standards were relaxed and the bank is chasing the business. After all, how did this bank all of sudden find so many good borrowers, especially when its competitors are doing the same?

If you placed one chart over the other, you could see that the peaks and valleys of different time periods and investments have an eerie similarity. Such a chart was developed by Francoise Trahan (then at Bear Stearns), and was published in *Barron's* in July 2004. Trahan indicated such similar patterns from prior bubbles in the Nikkei, gold, oil, and the 1920's Dow.

Given the various fundamental tools used to estimate the values in each market, the similarities can be haunting. "It is different this time" say the fundamental models, yet the chart patterns are almost identical. We can certainly sympathize with the United States when the oil shock came; Nixon resigned and oil prices skyrocketed in the 1970s. Gold also rose as

FIGURE 10.11 Gold, 1975 to 1984

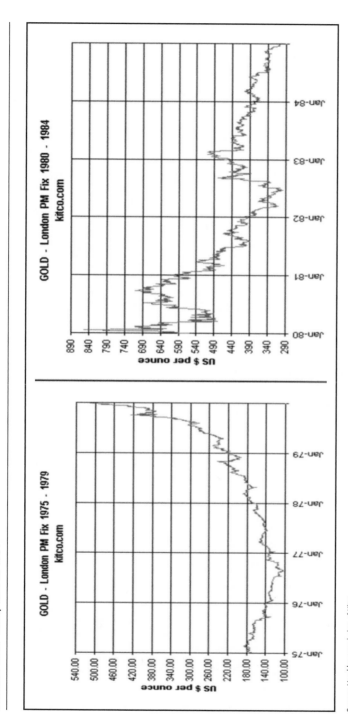

239

FIGURE 10.12 Japan Nikkei 225 Index, 1970 to 2010

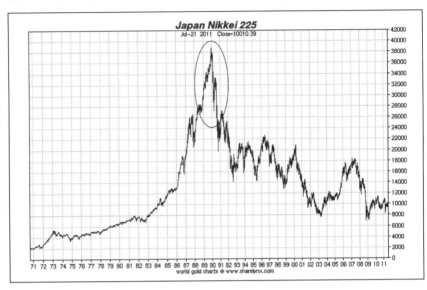

Source: Used by permission of Sharelynx.com

FIGURE 10.13 Monthly Crude Oil Prices, 1946 to 2010

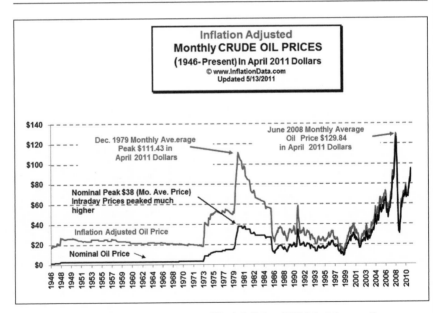

Source: Used by permission of Oil Prices – www.ioga.com/Special/crudeoil_Hist.htm; CPI-U Inflation Index – www.bls.gov

the recession of the mid-1970s took hold and investors felt an era of high inflation was near. And, of course, Japan was going to run the world, and unless you did business like the Japanese, you were finished. (Don't look at the high P/Es of Japan, as you can't evaluate Japan or the new economy in this manner. The same applies to Internet stocks in the 1990s.)

Of course, post-bubble predictions abound, but there can be a decoupling of exact rebound patterns for various reasons, such as inflation and a reaction to the severity of the action. That is: Steep in, steep out; less steep-in, less steep-out, to some extent. For example, there was a steep rise of the NASDAQ in 2000 that gave the steep selloff more than that of the milder Nikkei, which went in less steep and came out less steep. The Dow (the 1929 one) was in the middle of the NASDAQ going in, but about the same going out they all bottomed close to each other, except for the 1929 Dow, which came a year later and at much lower prices, thanks to the Fed tightening the money supply instead of easing it.

So while there is a spiky top with various bubbles, we still wonder why. A disturbing technical explanation is the human fear/greed nature of investors.

Recent Bubbles

Other explanations for more recent bubbles are that barriers to investing were lessened and so a filter that may have stopped people from investing was now removed. Consider the day trader of 1999 who only needed to click a buy or sell button on the computer. However, in the old days there was a human broker, who would somewhat discourage some of the reckless investments or try to tone down the greedy investor.

What about 1929? Again, with the greed for brokerage profits and little, if any, margin requirements, there were also low barriers to make trades. If brokers started to rubber-stamp orders, they could have been just like another buy or sell button on the computer that happened to be human and programmed not to ask questions. In the case of the recent real estate bubble, you could see mortgage brokers basically rubber-stamping applications to get their commissions. Then banks securitizing the loans. Who cared if they were good or not at this point? In the old days when the banker made the loan and investigated the borrower's credit and then booked it on the balance sheet of the bank, perhaps there was more care in residential real estate loans.

Today user-friendly outlets for potential profits in the markets are easily communicated to the inexperienced via the Internet and business TV programs. Commercials claim investing can be so simple. Joe So-and-So who can hardly string together a coherent sentence is already on Easy Street, and another investor is retiring early to trade stocks. And how about the Hawaiian-shirt guy, who can make any slob rich in real estate if he would only watch a few of his DVDs (that can, of course, be bought in installments)?

11

SENTIMENT AND
TECHNICAL TOOLS

The ability to be so obsessed with an asset price as to drive it up and then down again out of proportion to its intrinsic value shows that emotions are highly volatile. For example, an item such as a pack of chewing gum is selling for $1.00. You certainly do not wait in line all night to buy it. In fact, there is no line because that is the market value and you expect it to be there, at the same price, next time you want some gum. Now, if some magic gum could grow hair on your head, then there would likely be a shortage—and a line. Some would actually buy the item to use on their heads; others would try to purchase a large quantity of the gum in order to sell it on eBay at a premium.

This is what happened in 2007 with the iPhone release and with the 2009 platinum coins from the U.S. Mint, as well other hot items. In the case of the iPhone the line was longer at the Apple store in the Menlo Park Mall in Edison, New Jersey, than at the AT&T store in the same mall (actually 250 to 78 according to one observer). This was because one could buy two phones at the Apple store, but only one at AT&T. Was the extra phone for a friend? No, as one enthusiastic customer pointed out. They were reselling them (presumably on eBay).[1]

In the real estate frenzy over recent years, not only were many people ready to place deposits on not-yet-built condos with unseen floor plans, there actually had to be a lottery created to determine who could have the right to stand in line and make the deposit. This assumed that if you did not get in the line, you would have little, if any, chance to make a down payment. As with other products, not all desired to live in the condo but just wanted to flip it for a quick profit.

Sadly, fearful emotions may also account for increases in church attendance in economic crises. Recall Pascal's Wager. Religious leaders probably pull their hair out when they get new "converts" during hard times. While we are supposed to lead good lives and follow religious teachings, the leaders will say it should not only be when we need something, are unemployed, or are going into bankruptcy proceedings. In a study by David Beckworth, assistant professor of economics at Texas State University, that was quoted in the *New York Times*, it appears that church attendance goes up in hard times.[2]

Some, like Dr. Beckworth, a macroeconomist, make the further case that Evangelical churches see greater attendance in recession years and among the unemployed in Evangelical churches because they are less affluent than mainline churches and need more church support. There could certainly be more complex issues that determine church attendance, such as teachings on certain social issues. Still, the old saying of one getting religion, in reality is only an emotional event. For some the religious belief is permanent, but for others it soon dissolves once the crisis has past. In that case we have a sort of sentiment indicator. Perhaps if the empty churches are all of a sudden full, we have gone from greed to fear, and probably good times to bad ones.

There are many sentiment indicators that attempt to capture fear and greed or bullishness and bearishness. Long waiting times at top restaurants indicate a bull market that may be nearing an end.

Contrary Opinion and Indicators

In general, technicians will use contrary opinion. So, when all are bullish, you sell and when all are bearish, you buy. Another way of saying this is: "When everybody is crying, start buying, and when everybody is smiling, start selling." Keep in mind, however, that contrary opinion is not an exact measuring tool that gives us the date and time the market will move. Also, we have to use only extreme readings that persist for a while and then smooth the data.

So if bulls go from 38 percent to 39 percent from one week to another, it would be foolish to expect that the market would automatically go down as you attempt to use contrary opinion to find the direction of the market. In fact, you want the bullish reading to go up, since this will give more confidence to buyers of stocks and send the prices higher. First the readings are neutral and not near extremes; they also should persist and then be smoothed. Only then can you expect some sort of counterreaction down the road.

One long-standing measure of investment sentiment is the survey done by Investors Intelligence, a leading technical analysis provider that uses investor sentiment group.

The Investors Intelligence of sentiment reading, called the Advisors Sentiment Report, surveys over 120 newsletter writers, who provide market advice to determine if they are bullish, bearish, or neutral.[3] They have been doing this since the 1960s. They do not survey economists or strategists on Wall Street, as this group tends to be usually bullish and have small refinements among their outlooks. They emphasize that extreme readings are to be used for contrary opinion investing. Also, when market tops and bottoms are not confirmed by sentiment readings, you get divergences. They can be bullish, such as when a lower low in a market index is not confirmed by a lower low in bullish divergence. Bullish divergence is the difference between bulls and bears readings. So if the stock index goes from 1000 to 900, but the bullish divergence goes from 30 to 10, that is positive and one would expect to see a potential turning point upward in the market index. Using the absolute levels, as compared to divergence, buy signals occur when absolute bearish readings are above 45 percent and are further reinforced by low bullish readings of under 25 percent. Sell signals are when bullish readings are over 55 percent, and it is reinforced by bears being under 20 percent.

As mentioned, sentiment is not necessarily an exact timing tool, and studies on sentiment have to realize that only extremes count. One academic study found little benefit in the Investor Intelligence data, but Investor Intelligence has in the past responded to the testing of its survey results that the data has to be properly used, similar to the methods just described.[4] The fact that it has survived all these years and is easily seen by observation lends credence to the service and others like it. In general, there are other services that offer sentiment surveys, and these are well discussed in Kirkpatrick's and Pring's chapters on sentiment (see Endnotes for this chapter). Investors Intelligence also provides specific readings on more than just one index, and it can attempt to smooth the readings with the use of point and figure charts.

Sentiment can be followed broadly with certain categories, even though there are many specific uses. We have already mentioned that high levels of margin or heavy borrowings indicate a market top. Likewise, cash should be heavy at tops but is usually not and vice versa. In other words, you want to be in cash just before the market falls and be fully invested just before it rises. We can use activity such as the number of new IPOs, money flowing into a sector, and asset overweighting. Usually, a high number of IPOs indicate we are near a market top. Money gushing into a popular area also is a danger sign, as is being overweighed heavily in some asset.

Yields are another good indicator; the Fed model is also a guide. Also, when investors pay a small premium over the risk-free rate, then you can assume bullishness on debt—when the spread widens, there is more fear. Technicians use the TED spread, which is the spread of T-bills over euro deposit rates.

Events are another good guide. When the conference halls are packed with newbies taking real estate crash courses, that is a dangerous sign that we are near the end of a real estate uptrend. Pring quotes David Dreman's book *Psychology and the Stock Market* that during the 1920s real estate boom in Florida, it "was reported that there were 25,000 brokers in Miami, an equivalent of one third of the population."[5] And consider that this type of broker count phenomena took place in other areas, such as Spain, which was especially hard hit once real estate topped out.

Consider real estate licensing in California near the housing boom peak in 2005:[6]

> *More than 22,000 applicants took the state's real estate exam in April, nearly three times as many as in April 2003, according to the Department of Real Estate. To handle the surge, the department has rented six test centers around the state to supplement the five it already has.*

The last time so many people wanted to sell real estate in California was in 1990. In what might be an ominous sign for the current boom, that year marked a peak in the housing market.

There are 437,000 agents in California, enough to form the state's eighth-largest city ... Only a handful of other fields is growing faster, **including debt collection and waste collection,** *according to the state Employment (department).*

We can also make the case that if there is consensus of buying a stock or asset at a cocktail party, then watch out; it probably is near its peak. Brokers also tell me that they know dumb money among their many clients, meaning these investors come "late to the party" and end up buying at tops and selling at bottoms. Once they start to buy or sell, one should get the signal to do the opposite.

Magazine covers are also a kiss of death. Once a theme or company makes the cover of a major magazine, it's all over in terms of getting superior returns.[7] The glory days are mostly behind the company by that time.

We can also use put/call ratios, where you buy puts if bearish on the stocks, as compared to calls on being bullish. (Some of these indicators have lost their edge, however, because with many program trades the use of puts and calls may involve complex hedging strategies.) One can also view the VIX (Chicago Board Options Exchange Market Volatility Index) as a measure of volatility, where high readings over 40 indicate fear and low readings under 15 may indicate complacency and bullishness. Again, they may not be exact, as for two years prior to the 2007 selloff, the VIX had low numbers.

Kirkpatrick cites Ned Davis Research which shows the benefits of tracking Rydex funds.[8] The Nova mirrors the S&P 500 Index, and the Ursa replicates the short side of the index. As investors become bullish, they buy Nova, and when bearish, they buy Ursa. Davis found that their initial outlook on the market is subsequently found to be the opposite. With more long and short funds coming out, this can be a good technical tool.

We can also monitor corporate insider sales and purchases to see if the smart money is buying or selling. We must take care here, as many transactions are option oriented and may have tax requirements on the options. So I would use major transactions beyond this, as this may tell me if the insiders have some feeling on their company. Specialists are considered smart money, but their ranks and trade numbers are dwindling due to algorithmic trading. So I would not use them as much when comparing their short numbers to those of average retail.

Contrary Investing

Among the more popular technical sentiment measures is the use of sentiment and the ensuing contrary investing concept. Fear is expressed at bottoms; confidence and greed shows at the tops. This has led to contrary investing.

Figure 11.1 shows the use of technical analysis with a market index to make turning point decisions. The top part of the chart is the NYSE Composite Average. It covers the bear market that bottomed in 1974. Note it took about two years to bottom from the prior high. The Dow went from roughly 1000 to under 600 during this same period.

FIGURE 11.1 Technical Analysis with a Market Index

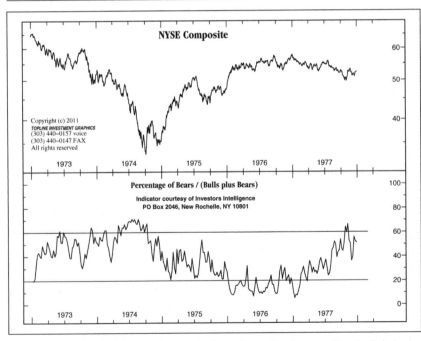

Source: Used by permission. Chart is from Topline Investment Graphics; NYCE Composite and Percentage of Bears / (Bulls plus Bears), 1970–1980. Indicator courtesy of Investor's Intelligence, PO Box 2046, New Rochelle, NY 10801.

The bottom line shows bears expressed as a percentage of bulls plus bears (Advisory Sentiment from Chartcraft). Note that near the top in early 1973, the bears were rather low at 20 percent. At the bottom in 1974 the reading jumped up over 60 percent. Then, as the market rallied again, investors became more complacent and the bears dropped under 20. Again, the bears rose to over 60 percent in 1977, as the market weakened and investors started to see October massacres, where the market dropped sharply in a few weeks.

Recall that technicians will confront fundamentalists with perhaps opposite sides of the arguments. The fundamentalists may talk about the lousy economic numbers, but the technicians may talk about the bullish sentiment readings. One thus will say buy (technician), and the other may say not yet or even sell (fundamentalist).

American Association of Individual Investors

Another measure of sentiment is a broader survey from the American Association of Individual Investors (AAII). It was founded for individual investors in 1978 and recently had 150,000 members.[9] AAII attempts to provide investment education and information to the average individual investor. This includes providing some investment basics, such as guidance for selecting stocks with screens and evaluating ETFS and bonds. AAII surveys its members each week. They are asked the question whether they are bullish, bearish, or neutral six months out on the market. You can then measure bulls as a percentage of bulls and bears. Weekly noise makes for fluctuations, so some smoothing is desired.

What can we conclude from this measure based on Figure 11.2? The bullish level is represented by the boxy lines, with its scale on the left. The S&P 500 Index is represented by the other line, with the market level on the right. The 1½-year period ends July 28, 2003. Note that even though the sentiment in the white line is jagged, the smoothing of the white sentiment levels indicates contrary opinion. Bulls are near the market top on the graph in March 2002, then drop to a low in July 2002. As the market rallies, the bulls also rally. (Once again, you would use a smoothing line, such as the moving average.)

FIGURE 11.2 Measuring Bulls as Percentage of Bears and Bulls

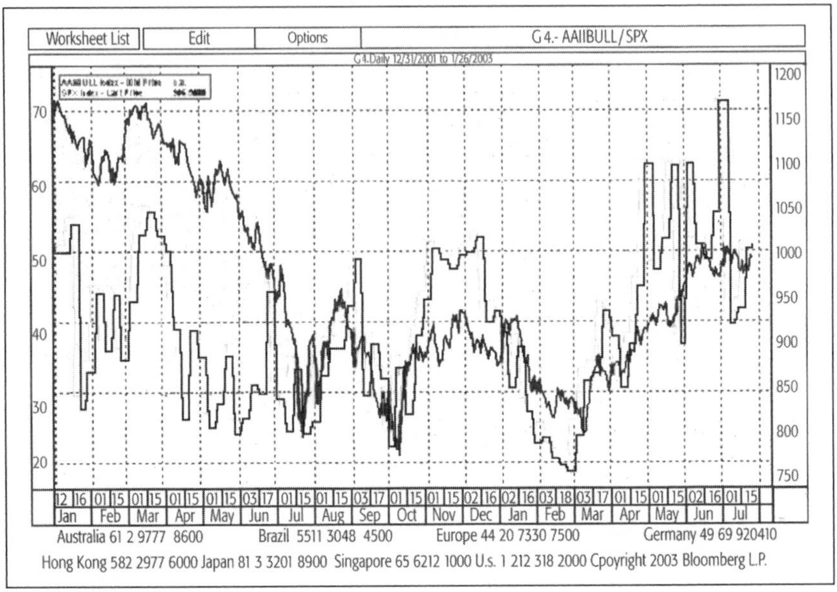

Source: Used by permission of Bloomberg and AAII

On extreme market levels of major tops and bottoms, bullish levels for the market highs near 1550 on the S&P 500 Index in October 4 and 11 of 2007 were 51.8 percent and 54.6 percent, respectively. These were relatively near their highs for the several months before and after the peaks. The 8-week moving average of the bulls was around a high level of 43 percent, and the lows were near 670 for the S&P 500 Index in March 2008. The bulls were near the lows, with March 5 and 12 of 2008 showing readings of 18.9 percent and 27.6 percent, respectively. The 8-week moving average of the bulls was near low levels of 25 percent for these dates.

Emotional Volatility

So what causes emotional volatility of investment decisions? Is it the fundamental news of the movement of the market? We can do an exercise using sentiment.

In looking at Figure 11.3, we see that for the 4½ months ending July 14, 2003, the S&P 500 Index ETF, SPY, went from the 70s in March to over 90 in June. The AAII reading of the difference of the bulls minus the bears averaged near the low for the month of March, and at the high in June. Near the low, the reading was −3 percent, but near the high, it was +34 percent. There were more bulls relative to bears near the top after the market rose versus the bottom. Note that the RSI stalled over 70 in June and showed a negative divergence, as higher highs in the ETF were not matched by the RSI, which showed lower highs. This proves that you can blend varied technical indicators to support a sentiment indicator.

One can then establish ranges of sentiment readings with chart patterns. You can perhaps blend more than one sentiment indicator in order to get a buy/sell reading. Should you add other sentiment readings from

FIGURE 11.3 S&P 500, March to July, 2003

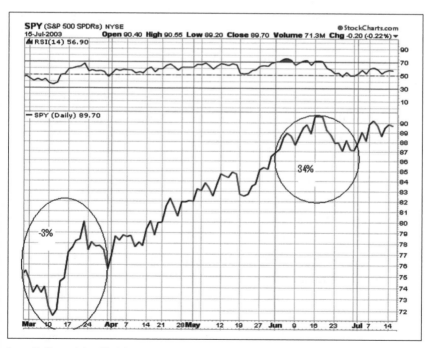

Source: Used by permission of Stockcharts.com

other sources? Should you also add other factors, like we did with our RSI? If so, which ones? This begins the process of creating a technical discipline in Fusion analysis (which will be tackled in Part 4). Naturally, this needs to be properly back-tested to see if it adds value.

Sentiment is constantly changing, but at the same time it is being measured in some manner. Using sentiment assumes that the markets are not efficient and investors are not rational in their actions, investing included. This could be more useful in certain segments of the market like small company stocks, which are especially prone to sentiment moods, as they attract more gut players, story stock investors, and the get-rich-quick crowd who wants instant action. Studies on small companies that are speculative and unseasoned have shown that high positive investor sentiment leads to rather low results as compared to when the sentiment is low.[10] This shows that when, for example, the story stocks are the rage it probably indicates the turning point and the returns would be expected to then be dismal. So the key point is to get the major direction correct.

Imagine if you were thirsty in a desert. As you plod along with the hot sun beating down, only one thought is on your mind—water. Your thirst is incredible and your knees are weak. You may fall in the sand, but not getting up can mean the end of your life. You get up and keep moving forward. If you can find an oasis, you can change your situation from weakness to strength. You do not care about the palm trees or how many fronds are on them (assuming, of course, they are not coconut palms, which would supply nourishment). You only care about finding water.

We can use this story as an allegory for seeking market direction. Instead of investors looking for an oasis to change their physical direction, they may only be looking for a change in their investment direction. They only want to know if the market is turning up or down.

Naturally there are many fundamental indicators such as unemployment data, production data, and inflation data. Sometimes this looks like all the fronds on a tree. Using all of these indicators may not tell us if the market trend is changing. Would lots of fundamental analysis be better? Probably not, as the bubbles are analyzed fundamentally to begin with. The believers already have justified their decision with some fundamental numbers. In other words, they have made their decision ahead of time and then work backward in attempts to find data that supports that decision.

Then we can return to technical indicators such as the MACD, moving averages, Stochastics, the patterns, and others. These could be like counting the fronds on a tree if they show multicollinearity. Again, counting all these indicators may not tell us the most important thing. Is the market changing?

This was the case with Japanese stocks in the late 1980s, the NASDAQ in the late 1990s, and the real estate market in the first part of the 2000 decade. These markets just kept going up. Prices that seemed expensive already got more expensive. Then, when the bubble burst and prices started to drop, what seemed cheap only got cheaper.

Investors were bombarded with both fundamental and technical data, with some of it, for example, Stochastics, likely showing oversold conditions for quite a while. Of course, technicians would rightly say that major turning points would be better served by using pattern, rather than Fast Stochastics that is better used for day trading than asset allocation. Even fundamental data, as we have seen, may be revised and delayed, which makes turning points difficult to ascertain. Sure, in hindsight we may use some moving average of earnings to show that P/E ratios were either too high or too low. But are P/E ratios properly smoothed, earnings adjusted for quality, and should there be other fundamental data?

Again, we are counting fronds on a palm tree instead of looking for the water; the more indicators we have, more time we spend counting them and less time looking for market direction.

So, while discussing the role of sentiment, we can summarize the key issues. How many measures should we use? One? More than one? How do we then adjust the data? Keep in mind that when we use more than one sentiment factor, or for that matter, more than one technical factor, we must consider whether they are adding value individually as well as collectively. Is it better to use just one or blend with more than one? Are many or even all just duplicating the decision? That would lead to the statistical issue of multicollinearity. More broadly, should we also add other technical factors such as patterns? After all, sentiment is not an exact timing tool;

a pattern may be in a better position of indicating a trend change. Should we then skip sentiment surveys and just look at chart patterns or perhaps momentum indicators? Or should we also look at fundamental estimates? This is the tricky area of Fusion. We could say that more than one technical indicator that confirms a trend is better than just one. Also, since some fundamental indicators also have backdoor sentiment indicators, we should not totally dismiss these.

Looking for the Oasis

What if we could eliminate the noise, frond-counting, and just look for the oasis? Which technical methods can we use? Is there something simpler to use than a complex system of many indicators? These are interesting questions for technicians.

What if one has the choice of using several technical indicators versus another method that is simpler in nature? There are technical systems that attempt to do this, and they have features for those still wishing to count the fronds on the palm tree. Perhaps these other technical methods will be better in the eyes of those who want to capture more major turning points. Some examples of technical tools that can better capture trends and turning points are the use of point and figure charts and GANN analysis. While some of these tools can be quite complex for trading, they offer analytical simplicity.

Case Study: Point and Figure

To avoid whipsaws in economic thinking and thus whipsaw forecasts on stock prices, some technicians use point and figure (PF) charts. They can also be suited to capture broad turning points that may indicate the future trend of the market. So if economic results are deterministic, like cycles, and they then influence charts, these inevitable trends can be captured and become more predictable.

Figure 11.4 is a PF chart that is easy to use for buy/sell decisions and capturing turning points. Note the 2002–2003 bottom. Since PF makes only

FIGURE 11.4 Point and Figure Chart

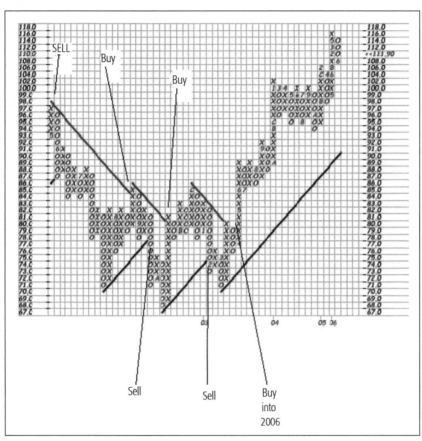

Source: Used by permission of Stockcharts.com

meaningful marks based on a reversal box method (here three), we only make
a mark on the chart when there is a meaningful move.[11] (So, in this way we
avoid counting the palm fronds and start looking for the oasis.) The chart
is pure simplicity, as it shows an inverse Head and Shoulders. Also, during
this four-year period, there are very few decisions to be made. Figure 11.4
represents the bear market low of the 2002 recession and its subsequent rally.
Breaking the downward 45 degree (the degrees are simplicity in itself) on the
upside in 2003 creates a buy decision until the chart breaks the line on the
downside, and so forth. In early 2003, the chart is near the bottom. You have a

buy decision and ride the price up into 2006. You found the oasis! This shows that one does not have to keep buying and selling each week based on fleeting economic data or short-term technical indicators. Believing in a deterministic economic model that leads to stock patterns can be captured easily in the chart.

PF charts have the challenge of deciding the appropriate reversal rule and thus decide whether to be more short-term oriented versus long-term. A small reversal box would give more buy and sell decisions and could lead to whipsaws. If you are a short-term trader, you may feel more comfortable with tools of momentum which PF does not use. Also, PF does not use volume. This may be disturbing for traditional technical analysts who wish to see moves made with volume confirmations. As we discussed earlier in Chapter 6 on gold, PF can provide measurement rules, but determining the walls for the column measurement may cause some disagreements, and so result in different price objectives.

GANN Analysis

Gann analysis is another tool used to catch changing trends by both traders and longer-term investors. We showed its use earlier with the stock VIP. Gann analysis can be quite complex and often oriented to short-term traders, but there are also parts of it that are quite simple and elegant in use. William Delbert Gann (1878–1955) was reported to have made over $50 million by trading stocks and commodities with his mathematical system. In it he acknowledged the cyclical nature of investing based on nature's laws and human nature.[12] (Seems one has a deterministic approach to investing.)

One simple Gann method is the use of angles, especially the 45-degree angle. One can then make buy/sell decisions with other angles. More simply, picking a bottom, one buys until the angle is broken on the downside by the price. Then one takes a protractor and draws a 45-degree line from the prior peek. Should the stock break this line on the upside, one gets a buy.

Looking at the NASDAQ top in 2000 shown in Figure 11.5, you can see that it created a bubble. Certainly the very high P/E of the NASDAQ was a warning, yet recall things can get more expensive. So when does one get in and out?

FIGURE 11.5 NASDAQ, April 1999 to July 2002

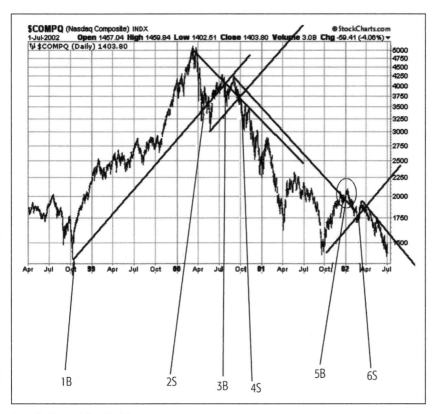

Source: Used by permission of Stockcharts.com

Using GANN analysis, you could have made only six decisions that would have profited from the bubble. One could have made buy and sell decisions to earn a profit yet not be concerned with all the fundamental issues. Technically, the buy/sell decision was also helped by other tools, but we shall concentrate only on the use of GANN.

To illustrate, let's review the numbers and the buy/sell decisions identified in Figure 11.5:

1B: Buy at 1350 on October 1999, as you make the assumption that this is a bottom (not necessarily *the* bottom). Take a protractor and draw a 45-degree line upward. Once the price falls below the line, you get a sell signal.

2S: The index price broke the upward line and gave a sell signal at 3375 on April 2000. Draw a downward 45-degree line from the prior peak to around 5000.

3B: You buy at 4100 in July 2000 and stay long until the prior lows uptrend (started in April 2000) is broken on the downside.

4S: You then sell at 3750 in October 2000, as the price breaks on the downside the upward trend line started in April 2000.

5B: Stay out of the market and buy at 2000 in October 2001, as the price breaks the downward 45-degree line that was started in October 2000.

6S: You then sell at 1750 in February 2002, as the price breaks the uptrend line that was started in October 2001. Because the price has yet to break the downtrend line started in March 2002, you still stay out of the market and avoid further declines.

Recapping the gains and losses:

1B–2S: Buy at 1350 and sell at 3375 = + 2025
2S–3B: Sell at 3375 and buy at 4100 = −725 (Opportunity gained)
3B–4S: Buy at 4100 and sell at 3750 = −350 Loss
4S–5B: Sell at 3750 and buy at 2000 = +1750 (Loss avoided)
5B–6S: Buy at 2000 and sell at 1750 = −200 Loss

Then, 6S on the chart: Sell at 1750 and then again at 1400 = + 350

Total gain = +2850

Roughly, an investor could have more than doubled her money in about 3.5 years. Also, you can play the NASDAQ via the ETF, QQQQ, and not bother reading all the research reports or looking at the business channels. Imagine, you can take walks on the beach and see the sunset instead!

OK, so what's the catch? There is none in a trending market; however, there is some volatility in terms of big swings, and you have to start at a bottom. The latter is not that hard, but what if the trend has more of a sideways move with little fluctuations? Then you can have each week, buy … sell … buy … sell. In the end, you can be eaten alive by transaction costs.

So now what? Most likely, the technical investor would add other technical measures to confirm buys and sells. Also, you may start to smooth the data. Instead of an actual break in the trend line, you may use some form of a filter—that is, you decide a break only counts if it is some percentage of the actual break. So, for example, if it is not more than 5 percent, you do nothing.

You can use some form of approximation or some smoothing of the lines to get the ultimate 45-degree line. For example, the sell at 6S is pretty close to just breaking the downtrend line in April. We actually took a liberty here and made an assessment that the break is not enough to justify a sell.

Note in Figure 11.6 that if the price actually broke the uptrend in April 2002, you should draw the downward 45-degree line starting in very

FIGURE 11.6 NASDAQ, April 1999 to July 2002, 45 Degree Line

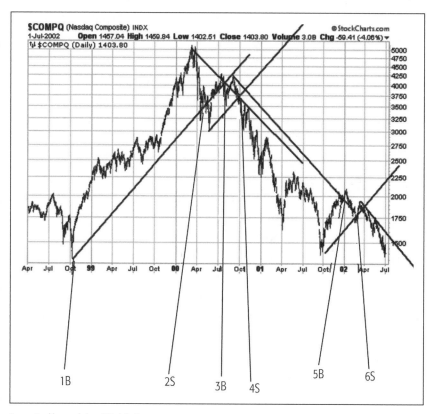

Source: Used by permission of Stockcharts.com

early January 2002 (see ellipse). You would still stay out of the market, as since January 2002, the price trend is still below the downward 45-degree line. It may still appear to scrape this line, and so you may again wrestle with the degree of the breaking line. So, we have a question mark on the downward 45-degree line that started in early January 2002.

GANN, as mentioned earlier, has more features that can create complex trading decisions. Notice that we used a log scale on the NASDAQ so each price box was not equal in points but is equal in percentage terms. Gann seeks a symmetrical trade-off between time and price, and thus an arithmetic scale is used. However, some may question this, as price change does not equal percentage change. Also, it is intended to be a shorter-term type of analysis, and weekly pricing is preferred by some Gann users than daily prices. Also, one has the various angles mentioned earlier. So, if the 45 degree is broken, a trend is called for, but then a trader may expect the next support at a 2:1 ratio. Here two units of time are compared to one unit of price. This then creates an angle of 26.25 degrees.

Figure 11.7 shows a more simplified chart of Gann. The 45 degree starts in October 1999. At point 2 one now must decide to trade on the breech, as discussed before in our log charts. A trader may sell at 4000 and wait for the 2:1 line test, as this should be the next support. This occurs later in April 2002 at 3800.

There are nine major angles, and they can create rather complex trading decisions if one plays each angle. For some, this is too complex and there is a feeling that geometry has little validity in technical analysis. Still, a 45-degree line has an intuitive appeal. It is the border perhaps between those who missed a move and those who may want to cash in a preserve to gain on position (upward line) and vice versa on a downside line. Other technical studies also adopt the 50 percent move shown in a 1:1 Gann proportion that gives the 45-degree line. These include the Dow Theory and Elliott Wave. If this concept of saving what one has versus the opportunity to get in (and again vice-versa) that would imply a behavioral concept to investing. It would also imply a cyclical pattern and a by-product of determinism.

However, a complex system often leaves a bad taste in technical users' mouths. If something is too complex, what's the use of using it, as there may be too many interpretations to see if the tool is valid? Also, some feel

FIGURE 11.7 Simplified GANN Chart

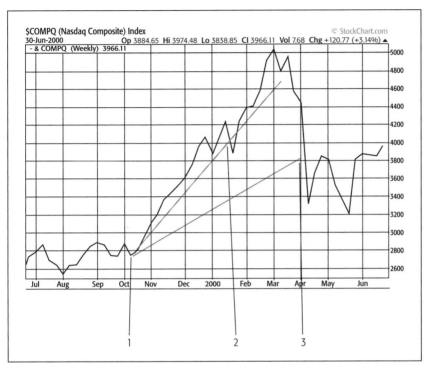

Source: Used by permission of Stockcharts.com

the universe is rather simple and thus complex systems must be ruled out. $E = MC^2$ is a simple formula to determine the relationship between matter and energy. For this reason, some may rule out the many world theory found in parallel universes of time travel. It is just too complex.

By noting the great rise and fall of Cisco in the period from 1998 to 2002, we can appreciate the complexity of Gann. Cisco was the darling of the Internet players, as it had a real business with a tangible product and was considered a surefire way to play the Internet. After all, one could see their routers every day in one's office or home. These, naturally, would connect one to the exciting world of the Internet.

12

ELLIOTT WAVE PRINCIPLE AND REAL ESTATE: MIXING A TECHNICAL TOOL AND A FUNDAMENTAL

Rather than my rattling off some of the technical approaches, we should spend time blending an exotic technical tool with the fundamentals within the context of determinism. To do this, we shall take a controversial technical approach, the Elliott Wave (EW), and apply it to the fundamentals of real estate. We shall briefly summarize some of the salient features of the EW and then apply them to the analysis of real estate. The objective is to measure extreme valuations and turning points in real estate prices. As the reader knows, real estate shook the world by putting the financial system on the brink and created much controversy on its appeal and valuation. Perhaps its influences are not over. This would invite further study of EW, which has been predicting further misery.

EW analysis is a major technical tool used to measure market direction significance. EW analysis can be used by long-term strategists who wish to make predictions of upcoming bull or bear markets. EW is used to make price predictions for various assets, such as commodities, stock indices, and FX in business journals and is often used by traders for various time frame predictions.

EW uses a mathematical method that accepts recurring waves that generate prices based on laws of nature that never change. These create predictable waves that investors can exploit. While some of the prior cycles were economically based, EW acknowledges economic effects but is mathematically based. (EW would probably say that the economic actions are the result of waves based on the emotions of market participants.)

The Wave Principle was popularized in *EW Principle* by Alfred J. Frost and Robert R. Prechter. It is based on the writings of Ralph Nelson Elliott, who wrote the books *Wave Principle* in 1939 and *Nature's Laws: The Secrets of the Universe* in 1946.[1] Today, Prechter is considered the guru of Elliott Wave. He has a broad following of his investment service, Elliotwave International (www.elliottwave.com). He appears to have generated some very successful investment results. As shown in his bio on his Web site, Prechter won the U.S. Trading Championship in 1984 with a then-record 444 percent return in four months on a monitored, real-money, options trading account. His publication, *The EW Theorist*, won numerous speaking, timing, and publishing awards during the 1980s. In 1989 he was named "Guru of the Decade" by the Financial News Network (now CNBC). In 1999, Prechter received the Canadian Society of Technical Analysts' inaugural A.J. Frost Memorial Award for Outstanding Contribution to the Development of Technical Analysis. In 2003, Traders Library granted him its Hall of Fame award. data from newsletter tracker Mark Hulbert, syndicated columnist Eric Tyson showed that Prechter underperformed the market from 1985 to 2009 with a negative return, while the market had a positive return.

It could be that he had been bearish for longer than most and maybe missed the up markets. However, he appears to have called the 2008 selloff correctly and thus conserved the capital of many investors. He warned of a market meltdown in 2006, when he indicated investors were in the worst bear market in 300 years.[2] The market crash of 2008 seemed to be on the mark.

Graduating with a psychology degree from Yale, Prechter developed Socionomics, which took into account "the character of trends and events in finance, macroeconomics, politics, fashion, entertainment, demographics and other aspects of human social history. His 'socionomic hypothesis' is that social mood is endogenously regulated and is the primary driver of social action."[3] These moods may lead to actions that make fertile the conditions for a bear or bull market. On May 7, 2010, Prechter stated that the then market rally would soon unravel as deflation takes hold. While deflation is not the intention of economic plans of governments, as they respond to country debt issues such as Greece, they may have to cut their spending and thus lower overall demand. This would cause the deflation that would take the market strongly lower to 2016.

The EW is deterministic in that actions make predictable effects. Prechter states:[4]

> *Under the EW or as some call it, the Wave Principle, every market decision is both produced by meaningful information and produces meaningful information. Each transaction, while at once an effect, enters the fabric of the market and, by communicating transactional data to investors, joins the chain of causes of others' behavior. This feedback loop is governed by man's social nature, and since he has such a nature, the process generates forms. As the forms are repetitive, they have predictive value.*

Jordan Kotick, past president of the Market Technicians Association and presently global head of technical analysis of Barclays Capital, sees the EW compatible with determinism.[5] While individual free will may allow one to choose, collective behavior is impulsive and therefore determined. So while we cannot predict individual behavior, collective actions can be predicted.

Although EW analysis can be quite complex, there are some very simple uses that can prove to be beneficial to the investor. For example, EW has similarities with the Dow Theory, as it too has three major up moves and then corrective phases. It also accepts patterns such as Head and Shoulders. It does not accept all bodies of technical analysis, as volume is not key to EW analysis nor is momentum. EW does not yet accept cyclic patterns. Prechter has stated the EW can be the primary market pattern for some major, traditional, technical chart patterns. If so, then other traditional methods can be "either spurious or fall within the structure of the Wave Principle."[6]

The EW has been used to predict both financial and social matters; however, here we shall only concentrate on the financial. It uses an 8-wave convention and the implications of special mathematical numbers called Fibonacci numbers. The numbers, and more importantly their ratios, are also found in nature. This implies that the cause and effect of the EW is rooted in the broad structure of the universe. So right away, you can see that this is a deeply analytical concept that some may accept but others may not.

As seen in Figure 12.1, the EW Chart forms a 1, 2, 3, 4, 5 and A, B, C cycle. Waves 1, 3, and 5 represent the "impulse" or minor upwaves in a major bull move. Waves 2 and 4 represent the "corrective" or minor downwaves in the major bull move.

The waves lettered A and C represent the minor downwaves in a major bear move, while B represents the one upwave in a minor bear move. Waves are fractals—that is, larger waves can assume smaller waves (somewhat like Russian nesting dolls where when each doll is opened, a smaller doll is revealed within it). Elliott proposed that the waves existed at many levels, meaning there could be waves within waves. This means that Figure 12.1 not only represents the primary wave pattern, but it could also represent what occurs just between points 2 and 4.

FIGURE 12.1 The Elliot Wave Chart

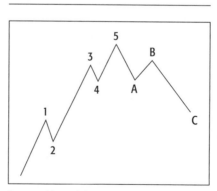

Source: Used by permission of Stockcharts.com - Charts School

FIGURE 12.2 Elliot Waves Broken Down

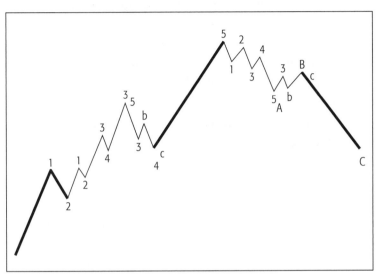

Source: Used by permission of Stockcharts.com - Charts School

Figure 12.2 shows how primary waves could be broken down into smaller waves. EW theory ascribes names to the waves in order of descending size:

- Supercycle
- Cycle
- Primary
- Intermediate
- Minor
- Minute
- Minuette
- Sub-minuette

Let's see why this may be important. EW assumes that the smaller wave takes on the size of the next larger wave. So from 2 to 3 is an up move or a bull market, but there are corrective phases. These would be 2, 1 to 2, 2 and 2, 3 to 2, 4. Therefore, while this may seem like a bear market, we are actually in a broad bull market, as the movement of 4 to 5 is still left. Then there is a correction of A, B, and C. After that, we could go to the next up cycle of 1, 2, 3, 4, 5, A, B, C, and so on.

Now if we complete the largest cycle, the Grand Supercycle, we can speculate that the future cycles will be on the downside, similar to 5 from A in a 1, 2, 3, 4, 5 pattern. Fake bull rallies would be A, B, C, and then we go down again from B to C. Completing the Grand Supercycle would indicate the end of an empire, it would seem. Similar to past Chinese dynasties and the Roman Empire, you can see the decline of a major civilization.

Prechter, as mentioned, predicted a massive declining market that would take out the March 2009 lows. It topped out near the year 2000, which was the end of the Supercycle that started circa 1784. It also made a broad 8-wave pattern with smaller waves. Also, all waves are fractals, so the top of wave 3 occurs at the midpoint of an 8-wave pattern.

In November 2007, Prechter was interviewed by Molly Schilling in "Technically Speaking," a newsletter for the Market Technicians Association.[7] Recall, he projected the end of the Supercycle near 2000, yet the Dow Jones, at the time of the interview, was making new highs. Prechter said the Dow was high in dollars, but since the dollar had been collapsing since 2000, the Dow once converted into gold was actually near a low. In Chapter 6, we compared the stock index with gold prices. While the index may go up, in gold terms, it may actually be going down. So it would seem that the decline in the dollar is a symptom of a decaying economy that eventually will make the economic problems very real. (No doubt, with the collapse of the stock markets the following year, Prechter looked like a genius!)

There are certain rules in Wave Principle analysis that can get quite complex. We have rules for complex systems that have simple objectives; for example, in chess one only has to capture the opponent's king. While opening moves follow conventional rules, deviating from these moves invites weakness that an opponent can then exploit, as the moves are not optimal. They are not optimal because over time we have experience from players that if they use the non-beaten path moves, they tend to suffer a positional disadvantage.

Rules of Elliott Wave

Following are some of the EW rules:

- Waves 2, 4 are called corrective waves because they correct waves 1 and 3. Wave 2 does not retrace more than 100 percent of wave 1.
- Within an impulse wave, subwave 3 is always an impulse wave.
- In cash markets, subwave 4 never overlaps any portion of subwave 1 (not always true in futures markets).
- Per Prechter, the apex of the triangle (the point where the two converging trend lines meet) often marks the timing for the completion of the final, fifth wave. The end of the fifth wave can therefore also be the head of a Head and Shoulders. Review the 8-wave pattern in Figure 12.2, and note the Head and Shoulders, with the peak at 3 being the left shoulder and the peak at B being the right shoulder.
- With regard to extensions, only one of the impulse waves may extend. While Waves 1, 3, 5 may take an elongated form by breaking down into five additional waves, only one impulse wave should extend.
- The remaining two impulse waves that do not extend tend toward equality.
- In a bear market, wave 5 does not violate the low of wave 3.
- Wave 4 is seen as support area in subsequent bear markets. The larger wave 4 should hold above lesser wave (in larger wave 3).[8] Once five upwaves have been completed and a bear trend has begun, the bear market will usually not move below the previous fourth wave by one of lesser degree—that is, the last fourth wave that was formed during the previous bull advance. Usually the bottom of the fourth wave contains the bear market.

There are also various measurement tools to indicate turning points and price objectives. For example, if wave 1 and wave 3 are about equal, and wave 5 is expected to extend, then the bottom of wave 1 to the top of wave 3 is multiplied by 1.618. The result is added to the bottom of wave 4 to get a price objective.[9] We shall see the use of this formula in our real estate example that is discussed further in this chapter.

The waves can also coincide with traditional patterns and sentiment moods.

Using comments from Kirkpatrick and Murphy, we can show the waves as follows:

Wave 1: Basing process and shortest. Diagonal patterns appear.[10]

Wave 2: Retracements and holding above bottom of wave 1 produces double/triple bottoms and inverse Head and Shoulders

Wave 3: The longest, traditional breakout; Dow Theory buy signals, trend followers jump in, gaps, heavy volume.

Wave 4: Consolidation patterns, bottom of wave 4 can never overlap the top of wave 1. Triangles usually appear and precede a move in the direction of the major trend.[11]

Wave 5: Lack of confirmations from indicators such as OBV and oscillators. Diagonal patterns appear.

We could also add that the beginning of wave 1 would have the most negative sentiment and the top of wave 5, the most bullish. Most likely, dumb money would be buying in wave 5 and smart money in wave 1.

Traders can also play the Wave with special A-B-C patterns as a Zig Zag, Flats, and Triangles, which may indicate opposite moves to the prevailing trend.[12] For example, if one sees a flat, that may indicate a sideways pause of an up move and imply that the trend is changing to a down move.

Fibonacci Numbers

Enough rules? Well, we still do not know how to make money with the rules. To do this, we need to introduce the math behind the EW—Fibonacci numbers and the ratios of those numbers.

Fibonacci numbers were introduced to Europe by Leonardo of Pisa (1170–1240; he became better known as his nickname "Fibonacci"). He wrote *Liber Abaci* in 1202 and basically developed a number system. These numbers were supposedly developed to solve a mathematical problem associated with observing rabbits reproduce.

The sequence of the Fibonacci numbers is as follows:

0, 1, 1, 2, 3, 5, 8, 13, 21, 34, 55, 89, 144 . . . up to infinity

To get these numbers, we start with zero and add one to begin the series. The calculation takes the sum of the two numbers, which is 0 +1 to equal 1. Then we take the second number in the prior sequence, 1, and add it to the recent total of 1 to get 2. Then we add the second number of the prior sequence of 1 to the recent total of 2 to get 3. Then we add 2 to the recent totals of 3 to get 5. Thus:

$$(0 + 1 = 1) \ldots (1 + 1 = 2) \ldots (1 + 2 = 3) \ldots$$
$$(2 + 3 = 5) \ldots (3 + 5 = 8) \ldots (5 + 8 = 13) \ldots (8+13=21)$$

The numbers are the basis for ratios that are important in technical analysis, as they provide the means to measuring price moves.

After the eighth sequence of calculations, there are constant relationships that can be derived from the series. For example, if you divide the former number by the latter, it yields 0.618. This then becomes phi (1.618) when 1 is added to the Fibonacci ratio of ... 618. It is the only number that when added to 1 yields its inverse as 1 + 0.618 = 1/0.618. The ratios are as follows:

$$34/55 = 0.618181 \sim 0.618$$
$$55/89 = 0.617977 \sim 0.618$$
$$89/144 = 0.618055 \sim 0.618$$

Dividing the latter number by the former number derives another relationship from the sequence. This relationship yields approximately 1.618.

$$55/34 = 1.617647 \sim 1.618$$
$$89/55 = 1.618181 \sim 1.618$$
$$144/89 = 1.617977 \sim 1.618$$

We can also create other ratios. The ratio of alternate numbers approach 2.618, or its inverse, 0.382. For example, 13/34 is 0.382, 34/13 is 2.615. Two other numbers often used when applying Fibonacci numbers to chart analysis, 0.786 and 1.27, are the square roots of 0.618 and 1.618.

Prechter notes the use of these numbers for measuring price moves. For example, when wave 3 is extended, waves 1 and 5 tend toward equality, or a 0.618 relationship. He adds that all three motive waves tend to be related by Fibonacci mathematics, whether by equality, 1.618, or 2.618 (whose inverse are 0.618 and 0.382).[13]

Fibonacci "rediscovered" the number sequence because 1.618 and 0.618 were known to the ancient Greek and Egyptian mathematicians. The ratio 1.618 was known as the Golden Ratio or Golden Mean. It is known to have applications in music, art, architecture, and biology. Greeks used the Golden Mean to construct the Parthenon. Egyptians used the Golden Ratio in building the Great Pyramid of Giza.

Now here is where things get spooky. As described by Prechter, the numbers and the ratios are found extensively in nature.[14] They are found in spiraling patterns of the galaxies, sunflowers, DNA patterns, and body parts.

The implication of these ratios appearing in nature is that they reflect some common and deterministic force. This force would guide all cause and effect in the universe; thus, this force would guide all human emotion that causes fear and greed. Recall the prior mentioned ratio formula for a price measurement: If wave 1 and wave 3 are about equal, and wave 5 is expected to extend, then the bottom of wave 1 to the top of wave 3 is multiplied by 1.618. The result is added to the bottom of wave 4 to get a price objective.[15]

So, not only are investor actions deterministic, but can they be explained by the math? As a side question, are we predestined, but by some number system? This may be a solid argument to use the EW, as it is objective and takes into account the recurring nature of human fear and greed. Yet at the same time, it can raise major objections, as it sounds too mechanical and contrived for some. For this reason, EW is not everyone's cup of tea, but the practical applications are being used by investors.

In the upcoming case, we will review the controversy surrounding the U.S. "housing bubble." Initially, fundamentals such as NOI/ATCF valuations, Price/Rent Index, and so on were stretched, yet prices escalated despite the talk of a bubble. This is not surprising from a technical perspective. However, perhaps, EW analysis is a better measure of the real estate top than were fundamental methods.

Real Estate Overview and Net Operating Income Valuation

Real estate is a tangible asset, including land, warehouses, retail space, and apartment buildings. As we shall see, real estate valuation depends on several factors:

- Other than emotion, rental income is an underpinning to values. (Rental income is stated contractually or implied by looking at similar rental properties.)
- Interest rates affect capitalization rates and lending policies.
- Income and wealth levels affect the ability to pay rents.
- Tax policy affects net cash flows.
- Local knowledge is important in terms of zoning and economics.
- Perception of quality (e.g., the Trump name).

Real estate objectives include being a hedge against inflation. (Providing cash flows from rent rolls would enable an investor to have a current yield.) Real estate can also reduce overall portfolio risk. Properties may have various degrees of correlation with traditional stocks and bonds. It can provide high absolute returns.

Forms of real estate are as follows:

- *Free and clear equity.* Full ownership rights for an indefinite period.
- *Leveraged equity.* Full ownership rights, but with a mortgage to hand over rights if the terms of the loan are not met.

- *Mortgages.* A debt investment (usually pooled) that includes interest and principal repayments.
- *Aggregation vehicles.* Pooled diversified real estate investments through a partnership, commingled funds (of institutional investors), or a closed-end investment company.
- *Real Estate Investment Trusts (REITS).* Include various property types. For example, the Morgan Stanley REIT Index (RMZ) enables one to 'index" a broad array of real estate properties via REITS.

Characteristics and risks of real estate as an asset class include the following:

- Properties are immovable and indivisible (unlike financial assets).
- Properties are unique and approximately comparable to other properties.
- Real estate can be a good inflation hedge.
- There may be good tax advantages for investors.
- There is no national market for properties (unlike exchanges for stocks).
- Transaction costs and management fees are high.
- Lack of information creates pricing inefficiencies.
- Some properties may be illiquid.
- Real estate purchased with leverage (debt) can create losses.
- Real estate prices can decline.

The major valuation methods include the following:

- *Cost approach.* Property value is the cost to rebuild a property. This is inappropriate for older buildings.
- *Sales comparison approach.* Property value is based on sales price of similar properties recently sold but can exclude unique features. One can get this data from various data bases and for homes on the Zillow Web site (www.zillow.com).
- *Income approach.* Property value is the present value of all estimated future income, similar in many respects to private equity valuations.

Properties can be valued quickly with a Net Operating Income (NOI) or sales comparison method, but most likely are assessed with methods that include parts of more than one approach. Realize that some firms may have their own method of valuation, similar to using corporate finance methods for discounting free cash flows. However, simply stated:

NOI = Gross rental income, minus
Vacancy and collection losses, minus
Operating expenses (e.g., utilities, repairs, insurance, taxes)

(Items to exclude from NOI calculations are depreciation and financing costs.)

As you can see, interest and depreciation are not included, but these are later used to obtain a tax shield when seeking an internal rate of return. However, NOI for many properties is a very good starting point and captures most of the valuation of the property.

NOI/capitalization rate yields the property value. If the NOI is $100,000 and the capitalization rate is 10 percent, then the property would be valued at $1 million.

If rental income increases and all else remains the same, the value of the property increases. If interest rates decrease, this would tend to lower the capitalization rate, and the property value increases.

Cash Flow Analysis

Real estate valuation is a simple cash flow analysis. While other valuation techniques may be used, they eventually rest on the notion of cash flow. After all, real estate investments are like any other investment—cash investment and cash returns.

The assumptions lead to technical/behavioral issues that can warp the fundamental analysis. Compounding the problem, some purchasers of property buy what they "want" and not what they "need." Housing purchases are not always made for utility, but for emotional and behavioral reasons, such as ego or the demonstration of independence. This situation also contributes to the emotional equation that may warp the fundamentals.

Real estate is sometimes perceived as a sort of sacred cow. It is assumed that people need to own it. Some even consider renting as generally a bad decision and indicative of poor economic health. Then consider wealth families that may own homes they barely live in. Or people who flaunt their wealth by buying a large house. There's also been the opinion, especially until the housing crisis, that owning a home was a safe, solid investment—something you could touch and feel (as compared to, say, an Internet stock). Compounding this comfort was the ease of getting mortgages. Herd mentality also plays a role.

All of these potential factors lead to cycles that are exacerbated by reckless lending strategies of profit-seeking institutions. Welcome to not only the recent United States but also to global real estate bubbles.

The recent decline in real estate prices may have surprised many. Not only did they go down, but they dropped sharply in a short period of time, bursting the notion that real estate prices never go down. The decline also made some investors uneasy about the future. If prices can drop, then the stability factor or the seemingly ballast nature of real estate in a family's total assets is now questioned. So even if real estate prices recover, perhaps down the road there will be another decline. You may have to reconsider a house as not just a place to live but as a savings vehicle. Either that or you might need to diversify your family portfolio with more stable assets such as cash. This is easier said than done, as most first-time home buyers just squeak through in a home purchase with a down payment. Perhaps empty nesters can afford this diversification, but first-time buyers who purchase real estate on a highly leveraged basis carry financial-leverage risk. They cannot diversify their home (which is the vast majority of their assets) with T-bills because it is unlikely they have piles of cash lying around. They also hope they will not lose their jobs from a recession or suffer stock market declines in their small IRA accounts. So, this disastrous scenario occurred after the top was made, taking many victims with it, as housing and stock prices spiraled downward.

Contrary to more recent belief, real estate prices have fluctuated in history and in popular areas. They don't necessarily lead to riches, and they don't always go up in a straight line. In the United States, one can measure the decline in housing prices by using the S&P/Case-Shiller Home Price Indices housing index shown in Figure 12.3.

Note the rate of negative change between 1990 and 1992, but it was not that much given the prior year gains and then the rebound into bubble territory by 2006. Then came the crunch as prices declined sharply post-2006. A 20 percent annual rate of decline was shown after 2008. While price declines were mitigated after this period, they were still declining, but at a lesser rate. We could also make an observation on the period of 1990 to 1998, as real estate price changes were rather listless. This may have set up the greed factor for individuals to play the rising NASDAQ and the eventual bubble stocks in the Internet arena.

So if we look at the housing index in Figure 12.4, we can see that prices peaked in 2005, but by year end 2009, they were back to 2003 levels. Near the end of 2011, prices fell over 30 percent from the peak per Case-Shiller. Therefore, if one bought in 1988 (we shall use the starting date

FIGURE 12.3 S&P/Case-Shiller Home Price Indices–Housing Index

Source: Used by permission of Standard & Poor's & Fiserv

FIGURE 12.4 U.S. National Home Price Index

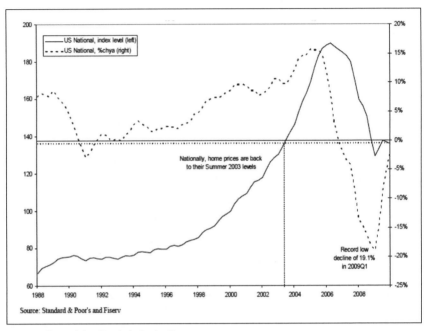

Source: Standard & Poor's and Fiserv

Source: Used by permission of Standard & Poor's & Fiserv

on the chart), one would have developed equity and still had some gains to show, roughly 3.6 percent per annum. This seems to mirror inflation returns, but it is not exactly a great way to become rich. We would have suffered with anemic results for about 10 years, 1988 to 1998, but then would be rewarded as the bubble prices took hold in 2006. Then we would again be punished with the sharp drop. We must realize that these returns do not include various levels of maintenance to keep up the property, the real estate taxes, the utility bills, and so on. Since we buy a house to get into a good school district, we may overpay for a house, as others in the neighborhood also are overpaying to get their kids into the good schools. Once the kids are grown up and leave, we move into another district that may have much lower housing prices, as it is more a retirement community and does not require all those premiums and real estate taxes. Well, again, since buyers are factoring affordability, they may really look at their after-tax cash flows (ATCFs) to service the mortgage. Since other buyers are in the same boat, we may actually pay for this tax deduction by paying more for the house.

You start surmising that a financially savvy person may start to rent and invest their money elsewhere, especially if the person has accumulated financial assets. At this point, you must use these buy/rent formulas to determine if it is better for you to rent or buy and covers things like the alternative returns you can get on the down payment, utility costs, expected housing prices, and so on.

So you can assume anything and get any results you want. Most likely with the higher returns of stocks over longer period and the fact that rents may also track inflation rates and that you can add lower correlated assets (gold), you may see that renting may be better than buying for some. However, would the memories of home life be the same in a rental as in an owned house? Can you get comparable properties? In some areas, yes, as homes are rented to executives, but some may be not, as rentals may not be as desirable given their perceived transient nature.

One can definitely make money by buying with little down in a neighborhood that is still not popular but may be turning up. These neighborhoods, such as SoHo in New York in the 1970s, can be found in many parts of the country and, of course, the world. This strategy may be a longer-term view, as one buys when the area is not that desirable or one is most likely using Contrary Opinion. To make this decision, you may have to be fortified psychologically to hang in there and even be lucky. SoHo and later other parts of New York City became chic. But realize during the mid–1970s, New York City was going bankrupt. It was considered to be dangerous with rampant crime, resembling the New York City portrayed in the high-grossing Charles Bronson movie *Death Wish*, released in 1974. Today wealthy socialites, celebrities, and investment bankers live in SoHo, and prices have skyrocketed into the millions for two-bedroom apartments. Other cities around the world have similar stories.

So by looking at the charts, we can see the real losers were the ninja types (no job, no income, no assets) who piled into real estate near the top. Some really did want a house but one that was larger than they could afford. Some of those early home buyers in 1988 started to take out second mortgage loans to fund necessary expenses such as college costs but also perhaps a vacation or two. Homes soon became an ATM machine for many people.

Prices and Inflation

Real estate prices are not always the same, and appraisals run along behavioral bias. The S&P Case-Shiller is considered one of the best methods for tracking real estate returns, as it uses transactions and also cleans up dubious flip transactions that can distort pricing. In addition, it attempts to measure houses with similar types of quality.[16]

You may have to factor this into the return equation, as homes have gotten much larger over the years and there are more desirable features in newer homes, like more than one bathroom and a two-car garage. Using U.S. government stats, you can see the median home price of new homes in 1963 was $18,000 and went through the severe recession of the mid-1970s without a hiccup by going up each year in the 1970s.[17] Prices peaked at $247,900 by 2007, and then declined to $216,500 by the end of 2009. So over this 46-year period, prices rose at a 5.5 percent annual rate. That is what real estate agents sell you—the nice gain! What they fail to tell you is that much, if not all, is inflation.

One can grow a dollar using CPI data during this period to $6.93 and get an annual return (geometric) of around 4.3 percent.[18] Realize that the index measures a basket of goods which may change over time. So, you might observe that with homes being larger, they most likely trailed inflation after adjusting for the size, as shown in Table 12.1. (But of course intangibles such as family memories cannot be downscaled in this manner.)

As we can see in the table, the average size of the home has increased over the years, from 983 sq ft. in 1950, to 2,349 sq. ft. in 2004.[19]

One could therefore even make the case that home prices are mostly a function of size and actually underperform inflation. In the real estate bubble players did not factor in the reality of investing in homes. They exhibited the behavioral trait of overconfidence. They also did the probability analysis when there were high probabilities that prices would increase and there were low probabilities that prices would decrease. And if they decreased, the prices would show only a mild dip. The real estate fallout is

TABLE 12.1 Average Square Footage of a New Single-Family U.S. Home

Year	Square Footage
1950	983 sq. ft.
1970	1500 sq. ft.
1990	2080 sq. ft.
2004	2349 sq. ft.

well documented, with record inventory, many upside downs (more debt than the house is worth), the vast government buying of over $41 trillion in mortgages to prop up the market, and on and on.

Other studies have also cast doubt on the value of real estate investing, including those pointing to the Herengracht neighborhood of Amsterdam,[20] undeveloped land in London,[21] and commercial real estate in New York City.[22] There have also been boom and busts in the late 1920s for the Florida land flippers, general U.S. real estate prices the 1930s, the 1970s, Texas in early 1980, Hong Kong in 2000, and Dubai in 2008 to 2009.

In 1999, as real estate prices declined moderately or languished, investors ironically withdrew a large $12 billion out of real estate mutual funds.[23] These investors subsequently missed the boom price increases over the following years. Then once they piled back in, prices peaked in the 2007 real estate bubble top. Technicians would see cash flows as a sentiment sign. Heavy money going into an asset at high prices is dangerous, and with withdrawals at seemingly low prices, it may indicate bullish opportunities.

So while one may feel that individuals are prone to buying high and selling low, especially in real estate, institutions are also as prone. Low interest rates and shoddy investing practices caused the real estate bubble. Both commercial and residential properties dropped considerably since 2007. So the damage was not just to home prices. This helped cause a major recession in many parts of the world, as country boundaries did not prevent real estate speculation throughout the world.

The point to realize in all this discourse is that real estate is an investment and proper assumptions will lead to correct valuations, which will lead in turn to proper returns, just like any other business. Buying on emotion can cloud this process, yet you can make a case that perhaps this is the main driver in real estate transactions.

Valuation Specifics

Rental income is tied to the ability to increase rents only so much in a given neighborhood. Generally, aside from exotic properties located in desirable locations, real estate, over the longer term, has matched income growth, which more or less tracks inflation in many areas.[24] Demographics can enhance or lower property values. Likewise, hedonic features (number of bedrooms, etc.) can influence real estate prices.

Sales Comparison Approach (Hedonic Price Estimation)

You may wish to compare features of a property in order to get a valuation. Is it worth more if it has more bedrooms, a pool, a deck, a finished basement, and so on? How much more? Local taste and desire goes into a regression equation. For example, a pool may add value in Florida but detract in the Northeast because of the short season and potential injury liabilities. Regression analysis of a large number of transactions can yield the following results:

> Each bedroom is worth $35,000.
> A garage is worth $12,000.
> Distance to nearest school declines by $5,000 per mile.

So, for a five-bedroom house with a garage, located 3 miles from the nearest school:

> Appraisal value $= (5 \times \$35,000) + (\$12,000) - (3 \times \$5000)$
> Appraisal value $= \$175,000 + \$12,000 - \$15,000$
> Appraisal value $= \$172,000$

After Tax Cash Flow

A better method may be the ATCF method. This is more useful if cash flows are expected to change substantially from the current ones. If not, you can use a perpetual model, like capitalizing the NOI. While the NOI assumes a more or less steady state (like a preferred stock) and is easy to do, the cash flow is more challenging. You assume a changing cash flow and make important assumptions on the development of that cash flow. Looking at the approach:[25]

- ***Start with NOI:***
  Calculate tax saving (from interest expense and depreciation). Calculate ATCF by subtracting the mortgage and adding the tax savings.
- ***Net present value (NPV)***
- Discount all future cash flows by an appropriate discount rate, and subtract today's equity investment amount for the property.
- ***Yield is the same as Internal Rate of Return (IRR).***

The upcoming example on Chelsea Inn is more detailed and takes in more variables such as interest rates, depreciation effects, taxes, and eventual selling price, in addition to the rent revenue and costs shown earlier.

Valuation Example: Chelsea Inn

To simplify with this example, we will not go into a more detailed analysis of depreciation recapture features to figure out the final tax. Let's assume our rate is the final blended rate.

- Initial investment: $120,000.
- $100,000 borrowed from bank: 10-year mortgage at a 5.0787 percent pretax interest rate. Annual level mortgage payments of $13,000 that include interest payments on the remaining principal at 5.0787 percent and a variable principal repayment that steps up over the life of the mortgage.
- $20,000 of equity used.
- Depreciation is straight line over 20 years.

Now to forecast inputs:

- NOIs for the next three years are shown in Table 12.2.
- Mortgage interest expense and depreciation is tax-deductible.

TABLE 12.2 Chelsea Inn Tax Calculations

Year	20×1	20×2	20×3
NOI	$10,000	$17,000	$21,000
Less: interest	$5,079	$4,676	$4,254
Less: depreciation	$6,000	$6,000	$6,000
Taxable income	($1,079)	$6,324	$10,746
Marginal tax rate	0.35	0.35	0.35
Tax (+) savings Tax (−) payable	+$378	−$2,213	−$3,761

TABLE 12.3 Chelsea Inn ATCF Calculations

Year	20×1	20×2	20×3
NOI	$10,000	$17,000	$21,000
Mortgage payment	($13,000)	($13,000)	($13,000)
Before-tax cash	−$3,000	$4,000	$8,000
Tax (+) savings	+$378		
Tax (−) payable		−$2,213	−$3,761
ATCF	**−$2622**	**$1,787**	**$4,239**

- Tax savings/payable used in cash flow calculations.
- ATCF (from NOI) = NOI – Mortgage payment +/– tax charge
- Cash flow analysis: Tax calculations for Chelsea Inn.
- Cash flow analysis: ATCF calculations for Chelsea Inn

Chelsea Inn assumptions:

- Assume that the property will be sold by the owners for $200,000 at the end of three years; assume no sales commission, transfer taxes, selling costs; the required return is 12 percent.

- The book value of property at the end of three years = Purchase price – Accumulated depreciation. (Note: We exclude land costs in this example, as land is not depreciable.)

  = $120,000 – (3 × $6000)

  = $120,000 – $18,000

  = $102,000

- If capital gains tax is 28 percent (excludes complexities of depreciation recapture), then tax payable = 0.28 × ($200,000 – $102,000) = $27,440.

- Repay outstanding principal on the mortgage (there have been principal repayments in each of the three years and interest plus principle payments each year total $13,000).

- $100,000 – $7921 – $8323 – $8746 = $75,010

- ATCF from property sale = Property selling price – Capital gains tax – Payment mortgage balance

  = $200,000 – $27,440 – $75,010

  = $97,550

- NPV and discounted cash flows:

$$NPV = \frac{CF_1}{(1+r)^1} + \frac{CF_2}{(1+r)^2} + \frac{CF_3 + CF_{sale}}{(1+r)^3} - I_0$$

$$NPV = \frac{-\$2,622}{1.12^1} + \frac{\$1,787}{1.12^2} + \frac{\$4,239 + \$97,550}{1.12^3} - \$20,000$$

$$NPV = \$2,341 + \$1,425 + \$72,451 - \$20,000$$

$$NPV = +\$51,535$$

Yield or IRR = 69.4%

Thus, one would proceed with the project as the NPV is positive. The IRR also appears to be very attractive at over 69 percent. Now let's see how the real estate valuation is affected.

If interest rates rise, the project may be less desirable unless rents can be increased. In the past, real estate was an interest rate situation, as lower interest rates made real estate more desirable. Yet interest rates were rather tame in the latest cycle; this confounded many investors who thought that the real estate investments had good potential.

Other Valuation Factors

Tax and depreciation schedules can also affect the return. Some countries have done away with the tax deduction on a gradual basis. In the United States, while it still exists, but there are caps. So for real estate, extensive tax law changes over the years have affected property values. Note that you also assume a resale price that can be subject to change as future economic events unfold.

Bank lending policy may require stricter requirements, as a higher down payment would reduce the IRR. Note that the bank lending policy could follow technical sentiments, as money would be crammed down borrowers' necks in boom times with low valuations and, of course, shunned in distressed times when valuations are attractive. Given the high IRR, you could enhance the value by putting even less down. Technicians would view this as a sell signal warning, as you would take on more downside risk. Being convinced of high returns is what entices investors and flippers to accept little or no down payments.

Since much real estate is financed by loans, the role of the financial intermediary (the bank making the mortgage loan) is important. Conservative measures require adequate income, sufficient value in the property to secure the mortgage loan, and the borrowers' commitment to live in or operate the property for several years in order to generate equity.

Technically, this does not always happen, and so the creation of booms and busts in various property values. Optimistic outlooks by lenders and borrowers tend to cause loose requirements on loans. A rapid rise in real estate loans (or even other loans) is a clue that perhaps standards are perhaps being lowered.

Similar to the mid-1970s with REITS, the Texas bust in the 1980s, and the S&L crisis (enhanced by fraud) contributed to a fall in property values. Yet prior to the decline, technical bullishness exhibited by loose lending standards was evident. At bottoms, standards become strict again and even investors shun property values, just before the next wave of price increases.

In 1999, Lipper reported investors pulled out a net $12 billion out of real estate funds at the bottom, as the funds significantly lagged the stock market bubble. These real estate funds were one of the top-performing sectors over the subsequent five years, confirming Contrary Opinion.

Technically, you can expect a predictable pattern of boom/bust prices. Reviewing historical data, you see the REIT bust in the 1970s, later in the S&L crisis, and more recently in the housing bubble.

Technical Weaknesses

Let's review some technical weaknesses also seen in other capital markets. Increasingly lower property down payments were a negative. It was similar to margin buying on stocks. Technicians would use this as sign of euphoria when margin levels got high. It was associated with stock downdrafts such as in 1929. At the top, instead of shoeshine guys giving stock tips as in the Saudi stock market top where we saw cab drivers giving stock tips. There were delayed payments for stocks, as only a small portion had to be placed in cash and the rest could be delivered a few months later of the stock purchase. This basically was equivalent to a leveraged futures purchase.

Usually, bull markets end with high margin buying, such as in 1929. A significant amount of property flipping was another negative. A plethora of initial public offering (IPO) flipping usually precedes market tops, such as near the 2000 market top.

In real estate, a hot property market in GCC countries has been Dubai, UAE. There were signs of heavy property flipping by foreigners in Dubai in late 2004. Within a half a year, EMAAR, a leading real estate company, was around 20 and then plunged to 10 about a year later. EMAAR proceeded to decline to under 2 by 2009 and participated in a bailout plan from Abu Dhabi when Dubai had to restructure its debts.

One can add other measures such as extreme bullishness. Ratio of buy/sell opinions were very high. Both stock opinions and property appraisals were not only marked up with rising prices, but as discussed, pressure was placed on appraisers and analysts to be more bullish or risk losing fee business. This is similar to the MAI (Made As Instructed) real estate problem in the 1970s, and appeared again in the recent real estate bubble. Thus starting this year all appraisals must be only paid by banks and not by mortgage companies. One can speculate that all over the world the appraisals were phony also for the same reasons. Note also the terminal value bias in the valuation.

Hot money usually comes in the top and gets out at the bottom. Note that record real estate dollars were withdrawn in 1999, just before the real estate rally. Where did money go into at the time? Right at the top of the stock bubble, especially the Internet stocks. Note also the many conferences near the top of the real estate cycle that were jammed by ordinary investors taking seminars from experts on how to cash in on the real estate boom.

What we see in real estate is similar to other markets like stocks. Fundamental projections, while rosy, may conflict with technical indicators near tops.

Real estate tends to come in 18-year cycles. You can also analyze the commercial real estate top by using a real estate proxy that captures a cycle with EW analysis. Note that the RMS (now RMZ) is a proxy for REITS of many different commercial real estate styles. However, more specific ETFs (XHB) were established in the housing industry, which should help future analysis.

U.S. homebuilding stocks peaked around August 2005, with leading homebuilders like TOL falling by more than 50 percent a year later. On another technical measure, smart money tends to buy at bottoms and sell near tops. Insiders in the homebuilders industry were large sellers near the 2005 top. In the case of Toll Brothers, insiders were reported to be among the most active sellers of stock in 2005. They sold nearly six million shares, worth more than $468 million by October 2005. That was three times the number of shares that netted Toll insiders $158 million last year. This led a leading analyst, Richard Bernstein, chief United States strategist at Merrill Lynch, to comment "if the market is so great and if, as most homebuilders argue, their stocks are undervalued, why are executives selling now?" He issued a report in late August saying that insider sales at homebuilders mimicked what happened in the technology sector before those stocks peaked in 2000.[26]

Housing stocks peaked around 2005, while commercial real estate stocks peaked a few years. Again, the feeling was that commercial real estate had more sophisticated investors (institutions) and hence would not be vulnerable to the hype that we saw in residential real estate.

Elliot Wave and Commercial Real Estate

It seemed in 2006 that commercial real estate was about to peak. Figure 12.5 shows the chart under EW analysis. The RMZ at 960 was approaching a top in mid–2006, assuming an EW measurement rule. You can see an extended fifth wave using Wave analysis. A top price of 1188 was forecast.

FIGURE 12.5 MSCI U.S. REIT Index, August 2, 2006

Source: Used by permission of Stockcharts.com

Figure 12.6 shows the 5th wave drawn. For an extended 5th wave, the rule is as follows:[27]

- If wave 1 and wave 3 are about equal, and wave 5 is expected to extend, then the bottom of wave 1 to the top of wave 3 is multiplied by 1.618. The result is added to the bottom of wave 4 to get a price objective.
- Thus, wave 1's bottom is about 250 (early 2000) and wave 3's top is 660 (early 2004). So, (660 – 250) × 1.618= 663 points.
- Added to the bottom of wave 4's 525 (near mid-2004), we get 1188, which is pretty near the top price of 1225 in early 2007, once we view post-2006 data in Figure 12.7.

Along with homebuilders and the stock market, commercial properties also weakened considerably. Prices for the REIT Index dropped about

FIGURE 12.6 MSCI U.S. REIT Index, August 2, 2006, With Fifth Wave

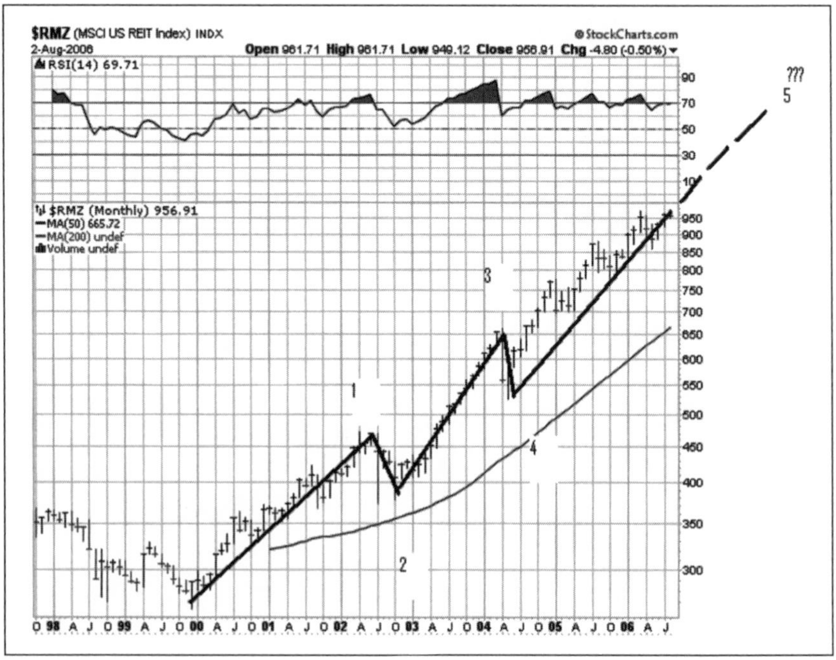

Source: Used by permission of Stockcharts.com

FIGURE 12.7 MSCI U.S. REIT Index, March 25, 2010

Source: Used by permission of Stockcharts.com

80 percent from the 2007 peak. Those fortunate enough to have sold near the top saved themselves great losses. Once the market rallied and the economy began to improve, the REIT Index rallied nicely for those fortunate enough to have bought near the bottom.

So who sold near the top of the REIT Index?

Sam Zell. He is a savvy commercial investor who is called the Grave Dancer. He got this name for building a multibillion-dollar net worth through buying commercial properties near cycle bottoms.

On November 19, 2006, Zell sold Equity Office Properties Trust, a portfolio of 573 properties (assembled over three decades) to the Blackstone Group for $39 billion. (It was the largest private equity deal in history.) In February 2007, Blackstone immediately flipped hundreds of the

292 · Fusion Analysis

buildings for $27 billion. Subsequently, the values of the properties began to crumble, as many had high levels of debt, and in retrospect, buyers made purchases at vastly inflated prices. It was thought that lenders not only provided lavish financing, but "excessive" financing based on unrealistic rental projections.[28] Blackstone reportedly paid a high 33.8 times Equity Office's funds from operations (a measure of cash flow) in the $39 billion takeover. (The ratio was about double the average for shares of companies in the Bloomberg Real Estate Investment Trust Index.)

Obviously, buyers expected nice growth in earnings and cash flow. This did not happen, as rents fell and vacancies subsequently rose. Some buyers found lenders only too willing to finance as much as 90 percent or more of the purchase price, even as profit margins shrank. The investment banks included Morgan Stanley, Wachovia, Goldman Sachs, Bear Stearns, and Lehman Brothers. In turn, they collected fees as they packaged the loans as securities and sold them to investors. Naturally, the bad paper contributed to the demise of Bear Stearns and Lehman Brothers.[29]

So both institutions and the amateur investors were now confronted by a crashing real estate market with declining rents and rising vacancies as the economy weakened. Both fell to technical and behavioral factors.

Let's pause here. So what do you believe? Fundamental projections or wave 5 implications of being near the top, behaviorally biasing the cash flows upward in order to get deals done, and the emotional nature of last-minute bidding and flipping? This is only easy to see in hindsight, except it would seem that seasoned technicians should not get swayed by the fundamental projections.

Fundamentally, REIT valuations were also showing relatively high levels. This would seem to support the EW top in Figure 12.6. The REIT dividend yield was at record low levels in 2006. Also, a specific valuation measure for REITS, Price to Projected AFFO (Adjusted Funds From Operations),[30] for the next 12 months showed that from the low level of 10 times in 2000, this measure had escalated to a high level of 24 in the latter part of 2006. This compares to a projected S&P 500 P/E of 25 at the stock market top in 2000 to a level of 14 in 2006.[31]

Technicians observe that large sums of money were withdrawn from real estate funds in 2000 at the bottom and placed into the stock market at the top. Then large sums of money flowed back into real estate near the high levels a few years later. (Generally this coincides with market sentiment and is a contrary indicator.)

Other Number Sets

So real estate was analyzed with a wave or cycle that carries deterministic implications. Going back to cycles and waves, it does offer the solution to bubbles and manias, or at least periods of great over- or undervaluation. Using EW or cycle analysis may be the dominant use of some technicians in that they support the notion that history repeats and moods of investors always show fear and greed. If these approaches capture the essence of investing, it makes the whole process rather simple. If the Wave can subsume other patterns, one needs to only study it, rather than be bogged down by many approaches.

However, there are some serious concerns in using the Wave. There can be disagreements among technicians and Wave users as to where wave 1 actually begins. That can change the outlook of market direction of the assumed next larger wave. Also, sometimes it is not clear if an A-B-C pattern is really the beginning of a wave that will show 1–2–3. Thus, it may seem the analysis is retro, or it fits the pattern after the fact. So what seems like a simple approach gets into more complex analysis and the need to know all the rules. This may turn off some technicians who don't want to use EW, as it may be too ambiguous and even complicated for trading.

However, the numbers and ratios of the EW are not the dominant or even ultimate number set that manifests. There are other number sets, such as Pascal's Triangle, shown in Figure 12.8.

Like Fibonacci numbers, it was known about in other countries for centuries. Named after its developer, Blaise Pascal, the number system first appeared in *Traité du triangle arithmétique* (*Treatise on the Arithmetical Triangle*) in 1653.

Pascal's Triangle has many uses, including statistics; however, it is not used in technical analysis, but we can derive the Fibonacci numbers from it. The numbers are created by starting with the top two rows: 1 and 1 1.

FIGURE 12.8 Pascal's Triangle

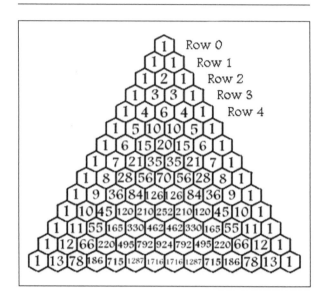

Then, in order to construct the next row, you look at the two entries above it (i.e., the one above it and to the right, and the one above it and to the left). So 3 has a 1 to the left and a 2 to the right above it. At the beginning and end of each row, where there's only one number above, put a 1. You might even think of this rule (for placing the 1's) as included in the first rule: for instance, to get the first 1 in any line, you add up the number above and to the left (since there is no number there, pretend it's zero) and the number above and to the right (1), and get a sum of 1.[32]

Now, review the Fibonacci number sequence in Figure 12.9.

The sum of the numbers in the consecutive rows shown in Figure 12.9 are the first numbers of the Fibonacci sequence. The sequence can also be formed in a more direct way, very similar to the method used to form the Triangle, by adding two consecutive numbers in the sequence to produce the next number. This creates the sequence: 1, 1, 2, 3, 5, 8, 13, 21, 34, 55, 89, 144, 233, and so on.[33] So the top number 1 is 0 + 1 =1; the next line is just 1, as we don't use numbers already used. The third line is 1+1 =2; then 1 + 3 + 1 =5 ... and skipping down to the last line, we get 1 + 7 + 15 + 10 + 1= 34.

FIGURE 12.9 Fibonacci Number Sequence

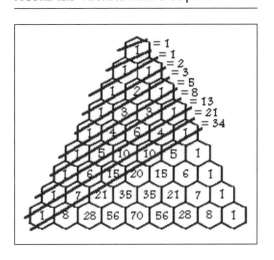

Are there other number systems better than Fibonacci? Perhaps there is one that technicians don't know about that explains prices in the markets.

Kirkpatrick states that the "tenets of any technical theory are that the principles must make sense."[34] Kirkpatrick also shows that "if you take any two whole numbers and add them together, then add to the sum the previous higher number, eventually you will arrive at phi, the Fibonacci ratio (1.618).[35]

If the EW is based on the nature of the universe, there can be some puzzling omissions of it in major religions. If we assume that the major religions represent signs from God, and realize one is not picking sides on whose God is the right one, then we have to do some shuffling with EW.

To begin with, if one is an atheist or agnostic, there is the puzzling problem of how to explain some order and repetition in the world. Certainly, the Fibonacci numbers and ratios cannot be just chance. They certainly must be a manifestation of a deity to create a complex universe but still install signs that were created. You could argue that chance can produce anything, even ratios.

In terms of religion, the Christian religion is replete with numbers in the Bible. The numbers may have been chosen to describe events or merely chosen by the authors to represent a concept. In the work called *Number in*

Scripture: Its Supernatural Design and Spiritual Significance, E.W. Bullinger, an Anglican clergyman and biblical scholar, explains the major numbers of the bible.[36]

For example, one is a Fibonacci number and one is in his work. One naturally represents the concept that there is only one God. We also have common numbers of 2, 3, 5, 8, and 13. On the number 13, an unlucky number in Western culture, also shows the 13 famines recorded in scripture as:

1. Genesis 12:10
2. Genesis 26:1
3. Genesis 41:54
4. Ruth 1:1
5. 2 Samuel 21:1
6. 1 Kings 18:1
7. 2 Kings 4:38
8. 2 Kings 7:4
9. 2 Kings 25:3
10. Nehemiah 5:3
11. Jeremiah 14:1
12. Luke 15:14
13. Acts 11:28

Puzzling is the number 40, which at first glance is not a Fibonacci number. Bullinger states that 40 "has long been universally recognized as an important number, both on account of the frequency of its occurrence and the uniformity of its association with a period of *probation, trial,* and *chastisement.*" Note that 40 is shown as:

- *Forty* days Moses was in the mount, Exodus 24:18; and to receive the Law, Exodus 24:18
- *Forty* days Moses was in the mount after the sin of the Golden Calf, Deuteronomy 9:18,25
- *Forty* days of the spies, issuing in the penal sentence of the 40 years, Numbers 13:26, 14:34

- *Forty* days of Elijah in Horeb, 1 Kings 19:8.
- *Forty* days of Jonah and Nineveh, Jonah 3:4
- *Forty* days Ezekiel lay on his right side to symbolize the 40 years of Judah's transgression
- *Forty* days Jesus was tempted of the Devil, Matthew 4:2
- *Forty* days Jesus was seen of His disciples, speaking of the things pertaining to the kingdom of God, Acts 1:2

Note that I said at first glance, but then Bullinger states that 40 "is the product of 5 and 8 (which are Fibonacci numbers), and points to the action of *grace* (5), leading to and ending in *revival* and *renewal* (8)."

Now other numbers are not Fibonacci numbers such as 42, which is explained as a number associated with the Antichrist. It is the product of 6 and 7, which are not Fibonacci numbers.

There others numbers and we can then start to figure out ways to make them work or abandon the whole notion of this exercise as being nonsensical. One can also get into the study of Gematria and the study of Kabbalah in the Jewish faith. The best-known example of Gematria is the Hebrew word chai ("life"), which is composed of two letters which add up to 18. This has made 18 a "lucky number" among Jewish people, and gifts in multiples of $18 are very common for them.[37] Obviously 18 is not a Fibonacci number.

In the Quran, we find both Fibonacci numbers and non-Fibonacci, but one of the more important numbers, 19, is not a Fibonacci number. There are 30 whole numbers in the Quran. The total of these 30 whole numbers is the multiple of 19.[38]

In Hinduism, we can see explanations for Fibonacci numbers such as 1, 2, but then we get 7, which is not. 7 is called Saptan, which is a symbolic representation of the earth. There are 6 higher planes and 7 lower planes.[39] Numbers help one to better grasp the beliefs. With its henotheistic (worshipping one God while accepting the possibility of others) nature, Hinduism can be more complex to make a case that numbers are a sign from a deity.

So, to make the case of a number system as the window to the laws of nature that guide human emotions is plausible but also rather dubious.

Which number system and how does one account for the inconsistencies? True, the Golden Mean is talked about more than the number 18 in technical analysis, and we find its ratio in many diverse places in the universe. But do we want to become religious scholars to make the nuances and inconsistencies prove out to using this type of analysis?

Then again, maybe there will be another religion in the future that will really tie up loose ends. But that is the case; it is inconsistent with a deity's master plan to give us the number sequence but give us the religion eons later. What sense does that make on the poor souls who followed the erroneous religions of the past?

OK, what if one of the religions is true and that atheism is false? This therefore poses the other problem. Why give us the true religion then bombard us with the inconsistencies? If the deity is perfect, why make the flaws?

All of this could lead to some gainful employment for philosophy majors, in some form. Perhaps the better technical analysts will come from not the investment banking and trading firms but from the Ivory Halls and religious organizations. Others would say that there cannot be a link, as that would be too easy. Imagine making money on earth and getting into a heaven. One must struggle with the concept of what does it profit a man to gain the whole world and lose his own soul (Mark 9:36)?

Final Comments

Part 3 has opened the door to various controversial philosophical theories about human behavior in general. This has also spilled into investment behavior. The concept that one is a cog in a machine that grinds away to a definite conclusion is not acceptable to many. In economics, the feeling that the economic cycle also acts in the same manner is also not exactly the beaten path of economists and political leaders.

Part 3 has demonstrated some technical disciplines that may reflect and resolve for investors these controversial philosophical notions. The wave/cycle technical disciplines have various loyal followers, but the disciplines still use some key concepts from the prior sessions that we have seen. Many technicians use their primary approach, and then may use the disciplines of the third session as a "backup" or second opinion. There is an unease to use the disciplines as a primary approach. Still others would use the Wave and ignore other methods.

In general, more interdisciplinary and intermarket analysis is being done, and this may require the blending of several technical disciplines. In any case, Part 3 has amplified the issue of the extent and usefulness of fundamental analysis in the first place.

Part 4

FUSION PROCESS

In Part 4, we review some quantitative issues that can be applied to investing. We already have been exposed to numbers as a decision-making tool in investing. These included Fibonacci ratios, cycle lengths, and GANN angles. In this part, we see how numbers can be packaged to create a Fusion buy or sell decision. Quantitative methods are often used in non-investing situations like shopping. You have a budget, but you want to maximize your satisfaction (or utility) with buying goods within budget.

You can also apply this quantitative method to sports. A team can pay a large sum of money to acquire a superstar player or can spend the same, or even a lesser, total amount, picking reasonably good players who play well together and have the potential to be successful.

Consider the current state of college basketball. Coaches are increasingly encountering a problem when recruiting exceptional players who are eligible to enter the NBA draft after their sophomore year. Coaches then lose these players' valuable skills. Perhaps a better recruitment strategy would be to select not necessarily the best players but solid players who perform well together yet cannot take the instant path to the pros. For example, the 2010 NCAA Champion team Duke probably exhibited this feature when it beat Butler 61–59. It was reported by the *New York Times* that three members of the team carried Duke all season: Jon Scheyer, Kyle Singler, and Nolan Smith. Scheyer was not expected to be drafted by the NBA, though Singler and Smith were mentioned as possible second-round picks in the June 2010 NBA draft if they left school early. While not considered the most talented players, they displayed the attributes of "athleticism, quickness and the ability to score the basketball in just so many ways . . . Each player lacks a dominant skill, but their chemistry is unquestionable."[1]

We also see these challenges in other areas, such as in the development of cancer drugs. It could be that one drug alone is not that effective but when combined with two others, the results are dramatic in helping to arrest and even cure cancer. (This is the case with testicular cancer where a combo of three drugs is the most effective.) We then run into other issues such as optimal dosing. If the dosage is too high, the drug can kill the patient and thus be of little use. Likewise, too low a dose can be ineffective. Thus, permutation analysis is a required phase of drug trials.

You can draw the conclusion from these examples in establishing investment criteria. Which criteria or factors should be used? In the case of Fusion, should you include technical and behavioral factors? What about weight? Is it better to have factors that work well together and have good chemistry rather than to have one super factor that solves all? Most likely, since all investing is a function of probabilities, you will likely decide to seek good chemistry.

In doing so, should you use P/B but downplay growth in fundamentals? In technicals, should you use patterns, momentum, Elliott Wave, some other factors, or even a combination of all of them? How should you handle behavioral factors? How should you blend all of this in a quant model, and should the model be oriented for trading or for long-term investing? Would you change your factors if the time horizon changes? That is, would you be as concerned with earnings forecasts and chart patterns, as compared to event announcements and Stochastics, if you are a short-term trader?

In addition, should Artificial Intelligence systems be used? Can effective screens be designed to optimize investment decisions? Due to complex and fast-moving markets, Artificial Intelligence and Quant Expert Systems may prove advantageous, as they can quickly program and execute trades on many factors. But if we allow human decision making, does that invite emotions and then lead to the herd mentality. These issues may give grief to many who try to use a bit of some, or all, approaches. It is not surprising to hear that some believe in technicals and fundamentals but they gave up using both, as they can't seem to put them together. Looking for the secret formula for success is not easy.

13

QUANT SYSTEMS

The use of quant (short for quantitative) systems should overcome behavioral bias. However, while they appear to be objective and mechanical, my personal experience with quant funds and their programs is they are likely to be an evolving situation. The programs are updated and revised to give better results, or at least in the hope of better results. It could be that results are not that good, and we are not quite sure if we need more time or if the program is just GIGO (garbage in, garbage out). At this point, we can start to program a system to take "advantage" of new information. However, it could actually just show our prejudices.

Problems with Quant Systems

If we use a low P/B ratio, we may omit many service and technology firms. If these areas are hot in the market but are being underweighted by the portfolio manager, we see underperformance. So then we make a behavioral decision: If we keep the criteria, then our job will be at stake at the end of the year. Yet if we change the criteria, it will seem that we don't know what we're doing. So what can we do to look like we can participate in this trend and yet not appear to have changed our criteria? Aha! We will no longer use accounting book value, as book is always low in these areas. We will now use price-to-enterprise value. Since enterprise value is the PV of the cash flows, we can rationalize that it better captures the real "book" value of a company, as it deals with market value as compared to a historical basis under accounting. Here we subtract the market value of the debt from the enterprise value to get close to an "equity" value of book value (I will leave out excess cash and non-operating assets to keep our analysis simple). Now we can start to massage approaches.

Let's say we have a P/B value but decide to use one that is more in tune with the times. Or some would say we found a way to rationalize our decision in order to enter an area we wanted to get into from the outset. These little tricks are dangerous because by the time we get to the point of changing the formula and buying assets with the revision, the market may change and all of a sudden tech and service is out of favor. In fact, we could get whipsawed. This happened in the late 1980s when managers avoided Japan due to its high P/E, but as they fell farther behind the EAFE index, they started to use creative ways to justify the P/E (such as bringing in land values), only to get slammed at the top near 1990.

So we can program a quant system to give the answer that we already expect. Knowing which valuation methods will be used can make certain assets unattractive and other assets more attractive. These games are also played in "fairness opinions," where you can start to cherry-pick a peer group to make your company more or less attractive than the peer group and so one can reject or accept a takeover offer. By adding certain companies that seem to be competitors, you can change the mean values. This is especially problematic when a company does not have exact competitors. The peer group could then represent similar types of companies. Sometimes this is a judgment call that may not satisfy all.

For example, Kroll, an investigative company that performs background checks, had a fairness opinion done by Goldman Sachs. There were virtually no pure plays that were publicly traded. So the peer group that Goldman selected included companies like Lab One, which did health-related laboratory tests such as blood and urine. While we could make a case that Kroll represented a type of security for one's health, others would see this as a stretch.

Job interviewers have used these types of tricks for years. If a company wants to hire a young person, they cannot discriminate on the basis of age, as this is illegal. Instead the company could say that the older candidate is overqualified. So the quant criteria cannot specify age. It can work through the backdoor spin by seeking a certain level of experience, which can then be massaged into the form that one wants.

Recall our discussions of the subprime mess that crippled the financial system. Bankers who wanted to capitalize on this seemingly lucrative boom would have reverse-engineered their algorithms to give themselves the answers they wanted. They wanted to make more loans that generated more commissions and that appeared to be safe investments. Thus, you can program a scoring system to pick these loans by making some simple assumptions and then massaging the data to get the desired results. For example, it was reported by the *New York Times* that some algorithmic programs assumed that home prices were unlikely to decline. Yes, "real estate never goes down" was the mantra for the gullible. Then they would massage data to give the desired results. The *New York Times* reported:[1]

> For example, a top concern of investors was that mortgage deals be under-pinned by a variety of loans. Few wanted investments backed by loans from only one part of the country or handled by one mortgage servicer. But some bankers would simply list a different servicer, even though the bonds were serviced by the same institution, and thus produce a better rating, former agency employees said. Others relabeled parts of collateralized debt obligations in two ways so they would not be recognized by the computer models as being the same, these people said.

Quant Systems that use historical data seem to violate the semi-strong version of the EMH. After all, most quant systems look backward at historical financial data. You cannot use this information to generate risk-adjusted excess returns because the data is already reflected in the stock price. Some quant systems use earnings projections of IBES (*Institutional Brokers' Estimate System*) and other such services, but historical data in these studies has been successfully back-tested. These studies include financial criteria such as various uses of P/B or a low P/E strategy to value stocks. So it is no surprise there have been successful back-tests, as well as successful funds.[2]

In Favor of Quants

A 2005 study by Casey, Quirk & Associates gave a boost to quants.[3] It showed that quant managers had better performance than non-quant managers. Thirty-two managers who managed $132 billion for the three years through 2004 showed a median tracking error of 2.7 percent, compared to a median error of 4.5 percent for the non-quant managers who had $925 billion under management. Over the same time frame, the median quantitative management group returned an annualized 5.6 percent versus 4.5 percent for the median non-quant managed product. This resulted in a median information ratio (excess return of 1.2 percent for quant and about 0.2 percent for other, divided by their tracking errors) of 0.37 for quantitative-managed products versus 0.06 for non-quantitative-managed products. The good results were independent of investment style approaches. Also, assets of the quants over the prior three years doubled, compared to a growth of only 28.5 percent for the non-quants.

Quant Investing

Though quant investing goes back decades, it became very popular with hedge funds after 2005. However, many of the quant funds had large losses in 2007 and 2008. This may have surprised investors who felt that quants were somehow immune to market drops. Certainly a hedge fund using quant should have escaped a downdraft—but that did not happen. Professor Andrew W. Lo, the Director of the MIT Laboratory for Financial Engineering, pointed out the issue in August 2007,when in that month, we saw a drop in the returns of some major market-neutral funds during the following environment:

With laserlike precision, model-driven long/short equity funds were hit hard on Tuesday August 7th and Wednesday August 8th, despite relatively little movement in fixed-income and equity markets during those two days and no major losses reported in any other hedge fund sectors. Then, on Thursday August 9th when the S&P 500 lost nearly 3 percent, most of these market-neutral funds continued their losses, calling into question their market-neutral status.[4]

In other words, why were there losses, if the funds were market-neutral? They should have shown a positive return, regardless of the direction of the market. Lo implied there must have been systematic risk, or in other words, the funds were programmed the same way and thus suffered similar losses when certain market events occurred. Market-neutral and 130/30 funds have been rather popular, but they have their share of critics. While some defend 130/30 funds, where one goes long 130 percent of the portfolio by shorting 30 percent. Skepticism arises from the feeling that if distributions are not symmetrical or the standard deviations are skewed, then 130/30 strategies are not that beneficial. Some also say that market-neutral funds really need a beta to generate positive returns or an up market with a positive beta.

Appeal of Quant Investing

So if the programmers all think the same, hang out together, went to the same schools, and studied the same theory, it is possible that they programmed the computer more or less the same. Now quant funds still have a bad flavor for some investors. Investors again started to remember Long-Term Capital Management (LTCM), which was built on a quant model by Nobel Prize winners. It eventually crashed and burned after the Russian default in 1998 and had to be bailed out indirectly by the Fed. Some would say the Fed intervention was a dangerous move, and it led to the risk strategies that also crashed and burned in 2007 to 2008. Others believe that this also then led to massive Fed and government intervention, which would not have happened if they let LTCM just burn investors, thus making them more cautious for future leveraged endeavors.

Quant also has some very good appeal from a performance point of view. Imagine if you have a simple fundamental criteria such as buying all stocks that trade below book value and have a P/E below 10. How expensive would it be to do this? Not very, as many free Web sites and discount brokerage firms allow screens to be made on these two criteria. You could narrow the list by adding liquidity and market cap filters. You can say that below a certain level on a P/E (or some other financial ratio), you buy, and if the ratios go over a certain level, you sell. So, to keep things simple, if the stock is trading below book and the P/E is below 10, buy; if the price/book exceeds 1.5 and the P/E is over 15, sell. Of course, to get the maximum out of this strategy, you have to back-test your criteria over various market conditions in order to tweak the ratios for the best possible entry and exit points.

Should the P/E for the buy be 10 or even an absolute number? Should it be some percentage of the market index? So one could then make a criteria that if the P/E is less than 1.1 times the S&P 500 Index, you would buy. The risk here is that the market could be way overpriced like in 1999, and while you can find the P/E below 1.1 times, the P/E is still too high to substantiate the growth. Another problem is that certain industries tend to have lower P/E ratios than others. Technology would have a higher P/E ratio than chemical stocks, as they tend to have more growth prospects and perhaps be less cyclical in some cases.

Cost/Benefit of Quant Analysis

So far, this analysis would take only a few minutes using a portfolio manager who programs a computer. The cost would be minimal. However, let's say we decide to buy 40 stocks to diversify our portfolio. Using active management analysis, we would have many prospects and so would spend many hours reading their financials. Then there would be the obligatory visit to the company (where we would interview the management and kick the tires of the physical plant). We now need airfares, hotels, meals, and so on.

Since returns are after all fees and expenses, the quant would seem to have a big advantage here. Assuming 40 companies and $5000 per trip, we already have $200,000 in costs. Now we probably need analysts in each sector; they have to be paid and they need to get bonuses. Let's say 4 analysts at $250,000 a year, and now we are up to $1,200,000. Now we need $120,000,000 in assets that earn 1 percent—just to break even. However, in theory, we have almost zero costs on a relative basis using quant. One would allocate costs for the compensation to the portfolio manager, say, $250,000 a year. Perhaps we even add programming costs and the costs to buy the financial database. But you can see the cost/benefits using quant. OK, you get the idea: more trips, more meetings, more expenses. Do they really add value? Some analysts have done well kicking tires, and some program the computer and can play tennis all day.

Suppose the real value added is doing a good quant strategy. If we admit that, then we may have a harder time justifying a management fee at the current levels of 1 percent of assets. Savvy institutions may not care about the fee if the results are good, or they may start to select quant managers only if they also have lower fees than average. So it is possible we may have to lower our fees in order to avoid doing this, or at least in a significant amount, give the illusion of using active management that justifies the higher fees. Why not hire a few MBAs, set up offices in some major cities, and have them do some tire kicking to show the clients that what separates us from them is our sound research? The clients probably won't know any better, and still all the human bodies that are dashing around the office with great urgency and who are piling up research papers on their messy desks give a nice illusion to the client prospect.

As assets come pouring in, the cost of research becomes less of an issue, unless clients want lower fees based on the true costs of getting the investment results. Savvy clients will likely sniff around to see how much of a return comes from quant criteria and how much from that invaluable judgment. The smarter clients could set up "shadow portfolios" where they reverse-engineer the quant criteria a manager uses, and then see if the manager can beat that shadow portfolio, thus giving evidence that the humans add value after all. The savvy portfolio manager will thus be very reluctant to give all the quant criteria and state that certain issues such as company management and brand image is important to the investment process and can't be quantitatively measured. Usually, the client doesn't care as long as the returns are good. However, eventually, someone on the board of the investment committee may raise the issue of fees and alternatives such as quant funds with good records or even ETFs that may start to replicate some simple quant strategies. These could be real challenges and also create illusions of value added.

Imagine if my quant formula accounts for my good record, but I know that a potential client wants to see a bustling office abounding with researchers, not my one cubicle with a computer on my desk. So, I bite the bullet, hire a few bodies, and get a larger office space with nice flowers, paintings, and a receptionist. But they really do nothing; they are decorations. As money comes in, I may start to prune back a bit, stating that I am speeding up the decision-making process or getting efficiencies. Hopefully, I have by then proven a good record and the clients start not to care if there are fewer bodies in the office doing research.

Quant was certainly used prior to the more recent inflection dates of 2005, but since this period, many mutual funds introduced quant funds, and even discount brokers and index funds like Schwab and Vanguard increased their exposure. Again, the ethical procedure is to explain the investment process to prospective clients.

Programming plus selecting and massaging investment criteria is no easy matter. Many other issues like accounting and statistics can cloud the process.[5] When using fundamentals and technicals, one question that always comes up is how to blend them. You will hear statements like, "I tried combining fundamentals and technicals, but gave up because it didn't work." Technicals and fundamentals are like a button and cloth and the quant is the thread. You need the thread to secure the button onto the cloth. One problem many have is that technicals are at odds with fundamentals. So one will have their analyst tell the project manager how lousy business is, yet the technicals may show a positive sign. The opposite is also probable, as the analyst can get enthusiastic about a stock just as the technicals indicate a sell signal. Add to this the Wall of Worry and the Slope of Hope scenarios, and we can see all this makes the process understandably challenging. No wonder some just stay with fundamentals and most likely end up on the scrap heap of index chasers.

A quant system is the only way to properly balance all these issues—fundamentals, technicals, and behavioral aspects. Of course, they have to be correctly programmed, yet that need not be difficult. We already saw that when the P/E is rather low, we get a buy indication. Most likely, the analyst won't believe the low P/E. In other words, the analyst has already made up her mind and the financial data just clouds the picture—the decision to buy or sell has already been made on some uncertain basis. Quant has a certain basis and there can be no fudging the decision. For this reason, quant has the necessary fabric to hold the buttons on the clothes; you can't just have them floating around. Similarly, floating opinions don't make it in investing. Convictions on a sound investment approach do. You must stay with an investment discipline in order to be successful. Quant is the only way to make your discipline measurable and objective. Vacillating and making exceptions is a good recipe for being whipsawed and getting poor results.

The Quant Frontier of Technicals and Fundamentals

Combining fundamental and technical quant systems is entering virgin territory. Adding behavioral filters makes the process even more challenging. Quant deals mostly with fundamentals and perhaps some simple technical measures, such as relative strength to the market. Rarely do we see in academic literature or fund publicity complex technical strategies combined with fundamentals and behavioral considerations. A key challenge lies in programming technical rules. We shall examine some academic work in this area.

A common criticism of technical analysis is that it is too subjective, as one's interpretation of a chart pattern may not be in agreement with another's, even if both are technicians. It would be good to have some specific mathematical formula to select, say, a pattern more objectively; algorithms can help.[6] Fuzzy logic methods have been developed to detect technical patterns, such as the important Head and Shoulders. Computers are assigned a mathematical formula to describe the pattern. If certain lines of the pattern exceeded the formula, a trader could reject the pattern, but if the lines failed to exceed the pattern, the trader might accept the pattern. In the study, post-pattern abnormal returns were found on a quantitative basis without human judgment.[7]

We still need to select a technical approach and then to decide on the key inputs and their relative emphasis. Trading firms might ask if they should use Bollinger Bands in a certain instance, and if so, should they be one or two standard deviations?

Multicollinearity issues also can cloud the process. Which factors add value and which just duplicate other factors and don't really add anything to the business decision? For example, suppose you are not sure if it is raining outside. You may use a one-factor model by opening the window and stretching out your arm to see if your sleeve gets wet. Now, another person says he has a superior model called the two-factor model. He not only puts his left arm out the window, but to make sure, he also puts his right arm out the window. Since both sleeves are wet, he claims to have a superior model. Finally, a neighbor claims he has a superior model, the four factor model. Not only does he stretch both arms out the window, he also extends both legs. He then shows that his sleeves are wet and his pants are wet. While his four factor model appears to be superior, it is not. This example shows the effects of multicollinearity, as additional factors didn't actually contribute any real value.

Now, to impress clients, you can find a "quant-looking" guy with heavy glasses, speaking with a thick accent about many secret factors used to make investment decisions. Again, multicollineraity? Perhaps investing is simpler than that, no? But if you only show a few simple factors to the client, the client may feel he is overpaying. This client's feeling is, of course, a misconception—maybe you'd do better by showing him a room with computers whizzing and blinking and people yelling at each other in various languages and where there are all sorts of math formulas on the wall boards. The fact of the matter is that these additional "resources" are not contributing any additional value.

Statistics 101 and Quant

Statistics 101 comes into play when we back-test criteria, as we must be cognizant of the usual outliers like cherry-picking honeymoon periods when the market treated certain strategies favorably and of course got statistically valid results. Statistical measures must be developed to create levels of confidence in the data. Short periods of time can make certain results look good, but not statistically.

For example, a batter who gets 3 hits out of 10 at-bats, bats .300, a rather good batting average in professional baseball. No one would take that batting average seriously until a few hundred at bats are done, and for this reason, one needs over 500 at-bats to qualify for a batting crown.

What if the investment manager had a one-year record or a short back-test? This is suspect, as the results are not seasoned and may be just luck. We would seek t-stats and p-value confirmations. Consider that going into the 2008 crash, over one-half of the hedge funds had records of just a few years. Could one really be convinced that there was any skill even if collectively the hedge fund managers outperformed the S&P 500 Index?

Assume we use ANOVA (Analysis of Variance) and a manager shows an alpha of 1 percent per quarter with a t-stat of 1.5 and 2 is required for significance at the 95 percent confidence interval. Also the p-value is 0.30. Now to add more stats, the coefficient of determination is 0.50 with eight quarterly observations. What can we conclude?

Well, there is an alpha or the fund did better than the index. However, we cannot be sure if it was totally due to skill, as the t-test is below 2 and the p-value indicates a 30 percent chance it was due to luck. Also, the record is eight quarters, which is not particularly long and the coefficient of determination is 50 percent, which seems low. This would imply that the index only affected 50 percent of the performance of the fund. What about the other 50 percent? Is the fund placing assets in another index (known as performance drift)? If the index is large cap, but the manager places much in small-cap stocks, then the coefficient of determination with the S&P 500 Index most likely gets lower and lower as more is placed in the other index. Also, this short period of performance does not get into other risks that were taken to get this alpha—such as liquidity.

As one can see, Statistics 101 starts to get a good workout as we examine manager returns. There are many books on this process, but usually the basic college stats course is a good start. Usually, consultants and gatekeepers may require at least three years of a record to get over some of these statistical issues. Morningstar will not give its top rating of 5 stars to funds with less than 5 years of record, unless it is a new fund. Still, some may fund a manager with no record for other reasons. First, the approach may make good sense and is well back-tested on paper. While paper portfolios are never allowed as part of a fund's record, they can be shown as side exhibits to illustrate an investment approach. Limitations and economic issues such as transaction costs should be included to give prospective clients a feel for the risks, as well as the opportunities.

Another reason to pick a manager with a short-term or no record is behavioral. We suspend belief and proof as we are convinced that we must be investing in this specific area. (The glass becomes half full when investors want hedge funds; criteria can become more relaxed.) While the manager does not have a record, she may have been in the "business" of investing for "many" years. When an investor is emotionally ready to invest, he can rationalize an investment manager and her investment approach in many different ways.

Performance has to be measured to see if it is statistically significant. One way to do this is by looking at the t-test and p-value. Stats 101 gives us even more measures and these are used, or should be used, by sophisticated and knowledgeable consultants and gatekeepers. We can get a taste of some of the measures in reports like Morningstar and other reporting services.

Generally it is human nature to focus on absolute returns. Being up 30 percent seems very good as long-term results for blue-chip stocks and even small-cap stocks is about 10 to 12 percent per annum over the past decades. Being down 30 percent is then naturally not pleasant and looks bad.

Still, if one is up 30 percent, is that good? There is a feeling that naive clients tend to be happy. Up percent, wow! However, more cerebral analysis may indicate that this return by itself may not be that special or even good. This can happen when one does relative performance analysis and analysis adjusted for risk.

For example, if you are up 30 percent and the index is up 35 percent, then you can say that the performance was not that good, especially if you paid active management fees. In 2009, some of the stock indices were up over 30 percent (the NASDAQ was over 40 percent). The S&P 500 Index was up over 20 percent, but an equally weighed S&P 500 Index was up over 40 percent. So we cannot easily determine if a 30-plus return is good or bad, but it may be more or less in line with the stock market indices. Now suppose the index was up only 25 percent. Then we can see that the 30 percent looks good, as it is up and beating the index. However, you must adjust the return for the risks that were taken. If the same risks were taken as those in investing in the index, the results are still good. But if the risk taken was greater, then the results are not good.

So, as you can also gather, absolute returns, which are appealing to measure investment skill, are very misleading for longer-term results if you ignore risk. Let's demonstrate briefly. Imagine you are working at Burger Heaven earning $10.00 an hour. The job is boring and low paying, but if you are a student, it could be a good way to pick up some spending money and even pay for tuition. Feeding a family would make this job a dead end unless it leads to a management position and eventually a potentially rewarding franchise deal.

Now a friend of yours tells you that you can earn $100 per hour for "easy" work instead of sticking around your potentially dead-end job. Of course, you are interested and want to know more. "Is it drug trafficking?" you ask.

No, says your friend; he explains that it is legit and easy. You work in a tent each day with a blindfold over your eyes and an apple on your head. Now you may hear strange sounds. That is Hugo, sharpening his knife. You may ask what for. Once an hour, Hugo will throw the knife and split the apple in half, and then you collect $100. Your friend says that Hugo almost never misses. Almost?

"Are you crazy?" you ask your friend. You wouldn't take that job for $1000 an hour. You might end up dead!

Now, let's examine this problem in statistical terms. There is a return called throwing the knife and getting paid, and then there is risk, the volatility or dispersion from the midpoint of the apple. If there is no or a very tiny dispersion, you take the job, because you think it is foolproof. But what if the knife goes too far from the midpoint? (See Figure 13.1.)

In Figure 13.1, the letter g is good, as it splits the apple. X is not good, as it misses the apple, causes injury, or even death. As X gets wider from g, the risk increases. You can easily see that (X – g) is the beginning of the standard deviation formula, as:

$$\sigma = \sqrt{\frac{\sum (X_i - \mu)^2}{N}}$$

FIGURE 13.1 The Knife Throw

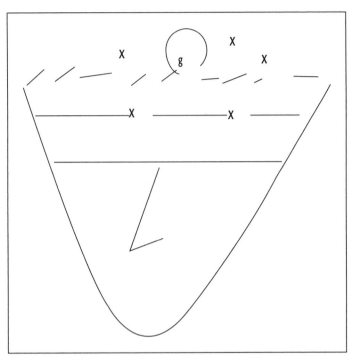

Source: Used by permission of Palicka/N/A

where:

σ	Standard Deviation
Σ	Total
X_i	Individual Number
μ	Arithmetic Mean
N	Number of Observations

What we see is that the return, while high, is unacceptable as $(X - g)$ continues to increase. In other words, if you divide the return by the dispersion, volatility, or a standard deviation, you start to make a trade-off between acceptable and unacceptable risk/reward ratios.

This then leads to the path of analyzing risk-adjusted excess returns. Now, not all jobs would have the same risk profile as working with Hugo; however, aggressive traders may still take on the job and live with Hugo's skill. Would you take the job if Hugo misses 1 out of 5 times? Most likely not. How about 1 out of 10, but you get $10,000 an hour? How about if he misses once out of 1000 times and you get $1,000,000 an hour and you can quit anytime you want? I hear takers! Of course, the business would not be profitable, as you may have to cap the payout based on the number of people who would be willing to pay to see the act.

Very conservative investors would stay away—no matter what the return. You would have to construct utility curves—in that investors may get more greedy emotionally and then become more aggressive. They then might be willing to consider working with Hugo. Initially, they may start out conservative but get more greedy and aggressive as time goes on. Perhaps they see others doing the same job with no accidents so far. Yet the day of reckoning may be just around the corner. You could say that private equity and hedge fund investors found this out in 2008. In the few years prior, there were no real accidents and returns looked good. However, 2008 showed steep losses and investments turned out to be illiquid. In the case of Hugo, as mentioned earlier in book, we are seeking an excess return to the risk-free rate per unit of risk. This is called reward-to-variability, or the Sharpe ratio.

Measuring for Risk-Adjusted Excess Returns

In investing, there are other measures for risk-adjusted excess returns: Sharpe, Treynor, Jensen Alpha, and Information Ratio. They all seek excess returns and compare them to risks. Which fund is better in terms of Sharpe, Treynor, Jensen Alpha, and the Information Ratio? An example follows.

Assumptions

- Return of the market (Rm) = 10 percent
- Risk-free rate (Rf) = 5 percent
- p = Portfolio return

- Standard deviation of the excess return (SDe)
- Fund A has a return (p) of 15 percent; standard deviation (SDa) of 10 percent, and a beta (Ba) of 1.2. Sde = 5 percent
- Fund B has a return (p) of 20 percent; standard deviation (SDb) of 25 percent, and a beta (Bb) of 2.0. Sde = 15 percent

SHARPE RATIO = (Rp – Rf) / SD portfolio a, b

Fund A = (15 – 5) / 10 = 1.0

Fund B = (20 – 5) / 25 = 0.6

Thus, *Fund A* is better.

TREYNOR RATIO = (Rp – Rf) / B portfolio a, b

Fund A = (15 – 5) / 1.2 = 8.3

Fund B = (20 – 5) / 2.0 = 7.5

Thus, *Fund A* is better.

JENSEN ALPHA = Rp − [CAPM]

(Note: CAPM = Rf + B a, b (Rm – Rf))

Fund A = 15 − [5 + 1.2(10.0–5.0)] = 4.0

Fund B = 20 − [5 + 2.0(10.0–5.0)] = 5.0

Thus, *Fund B* is better.

Assume the standard deviation of the excess return (SDe) for Fund A is 5 percent and for Fund B is 15 percent, then the Information Ratio is as follows:

INFORMATION RATIO = (Rp − Rm) / Sde

Fund A = (15 − 10) / 5 = 1.0

Fund B = (20 − 10) / 15 = 0.7

Thus, *Fund A* is better.

Consultants may emphasize one measure more than another. Note again, we are no longer just looking at absolute returns, but relative returns that are risk-adjusted. Except for the alpha (where the market produces no excess return or a result of zero), you should also do the Sharpe, Treynor, and Information Ratio on the index to see if it is the better deal. The higher the number the better, and of course, it should be higher than the benchmark, as well as similar competitors. It could be the managers show a ranking, but Fund A is still not as good, even if you only indexed. So, if the index had a standard deviation of 2.5, its Sharpe would be (10 − 2.5) / 5 = 1.5, a much better result than Fund A's 1.0 Sharpe. In this case, all things being equal, one would index rather than pick Fund A.

Fund Labels

This implies that returns alone actually shortchange buyers of funds. What we need is a list of risk-adjusted measures. These should be standardized for a specific type of fund with a label. Today we have food labels that tell us the ingredients and the calories. These also are of interest to those who cannot tolerate high salt or fat diets by stating these key measures in terms of sodium and fat content. So, too, we should have fund labels that can be standardized in terms of some basic measures. A label could look like the one shown in Table 13.1.

We could then add specific measures that may be of interest to specific types of funds. For example, we may add the time period the portfolio manager has run the fund and the amount of leverage used. If the fund is a bond fund, we would concentrate on its duration and its credit rating. If a hedge fund, we could add the length of the record, the left tail stress test and other measures for leverage considerations.

Market observers feel that investors chase absolute returns in the rearview mirror and don't do risk-adjusted analysis. Maybe they look at

TABLE 13.1 Performance Label for Fund XYZ

	Avg. Return	Standard Deviation	Beta	Sharpe	Treynor	Jensen	M^2
XYZ	.169	.244	1.21	.64	.13	.03	.02
SP 500	.114	.188	1	.54	.10	0	0
R^2	.54						

the index, but perhaps one stays with a fund if returns are positive and high. Quant programmers may also be biased by financial measures that seem to be working. So if technology is hot, one may raise the acceptable P/E ratio. In 2008, as the market went down, one still did better than the index on a relative basis, and even after adjusting for risk. This would be a "good" performance, but not in the eye of many fund investors. So managers that sidestep technology stocks by staying with their lower P/E ratios may look initially poor in terms of performance, as they lag the index that is being pushed up by the tech stocks. However, on the downside, there may be less of a casualty picture, and so over the course of a cycle, staying with our criteria may produce risk-adjusted returns.

While funds are relative performance vehicles, hedge funds tend to be viewed as absolute return vehicles. That is, we should have high positive returns no matter what direction of the market, as we can short stocks in down markets, and so on. We also realize that managers may take different risks in up markets and down markets. This would lead to up capture and down capture returns. Magazines such as *Forbes* give a grade to fund performance in up markets and then another grade in down markets. Getting a good grade in up markets but a low grade in down markets may indicate strong market risk via high leverage.

We can also view the situation where hedge funds may seek rather low-returning assets, but with leverage, they can either generate very high returns or disaster returns.

Note that in Figure 13.2, M has certain return with a risk shown on the horizon as the standard deviation. With true economic growth, the efficient frontier moves up where we should get more return for the same unit of risk. A good manager will produce an alpha by generating a return higher than the efficient frontier per unit of risk. By borrowing, we can move up the Capital Market Line (CML). We can keep investing with borrowed money into M, the optimal market portfolio. We can then move to the right, accept a higher standard deviation, and then get higher returns. (Note that the Sharpe ratio would be the same, even as the returns get higher.) Most likely, borrowing costs would increase with more debt and the returns to the right of M would slant down more as overall returns would be lowered with the higher borrowing costs. (Then the Sharpe ratio

FIGURE 13.2 The Efficient Frontier and Leverage

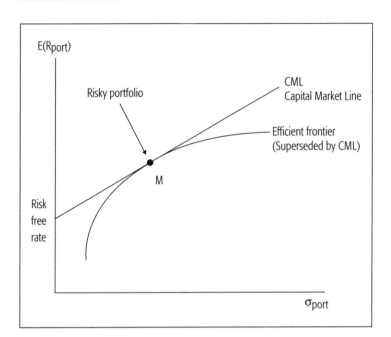

would decline from that of M.) So, we can see why the subprime mess faked out so many investors, including the no-money-down condo flippers. Using high leverage, a small decrease in value is greatly magnified into large losses.

When we get into back-testing quant strategies, we get into this type of analysis. Mainly, did the returns adjust for risk? One of the major risks that brought the economy to its knees in 2008 was the large amount of debt in the economy and in the funds, both visible and hidden. The visible debt was the obligation to service actual cash borrowings, and the hidden debt was the obligation to fulfill future swaps that were, in many cases, not shown or recorded. These swaps may have involved large amounts of future cash payments.

14

FINANCIAL AND EMOTIONAL BLEND AND TRADING STRATEGIES

OK, so we have had our taste of risk-adjusted returns. Let's introduce some other concepts. In formulating quant models and algorithms, we always run into the concept of limits. Is there a limit to the number of variables that can be used and still get a satisfactory answer? Can we be sure that while there is an answer, we can get a better answer if we only knew more factors? Can this be programmed in such a way that a machine can constantly improve its decision making and then eventually surpass human skill? Can a machine be programmed to even approach human skill in the first place?

These topics are popular with mathematicians and do not involve solely investment decisions. Investment decisions add more challenges than purely mathematical decisions, as there is an element of behavior that supposedly we must learn and anticipate. Whereas in physics we may see planets revolving around a sun in a predictable and mathematical model, the same cannot be said in investing. We have formulas that give us a projected path of earnings and valuation; however, investors perceive these paths differently, and so may over- or under-react to their paths. Thus, they may overpay or underpay for this anticipation. Although the stock or asset eventually reaches an intrinsic value, along the way it acts somewhat irrational to the expected path. Determinists would say that even with behavior anomalies, irrational paths may be an illusion, since behavioral patterns are repeatable. So emotional decision making must still exhibit the same, repeatable patterns. In that case you can then better predict the expected path to intrinsic valuation.

Consequently, it seems we need to consider the emotional factor, as it too can be a known. This emotional factor is a constant of the fear and greed profile that can be exploited by technicians. In that case, shouldn't we blend both financial and emotional factors together? Thus, the investment decision can be purely mathematically based using selected financial factors. This has been successfully used in the marketplace. But if there is a temporary insanity plea in investing, certainly it can and should be exploited by algorithms. In this way the decision may be improved. So, in addition to massive amounts of historical fundamental information, can we make good investment forecasts using all technical tools, or just a selective list?

The Gödel-Turing Argument

Mathematicians have always struggled with the question of just how provable math truly is in the first place. Is it all axiomatic, or can systems actually be proved? Worse yet, perhaps they can never be proved. Given a program and an input, will the program eventually halt when it runs through that input, or will it go forever? In 1936, Alan Turing, a British mathematician who formalized the concept of algorithms and played a significant role in the creation of the modern computer, proved that a general algorithm to solve the Halting Problem for *all* possible program-input pairs cannot exist. We can only make a specific program to halt for a specific algorithm. If never proved, it seems we cannot be certain a solution is correct or even the best one.

For example, consider a number sequence of 0 to a large number. Whatever sequence you have in mind, there then can be a larger number set, though it may make you scratch your head and wonder if it has any practical use. Now, imagine "1" followed by so many zeros that this book would become amazingly thick. What would this number represent and what could you use it for?

There are more general issues with answers as well, since knowledge of a broader universe can change a person's response. For example, say your friend asks you, "What shall I wear to the beach?" Note this is rather specific in terms of universe: the beach. Your first thoughts are along the lines of bathing suits, hats, and sunglasses. Now your friend asks the question again, but leaves out the words "to the beach": "What shall I wear?" At this point, you need a good idea of other specifics, as the answer can be much broader.

Up until a century ago if someone was asked what the square root of 4 was, the most common answer would have been 2. Yet it is not the best answer, as the more correct answer would be +2 *and* −2. Yet what do we need −2 for? It is certainly not necessary in business, but we do need it in physics for quantum theory and dealing with possible parallel universes.

Further knowledge of the universe creates different answers. Can you determine the entire universe and be sure that a math formula is the final answer?

Kurt Gödel, an Austrian-born mathematician, logician, and philosopher, proved that a complete and consistent set of axioms for all of mathematics is impossible, showing in his incompleteness theorems that there are limitations on math. While we may have an answer, we cannot be sure that a better answer does not exist. Gödel also said a computer cannot be programmed to get a final answer either. Another approach came from Turing, who felt a computer can keep learning and could get to a final answer. (Whether the computer gets real intelligence or is good at imitating human intelligence is another matter.)

The Gödel-Turing argument creates a problem for quantitative approaches. Turing's approach creates responses that can't be distinguished from human analysis. (Recall the movie *Blade Runner* where replicants who look like humans are interviewed to see if they are truly human or artificial creations of a company. The responses indicate whether the person is a machine or human.) So can we be certain these responses are reality, or just an *illusion* of reality? If we design a profile that a computer can act on, are we measuring the profile or the computer's ability to measure the profile? (If this is the case, I could program a drop in inventories to be good for rising oil prices. Then when the computer sees a drop in inventories it may thus conclude a rise in oil prices—is it really getting smarter and more human?)

The interaction of Gödel-Turing makes for interesting reading from Roger Penrose.[1] He proposed that algorithms cannot solely determine human thought, as there is more to it than some math formula. Algorithms can go only so far, but then there is the non-computational aspect of the brain. This aspect is based on quantum theory, which can circumvent cause and effect.

We may want to ask if we really need to get this deep into analysis. Why not just stay with the basics like devising a simple formula that shows rising oil prices and the factors that make this happen? The answer is that we can use simple formulas, but as we develop them, they will start to be tweaked and revised into more sophisticated versions in the hopes of getting better solutions. Now we can see how the Gödel-Turing arguments began to gain favor. Where does one stop in the tweaking and refining? Well, eventually one may accept the Gödel Theorem and say it is not worth tweaking anymore, as it adds no further value. But where is that line in the sand drawn? Does programming a computer with algorithms then matter?

Buy-hold versus trading is another issue to consider. I am often asked by traders, what is the optimum amount of trades? How many trades should be done per hour or per day? Still, a technical "black box" approach is gaining appeal because it can quickly spot investment opportunities and correctly calculate the vast number of probabilities and payoffs. Combined with fundamental black boxes, which have been around much longer, the investment appeal naturally increases. In using arbitrage pricing theory (APT) for CAPM formulas, how many factors should we have, which ones, and at what weight?

Black Swans

The nature of an efficient market is an issue in algorithms. If the market is that efficient, what is the use of developing an algorithm, as it would add no real value versus a random walk or indexing? Going back to the Gödel-Turing argument, we can also throw in another monkey wrench that has gained some popularity in the past few years: the Black Swan. Developed by Nassim Taleb, a practitioner of mathematical financial economics, the Black Swan idea takes an outlier approach to algorithms.

The idea is based on the notion that swans are only white; however, in Western Australia a black swan, an outlier, was surprisingly found. Taleb explains in his 2007 book *The Black Swan* that outlier events are of high impact, and hard to predict, like a meteor hitting the earth.

Asset managers may want to consider Black Swan theory in their approach. For example, were it not for 9/11 or the subprime catastrophe, asset managers' performance records would have been much better in recent years. Under Global Investment Performance Standards (GIPS), we cannot exclude outliers, but clients may use reasonable judgment to ascertain the outlier issue. Do we forgive a manager who has a great 10-year record but tries to get better performance by betting big on a certain industry and then fails when the industry crashes and burns? In such a case the result is that the manager goes from the top rankings to the lowest. Is this outlier action forgivable? What if the manager had an investment discipline that guided him well in the prior years, but all of a sudden a Black Swan screwed up the model? What should have never or very remotely had a chance to happen, happened. If only he anticipated this Black Swan that messed up the valuations. Taleb explains that since we don't know these high-impact areas, we should have high defenses. In other words, don't carry high leverage even if you are a big bank, as Black Swans can crush your business. Consider the surprise of investors with the failure of Lehman and Bear Stearns, which went down quickly.

Perhaps, however, there was a better solution we did not properly compute in the subprime catastrophe using the Gödel-Turing arguments. Some may say these Black Swans are not that surprising if we link and massage specific variables. For example, if the regulators did their job and analyzed the finances of the banks correctly, they should have seen the growing leverage risks and thus would have been in a position to stop the meltdown we saw in 2008. Without proper regulation, you may see the effect, but not the cause until it is too late.

Another intriguing look at Black Swan is in emerging market investing strategy that has gained popularity at times. It has been shown that outliers or Black Swan returns impact the returns of these markets so much that one may have a great change in performance depending on if they are trading on bad days or not trading on good days. According to the research of Javier Estrada, "an investor who missed the 10 best performance days in emerging markets would have had a portfolio that was 69% less valuable, on average, than a passive portfolio. Avoiding the 10 worst days would have resulted, on average, in a portfolio that was 337% more valuable than a passive investment. The 10 days account for only 0.15% of the study days, suggesting the odds against successful market timing are staggering."[2] Thus, like we saw earlier in small caps in Part 2, a very small number of days accounts for the majority of returns.

If Black Swans dictate alpha results, then perhaps you are better off indexing, since predicting the factors for alpha is not likely and may be a useless exercise. You can have fancy formulas, but they won't amount to much if a wrench stops the gears from turning. Others say that these Black Swans result from events that are known and predictable and that eventually surprise many but not all. Those that did better analysis may be ready to avoid and capitalize on these outliers. Statistically, one should learn from the past and adjust the probabilities using Bayes' theorem. But then again, maybe it is different this time. This possibility, of course, creates incentive to keep analyzing and performing algorithms.

Garbage In, Garbage Out ... Again

Based on my investing experience, all the points on math models, algorithms, or predictive analytics are basically useless if they are programmed with poor assumptions. I usually get bored MBA students in my classes who state that they already know all the formulas. What they don't realize is that they are being evaluated on the use of their assumptions in the formulas. In that case, indexing is the only solution for the investor, but thoughtful selection of proven factors will give you an advantage over indexing. We do not have to actually manage money to see the advantages of such thought based on the examples we have discussed and the research that has supported quant criteria that has generated risk-adjusted excess returns. If anything, they would seem to overcome some of the emotional traps that befall investors.

The use of quant Fusion analysis can be used in algorithmic trading techniques, as well as normal security selection for long-term horizons. For short-term trading, you could use algorithms to capture perceived pricing inefficiencies. (This could replace human eyeballs staring at a Bloomberg terminal.) One major cornerstone of client trading is capturing Best Execution. Algorithmic trading is a mathematical process that can be used to break up trades and execute them in a gradual manner in order to realize optimal profits.

The rapid growth of algorithmic trading was estimated by TABB Group to increase from 13 percent of U.S. equity orders to 23 percent within 2 years in 2008. By now, it is expected that this is even higher, as we can assume this number has been exceeded given greater interest by many buy and sell side firms in their trading decisions. The goal of algorithmic trading would be to meet established criteria on key factors, such as size, liquidity, and regulations.[3]

Now we need to step back a bit. OK, there are all kinds of algorithms for trading, but what purpose do they serve? Are they designed to get managers in and out of bad decisions? In other words, if the analysts had properly analyzed the asset, they would have had plenty of time to get in and out of the asset. If a client gives the manager money at the top and wants to withdraw it at the bottom, then the manager should have controlled money flows of the fund. However, we have already seen that technical and behavioral issues make this unlikely. So we have a situation where news may look good or bad, and as a result, the clients feel that now is the time to place money with the manager who may already be drooling over some good news stock.

So is buy-and-hold better than trading?

It has been considered by economists that having less turnover is better than more turnover in terms of seeking long-term performance. Of course, if the trader can buy low and sell high, then high turnovers are better strategies, but that is unlikely on a frequent basis. So, if she is not good at buying low and selling high, it may be better to just index and buy for the long term due to the transaction costs. Naturally, she may miss selling just before specific stocks or markets take a nosedive. Again, this can be a weak argument, as it assumes when she sells, the stock will actually go down, soon. It may sell off, but not till much later—and at a higher price. It also assumes the trader buys near the bottom. Quite possibly, she may be scared at the bottom and wait to see stocks or markets rise. Thus, market timing is not considered a good strategy for many, including professionally managed funds.

Morningstar made a study of comparing high-turnover funds with those that have lower turnover to see if the performance results are different and if they tend to favor either the high- or lower-turnover set of funds.[4]

Here funds using tactics were compared to those using strategies. Strategies were long-term plans, and tactics were more immediate and short term. As is common in some of these studies, the turnover ratio of trading was used as the criteria to ascertain which approach was better. Morningstar defines turnover as "a measure of a fund's trading activity, which is computed by taking the lesser of purchases or sales (excluding all securities with maturities of less than one year) and dividing by the average monthly net assets."[5] To keep things simple, if Manager A has trading activity of 1 and assets are 10, Manager A has a 10 percent turnover. This would be less than Manager B, who has a trading activity of 5 and assets of 10, or a 50 percent turnover. The higher turnover of Manager B would then be compared on performance returns in his fund against that of Manager A. We can then see who has the better performance. In Morningstar's study, tactical funds were defined as active funds with high turnovers and the strategic as low.

The funds in three categories were analyzed for the 10 years ending December 31, 2009: large-cap blend U.S. equity, large-cap blend non-U.S.equity, and U.S. intermediate bond funds. Looking at Table 14.1, we can see that higher-turnover funds had lower returns, as they were lower on a 3-, 5-, and 10-year time periods.

Generally, we can only surmise that funds emphasizing more trading in the hope of benefiting from some sort of short-term strategy make

TABLE 14.1 Funds froms Morningstar Study

EQUITIES AT HOME

With U.S. large-cap blend funds, a strategic approach (low turnover first quartile) outperformed a tactical approach (high turnover fourth quartile) over the past three, five, and 10 years.

Quartile (33 large-cap blend U.S. equity funds per quartile)	Average annual turnover ratio (%) from 2000-2009	Annualized % return as of Dec. 31, 2009		
		3-Year	5-Year	10-Year
1st	11.1	−42	12	10
4th	11.6	−57	0.3	−12

EQUITIES ABROAD

Turnover ratios in general were higher with non-U.S. large-cap blend funds than with domestic funds; again, strategic funds bested their tactical counterparts over all three time periods.

Quartile (13 large-cap blend non-U.S. equity funds per quartile)	Average annual turnover ratio (%) from 2000-2009	Annualized % return as of Dec. 31.2009		
		3-Year	5-Year	10-Year
1st	29.8	−3.5	5.4	1.9
4th	130.5	−6.5	3.4	0.3

BONDS AT HOME

Among U.S. intermediate bond funds, the performance differential between a low turnover strategic approach and a high turnover tactical approach is smaller.

Quartile (16 U.S. intermediate bond funds per qualified)	Average annual turnover ratio (%) from 2000-2009	Annualized % return as of Dec. 31. 2009		
		3-Year	5-Year	10-Year
1st	32.9	5.6	4.7	6.1
4th	436.7	5.3	4.3	5.9

Source: Dr. Craig L. Israelsen, reported in *Financial Planning*, June 2010, p. 140

returns worse. These short-term strategies could be reactions to news, earnings, perceptions of changes, and a host of other factors that lead to short-term valuations and, hence, subsequent trades. So why use these strategies? Again, one hires economists and strategists to create models that attempt to take advantage of changing economic winds.

Best Execution

A guiding requirement for client trading is the concept of Best Execution, and not necessarily Best Price. Best Price deals with trades at an immediate price that is the lowest for buying or the highest for selling. This can have drawbacks if the entire order is not executed, so subsequent orders may have to be executed at more unfavorable prices. The discovery of better prices may not be possible, as a large buy order may allow sellers to pull back in the hopes of getting higher prices. Best Execution is the better and required approach. It is governed in the United States by the Investment Advisers Act of 1940 and subsequent regulations. A broker has a duty to seek the best execution that is reasonably available for her customers' orders. Sometimes it is a judgment call between Best Price and Best Execution.

Some of the factors a broker considers when executing her customers' orders for best execution include the *opportunity* to get a better price than what is currently quoted, the *speed* of execution, and the *likelihood* the trade will be executed. Thus, a broker may pass on a current price for part of an order. (When I say broker, it can also mean a computerized trading system.) Instead, the broker may decide to pay a higher price if the entire order is executed and it is estimated that this action would save the client execution costs. So if the order is to buy 300,000 shares and stock is trading at 10.30, rather than risk doing half the order at 10.50 and the rest at 11.00, it would be better to do the whole order at 10.55. Thus, we pay up 0.25. How do we know that half may be done at 11? Well, it is not certain. We can wait and do the rest of the order at 10.50, but also it may go higher and then we may pay 11.25. So, there is uncertainty on getting size and price on an order. Sometimes this has led to illegal actions of paying for order flow on the pretext of Best Execution when the broker got commission for diverting a trade to an ECN and the client paid a higher price than he could have obtained elsewhere.

Trading Costs

A common misconception is that execution costs are only the brokerage commissions. However, professional traders realize this is the least important cost. In fact, trading costs include brokerage commissions, bid-ask spread, and market impact. Yes, brokerage commissions, but they are the smallest cost, usually 1 to 3 cents a share. (I will eliminate any exchange fees to keep our example simple.)

The next larger cost is the bid-ask spread, as regret trading may lead to a severe discount on sales, especially in small-cap stocks. So if one buys at 10.50, but then decides that the trade was a bad purchase and wants to unload the stock, the buyer may have to hit the bid at 10.40 or even lower if there is large size to sell.

Finally, the costliest part of trading can be the market impact. To buy 500,000 shares of a small-cap stock trading at 10, one may have to buy 100,000 at 10.25, 200,000 at 10.50, and the rest at 11.00. Once the order is filled, the stock may drift down to 10 again, so the buyer paid above the market to get the order off.

Trading analysis by firms like Abel/Noser have various ways to measure trading costs. For example, they may examine what percentage of the order was near the average price during a specific time period. Since the 1970s, trading costs have declined in terms of commission costs. Many discount firms now charge under $10.00 per trade, and some are even commission-free.

Electronic trading by networks like Archipelago and INET have attracted many traders. In addition, the NASDAQ has taken an increasing market share from NYSE listed stocks.

This has created a hybrid experiment where routine orders are done electronically in thousandths of a second or milliseconds (presumably the vast majority) and the rest that require special handling due to sensitive news is still handled by humans and specialists.[6]

So, what we have seen so far is the need to get Best Execution. Buy-side firms are especially cognizant of this, as they manage trillions of dollars for clients who are sophisticated enough to check the trading costs with firms like Abel/Noser.

Algorithmic Trading Strategies

Leading algorithmic trading strategies include pairs trading that involves trading in a non-market, directional basis, where a trader shorts one asset and buys another with the hope that the spread either expands or converges.

We may execute large blocks in stock with a trade involving volume weighted average price (VWAP). VWAP is a trading benchmark and is derived by dividing the dollar volume of a stock (Stock price × Number of shares traded) by the total corresponding shares traded over a designated trading period (Jefferies & Co. material). We can also buy time and get VTAP. Many trading companies have developed proprietary algorithms to guide traders on when to execute certain volumes and perhaps when to pass. Is it better to buy 500,000 shares now or do 5 trades at 100,000 apiece hopefully at better prices? Well, it appears that with algos we can start to split up orders and place them better. The average trade on the NYSE dropped from 1000 shares to only 250 shares from January 2004 to July 2009.[7]

Algorithmic trading has also led to high-frequency trading that examines real-time, tick-level data streams for trading opportunities. Orders can be placed and cancelled in milliseconds. Millisecond trading has created jobs for financial quants who can produce satisfactory algorithms that react quicker to market conditions. This has spawned algorithmic trading that attempts to capture the complete decision-making process for trade execution by the use of mathematical formulas. It is felt that machines using algorithmic trading will squeeze out the small human trader, since they will be able to more rapidly assimilate many variables into complex trading systems.

Algorithmic trading can squeeze the small human trader in terms of getting priority on an order and eventually force the small trader to assume more risk.[8]

Consider the rapid algorithmic growth in Euronext.liffe. In its market, a very large algorithmic order to buy 30,000 contracts of a short-term interest rate contract can squeeze a small human order of 100 contracts. Even if the large order, which can be the bulk of orders at a price, is placed after the small order of 100 contracts, it can be hit with most of a 100-contract sell order. The unfilled portion can then quickly be cancelled, and the small order may get only a partial fill. This can make spread trades (i.e., contracts with different expiration dates) difficult to do for the small trader. It also gives a false sense of liquidity, as the true buy order may not be real if it is quickly posted and then cancelled. The exchange has been reviewing its policies, but in the past, this situation doesn't violate its rules, as in theory the entire 30,000-contract order can be hit and filled.

The computerized order can also better "scalp" an order (playing the bid-ask spread). The small trader may have to develop her own algorithm, and even take on larger orders with more leverage risk. This implies that the trader can intensify bearishness or bullishness and thus contribute to abnormal pricing patterns that can be exploited by algorithms. So the trader goes further right on the CML line with leverage and thus takes more risk.

This has also led to probes and sniffer orders to get a feel of the real market. Similar to putting bait on a hook to test if the fish are biting, one can send small orders to test the market's real intentions. An example of that occurs in "dark pool trading." Dark pool trading matches buy and sell orders on proprietary trading systems that are not visible to outsiders. Trades are then required to be reported publicly within 90 seconds, although most are reported within a few seconds. There are 30 dark pools in operation within the United States (excluding overseas), and they execute about 10 percent of the consolidated volume. They are operated by broker/dealers, consortia, and independent firms.[9]

Broker-dealer dark books include Goldman Sachs' Sigma X, Credit Suisse's CrossFinder, Neovest (wholly owned by JP Morgan), and UBS's Price Improvement Network (PIN). This type of trading has taken share from crossing networks such as ITG's Posit, LiquidNet, Instinet Crossing, and Pipeline.

For example, in a game of stealth, some can try to ascertain the real market in a dark pool. Are there many buyers or sellers, and what price points are the critical ones? The average Joe Trader can't ascertain this type of information, but a sophisticated trading firm can. For example, dark pools don't post bid and asks and size similar to Level 2 quotes that a Joe Trader may see on his discount brokerage firm Web site. So a predatory trader may send out a small sell order and quickly see it snapped up by a buy order. The predator now knows there is a buy order and may then quickly turn about-face and take out the offer in the visible market (called lit), even above the current price. Joe Trader sees this and assumes the price is moving up; he starts to buy more, so as not to miss the up move. Then the predator returns to the dark pool and nails the large buyer at a higher price as the dark pool bid-ask has been raised, especially if the visible market is not that liquid and the bid-ask can be raised, easily. So the predator gets a higher price for a large order as the "investment" of a small order. This leads to a spy-versus-spy type of analysis. The pools may then have anti-gaming logic, with the buy side doing this as well. They may protect themselves by only taking an order in the dark pool that exceeds a certain size and thus not fall for the bait-on-a-hook trick of a small order, as at that point, it may not profit a predator.[10]

A large amount of data can be used in various algorithms, such as high-frequency or hyper trading. The appeal of this trading is that it purports to show low correlations to the movement of the market or the security itself, and at low volatility. It does not seek an intrinsic price, but just the ability to execute quickly in a mispriced market by jumping in with better quotes. Under Modern Portfolio Theory, this would be highly desirable in portfolio construction and could even lead to a separate asset class. Valuation of the security is not important, as the ability to play the bid-ask spread is the only thing that matters. High-frequency trading firms represent approximately 2 percent of the 20,000 or so trading firms operating in the U.S. markets today and account for 73 percent of all U.S. equity trading volume.

A major player in high-frequency trading is Tradebot Systems, Inc. Using a computer-based exchange such as Archipelago, Tradebot can trade in 1/1000 of a second. Its programmed computers can exploit fleeting differences between bid and offer prices by jumping on the purchase of one price and very quickly reselling at a fractionally higher price. At times, it trades 1000 times a minute and its trading can be as much as 5 percent of the volume of all NASDAQ trading.[11] Tradebot moved servers from Kansas City to buildings in New York that were closer to central computers of electronic exchanges, and thus captured an advantage of several thousandths of a second in terms of execution![12]

We can see that this can become a behavioral game where a trader may have to keep changing algorithms in response to the markets reacting to his orders. A successful leader in quant trading, Jim Simons of Renaissance, admitted on CNBC that unless he changed his algorithms in response to competitor moves who seemed to be tracking him, he would be showing lower returns.

Simpler Algorithm Example

Trading algorithms requires the creation of a strategy based on a perception of future market action. For example, using technical analysis, you can assume that a security will trend upward in the near future, and so may wish to buy each time a security hits a trend line. You can also develop a program to buy on a specific confirmation, such as the third touch after the prior two touches. Technically, the more times you bounce off a trend line, the more important it is. Conversely, a short trader may wish to short only after an important support has been broken.

In doing a formula for this strategy, we can set a linear regression in the form of:

$$Y = a + bx$$

where Y = Expected price, a = Intercept, b = Slope, and x = Time period in days. Thus, if a = \$10, b = 1.2, and x = 50 days, then Y = \$70.

We can now make a simple decision tool. If the price is too far above Y, it would not require a decision to buy/sell unless we are using our aforementioned envelope strategy.

A buy would be if the price (P) is equal to Y. If it falls below, it would break support and we would sell or not buy. Thus:

$$\text{If } P - (Y) = 0,$$

buy.

$$\text{If } P < Y \text{ or if } P > Y.$$

don't buy.

Of course, technicians may have a filter rule, so we can say:

$$\text{If } [1 - [(P - Y) / Y]] \times 100 \text{ is in a range of 98 to 102,}$$

buy.

$$\text{If } Y = \$70, P = \$69$$

then:

$$[1 - [(\$69 - \$70) / \$70]] \times 100 = 1 - (-0.0143) \times 100 = 101.43$$

therefore, buy.

$$\text{If } Y = \$70, P = \$71,$$

then:

$$[1 - [(\$71 - \$70) / \$70]] \times 100 = 1 - (0.0143) \times 100 = 98.57$$

therefore, buy.

One could narrow the filters and even add other indicators. For example, RSI would have to be attractive at 30 or lower. The math can then get more complex, and so would the computer programming. Proper statistical back tests would be required.

Again, the challenge would not be the math, but using the correct decision rule. This has caused angst to many quant funds.

News or pending news can also play a major factor in trading. Event players may speculate on the release of news to trigger a trading strategy. News services such as Reuters' NewsScope can be used to incorporate fundamental data into an algorithm. An expected strategy would be to play standard events, such as previously discussed SUE (Standardized Unexpected Earnings) announcements.

For example, if a press release shows XYZ Company just reported $1.00 EPS, we can program a trade based on beating or missing expectations. There would be a "machine" reader that not only scans immediate news but can take older news and create a thought process. Recent news can then create things such as "disappointments" that usually move trader sentiment.[13] There can also be a dissemination delay among various electronic sources.

Following the Reuters example would be another strategy using fundamental data.[14] Subscribers can set up automatic trading orders based on fundamental news events. Thus, an event can trigger buy or sell orders. Presumably, one can estimate how a stock reacted from similar past events.

For example, one may wish to trade TOL, the luxury housing stock. One can have the computer scan news events, such as housing starts, interest rates, and home inventory levels. Upon seeing how the stock has reacted in the past, one would program and tweak an algorithm to reflect one's best estimate of future reactions to news. The news can be visible, such as a broad government announcement (say, housing starts) or more hidden (say, TOL's sales progress in a specific project that is buried on page 98 of some newspaper). Putting together many various approaches is the responsibility of an algorithm trading desk.

An example of algorithmic trading is that of Knight Capital Group. With two dozen in-house PhDs, an algorithm is created to handle incoming order flows as follows:

1. Determine which can be matched with another client order.
2. Determine which Knight should take on its books for a day or for up to month.
3. Use some form of predictive analytics to determine the probability of waiting and finding a match.
4. Finally, send the order to an electronic platform and pay for execution.

Big investors have been expanding into various algo trading situations. Consider CalPERS, the largest pension plan in the United States. CalPERS is the California Public Employees' Retirement System, which manages $236 billion of pension and health benefits for the 1.6 million government employees, families, and retirees of California. They have been viewing high-frequency intraday trading strategies in the most liquid currency pairs as a source of alpha.

"We look at currencies as a source of Alpha," explained Omid Rezania, investment officer at CalPERS. "We've been doing that over the past few years—that's an ongoing effort within CalPERS."[15]

So how are they approaching this? First, they utilize various electronic trading platforms and a math algorithm tool MATLAB to analyze the tick-by-tick movement of the foreign exchange markets and perform intraday currency volatility Then, they use some correlation analysis:

"You see gold move closely with the S&P 500 futures," said Rezania. "You see the Australian dollar moving very closely ... with S&P futures. During the day, we notice the trade-weighted dollar index moves closely with S&P futures, and sometimes even oil moves in sync with the euro."

Let's point out some challenges. MATLAB can massage millions of data bits, but it does offer programmed trading programs, which run the risk of doing what others are doing and thus not getting an alpha. The reason they may be relying on MATLAB is because CalPERS admits that they can't hire many programmers; they have only a team of three people. Another challenge is to correctly model the correlations. For example, gold may go up when the dollar declines, but when the euro faltered, both gold and the dollar got stronger. So their correlation went from negative to positive. So, could they fall in the trap of using the same approach that we discussed earlier?

I feel that there will be both big winners and big losers in algo trading. The winners will be mostly institutions that have the deeper insight and can better surmount the Gödel-Turing limits. Perhaps they will be the first to see that the square root of 4 is also a minus 2. Perhaps the better decision is not to do this action and just index the S&P 500 Index!

15

DERIVATIVES INPUTS AND TRADING STRATEGIES

Complex trading strategies can also involve derivatives. This can make a trade invisible, as you would avoid the cash market. The shadow of the derivatives would eventually influence the cash market, but perhaps not immediately. On May 9, 2006, I made a technical market forecast called *Technical Outlook*.[1] The Dow closed near 11,650. (Several days later, on May 19, I presented this material at a seminar for the Market Technicians Association explaining what I had predicted.)

In my technical market outlook, I stated: "I continue to expect new highs by year end (2006), with a moderate correction in the second half being contained to the 10,600 level. I don't expect much progress in the market for the remainder of the year. My target for the Dow is 12,000 in the second half."

Figure 15.1 is how the chart looked at the time of my prediction.

So, while I expected to hit higher highs by the end of the year, I predicted a major curve ball. That curve ball would be a correction to 10,600 in the second half. Once that was made, then I expected a rise to 12,000 by year end 2006. Once the 12,000 was hit, then I expected not much progress for the remaining part of the year. (See Figure 15.2.)

I called for an immediate correction to about 10,600 and then a rally by year end to 12,000. The chart shows that my prediction was reasonably on the mark. The market made a double bottom near 10,700 in mid-June and then again in mid-July. It then rallied to 12,000 by mid-October.

FIGURE 15.1 Dow Jones Industrial Average, May 9, 2006

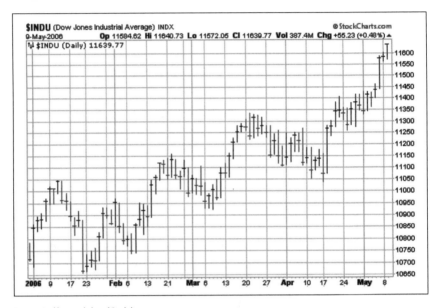

Source: Used by permission of Stockcharts.com

FIGURE 15.2 Dow Jones Industrial Average, December 29, 2006

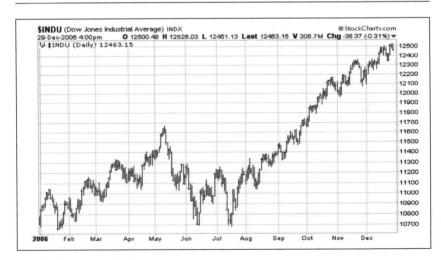

Source: Used by permission of Stockcharts.com

However, it did not stall here as I expected, but went higher by year end to 12,500.

While this market call is somewhat flattering, as the short-term is rather hard to do with the correction part, the purpose of this example is to demonstrate various derivative strategies that can be implemented by a portfolio manager. It can be assumed that a portfolio manager would come up with a similar outlook and decide to exploit it. Obviously, you can sell all stocks in anticipation of the correction to 10,600, park the proceeds in cash, and finally invest the cash just before the market rally begins. Recall that the tactics and strategy funds would have different time horizons, and so investors could also exploit this move, if they believed my forecast. This timing strategy involves cash trades. However, you may feel uncomfortable doing this, as the transaction costs could be considerable. So, depending on the size of the portfolio, you can entertain algorithmic trading or doing slices (or selling the whole portfolio in one shot).

Assuming 2 to 3 percent transaction cost on the sale and another similar amount on the purchase, you would not be too impressed given the 8.6 percent expected decline. If you did 2.5 percent on each side, that would equal 5 percent transaction cots. The profit would be 8.65 minus 5.0 percent, or a small 3.6 percent. (Probably not worth it for such a short-term strategy, but then again, there may be tactical funds that would feel comfortable with their models and would do this.)

Another strategy could be doing a guaranteed slice of 5 percent each way, but it would not be that attractive. A brokerage firm could give us closing prices at minus 5 percent. They in turn would have some way of deciding whether they could still make money on this, as liquid names would be worthwhile, but illiquid names could show further losses than the 5 percent. Adding round-trip transaction costs of 10 percent would make negative returns and thus make the cash strategy more appealing.

You can then entertain cash transaction costs against derivate trading costs by shorting futures in anticipation of the expected correction period, and then covering and staying long for the expected rebound. For example, if you have small-cap stocks, you may consider shorting Russell 2000 futures. This assumes that the portfolio has a high correlation to the index. If the correlation is low, you may have to blend various indices to better meet its characteristics. In the rather short-term horizon, the correlations could also weaken because of other market forces.

Of course, you must be a good market timer, as the short precludes any benefit in a surprising upside move. Also, you may have to pay a premium to the cash market in the futures. In addition, margin calls in a rising market would test the nerves of the portfolio manager. Would the manager hedge the upside? Would there be a disposition effect and allow the short position to show heavy losses, thus wiping out any gains from the long portfolio? Probably that should be done, but imagine if the market rallies 20 percent! While the losses would be almost eliminated, the portfolio would not share in this appreciation net of the cost of the short.

Protective Put Strategies

Insuring portfolio gains may then entail protective put strategies. Here you can only lose what you paid for the put. So, if the market really rallies, you still benefit on the upside once the cost of the put is covered. You can buy puts on the Russell 2000 Index. Again, the put must show a correlation to the portfolio, similar to shorting the future. (Recall that an option is the right but not the obligation to buy [call] or sell [put] a security at a certain price by a certain date. Thus, if one feels that a stock portfolio may decline, one may buy puts on the index that corresponds to ones portfolio.) Choosing the right strike price is important, as the puts may be so expensive in the short term that they wipe out gains. If you roll over the puts that are at the money on a regular basis, the costs become high. So, it may be better to use these only in selective market situations. Part of the expense of the put is the implied volatility, which can drive the put cost higher.

Let's make this point more interesting. Suppose the fund does performance drift and it is really a mid-cap fund; it could use the MDY puts. MDY is a type of ETF index called the SPDR S&P Mid-Cap 400. Just to give actual numbers to the concept, the analysis was done close of trading June 11, 2010, when the MDY was 136.95. The July 136 put was 7.00. Using rough numbers, we have about a month to get 136 protection on the price; this protection costs 7, or 5.1 percent. (We'll call it 5 percent for one month.) If we roll over this protection, then easily the cost is 12 times 5, or 60 percent per year. The MDY is lucky to generate 12 percent per annum over the long run—so this is costly. If the gain is 7 for one month, we basically break even. At this point, we can start to pay less insurance, such as 3.94 for a strike of 131.

Another concern is the open interest or how many puts are available to buy. The 136 had only 16, which is a puny amount to hedge a multi-million dollar portfolio. The 131 had 3001, which could cover $39 million, assuming we can buy all of them without moving the market. So, to get more open interest, we may have to create further transaction costs to move the market and thus give someone an incentive to write more puts. The solution is that if the portfolio is small and we can time markets in the short-term, a put could be the way to go.

On the other hand, why even bother with all these costs? Suck up the short-term loss (as the loss is unrealized anyway); then the market will rise if the outlook is correct. Yet, simple as this seems, fear, greed, and confidence in models makes some funds and some investors risk taking on trading situations even with the costs. The Morningstar study seems to support that notion.

Going back to the put option, this would safeguard the downside for a period of time (as we have the right to put a price back to the writer of the put by a certain date), but still allow participation on the upside if a market correction does not materialize, but instead the market goes up.

Option Prices

Option prices depend on six major factors: current stock price (S), exercise price (X), volatility of the stock price, time to expiration, interest rate, and dividend rate of the stock.

Option pricing can be derived from the Black-Scholes Formula. It is a more detailed version of the intrinsic value of a call option (C), where:

$$C = S - PV(X) - PV(D)$$

with PV being the present value discounted by the risk-free rate. D is the dividend.

Using the Put-Call Parity Relationship, we can derive the intrinsic value of put (P) as follows:

$$P = C - S + PV(X) + PV(D)$$

Options before expiry will trade at higher prices than the intrinsic value at expiration. For example, factors such as time will influence the price of a call by giving it a greater value the more time to expiry that exists. So if the strike price is $10 and the stock is $12, an option with three months before expiry would trade at a price greater than $2.00 ($12 to $10; all else being equal). Likewise, perceived greater volatility of a stock would increase the price of a call.

This means that a portfolio manager must do a trade-off on paying a premium on the option on factors like time. Buying a put with a year to expiry would carry a large premium and may not be justified if you only expect a small market correction, but it would be useful if you felt a large correction was looming.

Using basic intrinsic valuation, we can demonstrate some option strategies.

Assume that when the portfolio is worth $100, you pay $5 for a put to safeguard the portfolio at $95. Figure 15.3 shows the payoff on the expiry date of the option.

As the market declines below 95, the portfolio's maximum intrinsic loss would be $10: $5 for the put cost plus the capital loss of $5 ($100 – $95). Should the market rally, the portfolio would participate on the upside. Assuming participation point by point, you would only lose the cost of the put, or $5. At $110, the portfolio would gain $5.00 ($110 – $100 – $5).

Of course, the options value on the date of purchase will also be affected by the implied volatility expected by the market and other factors like time left to expiry. You must also see if enough options can be traded (hence transaction costs) based on the open interest.

Since you may expect a mild correction, portfolio gains may temporarily be sacrificed by writing a call for the expected period of correction.

FIGURE 15.3 Portfolio Worth

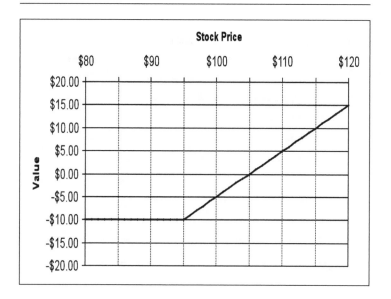

If you feel that a stock portfolio may decline, you write the call premium on the index that corresponds to the portfolio. This would safeguard some or all of the downside (depending on the call premium and the size of the correction) for a period of time but still allow participation on the upside once the call expires.

Assume the portfolio is again worth $100, but you write $5 for a call with a strike price of $105. You can see the payoff in Figure 15.4. As the market declines below 100, the portfolio's maximum intrinsic loss would be the $100 – Portfolio value, plus $5. So if the portfolio declines to $90, you would lose $5 ($100 – $90 + $5). (Obviously, in a sharp correction, writing calls would not be the best strategy to conserve capital.)

The prior derivative examples show choices for the portfolio manager that depend on market outlooks and the costs for the various derivative strategies, as well as doing cash trades. There can also be a blend of derivative strategies. Using statistics, we can better customize strategies.

For example, in 1987, a popular derivative strategy was to write deep out-of-the-money puts, on the assumption there was a low probability

FIGURE 15.4 Portfolio Worth

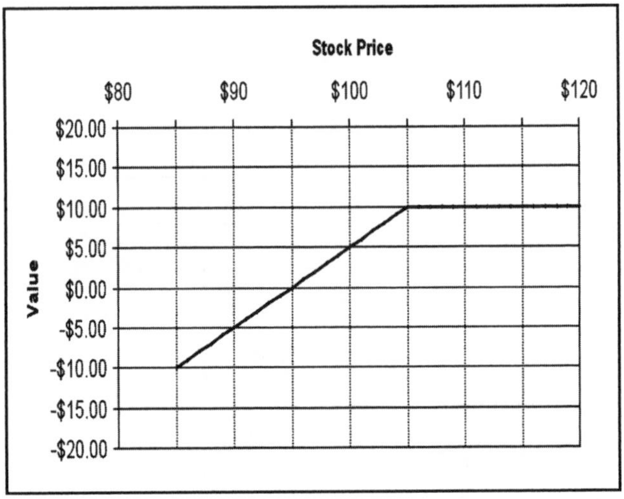

of a sizable market correction. When the market actually dropped about 20 percent in one day in 1987, there was a panic to raise funds to meet put obligations. More exotic types of derivatives have also blossomed. Insurance against disasters, such as hurricanes that can impact, say, oil service stocks in the Gulf of Mexico, can lead to buying CAT (Catastrophe) bonds.

Swaps

Another strategy for market timing is to enter swaps. These carry less transaction costs and have various time horizons. (They can also lead to potential problems if used poorly.) If you feel the market (and your corresponding portfolio) will underperform fixed income, you can swap the difference in the returns of the stocks versus a fixed income instrument.

So, in my market forecast to 10,600, I would trade the return of the market for a return in fixed income. To keep things simple, I would agree to pay (or get) the difference of the market indices. In return,

I would get LIBOR (London Interbank Offered Rate) interest returns, say, for three months. After that I would not be interested, as I would expect a market rally to 12,000. So, to keep things simple, if the market drops from 11,600 to 10,600, I get 8.6 percent of the notational amount (the amount we agree to change in dollars) plus LIBOR, say, 1 percent for the three months. I therefore collect 9.6 percent (not bad, since I don't touch my portfolio with transaction costs). But if the market rallies by 8.6 percent, then I pay 8.6 percent. After netting my return of 1 percent from LIBOR, I pay 7.6 percent. I may have cash or I may have to sell some of the portfolio to pay for this, thus generating some transaction costs.

Swaps is a broad subject, and many innovative instruments have been developed. For example, one can reverse engineer the equity value of a stock by analyzing the corresponding credit default swap (CDS).

In our swap example, let's change my market outlook, which now calls for a three-year bear market for stocks. Instead of selling stocks, buying market puts, or shorting financial futures, the manager has decided that swaps may provide the best execution. Also, reversing a bad decision on the market outlook may be easier with a swap. We would have to find another party to swap with to do the opposite trade, and of course, the counterparty credit risk would again come into play. (See Figures 15.5 and 15.6.)

Let's say the portfolio is now filled with S&P 500 stocks. The manager who handles the stock portfolio with the S&P 500 stocks has decided to enter the following equity swap:

One counterparty pays a fixed or floating rate.
One counterparty pays the return on an equity index (S&P 500, for example).

More specifically, the details of the equity swap are as follows:

Portfolio manager pays S&P 500.
Counterparty B pays 7.5 percent fixed rate.
Tenor is three years with annual payments.
Notional principal is $10 million.

FIGURE 15.5 Swap Market and Contracts Cash Flow Exchange

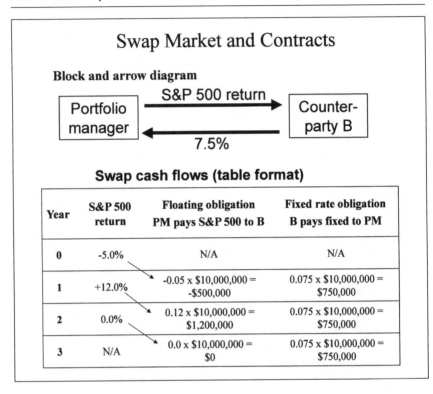

FIGURE 15.6 Swap Market and Contracts, Portfolio Manager Perspective

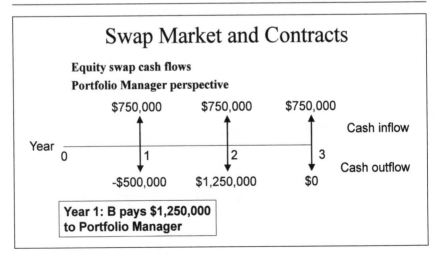

At the end of the three-year-period, the swap ends and the portfolio manager can fully participate in any potential market rally. If the portfolio manager wants to get out of the swap because she feels there will only be a two-year bear market, she can attempt to do a counter-swap with another party for the third year, where she will pay fixed income and get stock market returns.

Swaps have not been well regulated and rely on the creditworthiness of the counterparty. One can go to a "swap bank" or a major brokerage firm that can be ready to make good on one side of the swap, if the other party defaults. Of course, this can carry higher transaction costs in terms of a bid-ask on each side of the swap.

Moving forward, all credit default swaps will be required to trade on an exchange. The exchange will step in to honor the contract, so there will be much less credit risk. Also, the swaps will be transparent to outside parties.

Trading Decisions and Derivative Decision Trees

So, going back to our market timing example, we see the new challenges. As one may gather, the trader of old that just matches orders is a dying breed. Consider some of the choices to place a trade:

- Does a trader do a cash trade?
- Does a trader VWAP or TWAP an order?
- Short futures?
- Buys calls?
- Do swaps?
- Accept a firm discount for a slice?
- Incorporate technical analysis and use a Fusion algorithm? If so, what are the factors?

Here we are only looking at a market timing decision. You may also do this for investments or various portfolios rebalancing. Again, should one bother even doing a trade? Where does one draw line on trades, size of market moves, and risk/reward payoffs based on probabilities. Advanced academic training and the use of technical analysis is becoming important, especially among hedge funds. I doubt that this trading decision could be analyzed by fundamentals alone. I was allowed to observe a job interview for a trader by a leading asset management firm. The first question was asked what technical analysis tools the job candidate used? Many junior traders feel that they don't need to have financial and technical backgrounds, as compared to analysts. In my opinion, this is a big mistake. Both professional traders and managers must be well versed in trading alternatives, as well as programming and mathematics to increase investment returns.

16

DEVELOPING OUR MODEL

Algorithmic (or algo) trading is rapidly growing and the list of 46 algorithmic providers listed in Bloomberg is expected to increase, especially if regulations are changed. The quest to tap liquidity, hence lower transaction costs and beat an efficient market, is not a cheap process. It is estimated by experts in the field that one must spend $10 million to develop a system and another $5 million for annual maintenance. For some the costs will not be worthwhile. Aite Group, a leading independent research and advisory firm focused on business, technology, and regulatory issues and their impact on the financial services industry, sees algorithmic trading emphasizing global trades, more proprietary systems, less reliance on VWAP and more on statistical VARS, portfolio approaches as compared to single stock trading, and better methods to tap dark pools.

We can see that Joe Trader can be at a severe disadvantage to all this type of algo trading. The Aite group was reported as stating that certain types of algo trading in specific areas of arbitrage generated $21 billion in profits in 2009. Goldman Sachs, while certainly a beneficiary of prop trading, was also victim to possible algo theft when 32MB of Goldman Sachs' proprietary algorithmic trading code ("trading secrets") were allegedly stolen by Sergey Aleynikov.[1] (Now that Goldman Sachs is a bank, however, it must get out of prop trading.)

Because of the rapid growth of algorithmic trading and the many approaches, this area provides uncharted territory to the trading desk, especially with the use of Fusion analysis. For example, we may pass on trades when the RSI is in overbought situations or when the MACD declines below its moving average. These decisions would be reinforced if the fundamental valuations of stocks, whether on P/E, SUE results, or some blend of fundamental indicators, were excessive.

Back-testing of trading strategies with various programs, like Meta Stock, are always in demand. Statistical problems with back-testing could include such common problems as data mining and wrong correlation assumptions. These problems may explain the seemingly large losses of some hedge funds on market plunges.

Given the rapid developments in the market, exotic trading strategies may have to be constantly revised; however, this may only compound the problem if a systematic factor is missed and client credibility is jeopardized. Clients do not want to feel they are the guinea pigs who pays for a fund's R&D. While some traders may worry about losing jobs to rapid quant decisions, others will welcome the opportunity of selecting the appropriate algorithmic trading approach for a specific client need. Those welcoming the opportunity will generate more trading commissions.

For example, Client A could be a Market order, Client B a Limit order, and Client C a VWAP order. Some orders will also have more weights for technical factors for some clients. VWAP orders may not always be cancelled once entered but can provide various degrees of flexibility. A futuristic approach that is currently being studied is analyzing traders' emotions with the monitoring of brain waves. Charting a trading desk could allow a technician to create a Neuro-Brain Wave technical pattern to determine bullish/bearish sentiment.

While trading using algos is a broad topic and of interest to traders, it still remains to be seen if it can add value. As algos get smarter, it becomes a zero-sum game where some firms gain, but only at the expense of losers. Who will the losers be? Joe Trader, the mutual funds, other algo firms, or the buy-and-hold crowd?

We can see that trading has its own opportunities that some may not share. Investors may be more interested in long-term horizons and may have lower turnovers than day traders and even mutual funds. They may use more limits and be considered liquidity providers, as they choose their entry points more on some type of valuation rather than mispricing.

The next area of concern is using quant for investing as compared to just trading. Once the investment decision is made, there can very well be a follow-up algo trading decision. However, some may be quite patient, buying on bad news and selling on good news because they feel they have a good handle on the true valuation of the price.

As we discussed in Chapter 14 with the Gödel-Turing concepts, we can go deep into algorithms, but how deep? Is all this programming that useful in the first place? From my experience, you do not need many factors and the complexity can be rather simple. The algos themselves will not kill you, but second-guessing them due to sentiment can. That means you may fall into the hands of technicians who can exploit you, even if you are using algos.

Algorithmic System Model

Let's begin to develop a simple algorithmic system model that will give us a Fusion approach to investing. The horizon (for this model) is longer than just a few days or minutes, but it could easily cover those horizons as well. The time horizon would be several months to a year. We will create an AI model that is based on a scoring system. It is a sort of Zagat guide to investing where we will establish criteria for deciding if a stock is attractive or not. (I have used something like this for over 30 years, for both institutional money and for my personal portfolio.)

For investment decisions, the use of Fusion analysis consists of:

- Selecting technical indicators in a scoring system. This will also include some behavioral considerations.
- Deciding on what weights to give to these indicators.
- Selecting fundamental indicators in a scoring system.
- Deciding how much emphasis we will place on technical and fundamental factors. We also need to decide how to incorporate behavioral issues.
- Deciding which starts the process: technicals first or fundamentals first.
- Deciding on trading techniques.

The process can be elaborate and expensive. We can use data bases like Standard ampersand Poor's Compustat, which has many screening criteria.

Begun in 1962, it provides a database of some 75,000 global securities, covering 90 percent of the world's total market capitalization. It provides specific company data history back nearly 40 years that can easily be used for back-testing. Compustat is generally used by institutions that have large budgets, as costs can run into the many thousands per year to subscribe. There are also other databases to try. There are also other data bases to try. The output can be selected by specific criteria like picking companies with a certain range of P/E ratios.

Some funds have a plethora of mathematicians and programmers working as part of an investment team. The team's most effective members would be those that set the decision rules. They would then make special analytical rules for using the data to create investment decisions. For example, on a simple basis, you may decide not to use earnings or net income, but to use operating earnings to get a better feel of a company's earnings potential. For instance, this may be used if we feel the tax rates distort the true earnings picture. (Remember: Bad rules equal bad results. Computers and math formulas can't reverse bad rules.)

However, we will create a very simple quant screen for a technical scoring system. Similar to Zagat's guide or some travel guide to vacations, we have a scoring system. In the vacation guides one may see indicators such as price, friendliness of the staff, past feedback from guests, and so on. This process can be rather low-cost with short cuts or, as we have seen, very intensive and expensive. We may also have to be careful in interpreting bad reviews from those who had vacations in a hotel on rainy days, and good reviews from relatives of the hotel. Decisions will have to be made on the proper time horizon, as certain indicators may be more important for short horizons than others for longer terms. For example, technical screens using a shorter-term horizon may include indicators like Stochastics and RSI. For longer-term horizons, we may use factors such as the 200-day Moving Average and OBV. Technicians will disagree among themselves as to which are the best factors to use. This in itself makes the scoring system challenging. However, do the factors add value or just rehash the same results in a different format? In the end, the question will come back to the essential point of value added.

We will use a more affordable database, Morningstar, that suits our needs. There are plenty of inexpensive or even free databases to use for filtering tasks. While not as encompassing in breadth as Compustat, I feel Morningstar has the necessary data to get to the meat of the decision-making process. (I am seeking the oasis and am not concerned about how many fronds there are on each palm tree).

Selecting Indicators

We will only use four indicators. Is that too little? If so, how many more should we use? In addition, we will create weights for each indicator. Which will be weighted the most, the least, and how much? (All are good questions that challenge the quants, but we must move on.)

Our proposed indicators and weights are as follows:

- Head and Shoulder pattern, weighted at 45 percent
- Trend line, weighted at 20 percent
- Breakout, weighted at 10 percent
- Volume confirmation, weighted at 25 percent

These four indicators add up to 100 percent. We can explain the logic of our criteria as follows:

Head and Shoulders is well-tested, and thus a meaningful input. Thus, it has a high weight of 45 percent. Why not 50 or 60 percent? My feeling is that it should be near one-half of the weight because too much of one indicator is not likely to be statistically prudent unless we approach 100 percent of the results. When we have lower results, it pays to use additional indicators that can hopefully confirm. In addition, not all Head and Shoulders work, with upwardly sloping necklines being the least useful. Another weakness of using a Head and Shoulders pattern is that it does not appear that often. When I assign a large weight, I assume my time horizon is long and that I have little turnover, as periods of a few days or even a minute are useless, as they do not give the time required to create the necessary sentiment associated with the pattern.

The trend line has a 20 percent weight, as technicians feel trends can determine price direction. Breaking a trend is a serious matter, especially if the trend is long term. A trend of a few seconds, a few minutes, or even a few days is insignificant, so, we assume the trend is probably a year as the Head and Shoulders pattern tends to be a longer term indicator, evolving at least over a few weeks.

Breakouts from trends or support and resistances can be very meaningful. They are especially useful for long-term breakouts with serious support and resistance levels. Short-term patterns of support and resistance are likely to be broken, but are not as important.

The fourth factor is volume confirmation. Volume is a major ingredient of technical analysis, as it must confirm upside breakouts, but not necessarily downside ones. Volume is not important if we are using Japanese Candles, unless we are blending candles with a more traditional, technical measure like volume.

So, we already have some controversy in our model, and we only have four indicators. Each indicator will have its own challenges relating to interpretation for time horizons, for example. Some technicians will use approaches that other technicians may not use. It is odd to hear the criticism of technical analysis as being self-fulfilling prophecy. One would assume that all use the same indicators, have the same weights, and interpret the indicator the same. We could easily make a case as that there are at least 50 technical indicators. Permutations on selecting all or some with various weights would run into the many millions of possibilities. Then again, does one follow their indications?

Let's review our scoring system in Table 16.1. It represents a simple AI technical model. A 5 is a strong Buy, and a 1 is a strong Sell. (Depending on an investor's preference, one could also reverse the numbers to show a 1 as the best.) We can conclude the stock is attractive to purchase with a 4.35 rating, where 5 is a Buy. So what does this scoring system show? It could indicate an Inverse Head and Shoulders breaking a long downtrend, with good volume confirmation on the upside break of the downtrend.

Long- and Short-Term Horizons

If we are trading in a long-term horizon of six months to one year, I would use the following primary factors which have guided me over the years:

- 200-day, 50-day Exponential Moving Average (EMA)
- RSI

- MACD
- OBV
- Market relative (how the stock compares to the performance of an index)
- Patterns, including trends and support resistance levels.

TABLE 16.1 Simple AI Technical Model

	5 Is Bullish, 1 Bearish		
	Rating	Weight	Result
HS	5	0.45	2.25
Trend	4	0.2	0.8
Breakout	3	0.1	0.3
Volume	4	0.25	1
Sum			4.35
4.35 is a BUY RATING BUY STOCK XYZ			

I believe the factors I've listed show a good balance of momentum plus the benefits of patterns. Candles will give me more information on short-term timing decisions regarding to enter or exit the stock. Since I use global small-cap stocks, I feel EW cycle patterns are not useful given their exposure to specific risk. (But again, that is my opinion and quants would have to make their own decision.) I also feel that small-cap stocks should not be traded for short-term horizons, as they can entail high transaction costs given their possible illiquid nature. (Again, this is another decision for the quants.)

What about those who want to trade the short-term horizons? These would include short-term traders who are more day traders or swing traders than they are investors. I would then use the following that has been used in my consultations with trading firms:

- Fast or Slow Stochastics
- Triple Cross EMA
- Japanese Candles

- Fibonacci Ratios
- Support and resistance
- Events

For confirmation, I would use MACD and RSI.

Background or second opinion uses for traders should include long-term patterns, as ideally we trade in the direction of the long-term trend. Blending with GANN and sentiment is a good value added, as too many bulls in a stock mean we are asking for trouble if we are buying. Since some good opportunities are with stocks that show selling climaxes, GANN can help decide entry and exit points, as short-term momentum indicators may be distorted by being overbought or (in the case of a selling climax) being oversold. Skillful traders can take advantage of patterns such as channels combined with EW trading patterns.

Both investors and traders may wish to tweak momentum measures, such as moving averages, MACD, Stochastics, and RSI. For example, I have been asked if 10- and 50-day moving averages are better than 50- and 200-day. In my opinion, for longer-term investing they are not, as there are too many opportunities for being whipsawed. Once again, one would back-test all of one's theories on what makes the secret sauce.

Selecting Fundamental Indicators

We can conclude that given all the technical indicators, why not just use fundamentals? It must be simpler. Again, this can be a faulty decision, as there are many fundamental indicators, not to mention their interpretation—accounting versus economic.

Fundamentally, we can select key indicators that attempt to provide the best valuation model. This is both easy and difficult to do. For example, it is easy to select accounting metrics such as P/B or P/E ratios. What is difficult is to decide if we need to adjust these ratios for economic value. In my opinion, we need to adjust, as economic value is what we strive for because it is what the market interprets for correct pricing. The other difficult issue is that financial factors are only that—financial—and may not represent the hidden values. These hidden values may be issues dealing with brand image or management skill. The sudden loss of these may not be immediately reflected in the ratios. Initially, earnings may hold up, but as the brand image erodes, we can safely assume market share may be lost. This would result in lower sales, and hence earnings and cash flows being lower than expected.

Fundamental decisions require the determination of an investment approach, such as growth or value. Growth may select more measures on PEG analysis. Value may select more measures on low P/B and P/E ratio analysis. Fundamental approaches are based on either discounted cash flows or comparative peer group analysis, or both.

Fusion Decision

In Fusion, we combine a fundamental weight and a technical weight that results in a fusion decision. Table 16.2 shows five factors: short-term return, P/B, P/E ratio, a cash flow measure such as enterprise to EBITDA (called price to self financing), and then a blended technical rating.

I chose these measures because they are well back-tested in various formats. Also I have used these in various forms throughout my investing career. For technical, I say blended, because the technical rating is a weighted average of various technical measures that we discussed earlier. In the table, the technical measures are summarized into one rating, such as stock #1 having a technical rating of 2. This technical rating could be several technical factors and their weights, which then give the weighted average of 2.

We must decide on the sensitivity of the factors. For example, a P/B of 1.1 and 1.15 may be considered too close to each other, so the difference is not enough to create an ordinal differentiation. (It's similar to the expression you hear about splitting hairs.)

Now a P/B of 1.0 versus 2.0 is sufficiently large enough to indicate one is more attractive than the other, as 1 times book is certainly more attractive than 2 times book. But how does one decide the sensitivity? One way is to examine past histories to see what the extremes or foul lines would be.

TABLE 16.2 XYZ Portfolio Valuation Rating

| Portfolio Rating | Hold | | | | | | | | XYZ Portfolio Valuation Rating | | |
Name	Price 4/17/2010	Portfolio % TOT	Rating Change	Rating	Points	S.T Return	Price/Book	P/E N4qs	Price/Self Fin	Technical Rating
Stock #1	49.20	3.1	–	B/H	1.58	1.5	3	1	1	2
Stock #2	36.53	5.3	–	SELL	4.30	5.0	5	5	4	2
Stock #3	4.38	0.6	–	SELL	4.40	5.0	1	5	5	4
Stock #4	8.90	0.0	+	SELL	4.60	5.0	1	5	5	5
XYZ PORTFOLIO (Weighted Average)	26.72	100.0	+	HOLD	2.900	4.0	4	2	2	2

We can then back-test sensitivities to see if the effect on the ratings add any value to the pricing decision. Does 1.25 book add any value versus 1.0 times, and so on? This can be a challenging process, as we would have to back-test all factors on their sensitivity and then decide if the sensitivity is the cause of the valuation or if other factors not related to the P/B ratio are the cause. For example, it could be that one entered into a certain phase of the business cycle and the P/B is not as important as the effect commodity prices have on sales. Both a bank and material producer may have the same P/B of 1.5 times. But if commodity prices start to rise, this will help the commodity producer more than the bank, as the bank may be impacted more by the interest rate spread between its cost of money and the lending rate of its funds.

One can be generally comforted in knowing that low P/B and low P/E stocks tend to do better than high ones (over longer periods of time). This is possible because factors such as emotions cause valuations to be high or low. Investors can bid up the P/Es to high levels based on their optimism, rather than on the P/E's potential growth. So should we use some sentiment measure of bullish and bearish outlooks on an industry, rather than a P/E or P/B approach? The prominent economists Eugene Fama and Kenneth French seem to indicate in their research the optimism of investors that leads to high P/E ratio leads to underperformance, rather than the discount of low P/E ratio caused by pessimism.[2] So are we double-counting with technical analysis when using high and low P/B and P/E ratios. (More food for quant thought.) In any case, we must decide on the sensitivity ranges.

Table 16.3 shows the weights for each factor and the rating criteria based on the sensitivity for the factors. Thus, for price-to-book, the most desired stocks are those below 1.5, and the least desired are those with price-to-book over 3. (We can switch the ordinals, where now 1 is the most attractive ordinal and 5 is the least attractive. We can create any scoring system we want, and that's the point. Whether it works is another matter!) The weight is 10 percent for the price-to-book. This may be because the portfolio is more focused on growth, so price-to-book is not meaningful.

The technical rating is assigned a 20 percent weight by the Fusion portfolio manager. This low weight could be because the portfolio is more long-term oriented and deals with small-cap stocks. In dealing with small-cap stocks on a longer investment horizon, fundamental research may be very

TABLE 16.3 Weights and Rating Criteria

CATEGORY	Weight %	RATING				
		1	2	3	4	5
S.T. RETURN	35	>30	>10	>0	>−10	<−20
PRICE/BOOK	10	<1.5	<2	<2.5	<3	>3
N4QsP/E	25	<1.25	<1.5	<1.75	<2	>2
PRICE/SELF F.	10	<1	<1.5	<2	<2.5	>2.5
TECHNICAL	20	1	2	3	4	5

valuable, as these stocks are not that well researched or followed. On the other hand, large-cap stocks that have analysts following their fundamentals may not provide the analyst for discovering some factor that leads to insight on better valuation; all is already known. Therefore, one may conclude that well-researched stocks are better analyzed technically, whereas low-researched stocks are better analyzed fundamentally.

Refer back to Table 16.2 and note that stocks 1, 2, 3, and 4 have either Sell, Hold, or Buy/Hold decisions. Thus, the weights would be either 0 or a low number in a portfolio of 30 stocks. We can also rate the entire portfolio by taking the weighted average of the individual ratings. This is the bottom line of the chart where the portfolio is 100 percent and has a rating of Hold. We can then see which indicators have contributed to this decision.

Table 16.2 shows the short-term returns of stock 2 drag down the rating with a 4, while the other measures, such as the technicals, are favorable with a rating of 2. The short-term rating represents the price target over our time horizon. If it's one year in this model, we have projected stock prices one year from now that are not that attractive. It could be that we have used earnings-per-share estimates and applied a P/E ratio to them to get the price. So if the earnings projection is $1.00 and we give it a P/E of 15, we get a $15 price objective. If the price is now 15, then there is a zero return and the scoring system would give it a 3 rating. Since the rating is 4, it would appear that our portfolio has slightly negative return based on the prices of all the securities we are forecasting.

Let's move ahead. Imagine if a client gives you a big sum of money, but you have a Hold. It would be better for the client to wait until prices decline so that they get a better return. At this point, we have the behavioral trap. If we pump up our earnings estimates, then the short-term returns become attractive and the portfolio is now a Buy/Hold and we feel we can take the money in good faith. So did we do this for the client's benefit or our benefit? A savvy client would like to see these results at least weekly to see if we are gaming the system somehow. But then again, ignorance is bliss. We can also start to do sneaky things like only pumping up the earnings of the larger weights in the portfolio, as that may be enough to upgrade the portfolio rating.

Again, do we go back to the same question if checked by the client? We should explain the investment process and be true to it. Managers should be true to their discipline and notify clients of significant changes—ahead of time. Clients need to have some checks and balances and not just rely on the word of the manager. The scoring system is certainly a good start.

We combine a fundamental weight with a technical weight to get a Fusion decision. While this can be run daily, online, it is more practical for certain investors, such as small-cap managers, to use a weekly approach to save on cost. Also, one can temper market fluctuations.

The question after doing all of this is whether we stay the course with the quant model or start to second-guess it and make exceptions, especially if performance is trailing the index in the shorter term. We may then be exhibiting the anchoring effect where we start to change the criteria of the quant model so as to get the desired result based on present market trends. So if technology stocks are doing well, we can relax the P/E constraint and lower the weight of the P/B. This would make technology stocks more attractive in the quant model.

By valuing each stock in the portfolio with Fusion criteria (including both fundamentals and technicals), we can make a valuation for the entire portfolio. Relaxing criteria may be just the extra lift one needs to make the larger stocks change the portfolio rankings to meet anchoring goals.

In Table 16.2 the portfolio is rated as Hold (note top left portion). This rating is derived from the weighted average of the dollar value of each stock in the portfolio (see the bottom line). So if a stock is 2 percent of the $100,000 portfolio, then the stock would have a dollar value of $2000 in the portfolio. This stock would have twice as much influence on the portfolio's eventual rating as compared to another stock that was only 1 percent. If we had three stocks in a portfolio and two were rated as a Sell with each having 1 percent of the portfolio, but the third was 98 percent of the portfolio and had a Buy rating, the portfolio would be rated a Buy, even though the majority of the stocks were a Sell. (Of course, such a portfolio would be difficult to explain in terms of prudent diversification, but the example is used to make a point.) The portfolio is a weighted average, but not equally weighted, as the larger positions have the greater influence on the portfolio rating. For this reason, we can game the system by tweaking a few large holdings to get the result we really want.

We can also use this for attribution analysis by doing a retro analysis to see how the ratings did in terms of accuracy. Attribution analysis is used to measure skills of portfolio managers to see who and what contributed to portfolio results, meaning we can see how each factor, such as P/E, contributed to the final success of the decision. Think of a football team: Is it the offense, the defense, or the coach that made the difference in the team's success or failure?

For example, a stock may be rated as a Hold and so may not be bought, but if it is illiquid, it can be made an underweighted holding. So, if the normal weight was 3 percent, we could buy it at 0.5 percent. Then we could see how the stock did on a risk-adjusted basis a year later.

Before we looked only at an absolute return in our aforementioned $15.00 example, however, we should do the risk-adjusted return for a short-term return. So, using the CAPM, let's say the stock should have returned 20 percent if the beta was above 1. It would be rated as a Hold. The stock would then be completely avoided, with a zero weight in the portfolio. This may imply it is not attractive in the Fusion process, but we could still make a case to buy a small amount as the stock is not a full Sell. If we had a strong liquidity criteria, we can still buy a small amount, as the stock is difficult to buy and if a large block shows up, one can then take some position. This would be more prudent for long-term time horizons, as the manager can then afford to sit on the position for a while and hope fundamentals turn around. For short-term horizons, this would not be prudent.

We could further reverse-engineer all the factors of the Fusion process to see what caused the miss. Perhaps the short-term return was estimated to be negative because the analyst estimated too low on the earnings and the estimated stock price was therefore too low. In hindsight, we may see if the earnings was correctly estimated, as the company reported actual earnings much higher than the analyst; the rating would have been high for the short-term total return, or S.T. Returns (the total return of the stock in a time period, usually in one year) *and* the stock would have had a Buy rating. (If there are enough such misses one can then dismiss the analyst.) We can program a computer to pick the P/B ratio, but the value added, the S.T. Return is the responsibility of the analyst.

It could also be that the technical analyst used the wrong blend of technical factors. So the fundamental analyst may have done well, but the technician did poorly. Perhaps the technician should have used more weight on a moving average rather than a Fast Stochastic. Perhaps the weights were wrong and the S.T. Returns should have a higher weight in the stock rating—then the quant is to blame. We may also find that the analyst was correct, the stock was a Buy but instead of putting 3 percent of the stock into the portfolio, the manager put only 0.5 percent. Then the portfolio manager is to blame. Enough of these misses and the portfolio manager should be replaced.

As we can see, there are many permutations on attribution analysis. In tops down analysis, the key ones involve market timing. It could be the stocks were rated correctly as a Buy, but the portfolio manager had too much cash in an up market and this caused performance to lag. Some portfolios are always run fully invested, as the manager may be part of an asset allocation strategy where other managers decide market timing and asset allocation. So if they get more bearish, they would withdraw funds from the stock portfolios and place it in cash or some fixed income funds. Because this is not only possible but likely in small-cap funds, a manager then would be evaluated more on the second major factor, sector or industry selection. So if technology stocks did well, were the technology stocks in the portfolio overweighted to take advantage of this result? Some limits may be placed on making industry bets, as large bets may not be allowed or it may not even be prudent.

We are now ready to review stock selection. Usually, bottom-up funds tend to place the most emphasis on the stock selection skills portion of the total attribution analysis process. Some firms may be required to prepare attribution reports for clients who insist on it, as the clients themselves want to know what makes the fund tick.

One challenge for the portfolio manager in evaluating the analysts is the time horizon. If a fund attempts to show low transaction costs with low turnovers, the fund will select a longer-term horizon, rather than a few days or even a few weeks. If one manages a large sum of money where the stocks are not that liquid, a year horizon may be wise in order to avoid transaction costs. For many analysts, having a year-out view is challenging, as they tend to view stocks in the rearview mirror or some near-term time period. A seasoned analyst may be good at discounting immediate news that only affects the stock in the short term, as compared to the desire of getting good, longer-term results. Junior analysts often say, "See, the stock is up a point or so," but of course, we do not hear from them when it returns to the original or even lower price. The analysts then want to trade on short-term news, but eventually this leads to a trading strategy that may not be within the skill set of the analyst.

Our simple Fusion discipline could have even more bells and whistles. For example, we can add the criteria of ownership. If the stock is not held by institutions, or if only a few funds own it and they have an excellent track record, that will help the process, as either the stock will benefit from the neglect concept or the smart money crowd concept. But don't we want institutions to own it and support it? Not until one has a position. Then you want the elephant funds to clamor in and push up the price. Once again, this may require time to not only get the position in case of illiquid stocks but to disguise intentions so as not to get run over by others who may sniff out that we are buying. So, we return to algo trading strategies.

How do we know if a fund is good or bad? The holdings of funds is usually shown in several documents such as a SEC 13-d filing or even a listing in Yahoo (despite some lag). If they are mutual funds, their record can be seen in Morningstar or Lipper. A professional manager also knows the good funds by name.

We can also be creative and add factors that could influence the portfolio ranking. For example, how do we measure a factor such as "good management?" Cynics may state that if the stock price goes up, the management is good and if it goes down, management is bad. We'd like more objective criteria that can be derived from databases.

For example, we may decide that years of experience is a criteria, so holding a serious position of employment for 10 years would get a higher rating than one being held for 3 years. We may filter academic degrees where top schools may lead us to feel management is better than those who get degrees from lesser schools. We may also look at deal flow. Did the manager have past successes with other companies? If so, that could lead to a higher rating.

We may also wish to have a governance rating. These ratings are being increasingly circulated. It has been found that the stock of firms with poor governance ratings do worse than companies that have high governance ratings.

We have also discussed other important topics such as brand image. An objective decision has to be made on this item, as we can easily have stars in our eyes with a stock that is going up and appears to then have good brand image. We can think of past-glory stocks such as Xerox and Kodak that had good brand image but seem to have lost it when the stock was at lower levels after competition eroded their market share.

In general, there can be many more factors, but one may wish to know if they really add more value than a few key ones. Again, back-testing could help in this area. From my perspective, I tried to keep things simple. Keeping things simple may be more effective than contriving some complicated algo that only confuses the real issue.

Balancing Fusion Factors

The flowchart in Figure 16.1 illustrates a method to balance the various issues discussed in the previous chapter.

First, we use Fusion with quant criteria on our fundamentals and technicals. This gives us a list of stocks that either can be purchased now or sometime in the future—once the price is right. I call future stocks the bullpen.

FIGURE 16.1 Balancing Fusion Factors

Then we have a qualitative filter that either accepts or rejects a stock even if the quant is good. For example, we will not buy "me too" stocks that lack brand image. We are not interested in buying the 7th regional bank in Rhode Island because it is cheap. Each company must be special as either a one-of-a-kind or a major leader in its market. In this way, brand image comes in the back door. We also reject any company with management imbroglios or that seemed to have violated shareholder governance.

To this I would add any factor that is not yet visible in the financials but can impact business down the road. This could be lawsuits, environmental issues, or quality of product issues that can result in product recalls and eventual erosion of the brand. Recall our analysis of economic earnings. Any issues that may significantly cast doubt on the quant criteria are immediately filtered into the equation through this qualitative cut.

Now we may add the issue of liquidity. (When I ran large sums for institutions, I saw stocks that were traded by appointment-only or I had to buy on the bad news and on the good news. Now that I manage much smaller amounts, liquidity is not really an issue.)

Once again, doing this in a disciplined manner through good markets and bad is the key. Making exceptions and constantly redoing your quant is a danger that can result in nothing more than just chasing yesterday's news. Of course, in the beginning, you still do not know if your quant and qualitative criteria will work.

17

FUSION PROCESS AND STEVE MADDEN CASE STUDY

We can do a Fusion process example on Steven Madden (symbol: SHOO). SHOO makes shoes for tweenies (mostly teenage and twenty-something women). Steve Madden, its designer, successfully developed and expanded this company from one store in New York to over 100 stores nationwide, with some initial distribution overseas. SHOO also does a line of men's shoes and a line for older women. In addition, he has garnered licensing fees through the development of clothing and accessories.

The shoe business is very competitive, yet he has developed a successful brand with low price points that appeal to students and first-time job holders. In addition, he has a reputation for trendy fashion that makes SHOO a destination store for many young shoppers. While the quality of the shoes is not high, they do have affordability and are looked upon as a good value. According to a 2007 poll by the Consumer Reports National Research Center for *ShopSmart* magazine, the average woman owns 19 pairs of shoes (excluding sneakers), with 15 percent of women owning 30 or more pairs. Four pairs are worn regularly, and the average women buys four pairs of shoes a year. A quarter of their shoes are worn only once. In 2005, 1.4 billion pairs of shoes (for women) were sold with a value of $42 billion.[1]

The price points of SHOO are higher than the implied $30 a pair, as they are mostly in the $75 to $150 range. Thus, they are less than Chanel shoes that can easily start at $600 or Jimmy Choo shoes that may start at

$300. Higher-end shoes for fashionistas are Manolo Blahnik and Christian Louboutin shoes, which can also start over $500 and go much higher. SHOO satisfies a need for budget-conscious women who seek good values but may not be interested in the longevity of shoes. Hence, not factored into SHOO's financials is the ability to capture the fashion and value need of women. This makes it an interesting brand.

A shocking highlight of SHOO is that its chief designer and major stockholder (near 20 percent) Steven Madden was convicted in 2002 for securities fraud and went to jail for a few years. His conviction could be mitigated in the context that as a non-financial person he was unfortunately influenced by his childhood friend who cofounded an unscrupulous brokerage firm, Stratton Oakmont. Stratton did the SHOO IPO in 1993. Thus, he cannot be an officer of the company, but he has a long creative consultant contract. Once released from jail, Steve's creative juices apparently have not missed a beat. Other management runs the day-to-day operations of SHOO, but Steve is considered the essence of the company's success.

SHOO does not own any factories, as it outsources its production to China and other countries. Hence, it has an advantage of operational leverage. One reason for SHOO's success is the ability of its designer Steve to see a fashion trend and have a test sample in the store, in less than two months, sometimes even sooner. Thus, he can then expand its release into other stores if the reception is good and this quick turnaround gives the company a marketing advantage. On SHOO's Web site, one can see the various actresses, models, and personalities who have bought SHOO shoes by the type and in what SHOO store location, indicating the brand's appeal.

The stock has been volatile but has compiled a good record (or earnings growth) and has generated good amounts of cash that have been used to buy back stock and pay out a special dividend.

The top chart in Figure 17.1 represents SHOO's long-term stock activity through December 2009. As we can see, the stock had a good rise from the early days of its public trading history of a few dollars, to around 30 by 2009. I have ended the chart at this period to illustrate an actual class case around that timeline. In actuality, the stock subsequently split 3 for 2 and the chart should be adjusted for a price around 17 and not the shown price of 26. By the end of October , 2011 the stock went even higher, topping 37 on a split-adjusted basis. This would substantially

FIGURE 17.1 Steve Madden Limited Stock, NASDAQ

Source: Used by permission of Stockcharts.com

increase the returns discussed below. There were volatile periods which gave opportunities to take advantage of valuation analysis by buying low and selling high. Still, if we just bought near the IPO period of 3 and then held to the 30 level about 15 years later, we would have obtained a 16.6 percent annual compounded return. Recall our discussion on the stock split and the comments on the updated and higher stock price.

Now, using a simple comparison (unadjusted for risk and the appropriate index of small-cap stocks), we can eyeball performance against the usual benchmark of the S&P 500 Index and see that it would pay to buy low and sell high for the years in the 1990s, as the stock basically tracked the index (see bottom chart in Figure 17.1.) Later, it either greatly outperformed or underperformed in shorter periods, but overall well outperformed. The same could be said for the small-cap index, the Russell 2000 Index (see middle chart in Figure 17.1). So buy-and-hold investors did well, but mostly on the performance of the latter years. Those who did good valuation should have done better by taking advantage of overvaluations and undervaluations to trade the stock. Note the market plunge in the post-2000 Internet bubble fallout; the stock went from around 9 in 2000 to a little over 2 about six months later, and then a year later the stock skyrocketed to over 8.

So, opportunistic trading on valuation could certainly improve the performance of a portfolio manager. We can use my Fusion system for the valuation approach.

This is a stock study I use in my Equity Portfolio class at NYIF.[2] I took some liberties to make an estimate for certain financial measures as though we had the 2009 annual report, even though the actual 2009 financials would not be reported till early 2010, I analyzed this stock at the end of November 2009. Using a proposed scoring system, we shall determine a rating, but my actual and proprietary system may differ from that illustrated for confidentiality reasons.

For this 2009 base (year 0), I made cash flow projections going forward. I used the price of $37 as a rounded number for analysis purposes. Note that this was before a 3:2 split, as I did not have the news of the split at that time. (Since the chart I showed was pre-split, the $37 was really $24.67.)

Going back to the fundamentals, we can review the stock price of late November 2009, compared to preliminary estimates for financial data of 12/31/09 as:

$$P/B \; = \; \$37/ \, \$14.85 = 2.5\times$$
$$\text{P/E ratio (forward year)} \; = \; \$37/ \, \$49.95 \, M/18.1M = 13.4\times$$
$$\text{Stock price/equity value}^3 \; = \; \$37 \, / \, \$41.15 = 0.9\times$$
$$\text{S.T. return (one year out)} \; = \; 11.2\%$$

So now, going to our scoring system, we can translate the ratios to ratings as follows. (See Table 17.1.) Price-to-book is 2.5x, so that is a 3, as it is between a P/B of 2.0x to 2.5x. (We can interpolate or just

TABLE 17.1 Category, Weight, and Rating

Category	Weight %	Rating				
		1	2	3	4	5
S.T. RETURN	35	>30	>10	>0	−10	<−20
PRICE/BOOK	10	<1.5	<2	<2.5	<3	>3
N4QsP/E	25	<1.25	<1.5	<1.75	<2	>2
PRICE/ SELF F.	10	<1	<1.5	<2	<2.5	>2.5
TECHNICAL	20	1	2	3	4	5

round to the nearest number or use the lower number, unless a barrier is breached.)

P/E was 13.4×, and this compares to an expected P/E on the S&P 500 Index of 14.1 times forward earnings (index of 1085/$77 earnings). So the relative P/E was 13.4/14.1 or 0.95. This is below 1.25, thus the rating is a 1.

The short-term return is 11.2 percent and this scores a 2. (Generally, small-cap stocks return 12 percent per annum over a long period of time, so this thought goes into my rating.)

The price-to-cash flow was 0.9×; it is less than 1.0× and gets a 1 rating.

For the technical rating, we shall use the actual one derived in Figure 4.20. We shall discuss the technicals later in this chapter.

I chose the P/B, P/E ratios because they were well tested in academic literature for determining excessive returns. Short-term returns are not well tested, as the management tends to have the better estimates. Thus, we need a good analyst to have confidence in using this measure. The cash flow portion is, to some extent, the same concept as the earnings estimate.

So putting all factors together:

$$\text{P/B rating times weight} = 3.0 \times 0.10 = 0.30$$
$$\text{P/E rating times weight} = 1.0 \times 0.25 = 0.25$$
$$\text{ST rating times weight} = 2.0 \times 0.35 = 0.70$$
$$\text{Price/CF rating times weight} = 1.0 \times 0.10 = 0.10$$
$$\text{Technical rating times weight} = 2.35 \times 0.20 = 0.47$$
$$\text{Total Rating 1.00} = 1.82$$

So referring to Table 17.2, a rating of 1.82 results in a Buy/Hold decision. Once again, a 1 is the best rating, or a Buy, and 5 is the worst rating, or a Sell. The investment decision table is shown in Table 17.2.

If the rating is below 1.5, then the stock is a Buy and we overweight the stock in the portfolio. Thus, if a normal weight is 3 percent, we may weigh the stock up to 5 percent (as beyond may take on too much specific risk). If the rating is 1.5 or greater but less than 2.25, we can rate the stock as Buy/Hold. Then we could buy the stock, overweight a bit, but not as much as a Buy. Thus, if 3 percent is a normal weight, we may place say 3.5 percent to 4.0 percent.

The ranges can be equal in size of the spread or based more on a normal distribution. Note that a Buy is 1.5 points, and a Buy/Hold is 0.75 points in terms of range; a hold is 1.5, but then a Sell/Hold is 0.50 points and a Sell is over 0.50 points. Thus, our decision table appears to follow a near normal distribution type. Thus, the bulk of the rating hovers around neutral. Only when it exceeds this normal range (say 2.25 or greater, but less than 3.75) do we get various intense Buy and Sell decisions.

Thus, 3.75 or greater, but less than 4.25, is a Sell/Hold and 4.25 or greater is a Sell rating. The sell decisions mean we would sell some or all of our position in the stock. If the stock is not in the portfolio, the stock would not be purchased. So the range itself should be backtested to see how sensitive we want the investment decision. (Note that if the stocks keep coming up neutral, we should index, as there would

TABLE 17.2 Rating and Points

RATING	POINTS
BUY	<1.5
B/H	1.50–2.25
HOLD	2.25–3.75
S/H	3.75–4.25
SELL	>4.25

be no value added to the portfolio by adding stocks that don't have a buy rating).

Using Modern Portfolio Theory

We can optimize our portfolio by using Modern Portfolio Theory (MPT). However, portfolio theory only works if the assumptions are correct on each stock's expected return, standard deviation, and correlation to the index.

MPT was developed in the 1950s and 1960s by leading scholars of Markowitz and Sharpe and was designed to show the optimum construction of a portfolio of assets, such as stocks. By estimating their returns, standard deviations, and correlations among each other, we can then weight them properly in a portfolio to achieve the highest risk-adjusted returns, on a measure such as the Sharpe. We can then do "what ifs" by eliminating one stock and adding another to see if the Sharpe increases or decreases. If it increases, then the stock is desirable and we would substitute it for the other.

MPT follows some basic assumptions such as normal distribution of the standard deviations and investors having common time horizons, among others. The portfolio return is simply a weighted average of all the securities. (This is similar to your grade in school, where the final grade was the weighted average of the term paper, mid-term, quizzes, and final exam. Usually, the final exam carried more weight than a quiz.)

In a two-asset portfolio or a portfolio having only two stocks or an index and a stock, the math is rather complex, but still basic; for more than two assets, we start to use more complex calculations of matrix algebra. This is rather easy to do in Excel; however, it is difficult to correctly estimate each asset's return, standard deviation, and correlation with all of the other assets.

$$E\left(R_{port}\right) = w_1 E\left(R_1\right) + w_2 E\left(R_2\right)$$

$$\sigma_{port} = \sqrt{w_1^2 \sigma_1^2 + w_2^2 \sigma_2^2 + 2 w_1 w_2 \, \mathrm{cov}_{12}}$$

$$\sigma_{port} = \sqrt{w_1^2 \sigma_1^2 + w_2^2 \sigma_2^2 + 2 w_1 w_2 r_{12} \sigma_1 \sigma_2}$$

where:

$$
\begin{aligned}
E(R_1), E(R_2) &= \text{Expected rate of return of assets 1 and 2} \\
w_1, w_2 &= \text{Portfolio weight of assets 1 and 2} \\
\sigma_1, \sigma_2 &= \text{Standard deviation of assets 1 and 2} \\
\text{cov}_{12} &= \text{Covariance between assets 1 and 2} \\
r_{12} &= \text{Correlation between assets 1 and 2}
\end{aligned}
$$

The equation shows the mathematical method of getting the portfolio return and risk (standard deviation) of two assets. Note: The standard deviation formula is shown *both* with covariance and correlation.

We see that returns are weighted averages. The standard deviation is also the same, but we add the effect of its correlation to another asset in a two-asset portfolio. So if they dance together, we do not get the same benefit as if they danced in opposite directions (negative correlation).

As an example, let's assume an investor, in an effort to meet investment objectives, can choose between two assets or securities: GEGC, a stock, and the S&P 500 Index. See Table 17.3. What is the best risk/reward blend? What is the best blend given return and risk constraints of the investor? This example will also introduce some risk measures.

The risk/return/correlation profile is seen in Figure 17.3.

The Efficient Frontier (created from our prior return/risk formulas) is almost linear due to the high correlation between GEGC and the S&P 500, where GEGC is a dummy name for a proposed stock. The highest Sharpe ratio (reward-to-variability) of 1.30544 shows the optimal portfolio at about 20 percent allocation to GEGC and 80 percent to the S&P 500 Index. It shows the best trade-off of accepting higher

TABLE 17.3 Asset Allocation Analysis: Risk and Return

	Expected Return	Standard Deviation	Corr. Coeff s, b	Covariance
GEGC-Sec#1	0.1687	0.138	0.71	0.0078384
SP 500-Sec#2	0.1135	0.08		
T-Bill	0.0125	0		

FIGURE 17.2 GEGC and SP 500 Opportunity Set

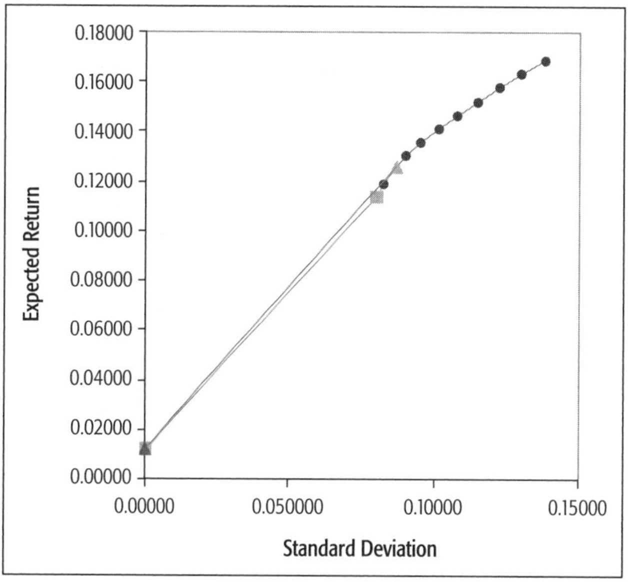

returns with higher risk. The optimal portfolio has a return of 12.5 percent and a standard deviation of 8.6 percent from the schedule shown in Table 17.4.

If we had both securities and all was the same Buy, they correlated not 0.71, but by –0.5, we would have a better Sharpe.

Note that the Efficient Frontier forms a boomerang shape due to the less positive and even negative correlation between GEGC and the S&P 500 in Figure 17.3.

The Sharpe ratio shows the optimal portfolio at about 40 percent allocation to GEGC and 60 percent to the S&P 500 Index. It is now higher with a reading of 2.36804 as compared to the prior example of 1.30544. Note that the optimal portfolio now has a return of 13.6 percent and a standard deviation of 5.2 percent, compared with the original return of 12.5 percent and a standard deviation of 8.6 percent. So, the investor picked up more risk-adjusted return. Thus, the second investment is more favorable.

TABLE 17.4 Returns, Standard Deviations, and Reward to Variability Results

(A):

Weight Security 1	Weight Security 2	Expected Return	Standard Deviation	Reward to Variability
1	0	0.16870	0.13800	1.13188
0.9	0.1	0.16318	0.12040	1.25150
0.8	0.2	0.15766	0.10333	1.40478
0.7	0.3	0.15214	0.08712	1.60292
0.6	0.4	0.14662	0.07232	1.85453
0.5	0.5	0.14110	0.06001	2.14304
0.4	0.6	0.13558	0.05198	2.36804
0.3	0.7	0.13006	0.05031	2.33650
0.2	0.8	0.12454	0.05560	2.01511
0.1	0.9	0.11902	0.06619	1.60936
0	1	0.11350	0.08000	1.26250

(B):

Weight Security 1	Weight Security 2	Expected Return	Standard Deviation	Reward to Variability
1	0	0.16870	0.13800	1.13188
0.9	0.1	0.16318	0.13000	1.15906
0.8	0.2	0.15766	0.12228	1.18711
0.7	0.3	0.15214	0.11489	1.21542
0.6	0.4	0.14662	0.10790	1.24301
0.5	0.5	0.14110	0.10139	1.26835
0.4	0.6	0.13558	0.09546	1.28927
0.3	0.7	0.13006	0.09023	1.30284
0.2	0.8	0.12454	0.08583	1.30544
0.1	0.9	0.11902	0.08237	1.29314
0	1	0.11350	0.08000	1.26250

FIGURE 17.3 GEGC and S&P 500 Opportunity Set (2)

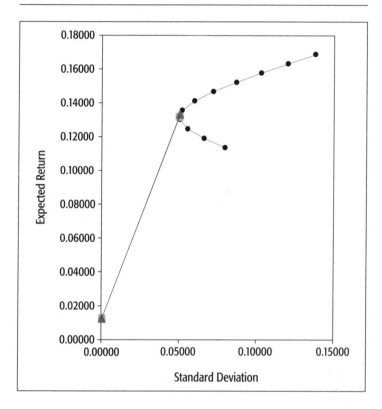

So, in a Fusion process we can start to make decisions on which stocks to add to the portfolio and the weights for those stocks. We may be influenced by past results when we input expected returns, standard deviations, and correlations—yet we must be aware that the past may not continue. A large change in these inputs will certainly mess up the results.

Critics of MPT point out that if the standard deviation is not symmetrical or is skewed, then the results can lose their effectiveness in determining a portfolio. Now skewed results may mean that behavioral bias shows more fear on the downside, for example, or returns end up more on the left tail of a distribution, as shown in Figure 17.4.

With greater use of leverage, returns can then be more sensitive to the left tail, and thus we get stress tests for the left tail. Even if there is small chance of a loss, the loss would be so large it wipes us nearly out. Hence, more conservative utility curve investors would shun these investments.

FIGURE 17.4 Skewed Standard Deviation

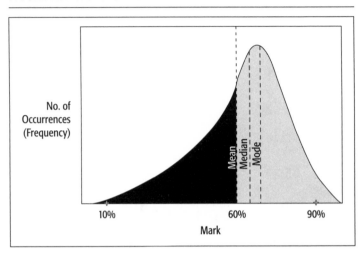

No. of Occurrences (Frequency)

Mean Median Mode

10%   60%   90%

Mark

These investments could be some of the toxic mortgages and hedge funds that had high leverage.

Let's return to our SHOO stock. The financials from the 10-K that was issued in early 2010. Again, I made some estimates in my cash flow of the final earnings and book values, but the data is fairly close to the actual results at year end. So my numbers may differ from 2009 a bit. For example, I used $500 million for estimated sales for 2009 or my Base 0 Year, but the actual sales were $503 million. I estimated $45 in Net Income, but it did better than expected and ended the year with $50.1 million. SHOO has no real debt, but I included a hypothetical amount of $10 million so my students could see how to calculate a WACC. (For simplicity, I have not calculated a new WACC each year nor adjusted the beta for expected levels of debt.)

SHOO spent over $7 million on advertising, but this is rather low relative to sales of $500 million. We must accept its brand-image strength; if that erodes then we can make the case that the cash flows are overstated. SHOO would then have to reposition its brand. This may entail advertising expenses well over the 1.5 percent of sales. In that case, we would question management's advertising budget and plans, and so downgrade any actual cash flow number if we feel the advertising is too low. Recall our comments on economic accounting. The data in Table 17.5 has been derived from our audited Consolidated Financial Statements.

TABLE 17.5 Income Statement Data, Year Ended December 31 (in thousands except per share data)

	2009	2008	2007	2006	2005
Net sales	$503,550	$457,046	$431,050	$475,163	$375,786
Cost of sales	287,361	270,222	257,646	276,734	236,631
Gross profit	216,189	186,824	173,404	198,429	139,155
Commissions and licensing fee income—net	19,928	14,294	18,351	14,246	7,119
Operating expenses	(157,149)	(156,212)	(138,841)	(134,377)	(114,185)
Impairment of goodwill	–	–	–	–	(519)
Income from operations	78,968	44,906	52,914	78,298	31,570
Interest income	2,096	2,620	3,876	3,703	2,554
Interest expense	(93)	(207)	(65)	(100)	(164)
Loss on sale of marketable securities	(182)	(1,013)	(589)	(967)	(500)
Income before provision for income taxes	80,789	46,306	56,136	80,934	33,460
Provision for income taxes	30,682	18,330	20,446	34,684	14,260
Net income	$50,107	$27,976	$35,690	$46,250	$19,200
Basic income per share	$2.78	$1.53	$1.73	$2.21	$0.95
Diluted income per share	$2.73	$1.51	$1.68	$2.09	$0.92
Basic weighted average shares of common stock	18,045	18,325	20,647	20,906	20,112
Effect of potential shares of common stock from exercise of options	278	194	645	1,195	806
Diluted weighted average shares of common stock outstanding	18,323	18,519	21,292	22,101	20,918
Dividends paid per share of common stock	$0.00	$0.00	$0.00	$1.00	$0.67

	BALANCE SHEET DATA (At December 31)				
	2009	**2008**	**2007**	**2006**	**2005**
Total assets	$326,859	$284,693	$266,521	$251,392	$211,728
Working capital	139,007	122,086	121,138	151,711	114,066
Noncurrent liabilities	6,710	5,801	3,470	3,136	2,757
Stockholders' equity	$267,787	$206,242	$215,334	$211,924	$182,065

TABLE 17.6 Technical Rating Decision Table

	1 is Bullish, 5 Bearish		
	Rating	Weight	Result
MA	1	0.35	0.35
Support/Resistance	2	0.15	0.3
MACD	4	0.1	0.4
OBV	3	0.2	0.6
Market Relative	4	0.1	0.4
Fibonacci	3	0.1	0.3
Sum		1.00	2.35

2.35 is BUY/HOLD RATING
BUY/HOLD STOCK SHOO

The SHOO chart looked like Figure 17.5 on November 27, 2009 (remember pre-split of 3:2), as we did not have split chart yet. We have to select and annotate factors to determine the technical rating. Figure 17.6 is the annotated chart that we can use to do so. The technical rating is based on the decision in Table 17.6.

So how did we get a Buy/Hold rating on SHOO? The largest weight is on the moving averages, which have a 35 percent weight. The stock is still above the 200-day MA, with a Golden Cross. The 50-day MA is still above the 200-day MA. This would be more important for long-term hold-

FIGURE 17.5 SHOO, November 27, 2009

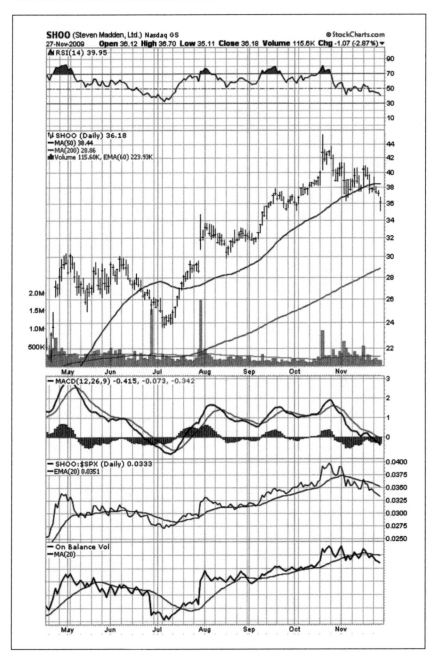

Source: Used by permission of Stockcharts.com

FIGURE 17.6 SHOO, November 27, 2009 (Annotated)

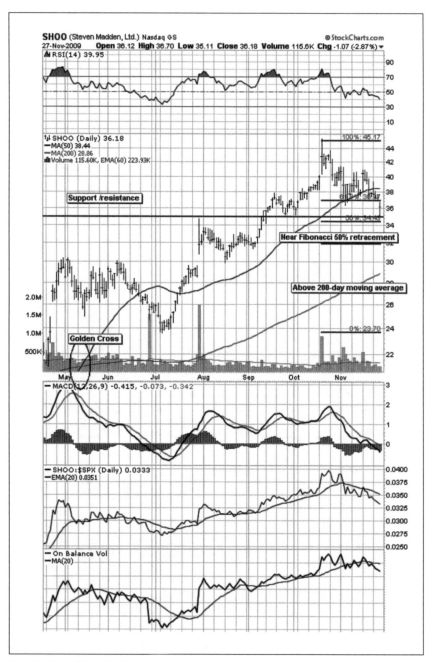

Source: Used by permission of Stockcharts.com

ers than for the short-term holders who may place more weight on other measures like MACD, which is negative. (Note: stocks may appear attractive for long-term holders but unattractive for traders.)

The market relative shows the stock is performing negatively in relation to the S&P 500 Index. It has turned into a downtrend but also broke support levels of October and November. So, Market Relative gets a 4 rating.

OBV (volume indicator) is about neutral, as it is trending sideways and still holding above resistance levels of September and October. OBV therefore gets a 3 rating.

The Fibonacci retracement is at a crucial support near the 50 percent level. At this level, there is support from the prior resistance price of 35 of August and the more recent support levels of 35 of September and October. This indicates a good time to buy, as the stock got overextended to 45 because it got too far above its 200-day MA. But now it has pulled back and is near interesting support areas and ready to be bought. So support/resistance gets a 2 rating. The Fibonacci gets a 3, as the 62 percent support did not hold near the 37 level. (This is somewhat disappointing.)

We then take a weighted average of the technical factors and get 2.35. Actually 2.35 is a NEUTRAL rating but close to the cut-off point. Based on our discussions of trading, because SHOO is not that liquid we can then treat it as Buy/Hold and nibble with some algo buys. Because 2.35 is closer to 2, we rate it Buy/Hold. We can also do numerical rounding and treat it as a 2.

Cash Flow Ratings

Going back to fundamentals, let's take a more thorough look of the cash flow rating. (We will use a discounted cash flow for our cash flow analysis.)

A simple and brief discounted cash flow analysis is shown in Table 17.7. Sales are summarized together, but an analyst would break down sales into various categories like product lines, licensing fees, and sales channels. We need to make estimates on major inputs like margins, growth rates, working capital needs, and CAPX. I used a terminal value based on earnings,

TABLE 17.7 Cash Flow Analysis

VALUATION

COMPANY INPUTS			YR 0	%growth 1	YR 1	%growth	YR2	TV YR2
Stock Price	37							
Shares O/S	18.1		SALES	500.0	0.08	540	0.11	599.4	
	Yr1	Yr2	NI %	0.09		0.0925		0.1	
Growth	0.08	0.11	Net Income	45		49.95		59.94	
NI %	0.0925	0.1							
			"+ NCC	10		10		11	
MV debt	10		"+ INT(1-T)	0.1		0.2		0.2	
MV equity	669.7		Chng WC	−8		−12		−15	
Beta	1.3		"−CAPX	−12		−10		−15	
K debt (pre-tax)	0.06		FCF (F)	35.1		38.15		41.14	839.16
Ke CAPM	0.1065		PV CF			34.51		720.29	
Tax Rate	0.35								
Excess Cash	0		Sum of PV FCF	754.80					
Non-Oper	0		add Excess Cash	0					
			add Non-Oper	0					
WACC	0.105507		ENTERPRISE VALUE	754.80					

MARKET INPUTS

Rf Rate	0.035		
EMR	0.055	less Debt	−10
		EQUITY VALUE (EV)	744.80
		EV per share	**41.15**
		Expected Return % =	11.2

CALCULATIONS

	Rf+	Beta (EMR)	
Ke CAPM =	**0.1065**	0.035	0.0715

		MVd $(MVd+MVe) \times$	Kd(1-t)	MVe/ $MVd+MVe) \times$	Ke
WACC=	0.105507	0.015	0.039	0.985	0.1065

TV =	p/e x	NI
839.16	14	59.94

FIGURE 17.7 SHOO, April 16, 2010

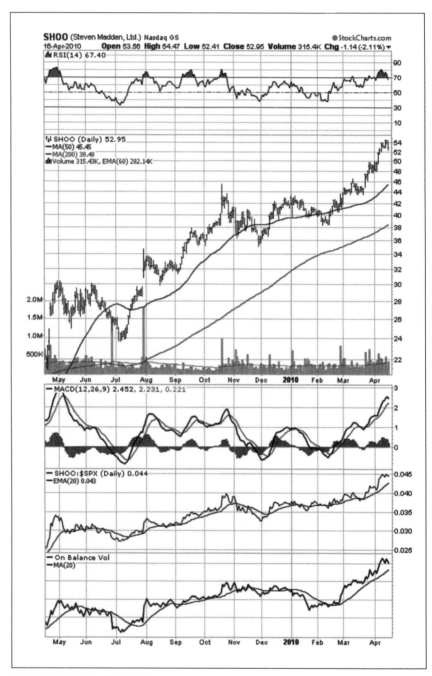

but some might have used EBITDA or a combination of both. We must also get the cost of capital (WACC) in order to discount the cash flows that need to be adjusted.

Based on this, we see a buy, as the expected return is 11.2 percent. Now one can also do comparable analysis to see how this compares to similar companies by using databases of Value Line. Again, one must be aware that not all databases adjust numbers on an economic basis to one's taste.

Post Mortem—The Results Were Good

Figure 17.7 is the SHOO stock as it unfolded through mid-April 2010. It would soon split 3:2. As you can see, the stock went up even more than the estimate. The Buy/Hold signal was correct, but rather conservative. The stock went from 36.18 to 52.95, or an increase of 46.4 percent.

So now what? Well, we can see the stock is already up considerably, even before the one-year anniversary in November 2010. Thus, we would run another Fusion analysis to see if the stock is still attractive.

Realize that by now there would be updated fundamentals and technicals, and so the inputs may change as well as their corresponding ratings. In general, I would run these evaluations each week on all the stocks in the portfolio. This can be highly automated by getting data feeds and even programming technical rules, but it may get expensive in terms of obtaining real-time data and using the computational power. Instead, we may wish to do reasonable shortcuts on the data in order to keep costs down. The decisions on all the stocks could then be done 100 percent automatically, with the stock being bought and sold by the computer (within certain dollar limits). Or we can use some judgment where only, say, 75 percent of the decision is done by computer. Once again, will emotions cause second-guessing of the results?

In addition, we must realize that not all data is worth massaging. Overanalyzing too much data is useless and may cause the manager to miss the basic thrust of the stock that can be influenced by just a few factors. Usually, correctly estimating sales is the key item that may move the stock. As the news got better, it would be hard to buy stock. Thus, the initial decision to a liquidity factor for the stock paid off.

Paralysis by Analysis

Too much data leads to what is called "paralysis by analysis." Seasoned analysts should be able to make this decision. Junior analysts may stay late hours analyzing all kinds of data that really don't mean much. I recall one junior analyst who was staying late and studying how money transfers are made, so I asked why this is important for a manufacturer. The analyst said by knowing how money clears the banks, one can perhaps do a better accounts receivable flow and thus working capital. In reality, time would have been better spent analyzing the future cost of materials. A portfolio manager or senior analyst must focus junior analysts. Some will not even hire them, as it takes too much time for this hand-holding, and prefer only to hire seasoned veterans. However, veterans can be set in their ways and lose that spark of creativity. Life is not easy!

Should the investor step back and ascertain if fundamental criteria are being clouded by a bubble and therefore fundamental weights be lowered? This was a criticism in 1999 when the Internet bubble caused valuations on factors like P/E to rise to lofty levels. An investor may then view financial factors as being rather stretched and of no particular usefulness, and he may be attracted to the cheaper stock in a forest of highly overpriced stocks. Yet the cheaper stock may be overpriced as well, even if it is not as overpriced as the forest. Therefore, a tech stock may have a P/E of only 30, even as the market is 40 and tech stocks are priced even higher. One could then say the fundamental weight should be lowered from 80 percent to only 30 percent, as the technical factors seem to be better indicators.

This is a possible solution to this predicament, but I am not in favor of doing this maneuver. First, this implies that we already know that the mark is high. Yes, it is higher than before, but it can go much higher and vice versa. It is better to keep a consistent discipline and stay with the 80/20 ratio or some ratio that has generally worked. If we are using adequate sensitivity on the filters, the technicals will allow some extra rise in expensive stocks and allow some bottom-fishing for declining stocks. We may not get into the bottom or out at the top, but this should not concern the investor, as over time, an alpha will be produced and beat the competition. Trying to make exact top/bottom strategies can jeopardize this, as we may cash out too soon and not be invested in a rising market.

This recalls behavioral issues with quant investing. For example, will the Prospect Theory (exaggerating true probabilities of events) cloud the eventual quant results? For example, per Montier, "they overestimate the small probability that the price of the underlying stock crosses the strike price [in an option], and underestimate the high probability that the price of the underlying stock stays on the same side of the strike price." Should one override the quant results? Changing the 80/20 mix of fundamental/technical or some other ratio could very well mean doing the Prospect Theory.

We could combine an effective use of derivative valuations with technical tools.

For example, the Head and Shoulders measurement objective may lead to an effective method of protecting losses with the use of derivatives. The trade-off of the cost of derivatives and the implementation of the technical decision can be done by using the technical price objectives and comparing them to the cost of the derivatives. So while derivatives may allow a rather low cost of fine-tuning a portfolio, it could very well lead to another form of the Prospect Theory. For example, let's say the technicals state the stock or portfolio is overpriced but the fundamentals still show good values. This most likely occurs near tops, as the portfolio team of analysts would feel positive about their stocks and mark them higher (behavioral analysis again). Then we may be tempted to increase the weight on the technicals, or we might be more bullish and would lower the weight of the technicals. This is not wise, as we get into market timing and the Prospect Theory. So why bother with quant?

We might then start to buy puts on the stock or portfolio and may seek a delta nearer to 1 to get better hedged on the downside. In effect, this is the same as mixing the technical/fundamental ratios. While the puts may be relatively low in cost to the portfolio, the cost can get quite large if we keep doing this on a regular basis over time. As we keep entering into the put contracts, the insurance costs start to add up. These costs are then compared to the actual up and down moves of the portfolio and therefore either eat into opportunity gains or provide needless insurance costs when the market goes in the opposite direction. We can see that constantly changing the mix can create whipsaws that detract from returns, and so can constantly using a derivatives strategy. It is better to use sensitive filters that provide a Buy and Sell and then occasionally use derivatives to enhance your portfolio's growth.

At this point, we are ready to do a Fusion screen that may search for new ideas instead of only valuing existing holdings in the portfolio. The method is the same, but there may be looser filters in order to get more ideas that can then be also rejected on qualitative features. The goal will be to get a promising list of investments that can generate risk-adjusted excess returns and beat indexing approaches. Again, one will try to create a diversified portfolio of say, 35 stocks, and thus the Fusion process should start to create a good batting average as much noise cancels out. The thrust of the discipline should be the basis of the expected portfolio alpha.

18

FUSION DEMONSTRATION FOR NEW IDEAS AND NECESSARY INVESTMENT KNOWLEDGE

Thus far we have discussed how to use the Fusion process on a current portfolio. We now will look at the Fusion approach from the perspective of selecting investment opportunities. Where do we begin? A Fusion filter or screen is a good start. We can also read an article on a company in a business publication, go to a stock conference, or even get a tip (legal) from a relative. We can then run these ideas through the Fusion process, using filter screens, both technical and fundamental. I personally run these screens on a weekly basis. Next, we evaluate the screens on technical indicators and incorporate the behavioral issues that are important. As we did with a current portfolio, we now create a scoring system in order to generate a list of buy and sell opportunities. It is important to then determine and implement an appropriate trading system and evaluate the potential use of derivatives. Then, we revalue the process for trade-offs on speed, detail, and cost. From various databases, we can start a very simple screening process.

Assume we are long-term investors. We start with fundamentals and use the weights seen in our earlier process, where technicals were 20 percent of the final score. (Note: A short-term trader will most likely start with technicals and then weight them well over 50 percent of the total score.) Fundamentally, we can select a popular approach like Growth at a Reasonable Price (GARP) in small-cap stocks. Given the past good record and the opportunities for profit, small-cap stocks may then be a destination center for the investor. Our screen may be as follows:

- Stocks under $1 billion market caps
- Operating earnings growth for the past three years of at least 10 percent
- P/E under 22 (or, say, no more than 1.25 × the SP 500 P/E)
- P/B under 3.5x
- Debt/capitalization under 50 percent
- ROE of 15 percent or more in the past year

Traders may seek stocks that are approaching reporting earnings dates, have high momentum in earnings growth, and are tied to news events.

TABLE 18.1 Morningstar Screen

5162		Market Capitalization (mil $) < = 1000)
2399	**and**	(Price/Earnings (Raito – Current < = 22)
1955	**and**	(Op Income % Growth Year 1/Year 2 > = 15)
2213	**and**	(Op Income % Growth Year 2/Year 3 > = 10)
1627	**and**	(Return on Equity % – Trailing 12 Months > = 15)
4415	**and**	(Price/Book Ratio – Current < = 3.5)
2910	**and**	(Relative Strength vs. S&P 500 – 3 Months > = 0)

Source: Morningstar

Table 18.1 is a screen from Morningstar.[1] The fundamental criteria will help us focus on a select group of 34 stocks (from over a beginning number of more than 5000). The column on the left indicates the number of stocks that pass each screening filter.

Table 18.2 is a partial list of the first few stock names (in alphabetical order). We can click on name to get more detailed information. Technically, we can select the following measures, which should show good trends, divergences, and so on.

TABLE 18.2 Morningstar Screen–Stocks

Stock Name	Morningstar Analyst Report	Morningstar Rating	Sector	Industry	Market Cap ($ mil)	Divided Yield %
Adams Resources & Energy	..	..	⬤ Energy	Oil/Gas	165	0.95
Alis-Chalmers Energy	..	..	▤ Business Svc	Security Svcs.	291	0
American Physicians Service Gr	..	..	💲 Financial Svc	Insurance (Property)	45	0
Avatar Holdings Barrett	..	..	💲 Financial Svc	Real Estate	522	0
Business Service	..	..	▤ Business Svc	Business Support	267	0

Source: Morningstar

- Moving average, 50-day and 200-day features
- Relative strength outperformance
- OBV measures
- MACD and RSI

Note that traders may seek stocks in climaxes, use oscillators like Fast Stochastics, seek channel trading, and/or apply measurement rules to patterns. Behaviorally, trading patterns of leading holders should be analyzed if event-driven strategies are used. If a trader is bottom fishing he may select stocks that are down 50 percent from 12 month highs. If seeking a short, one may select any stock that has exceeded its 50 day MA by 50 percent and has negative RSI divergence.

FIGURE 18.1 Avatar Holdings, November 2005 to October 2006

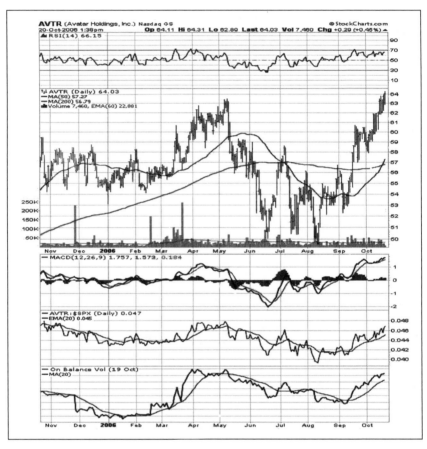

Source: Used by permission of Stockcharts.com

We can now take a name from the fundamental screen and create a stock chart. Figure 18.1 is a chart for Avatar Holdings. (Note that certain technical factors have already been selected and thus programmed by the stock manager.) Some positive features of Avatar are that it is trading above its 200-day moving average, taking out its prior May resistance and a rising OBV. As a result, Avatar would be a likely candidate for further analysis, as both fundamental and technical screens appear positive.

We then decide if Avatar is to be bought only on the quant factors. For example, Avatar is a real estate company, and so the accounting may

TABLE 18.3 Top Institutional Owners of Avatar

Holder	Shares	% Out	Value	Reported
Third Avenue Management, LLC	735,990	8.98	$41,929,350	30-Jun-06
Dimensional Fund Advisors INC.	408,038	4.98	$23,245,924	30-Jun-06
Sterling Capital Management Company	277,365	3.39	$15,801,484	30-Jun-06
Barclays Global Investors UK Holdings Ltd.	249,567	3.05	$14,217,831	30-Jun-06
Private Capital Management, INC.	1,861,680	22.72	$106,059,909	30-Jun-06
AXA	207,163	2.53	$11,802,076	30-Jun-06
First Manhattan Company	190,093	2.32	$11,226,892	30-Sep-06
Advisory Research, INC.	1,386,094	16.92	$78,965,775	30-Jun-06
Vanguard Group, INC. (THE)	121,885	1.49	$6,943,788	30-Jun-06
Wellington Management Company, LLP	96,996	1.18	$5,524,153	30-Jun-06

Source: Yahoo! Finance.

have to be adjusted to better reflect the industry. We may also add subjective judgments, such as the quality of management. Liquidity considerations would also be important. Pure quants may either ignore this or translate this into a quant screen. Behavioral factors can be considered. We may wish to know the answers to questions such as: Who are the large stockholders? Is it smart or dumb money? Will they be long-term holders or traders following behavioral movement? (All in all, establishing and interpreting quant factors can be both a science and an art.)

The top institutional holders of Avatar are shown in Table 18.3. We may also want to get top mutual fund holders. They are often close to being the same, as funds manage money for both institutions and mutual funds. The Avatar fund holders appear to be either long-term value investors or index funds, such as the Dimensional Fund advisors. We can get this data from Vickers or Yahoo. In addition, we can scan the recent SEC reports to determine the insider's trades. We can then research the records of the active managers to determine if the holders are dumb or smart money.

Since fundamentals and technicals never deal with certainties but probabilities, we should construct a diversified portfolio of about 35 stocks covering several industries. We should again review some of our aforementioned concepts of trading in order to keep transaction costs low.

Traders will probably be operating with leveraged positions. Therefore, betting the bank on two or three stocks is not prudent, especially as transaction costs can be high. The resulting portfolio should be measured against appropriate benchmarks, using proper performance reporting. Risk measures, such as Sharpe, need to be discussed.

You may wonder when to do these screens. Behaviorally, one may only seek to invest in new ideas if we are bullish. Recall that near market tops everybody has a stock pick. At bottoms, investors may be too tired, wiped out, or scared to search for new ideas. Thus, running screens in good times runs the risk of buying at the top.

A regular running of the stock prospect screen is required, and it should be followed closely by investors. In this way, investors are more likely to buy and sell at or near opportune times. This occurs when securities are truly valued incorrectly and not when we "feel" they are valued incorrectly.

Market outperformance is not an easy process. We have already discussed the efficiencies of the market. Indexing should be seriously considered by both novices and professionals who are too "tired" to do an investment discipline. Active management increases the risk that the portfolio will likely underperform. Thus, the outcome is worse and at the same time more costly when fees are calculated.

Still, there are those who have skill and do perform. We can assume that those with better knowledge will have an advantage over the naïve investor. Also, as shown in this book, a disciplined approach will also prove beneficial.

Hopefully, Fusion analysis will provide an edge in achieving outperformance.

Knowledge Base and Education

How does one capture this knowledge? The knowledge falls into two parts: information and use. In other words, one must get the knowledge and then have the skill and savvy to exploit it. Since investing is an art and science, it is not conducive to the physical sciences where there are clear end results. For example, H_2O is water. In investing, H_2O can be mud, gold, or water. In other words, one can follow proper procedures in physics and mix the elements and get water. Not so in investing. One may do a DCF and get a valuation and be way off. Thus, when students ask me if the answer they generated is right for a case in corporate finance, I can only answer that the procedure *looks* correct, but only the market gives the final grade. It could be that the data was misinterpreted and other inputs were left out that affected the valuation. In physics we can do experiments many times and get the same result. In investing we get a tendency. That is, it is likely that a low P/E ratio leads to outperformance relative to high P/E stocks, but not always. In fact, the P/E ratio may not be crucial for certain companies. For example, service companies may be affected more by the P/E valuation than banks, which may be affected more by P/B ratios.

One also speculates that future data may not resemble the past history. If it does, then forecasting is easier for valuations, but if not, then the results may be totally different and very surprising. Also, one must account for qualitative factors that initially don't show up in the financials but may down the road, such as brand image changes or environmental costs.

Hunches vs. Valuation Methods

Thus, some would say that stocks should be bought more on concept or hunch. This may not be a bad approach, as correctly predicting changes in lifestyles and technology may be all that one needs to be successful. So, if one makes the case that horseshoes are on the way out because there is a new industry, the automobile, then one may just avoid the losses of horseshoe companies, which may be closing by the droves, and then feast on the new auto companies that are starting to earn big profits. Some may say that is the way to play Apple. Stay with this company until it blows up, but as long it is a leader in its products, the stocks will go higher. As mentioned, in the past we saw glory stocks that eventually declined on this concept, such as Xerox and Polaroid. So the old-timer who exercises keen insight and good judgment may then have a good feel for investing.

For some, this approach seems too easy and not useful in terms of buying low and selling high, especially if one is monitored on performance for increasingly short-term periods. One needs a more exact valuation model. Sure, Apple is great, but it may be overpriced and thus you don't get an alpha. That certainly makes sense, but we end up in a chicken-and-egg game of what comes first. Is it the change in earnings, which is due to the changing attitude of the consumers of the stock, or is it just that the P/E is too high? That then means that earnings were either estimated as too low by investors, as the investor mood did not adversely change yet, or if it is still the same, investors got crazy and bid this stock up into the clouds.

So, for the most part, professional investors have valuation models based on the inputs of data. This data is inputted based on subjects such as accounting and corporate finance. Hunches and guesses are not the mainstream approaches of fund investing, or at least they are not advertised as such. One will see some investment discipline described to investors, and this assumes some body of knowledge that must be learned to do this properly.

Formal Training

Where does the investor turn in order to properly learn the science portion of investing, such as the accounting and corporate finance? In other words, can you pick up this information on your own over time, or do you need a formalized method of study? Certainly, the information can be picked up by some over time, but there is also the risk that it may not be. Thus, you may wish to see evidence that the formalized knowledge is known by an analyst before beginning to entrust funds to that person for investing. Funds themselves don't have all day to try out every crackpot who claims that he or she knows how to buy low and sell high, and also they must ensure that they do proper diligence with client money. Therefore, standards are set either officially or informally that make the process more scientific. For example, there may be required passing of exams or getting certain degrees, not to mention regulatory requirements. Also, while no agency or governmental regulations may apply to certain investment requirements, the industry may police itself by requiring some standards.

What we see are two types of union cards into the industry: regulatory and industry standards. Regulatory may include at times passing exams, such as the Series 7 and 63, which deal with trading and soliciting orders. The exams are administered by the Financial Industry Regulatory Authority, or FINRA (formerly the National Association of Securities Dealers). There are other required exams such as Series 86/87, which is the Research Analyst Qualification Examination. It is intended to ensure that research analysts of NYSE and NASDAQ member firms show some basic competency to perform their jobs. It was an exam designed to show that an analyst has some skill and is not just a cheerleader who was prevalent in the Internet bubble. (Cheerleaders were always bullish in order to drum up business but may not have been good analysts.)

The body of knowledge includes business topics such as using economic data and making valuation models. A candidate who has passed both Level I and Level II of the Chartered Financial Analyst (CFA) Examination (discussed below) may request an exemption from Part I (Series 86), the Analysis section of the Research Analyst Qualification Examination. The same applies to passing Levels I and II of the CMT Certification Examination (also discussed) in technical analysis. Other conditions are required, such as being a practicing research analyst. In addition to other regulatory exams, foreign countries may have exam requirements for its investment professionals. Some international investors may also take the U.S. exams.

While general regulatory exams are required, investment firms may decide to be selective and pick the cream of the crop. Here they may recruit investment professionals who have advance degrees and come from the best business schools. Also they may require that their analysts pass the CFA exam as well. For those who wish to learn fundamentals, an MBA and becoming a Chartered Financial Analyst charterholder is desirable in order to gain employment at leading funds and investment firms.

Some MBA programs may have watered down their courses to meet the skills ability of the students, and thus the degree is not that rigorous. More undesirable schools may leave frustrated students in a hole with tuition borrowings not covered by the expected extra income but the choice schools may result in signing bonuses that wipe out the school loans.

Earning the CFA designation is another route to getting good jobs at leading investment firms. Not all firms require this designation, but an increasingly large amount do. Also, in manager searches for investments, there is increasing interest in knowing that the firm has a certain number of CFA charterholders. In addition to a good core of financial subjects, the CFA program places good weight on ethics. It is felt by some clients that the CFA charterholder will adhere to ethics and thus avoid breeches in regulations and ethics. Hence, not having the proper amount or even any CFA charterholders may preclude the firm in a manager search. One question that almost appears on all investment questionnaires is whether the manager adheres to GIPS, the investment performance criteria of the CFA Institute.

The CFA designation is globally recognized and attests to a charterholder's success in a rigorous and comprehensive study program in the field of investment management and research analysis.[2] It was part of a vision of Benjamin Graham in 1942 that led to the creation of the CFA designation. The purpose was to make the investment management process a profession. The first charters were awarded in 1963. In more recent years the number of enrollees have escalated sharply, especially from abroad, and there are now over 100,000 candidates sitting for the CFA exams. There were 87,600 charterholders as of 2008.

Earning the right to use the CFA designation requires the passing of three levels of exams that cover subjects of ethics, quantitative methods, economics, financial reporting and analysis, corporate finance, portfolio management, equity and fixed income analysis, derivatives, and alternative investments. Ethics is usually 10 to 15 percent of the exam in each of the three levels, and is stressed as an advantage of the program. Recent pass rates on the first level of the exam has been around 35-40%. Needless to say, passing all three exams is a good accomplishment.

Is there any value in the CFA designation? If the market is efficient, does it make any difference if one has a CFA charterholder managing one's money? Obviously, there is no guarantee of an alpha as some funds have CFA charterholders and don't get alphas. Some studies imply that CFA charterholders add value. For example, CFA charterholders provide better earnings forecasts than those financial analysts who do not have the charter.[3] Therefore, the implication is that valuation models are more accurate. This could be due to the course training of the CFA program and the ethical requirements that require the analyst to use reasonable care and making a fair representation to clients.

Another study shows that sell-side analysts who are CFA charterholders issue forecasts that are timelier than those of non-charterholders. However, the results for accuracy were shown to be mixed. For a subsample of analysts, charterholders improve their timeliness after they receive their CFA charter. So this supports the effort to get the CFA designation. Also, in smaller firms, clients were more likely to be influenced by the recommendation because it was done with a credentialed person.[4]

For technicians, as mentioned, one could study for the Chartered Market Technician (CMT) designation. The CMT program is administered by the Market Technician Association, which was organized in 1973. It has 3000 members of market analysis professionals in over 70 countries around the globe.[5] About 63 percent of the members are in the United States and the rest are overseas, with Canada, Switzerland, and India having the most members. There are 817 active members with the CMT designation.

The CMT also has three levels of exams and covers a multitude of technical analysis topics. The first level consists of 120 multiple-choice questions to be answered in two hours. The cost is $500 including the test and registration. One must also pay annual dues of $300. Pass rates have been about 70 percent for Level 1 and lower on other levels. However, pass rates have been declining on Level 1 on more recent exams.

Since technical analysis has had resistance in business schools and from investment houses, its growth has been slower than that of the CFA program. However, with greater interest in the subject and behavioral finance, its enrollment has been increasing. In 2009, 700 candidates sat for the exam. While some of the technical practices have been studied in academic journals, to my knowledge, one does not have efficacy studies on the CMT value added that are similar to those in the CFA program. Since there are many users of technical analysis around the world, there is thus definite interest in a formal course of study. Many investment firms request a formal course in technical analysis, and some universities offer courses in technical analysis.

As one can see, the body of knowledge is considerable and not easily mastered. There can be unease in hiring people who have no formal skill set, as some of them are useless in terms of performance. Thus, it is a balancing act where some basics are the standard of the industry and the better firms can choose among the best candidates. If this formalized knowledge is an entry barrier, then many cannot perform in investments, much less consider generating an alpha. Fusion analysis then would require highly trained professionals, as it is unlikely that many can master all this knowledge in a short time with productive results. Thus, again, one should seriously consider investing with indexing approaches and not paying for this activity.

Conclusion

THE FUTURE AND THE GOLDEN BUTTERFLY

Do we need a Fusion approach in forecasting the future? Those who live day to day will not need this book. Those that wish to take their few limited financial resources and capitalize upon them for a better life, will. While Fusion is an investment method, forecasting with an investment method can naturally have good or bad results. Results may be wrong or correct for a while and then reverse. Similar to a basketball game, the score can keep changing and favor one side or the other. Unlike a basketball game, there is no buzzer or end of the game signal. So what do we mean by the future? One week, one year, one decade? The stock market can drop a year from now but rebound sharply over the course of a decade. As we have seen with large-cap stocks in the United States, it can also go down for a decade.

Usually in forecasting, the rule is to forecast price levels but not the date that the price level will be reached—or, conversely, forecast the dates but not the price levels. In this way, one has plenty of time to reach the decision, or investors may have long forgotten what the prediction was in the first place. Thus, one's reputation is intact and not tarnished. Predicting that the market will be up nicely over the coming years is therefore a good way to take advantage of the forecasting rule.

Because the market has unlimited life (or very long if one adopts the inflationary universe), what appears good in the short term may look bad in the longer term, and vice versa. Therefore, prognosticators who may follow the rule of forecasting on price levels and time horizons will probably also generalize caveats. For example, one can say something to the effect that while the market will be up nicely over the coming years, investors should expect some dips along the way. Thus, any market selloff could satisfy one's prediction. In this way, one can be safe in a prediction—though it would be rather useless. For this reason, one cherishes those who make specific significant market calls that are correct. The problem here is that even the best have flubbed at times. In terms of portfolio management, this may not be objectionable, as there would be a batting average that hopefully outperforms the index on a risk-adjusted basis. So even great ballplayers strike out, but they tend to do better than the other players and thus command higher compensation and help create winning teams.

Another way to get around forecasting is to make predictions with the "if" term. For example, if the Fed eases, the market will go up, but if it tightens, it will go down. If I have enough "ifs" and enough ensuing forecasts, I can start predicting some correct eventuality.

There is another method to duck the question that has been used on talking-head TV shows. It is rather humorous when reading the words actually said, but they seem to be a serious forecast if said quickly and with a straight face. (Also helping would be wearing red suspenders, having a Swiss accent, and wearing glasses and smoking a pipe.)

One can make some generalized predictions that mean nothing but look good for quick bursts on these business shows. In this way, a prediction is made but its results are never explained, since it did not predict any real results in the first place. I have list of some of these predictions that I have collected from various business forums, including the statements from past talking heads. (They are for your amusement, but can be used in emergency if cornered to make a prediction at a cocktail party.) Let's begin.

For example, following are some of my favorite gibberish answers to the question: "Where do you think the market is going and what is your investment strategy?"

- "My research has shown that we cannot make new highs unless we break the old highs."
- "The downtrend cannot end unless an uptrend begins."
- "I only concentrate on buying stocks that go up."
- "When gold goes up, it is no longer going down."

- "Rising prices mean only one thing, and this is important to know, the left side of the chart has lower prices than the right side of the chart."

- "Our firm is different in its investment approach. We only pick stocks that are attractive, have good management, and above all, are cheap."

At this point you may now be asking me what my opinions of the future of the market are and whether there is a place for Fusion within the market.

There have been many challenging economic times in our financial history. We have been in over the recent years. However, if past history is a guide, our financial markets can be a time for great opportunity to rebound and make money.

Using the next ten years as a time horizon, I feel that most investors should index their asset allocation and investments. However, if you feel that active management can add value, then I would certainly propose using Fusion analysis, as it combines the best of all investment approaches. It should capitalize on the repeating nature of investment psychology and not be sucked into emotional fallout from fear and greed.

In this book, as a byproduct of Fusion, the case was made that there can be two fundamental trends emerging that investors can benefit from in the coming years: higher inflation and the appeal of small-cap stock investing, especially as an alpha source. I expect inflation rates to at least double the historical long-term rates in developed countries—so, roughly over 6 percent. This should come about as a result of monetizing some of the current heavy burdens of debt. However, this will be deceptive, as the real inflation for desirable things will be even more than the 6 percent. Desirable things may be health care, tuition at Princeton, luxury items such as Patek Phillipe watches, and income tax rates on the upper quartile. This inflationary development will widen economic class distinctions between the haves and the have-nots. This will create a social unease and invite higher taxes and fees on the upper class.[1] I predicted this trend a few years back, and also it led me to introduce my course on Portable Wealth investing. Some would say that this is the only way to go to narrow the differentials. I disagree. In order to overcome this inflationary outlook, I would continue to diversify my portfolio with strategic buys in metals, especially in gold.

In addition, this diversification should also include a good alloca-tion in global small-cap growth stocks. I feel that smaller companies will innovate new products and services, like they have done in the past, and they have the potential to create new jobs and a larger tax base. They will also be good hedges for the obvious increasing levels of inflation. They can get operating leverage and be in a position to create efficiencies and raise prices, thus increasing stock prices, and so their profits.

Over long periods of time, small-cap stocks have outperformed large-cap stocks. More recent analysis of a near -term ten-year period has shown that small-cap stocks both in the United States and on a global basis have performed much better than large cap stocks by almost 2 to 1, and they have also provided satisfactory returns, with global small cap stocks show-ing annualized double-digit returns.[2]

While the markets will gyrate as this book goes to publication, a decade is already an indication that there may be a change in attitude. Bonds may get an attitude adjustment as well as the low rates, and this could change to higher rates as inflation picks up. Small-cap stocks have already done well and would be expected to do well in higher inflationary times as they would be in a better postion to pass along price increases and capitalize on their operating leverages.

Future Growth Companies

We also need to create investment incentives so people can start future growth companies. We need more FedExes, Microsofts, and Apples. These companies require both higher intelligence workers and basic-skilled employees. The government has to get out of the way and let such companies develop. The government should also adopt a Fusion approach. The government certainly needs some broad quant criteria to maintain financial order, such as capital requirements. Some tech-nocracy is good. But then they need to exit the picture and stop second-guessing investor sentiment. They don't need to bring diapers every time the baby cries. It needs to let the old trees die and let new ones grow. If not, we will have a dwindling forest. So a Fusion process for the government would include a smaller role of the Fed whose money supply targets are more quantitatively set; a flatter tax rate that gets out of the emotional support of select businesses; a currency backed by less emotional fiat and more objective measures, such as gold.

Today, that means it must avoid hiking taxes, or earmarking tax benefits to supposedly needy areas in order to spur demand, such as we saw with housing, and then create more bureaucracies that are prone to waste, inefficiency, and corruption. We already discussed the dubious skills of the Fed in taming the economic cycle, and one would doubt fiscal policy is any better. Let industry breathe and grow within broad and sound boundaries. Government needs to stop spending to bail out sunset companies and still expect future generations to shoulder the debt. This invites the likelihood that some of the government debt will have to be rationalized. Behaviorally and technically, this is a deterministic action that cannot be changed with just money printing. The calamities are the result of fear and greed. Overcoming the cycle makes it only worse, similar to the Fed action in the early '30s. Trees that are ready to die cannot be propped up with wooden splints. They still die.

Overcoming the debt burden by more monetization and rationalization, it is a better option than crushing the middle classes and the poor with austerity measures and letting bankers collect bonuses on their bailout situations. Let's not crucify growth on a cross of debt! Some would point out that certain geographic parts of the world could be better able to provide this growth. For example, China is cited as a future growth opportunity as compared to perhaps the United States. That could very well be, but this argument misses something: The growing company may have a headquarters in a country, but this headquarters can easily be moved— and so can its production and sales—becoming more global in scope. Thus, is Apple really a "U.S. company"? A cancer drug that is sold globally, for example, is really not a country's asset. Consequently, we need to get rid of capital controls and thoughts of currencies. We should realize that items sell at a global price because they are in demand and not because one buys them in dollars or euros. These currency transactions are really after the fact, as the prices are set to what the market will bear. Princeton tuition can be paid in gold or dollars. Still the same degree but the dollars are increased to meet market demand. This implies that currencies need to be pegged to gold and commodities and real earning assets, not government promises. This invites again the strongest of all currencies, small-cap growth stocks and hopefully their growing cash flows. Not sure? Would you rather buy an Apple-type stock 10 years later or government bonds?

The Era of the Golden Butterfly

I call the coming decade the potential era of the Golden Butterfly. These will help mitigate the threat of the Black Swan. Because accidents will be allowed, diapers will not be provided. Through Bayes' statistics one will get better probabilities of failure and thus become more defensive oriented. Golden because gold will hedge against the rising price levels, butterfly because many industries and country economies will be restructured from their ugliness, with a result of new companies springing up. This should result in beautiful butterflies whose growth will finally lift up from the ground. Of course, they won't live forever, but there will be the opportunity to renew the pool as the old ones die or fade away. These butterflies will include the sunrise companies—the small companies that will be encouraged to develop. They will create employment and a rising standard of living for many.

With this kind of investment approach, I therefore forecast a premium return of global small-cap companies of about 10 points per annum over the risk-free rate. Historically, U.S. small-cap stocks have generated about 12 percent per annum returns over many decades, with official inflation about 3 percent per year. So that is about a 9 percent premium over T-bills. If we use a U.S. government bond (say, 10-year) as the risk-free rate, it has generated about 5.5 percent annual return. Going forward, it may have to offer more, if it has to monetize debt. Thus, small-cap stocks have generated about 6.5 percent premium per year. I predict a 10 percent premium to long-term government bonds. Currently, valuations of stocks and especially small-cap stocks are low by historical measures and this low base should provide a good springboard for the future growth. Investor mood is on the gloomy side, and they are seeking safety in US government debt. These factors indicate a potential coming change from debt to equities. Since the rates should rise on these bonds because of some type of debt monetizing strategies, we could estimate another 3 percent added to government bonds to get 8.5 percent. Then add 10 percent premium to get 18.5 percent per annum nominal return for small-cap stock over the next decade. Yes, the Golden Butterfly!

It will be difficult for the investor to get an alpha, as obtaining and analyzing the data needed to make these decisions is rather challenging. Uncertain data or hidden data of sunrise companies will make this hard to do. Data from new companies will be the most difficult to analyze for their potential. Who will be the next Apple?

We would be better to pick certain quant criteria ahead of time, as these could lead one to the next Apple. The obvious, well-known companies will capture the interest of both investors and government policy. In a sense, the tail will wag the dog as weakness in prominent firms will shape companies and government policy, especially if they are closely correlated like a bank industry. This will lead to the repeating cycles we discussed.

Thus, we will seek new algos to find the growth companies. This will be challenging, as we will need to make creative judgments on the data. I have shown some of the criteria that I have used over my career, but there will be even better ones coming from even more skilled investors.It is unlikely that established large organizations, such as governments and institutions like the Fed, will be able to do this. Most likely, the comfort zone will be the Turing portion of the chart where massive amounts of data and beaten-path analysis exists. Behaviorally, we will attempt to place this data and analysis into expected square and round holes. This will cause technical and behavioral analysis to continue to flourish as they repeat cycles and past behavior in a determined fashion.

So in doing Fusion, we can have quant criteria to potentially capture the butterflies. It would be a quant net. For example, one can use a high ROE combined with a low P/E and a technical indicator of good market relative strength as a key input. This quant method could be a much better way of picking future growth companies and avoiding hype than just playing hunches or emotional appeals of logic. More perceptive filters could be created to scan for prospects of the coming decade, such as using the intellectual background of management. This would include their past records and educational levels that usually help predict future success. This may give a choice list of companies that may turn to the Golden Butterflies.

We could also buy the ETFs of Russell 2000 or the MDY to get some of the good, but also some of the bad, of small- and mid-cap stocks. An enhanced quant filter would then hopefully lead to the identification of better companies. From this, when I was at Prudential, we got good investment results by picking some winners and also avoiding some of the story stocks that were hyped but eventually failed.

The coming decade offers much promise, but only in certain areas. Thus, I would buy gold and small-cap growth stocks. If I am correct on my assumptions of 18.5 percent per annum growth, for the next ten years, the Russell 2000 Index, which now stands at 712 (10/14/11), can rise to over 3,500 in 10 years (and not counting a dividend yield of say 1 percent).

Perhaps it's time to stop worrying. Instead, it's time to get back to business and by using a Fusion approach one can hopefully enjoy the coming of the Golden Butterflies

APPENDIX

Back in the 1970s when I was recommending stocks to individuals, I created and printed some basic investment reports. These included a recommendation showing both fundamental and technical approaches to support the investment decision, my early garage days of development of a Fusion process. There was a basic report giving more detail on the company and then updated reports that tended to be shorter, but still covered both fundamental and technical decisions. Yes, today one can see learning curve challenges in the reports. We hopefully get wiser as we age.

Two investment report examples are FCA International and Mite. These reports eventually got into the hands of some Wall Street brokers who got to know my name and approach. They were Arnie Ursaner and Peter Scholtz of Smith Barney. They have since developed their own firms. I thank them very much, as they eventually recommended me to a major asset manager, at The Prudential Insurance Company, who eventually hired me to help develop its small-cap investments. These stocks ended in the Pru portfolio and made good money, as they rose in prices due to good fundamentals and eventual takeovers.

SITUATION REPORT ON: October 3, 1977
(An Advisory Service
of John Palicka)

                    MITE CORPORATION: Second Quarter Earnings
                    (ASE: MTE)

Dividend: $.28   Recent Price: 8 1/4
  P/E :   5.4X   1977 Price Range: 7 1/8-10 1/4

                        Recommendation

     We reinforce our buy recommendation for the long-term investor.
Despite a weak stock market, we are upgrading our short-term
opinion from hold to a mild buy. Our opinion stems from the good
operating performance of the company, its recent dividend increase,
overall good market prospects for its products, increasing downside
protection, and slightly better technical features of its stock.

     Second quarter earnings showed net income of $1,176,000 ($.50)
on sales of $11,016,000 versus $1,068,000 ($.32) on sales of
$9,747,000. The recent quarter had a gain from a tax settlement
of about $.04 a share, and of course there was the extra interest
expense of some $150,000 arising from the issue of debentures into
which 1-million shares were tendered late last fiscal year. Therefore, there were some 2.2-million shares in the current quarter
versus 3.3-million last year.

     Second quarter earnings (netting out the tax settlement) were
above our forecast by about $.04 a share, and a real operating
margin of 11% (not giving effect to the additional interest
expense) is the company's best showing in recent history. The
excellent profit margin is due to further improvements in the
company's operating leverage (as explained in our 6/2/77 report).
More important is the catapulting effect of the company's financial
leverage. Much credit must go to the Mite financial team, especially
to Mr. Marcel Lamy, for correctly seizing the opportunity to
enhance their book value and earnings per share with the adoption
of the recent financial tender. Management has indicated that there
is no evidence of inventory build-up by its customers. Mr. Robert
Blinken, Chairman, indicated that Mite's record first half
($2,066,000 or $.88 a share) resulted from improved business
conditions in Mite's market and "based on present indications we
expect a continuation of strong operating results in the balance of
our fiscal year." We continue to expect $1.75 for the year, plus
on minus 3%. Foreign imports are not having an adverse effect on
Mite's sales.

     Mite also increased the dividend to $.07 a share and this
increases the yield to 3.4%. We continue to feel that the dividend
will have to be increased to bring the yield more in line with that
of the industry: approximately 5.2% (Common Stock Reporter, 9/26/77,
page A-5). On the other hand, Mite's P/E is below the industry
average of 7.3. Given the fact that its 5-year growth rate is about
2.5 times the industry norm of 11%, that its return on equity and
profit margins are at the better end of the industry, the common
stock is undervalued strictly on a P/E basis. Therefore, we look
forward to an expansion of the multiple.

General Motors stated that 1978 will be a record year of
unit sales for the automotive and truck industry at 15.5-million.
This should bode well for Mite's fastners as even a fairly good
year should give the company adequate financial reserves to
weather the next downturn in this cyclical industry. Mite has
about $8,000,000 in cash and equivalents and this amount should
build up to over $11,000,000 by the fiscal date. Consequently,
its heavy cash reserve of say $4-5.00 a share also makes it an
attractive acquisition candidate. We expect that in a severe
recession that produces automative sales as low as the previous
one, Mite should earn about $1.00 a share. With a P/E of at
least 7 (P/Es are normally low at the peak and high in the valley
of a cyclical stock), Mite's cash reserve would certainly make a
tender offer attractive. Thus we feel that on the downside there
is limited risk.

Technically, Mite has reversed a downward field and is
currently in a neutral position with an OBV of +800. The 200-day
trend line continues in an upward direction and since mid-August
the stock price has stabilized at 7 1/2, a higher level than 7
1/8 in mid-April. Mite has pierced its 200-day trend line on the
downside at 8 in August but is now ready to pierce it on the
upside at 8 3/8. Because of the upward direction of the 200-day
trend line, we do not see any serious technical deterioration at
the present time. The stock appears to be in a neutral to slightly
bullish position. An overall negative aspect is that some
technicians feel that the market has run its course in the bull
phase and that we are now in a bear market. It should be noted
that the weakness of Dow Jones Industrial Index has not been as
strongly manifested in the broad-based averages of the market.

John Palicka

Special Note:

It is about one year that we first began to recommend and accumulate
Mite in the high 4's and low 5's. Our basis for purchasing Mite
was that it had a strong cash position, and in reading the 10-K,
the company had a successful history of investing in itself (buying
its own common etc.) We continue to feel that Mite is undervalued
and that these factors will continue to play a role in increasing
Mite's common stock to a realistic level. In view of today's spirit
of acquisitions, we especially feel that Mite rests in an attractive
financial position.

Situation Report On: February 7, 1978
(An Advisory Service
of John Palicka)

                    FCA INTERNATIONAL LTD. - 2nd Quarter Results

Dividend: $.12   Price As of 1/11/78 Recommendation: $1.95
Yield : 5.6%   Recent Price: $2.15
Current P/E: 5.8X   1977 Price Range: $1.40-$2.00
Estimated 1978 P/E: 5.2X   1972-1977 Price Range: $1.25-$15.00

        Note: Since our 1/11/78 BUY Recommendation, the price of
        FCA's common stock has increased from $1.95 to $2.15
        — some 10%; during this period, the Dow Jones
        Industrial Average declined from 773 to 764 — some 1%.

                            Recommendation

We continue our BUY recommendation as operations are progressing according to
expectations, FCA'S financial position continues to invite an external or
internal tender, and the stock is trading in a more favorable technical position.

                        Basis For Recommendation

An excellent second quarter has established a strong base which is expected to
support the optimism for the fiscal year ending 6/30/78, especially since FCA's
second half is usually supposed to be stronger than the first half of its
fiscal year. Management in its shareholder's report has stated "We are looking
forward with much confidence to a strong second half. All signs seem to
indicate excellent results for the year ending 6/30/78." (Although, for what it
is worth, notice the slightly more positive tone in the French "Nous prévoyons
avec beaucoup de confiance un duxième semestre tres positif. Tout semble
indiquer que nous obtiendrons d' excellents résultats pour l' année se terminant
le 30 juin 1978"). For the fiscal year we are forecasting aroung $.41 a share.
In the second quarter ended 12/31/77, EAT increased by 24% (despite a higher tax
rate) and the EBT and EAT margins showed healthy gains, as did revenues as a
percent of accounts for collection (from 6.6% to 7.2%).

                    (In 000's of Canadian Dollars)

| | First Quarter | | Second Quarter | |
	1976	1977	1976	1977
Accounts For Collection	56,000	68,000	58,000	61,000
Revenue	3,756	4,220	3,841	4,383
EBT	519	589	478	633
EAT	256	286	261	324
EPS	.06	.07	.06	.07
Tax Rate:	50.7%	51.4%	45.4%	48.8%

Although operating cost figures were not disclosed, they were not expected to show an adverse level. Again, a weakening Canadian dollar has contributed to FX earnings. All in all, as discussed in our 1/11/78 opinion, FCA has utilized its various measures of profitability to generate the above results. FCA's cash position is now $3,200,000 and is expected to reach $3,800,000 ($.88 a share) by 6/30/78.

Technical

Since our 1/11/78 report, the stock has not traded below $2.00, thereby confirming the surmountation of the near-term resistance level of $2.00 which has not been exceed in 18 months. Consequently, our advice for traders has been correct so far. The real test will now be at $2.30, which if exceeded, should signal a major"break-out". Since 1/11/78, the OBV is +7,900; however, due to the short time period and the low level of the OBV per share outstanding, we cannot attach significance to this measure at this time, although it is positive. A drawback to our technical analysis is the lack of a detailed chart with which we can analyze the 50-and 200-day trend line.

- John Palicka -

* * * * *

This opinion is based upon sources which we consider reliable, although accuracy cannot be guaranteed. The investor is requested to refer to the company's financial statements for full details, as the opinion is abbreviated. Also, considerations to country risk and foreign exchange fluctuations should be given. Prior to the publication of this opinion, select clients were verbally notified, in an immediate manner, of the opinion so as to be in a position of being able to act quickly in an everchanging market. We carry a postion in the common stock and have "made" the market at a price in excess of $2.00.

FURTHER READING

The following list of books provides further knowledge on the many of topics discussed throughout the book. A number of these works are referred to in the text.

Technical Analysis

For a foundation in the core body of technical analysis knowledge:

Edwards, Robert D., and John Magee, *Technical Analysis of Stock Trends.* Snowball Publishing, 2010. This work is a pillar of classical technical analysis with many illustrative charts from the 1930s to the 1950s, long before derivatives influenced charts. The book has been updated with later editions.

Frost, A. J., and Robert R. Prechter, *Elliott Wave Principle: Key To Market Behavior,* 10th ed., Gainesville, GA: New Classics Library: 2005. This work provides a good foundation in this specialized technical approach to investing.

Kirkpatrick, Charles D., and Julie R. Dahlquist, *Technical Analysis: The Complete Resource for Financial Market Technicians,* 2nd ed., (Upper Saddle River, NJ: Pearson Education, 2010). The authors discuss many technical approaches and examine evidence on their effectiveness. This book is by far one of the better books in terms of academic discussions.

Murphy, John J., *Technical Analysis of the Financial Markets: A Comprehensive Guide to Trading Methods and Applications* (New York: New York Institute of Finance, 1999).

————, *Intermarket Analysis: Profiting from Global Market Relationships*, (Hoboken, NJ: John Wiley & Sons, 2004).

These books lay the basic foundations of technical analysis and the growing use of inter-market trading strategies. The author's simple style of writing should especially be useful to novices.

Pring, Martin J., *Technical Analysis Explained: The Successful Investor's Guide to Spotting Investment Trends and Turning Points*, 4th ed., New York: McGraw-Hill, 2002).

The author clearly explains the basics of technical analysis and introduces some of his own proprietary investment tools (I especially like his sentiment section).

StockCharts.com, http://stockcharts.com, 2011.

This affordable and rich charting service also has a great tutorial.

Fundamental Analysis

Basic books on investing and portfolio theory are quite numerous on more advanced levels. I would try any book that a major business school has on its required list as a start. For a foundation in the core body of fundamental analysis knowledge:

Bodie, Zvi, Alex Kane, and Alan Marcus, *Investments*, 9th ed., New York: McGraw-Hill/Irwin, 2010.

Leading business schools use this book for general finance theory.

Ross, Stephen, Randolph Westerfield, and Bradford D. Jordan, *Fundamentals of Corporate Finance Standard Edition*, 9th ed. New York: McGraw-Hill/Irwin, 2009.

Leading business schools use this book for general corporate finance topics.

Sundem, Gary L., John A. Elliott, Donna R. Philbrick, and Charles T. Horngren, *Introduction to Financial Accounting*, 9th ed., New York: Pearson Education, 2008.
This textbook covers the core fundamental subjects in accounting. I also thank Dean Elliott for the opportunity to teach an advanced Fusion stock course for the top students at the MBA program at Baruch

Behavioral Finance Analysis

For a foundation in the core body of behavioral finance analysis knowledge:

Montier, James, *Behavioural Finance: Insights into Irrational Minds and Markets*, Hoboken, NJ: John Wiley & Sons, 2002.
This book is a collection of behavioral topics from this professional research manager's career. Currently he is the Global Equity Strategist at Dresdner Kleinwort Wasserstein in London.

Shefrin, Hersh, *Beyond Greed and Fear: Understanding Behavioral Finance and the Psychology of Investing*, New York: Oxford University Press, 2007.
This work provides good behavioral cases for financial practitioners.

Quant and Artificial Intelligence

The quant and artificial intelligence topic is very broad. Advanced math and statistical disciplines are required, so first review any basic college textbooks on math subjects, such as statistics.

ENDNOTES

Part 1

Chapter 1

1. Zvi Bodie, Alex Kane, and Alan Marcus. *Investments*, 7th ed. (New York: McGraw-Hill/Irwin, 2008), 132, 146, 148.

2. Detractors, such as Burton G. Malkiel, support the Efficient Market Hypothesis and refute the value of technical analysis, behavioral finance, and fundamental analysis. See Burton G. Malkiel, "The Efficient Market Hypothesis and Its Critics," *Journal of Economic Perspectives* 17, no. 1 (Winter 2003): 59–82. This is summarized in the *CFA Digest* (November 2003): 40–41.

3. Brad Barber, Reuven Lehawy, Maureen McNichols, and Brett Trueman, "Can Investors Profit from the Prophets? Security Analyst Recommendations and Stock Returns." Summarized by Bruce D. Phelps, *CFA Digest* 31, no. 4 (November 2001): 5–7.

4. Gordon J. Alexander, William F. Sharpe, and Jeffrey V. Bailey, *Fundamentals of Investments*, 3rd ed. (Upper Saddle River, NJ: Prentice Hall, 2001), 291–292.

5. Charles D. Kirkpatrick and Julie R. Dahlquist, *Technical Analysis* (Upper Saddle River, NJ: Pearson Education, 2007), 161–164.

Chapter 2

1. Jacob Thomas and Frank Zhang, "Don't Fight the Fed Model," April 2008 version, http://www.som.yale.edu/Faculty/jkt7/papers/fedmodel. pdf (accessed October 5, 2011).
2. Jonathan Clements, "The Fed Model: Fix It Before You Use It," *Wall Street Journal*, May 1, 2005, http://online.wsj.com/public/article/ SB111491292409921442.html (accessed October 5, 2011).
3. Conrad de Aenlle, "Model Contrasts Stocks and Bonds to Find Under- and Overvalued Markets : A Fed Formula Tests for Exuberance," *New York Times*, December 1, 2001.
4. See "Stock Market Gurus and Their Forecasts: Can You Use Them or Should You Just Flip a Coin?" The Motley Fool, December 22, 2007, http://caps.fool.com/blogs/stock-market-gurus-and-their/27516 (accessed October 5, 2011). The article quotes the work of CXO Advisory Group, http://www.cxoadvisory.com/gurus/#individuals (accessed October 5, 2011).
5. Reported by www.tradethe news. com December 12, 2007.
6. Dave Young, "Market Forecasting: Investor Beware," December 20, 2007, http://ezinearticles.com/?Market-Forecasting—Investor-Beware &id=907205 (accessed October 5, 2011).
7. Daniel L. Thornton, "Economic Outlook—2002." Remarks Made at the Annual "Power in Partnership" Meeting of the Paducah Kentucky Chamber of Commerce, December 6, 2001, http://research.stlouisfed.org/econ/ thornton/economicoutlook2002.pdf (accessed October 5, 2011).

Chapter 3

1. James Montier, *Behavioural Finance: Insights into Irrational Minds and Markets.* (Hoboken, NJ: John Wiley & Sons, 2002), 79.
2. Ryan Garvey and Anthony Murphy, "Are Professional Traders Too Slow To Realize Their Losses?" *Financial Analysts Journal* 60, no. 4. Quoted in www.cfapubs.org, July/August 2004, 35–43. The Disposition Effect is also discussed in Montier, 23–25.
3. Report of the Day Trading Project Group, North American Securities Administrators Association, August 9, 1999, 1.

4. Sandy Huffaker, "Day Traders 2.0: Wired, Angry, and Loving It," *New York Times*, March 28, 2010, New York edition, BU1.
5. Clifford S. Asness, "The Future Role of Hedge Funds," *CFA Institute Conference Proceedings* Quarterly 23, no. 2 (June 2006).
6. Gordon J. Alexander, William F. Sharpe, and Jeffrey V. Bailey, *Fundamentals of Investments*, 3rd ed. (Upper Saddle River, NJ: Prentice Hall, 2001), 291–292.
7. Russell Style Indexes, Russell Investments, January 31, 2010, http://russell.com.
8. Ibid.
9. Scott D. Stewart, John J. Neumann, Christopher R. Knittel, and Jeffrey Heisler, "Absence of Value: An Analysis of Investment Allocation Decisions by Institutional Plan Sponsors," *Financial Analysts Journal* 65, no. 6 (2009).
10. James M. Clash and Mark Tatge, "The Fund That Lost Its Way," *Forbes* (November 26, 2007). This article gives a good example of switching styles.
11. Simon Kwan, "The Stock Market: What a Difference a Year Makes," *Federal Reserve Bank of San Francisco*, June 1, 2001.
12. Floyd Norris, "Another Technology Victim: Top Soros Fund Manager Says He 'Overplayed' Hand," *New York Times*, April 29, 2000, C1.

Part 2

Chapter 4

1. Ray Wert, "New York City Taxi Medallion Goes for the Price of a Midtown One Bedroom!" *Jalopnik*, June 1, 2007, Jalopnik.com/265252 (accessed October 5, 2011).
2. *411 New York*, New York City and State Guide, May 16,2010, http://411newyork.org/guide/2008/03/30/new-york-taxi-cab-driver-salary/ (accessed October 5, 2011)
3. James Montier, *Behavioural Finance* (Hoboken, NJ: John Wiley & Sons, 2003), 79.
4. Ibid., 20–28.

5. Jing Liu, Doron Nissim, and Jacob Thomas, "Is Cash Flow King in Valuations?" *Financial Analysts Journal* 63, no. 2 (2007).

Chapter 5

1. Helen Coster and Daniel Fisher, "Does General Electric Deserve Its AAA rating?" *Forbes*, October 27, 2008.
2. VimpelCom year-end report 1998. http://about.beeline.ru/media/About_eng/annual%20reports/ar1998.pdf (accessed October 5, 2011).
3. "Interview with Mr. Jo Lunder, CEO of VimpelCom/Beeline," September 4, 2002, Winne, http://www.winne.com/topinterviews/beelineman.html (accessed October 5, 2011).
4. Ibid.
5. Andrei Musatov, "Vimpelcom 'Pulls Through' Despite Crisis Setbacks," *The Russian Journal*, October 18–24, 1999, 13.
6. Interview with Jo Lunder.
7. John Palicka, "Introduction to Fusion Analysis," *Technically Speaking*, June 2005.
8. John J. Murphy, *The Technical Analysis of the Financial Markets* (New York: New York Institute of Finance, 1999), 92.
9. Robert D. Edwards and John Magee, Technical Analysis of Stock Trends, 8th edition (New York: AMACOM, 2001), 171.
10. Eugene F. Fama and Kenneth R. French, "The Cross Section of Expected Stock Returns," *Journal of Finance* 47 (June 1992): 427–465. This is cited in a leading financial textbook, *Essentials of Investments* by Zvi Bodie, Alex Kane, and Alan Marcus, 5th ed. (New York: McGraw-Hill/Irwin, 2004), 241. There is ample literature exploring the Fama/French thesis. Note also that in the Bodie textbook, Chapter 19 is devoted to behavioral finance and technical analysis.
11. Ibid., "The Anatomy of Value and Growth Returns," *Financial Analysts Journal* 63, no. 6 (2007), CFA Institute.
12. James Montier, *Behavioural Finance* (Hoboken, NJ: John Wiley & Sons, 2002, 9, 11, 79.
13. Ibid.

14. Reviewed to 1997 by Lawrence D. Brown, "Earnings Surprise Research: Synthesis and Perspectives," *Financial Analysts Journal* (March/April 1997): 13–19.
15. Alina Lerman, Joshua Livnat, and Richard R. Mendenhall, "Double Surprise into Higher Future Returns," *Financial Analysts Journal* 63, no. 4 (July/August 2007): 63–71.
16. Quotes and example are from Gordon J. Alexander, William F. Sharpe, and Jeffrey V. Bailey, *Fundamentals of Investments*, 3rd ed. (Upper Saddle River, NJ: Prentice Hall, 2001), 374–377.
17. Ibid.
18. This concept is discussed in "Behavioral Biases and Investment Research" by Richard S. Pzena when he was director of U.S. Equity Investments, Sanford C. Bernstein & Company, Inc. http://www.cfapubs.org/doin/pdfplus/10.2469/CP.V1995.N7.7
19. Brown, et al.
20. "Economic Perspective," Mutual of America Capital Management Corporation, August 20, 2003.
21. "An Unwelcome Fall in Inflation?" Remarks by Governor Ben S. Bernanke, Before the Economics Roundtable, University of California, San Diego, La Jolla, CA, July 23, 2003.
22. A good source for technical intermarket analysis is John J. Murphy's *Intermarket Analysis* (Hoboken, NJ: John Wiley & Sons, 2004).

Chapter 6

1. Excerpts are from Terrance Odean, "Effect of Behavioral Biases on Market Efficiency and Investors' Welfare," *CFA Institute Conference Proceedings Quarterly* 24, no. 1 (March 2007).
2. "Dubai Property Prices Decline," *Dubai Chronicle*, January 22, 2009.
3. Bruno Solnik and Dennis McLeavy, *International Investments*, 5th ed. (New York: Addison-Wesley, 2003, 51 and Chapter 3.
4. Solnik and McLeavy, 51.
5. The book was revised in a later edition with the help of Jill Leyland, who was consultant to the World Gold Council, and covers the period

from 1560 to 2007. Sourced from "The Golden Constant," *World Gold Council*, July 2009.

6. Based on gold price data from World Gold Council, calculated by Global Emerging Growth Capital using portfolio risk measures. I did the calculations as proprietary work, using the world gold council only for their official gold price.

Chapter 7

1. Jill Leyland, "Jastram's Golden Constant: How Is It Relevant Today?" *Alchemist* 56, http://www.lbma.org.uk/assets/alc56_golden_constant. pdf (accessed October 5, 2011).
2. World Gold Council, third quarter, 2009. Tonnage is for 2008. Above-ground data is from World Gold Council as of 2008.
3. Ibid.
4. Ibid.
5. Ibid.
6. Mike Hewitt, "Global Money Supply" July 31, 2007. Estimate is as of July 25, 2007, www.marketoracle.co.uk/Article1700.html. The stats now show 60 trillion as of 2011, but we shall not update all as the trend and concept is still intact.
7. Ibid.
8. NowandFutures.com, "Pain and Misery Index (CPI + Unemployment Rate)," 2009; and BLS and shadowstats.com. Data from 1970–1993 interpolated from yearly BLS data.
9. John J. Murphy, *The Technical Analysis of the Financial Markets* (New York: New York Institute of Finance, 1999), 336.
10. Edmund L. Andrews, "Wave of Debt Payments Facing U.S. Government," *New York Times*, November 22, 2009.
11. Landon Thomas Jr., "Patchwork Pension Plan Adds to Greek Debt Woes," *New York Times*, March 12, 2010, A1.
12. "Gibson's Paradox and the Gold Standard," *Journal of Political Economy* 96 (June 1988): 528–550.
13. The World Bank, "Data Catalog—2011," http://data.worldbank.org/ data-catalog (accessed October 5, 2011).

14. Gold Eagle Technical Staff, http://www.gold-eagle.com, 1997.
15. Bank of Tokyo-Mitsubishi UFJ, 2006–late December 2008, cited in *Wall Street Journal*, March 16, 2009, C1.
16. World Gold Council, August 2007, using data as of year-end 2006.

Part 3

Introduction

1. Ryan Grim, "Priceless: How the Federal Reserve Bought the Economic Profession," *Huffington Post*, September 7, 2009; updated October 23, 2009, http://www.huffingtonpost.com/2009/09/07/priceless-how-the-federal_n_278805.html (accessed October 5, 2011).
2. "Milton Friedman @ Rest, Email from a Nobel Laureate," *Wall Street Journal*, from the WSJ Opinion Archives, January 22, 2007.

Chapter 8

1. Franz Kafka, *The Trial*, trans. Breon Mitchell (New York: Schocken Books, 1998).
2. Information Philosopher, "Determinism," http://www.informationphilosopher.com/freedom/determinism.html (accessed October 5, 2011)
3. See, for example, B.F. Skinner's *Beyond Freedom and Dignity* (1976) and *About Behaviorism* (1971).
4. News Staff, "The Big Bang Clock: A Thermodynamic Theory for the Origin of the Universe," *Scientific Blogging*, November 2, 2007, http://www.scientificblogging.com/news_account/the_big_bang_clock_a_thermodynamic_theory_for_the_origin_of_the_universe (accessed October 5, 2011).
5. Among many works on this idea, a good starting point is Alan H. Guth, *The Inflationary Universe*, (New York: Addison-Wesley 1997).
6. Brian Greene, *The Elegant Universe* (New York: Random House, 2000), 203–204.
7. Adapted from Alan Hajek's "Pascal's Wager," *Stanford Encyclopedia of Philosophy* (May 2, 1998; revised June 4, 2008).

8. "Vatican Announces Results of Pascal's Wager," *Sneer Review*, August 10, 2009, http://sneerreview.blogspot.com/2009/08/vatican-announces-final-results-of.html (accessed October 5, 2011).

9. Hajek, "Pascal's Wager."

10. Lawrence C. Strauss, "An Interview with Burton Malkiel," *Barron's*, July 7, 2009. Reprinted at SmartMoney.com, http://www.smartmoney.com/invest/funds/an-interview-with-burton-malkiel/?zone=intromessage (accessed October 5, 2011).

11. Burton G. Malkiel and Atanu Saha, "Hedge Funds: Risk and Return," *Financial Analysts Journal* 61, no. 6 (2005): 80–88.

12. Rajesh K. Aggarwal and Philippe Jorion, "Hidden Survivorship in Hedge Fund Returns," *Financial Analysts Journal* 66, no. 2 (March/April 2010).

13. *Webster's New World Finance and Investment Dictionary* (Indianapolis: Wiley, 2003).

14. Bloomberg, 2009, Global Capital Markets League Tables.

15. Gretchen Morgenson, "'100% Protected' Isn't as Safe as It Sounds," *New York Times*, May 21, 2010, BU 1.

Chapter 9

1. Raymond A. Serway, *Physics for Scientists and Engineers with Modern Physics*, 3rd ed., updated version (Fort Worth, TX: Saunders College Publishing, 1990), 1115–1117.

2. These concepts and definitions are derived from Brian Greene's *The Fabric of the Cosmos: Space, Time, and the Texture of Reality* (New York: Knopf, 2004).

3. Steve Nison, *Japanese Candlestick Charting Techniques*, 2nd ed. (New York: New York Institute of Finance, 2001), 104.

4. Kondratrieff Winter.Com. My interpretation of the wave is based on the description of the cycle found in www.kwave.com.

5. FedEx Corporation Web site. Microsoft numbers 2009 10-K; Millionaires and billionaires reported by Wikipedia.

6. William A. Galston, "The 'New Normal' for the U.S. Economy: What Will It Be?" *The Brookings Institution*, March 5, 2010, http://www.

brookings.edu/opinions/2009/0901_economy_galston.aspx (accessed October 5, 2011).

7. Ibid.

8. John L. Ward and Craig E. Aronoff, "Shirt Sleeves to Shirt Sleeves— Family Business," *Nation's Business*, September 1992.

9. Joseph Tracy and Henry Schneider, "Stocks in the Household Portfolio: A Look Back at the 1990s," *Current Issues in Economics and Finance* 7, no. 4 (April 2001), Federal Reserve Bank of New York.

10. Chris Isidore, "Home Ownership in Record Plunge," *CNNMoney.com*, (January 29, 2008).

Chapter 10

1. Arthur F. Burns and Wesley C. Mitchell, *Measuring Business Cycles* (Cambridge, MA: National Bureau of Economic Research, 1946).

2. Charles D. Kirkpatrick and Julie R. Dahlquist, *Technical Analysis* (Upper Saddle River, NJ: Pearson Education, 2007), 161–164.

3. John J. McConnell and Wei Xu, "Equity Returns at the Turn of the Month," *Financial Analysts Journal* 64, no. 2 (March/April 2008): 49–64. My discussion is based on this journal article.

4. Ibid., 63.

5. Martin J. Pring, *Technical Analysis Explained*, 4th ed. (New York: McGraw-Hill, 2002), 388–389. Pring cites the data from D. Klienand and R. Stambaugh, "A Further Investigation of the Weekend Effect in Stock Returns," *Journal of Finance*, July 1984, 819–837. Note again that some technical arguments are supported by studies done in finance rather than technical journals.

6. Tim Loughran and Paul Schultz, "Weather, Stock Returns, and the Impact of Localized Trading Behavior," *The Journal of Financial and Quantitative Analysis* 39, no. 2 (June 2004): 343–364.

7. Kirkpatrick, 456. He also cites the work of Al Lieber in the *Journal of Clinical Psychology*. Leiber, Alan. "Human Aggression and Lunar Synodic Cycle." Journal of Clinical Psychology 39,no.5 (1978): 385. Again, other academic disciplines are used to attempt to support technical observations.

8. Ingo Swann, "Arch Crawford Foresees the Unforeseen on Wall Street," *FATE Magazine* 46, no. 4, issue 517 (April 1993): 72–81.

9. Ibid.

10. Martin J. Pring, *Technical Analysis Explained*, 28–32.

11. John J. Murphy, *Intermarket Analysis* (Hoboken, NJ: John Wiley & Sons, 2004), 201–213.

12. P. Q. Wall, "Fire or Ice," *Barron's*, July 23, 2001.

13. David Chapman, "Technical Scoop: A Short Primer on Cycles in the Current Market," February 13, 2004, http://www.gold-eagle.com/editorials_04/chapmand021604.html (accessed October 5, 2011).

14. Charles Mackay, *Extraordinary Popular Delusions and the Madness of Crowds* (1841): 89.

15. Earl A. Thompson, "The Tulipmania: Fact or Artifact," *Public Choice*, June 26, 2006.

16. Discussed in many behavioral books, overconfidence is illustrated with a set of questions and market forecasts in Hersh Shefrin's book *Beyond Greed and Fear* (Oxford: Oxford University Press, 2002), 48–51.

17. James Montier, *Behavioural Finance*, 77. Montier is quoting from the work of Gundez Caginalp, David Porter, and Vernon Smith. (2000) "Overreaction, momentum,liquidity and price bubbles in laboratory and field asset markets". Journal of Psychology and Financial Markets.

Chapter 11

1. Richard Menta, "iPhone: Hundreds Come, Lines Orderly," June 29, 2007, *MP3newswire.net*, http://www.mp3newswire.net/stories/7002/iPhone-line.html (accessed October 5, 2011).

2. James Estrin, "Bad Times Draw Bigger Crowds to Churches," *New York Times*, December 13, 2008, A1.

3. Based on Advisor User Sentiment Guide, November 2009, *Investorsintelligence.com*.

4. Fisher and Meyer, Investor Sentiment and Stock Returns, *Financial Analysts Journal*, March/April 2000, 16–23, quoted from #cW2000, Association for Investment Management and Research.

5. Martin J. Pring, *Technical Analysis Explained*, 522.

6. Quoted from Paul Kedrosky, *Infectious Greed, paul.kedrosky.com*, citing David Streitfeld, "A Glut in the Market for Homes," *Los Angeles Times*, May 20, 2005.

7. Tom Arnold, John H. Earl, Jr., and David S. North, "Are Cover Stories Effective Contrarian Indicators?" *Financial Analysts Journal* 63, no. 2 (as corrected May 2007).

8. Kirkpatrick, 104.

9. Data on sentient readings from American Association of Individual Investor, http://www.aaii.com.

10. Malcolm Baker and Jeffrey Wurgler, "Investor Sentiment and the Cross Section of Stock Returns," *Journal of Finance* 6, no. 4 (August 2006): 1. Summarized in *CFA Digest*, February 2007, 49–50.

11. One-point box reversals are not used that much today. For an excellent book on PF, read Jeremy du Plessis, *The Definitive Guide to Point and Figure*, reprint ed. (Petersfield, Hampshire, U.K.: Harriman House Publishing, 2006).

12. 2003 Lambert-Gann Educators, http://www.lambertganneducators.com/pages/wdgann.php.

Chapter 12

1. Alfred J. Frost and Robert R. Prechter, *Elliott Wave Principle*, 20th anniversary ed. (Gainesville, GA, 1998; First Edition, 1978). Elliot Wave Principle is based on the writings of Ralph Nelson Elliott's *Wave Principle*, published in 1939, and *Nature's Laws: The Secrets of the Universe*, published in 1946.

2. Eric Tyson, "Update: Robert Prechter Predicts Dow 1000 and Depression," June 16, 2009, http://www.erictyson.com/articles/20090616 (accessed October 5, 2011).

3. Frost and Prechter, *Elliott Wave Principle*.

4. Prechter, *Elliott Wave Principle*, 20. Italics are those of authors.

5. Jordan E. Kotick, "The Metaphysical Implications of the Elliott Wave Principle," *MTA Journal*, Spring–Summer 2001, 21–26.

6. Robert R. Prechter Jr., "Does the Wave Principle Subsume All Valid Technical Chart Patterns?" *Journal of Technical Analysis*, no. 66 (Fall/Winter 2009): 28.

7. Molly Schilling, "In Depth with Robert R. Prechter Jr.," *Technically Speaking*, November 2007, 1–6.

8. Kirkpatrick, 497.

9. Murphy, 336.

10. Kirkpatrick, 489.

11. Murphy, 329.

12. Kirkpatrick, 491. Another good source is Rich Swannell's "Elliott Waves Vary Depending on the Time Frame and Direction of the Pattern," *Journal of Technical Analysis*, Summer–Fall 2003, 17–23.

13. Prechter, 128.

14. Prechter, 108–111.

15. Murphy, 336.

16. Standard & Poor's, "S&P Case-Shiller Home Price Indices Index Methodology," November 2009.

17. http://www.census.gov/const/uspriceann.pdf (accessed October 5, 2011). Actually, prices dipped in 1970.

18. InflationData.com. The pre-1975 data are the Consumer Price Index statistics from *Historical Statistics of the United States* (USGPO, 1975). All data since then are from the annual *Statistical Abstracts of the United States*, http://www.inflationdata.com.

19. Margot Adler, "Behind the Ever-Expanding American Dream House," *All Things Considered*, NPR, July 4, 2006, and National Association of Home Builders, "Housing Facts, Figures and Trends for March 2006."

20. Cited in Robert J. Shiller, *Irrational Exuberance Revisited*, September 2006, cfapubs.org.

21. Donald Olsen, *The City as a Work of Art* (New Haven, CT: Yale University Press, 1986), 22. Past performance is no guarantee of future results.

22. William C. Wheaton, Mark S. Baranski, and Cessarina Templeton, "100 years of Commercial Real Estate Prices in Manhattan," Draft: May 1, 2006.

23. Lipper, December 1999.

24. Robert J. Shiller, "Irrational Exuberance Revisited," September, 2006, cfapubs.org.

25. I wish to thank all my colleagues at New York Institute of Finance for help on this example, which is used in the CFA prep material.

26. Julie Creswell, "Home Builders' Stock Sales: Diversifying or Bailing Out?" *New York Times*, October 4, 2005.

27. Murphy, 336.

28. Charles V. Bagley, "Sam Zell's Empire: Underwater in a Big Way," *New York Times*, February 6, 2009.

29. Ibid.

30. AFFO for REITS is generally calculated as GAAP net income + Depreciation − Gains on property sales = Fund from operations (FFO) − Capital expenditures = AFFO.

31. Reported in *Barron's*, September 11, 2006, 19.

32. Drexel University, "Pascal's Triangle," *Ask Dr. Science*, http://mathforum.org/dr.math/faq/faq.pascal.triangle.html (accessed October 5, 2011).

33. Chart and explanation based on "Pascal's Triangle and Its Patterns," http://ptri1.tripod.com/#fib (accessed October 5, 2011).

34. Kirkpatrick, 504.

35. Kirkpatrick, 502–503.

36. Bible numbers based on the work of E. W. Bullinger, *Number in Scripture: Its Supernatural Design and Spiritual Significance*, 4th ed., revised (London: Eyre & Spottiswoode, 1921).

37. Ariela Pelaia, "Bar and Bat Mitzvah Gifts," *About.com Guide*, 2011, http://judaism.about.com/od/lifeevents/f/bmitzvah_gifts.htm.

38. Caner Taslaman, *The Quran: Unchallengeable Miracle* (Istanbul: Nettleberry/Citlembik, 2006), http://www.quranmiracles.com/19/19read.asp?id=8.

39. Jayaram V., "The Symbolic Significance of Numbers in Hinduism," http://www.hinduwebsite.com/numbers.asp (accessed October 5, 2011).

Part 4

Introduction

1. Thayer Evans, "Threesome Captures Title It Was Missing," *New York Times*, April 6, 2010, New York edition, B13.

Chapter 13

1. Gretchen Morgenson and Louise Story, "Rating Agency Data Aided Wall Street in Mortgage Deals," *New York Times*, April 24, 2010, New York edition, A1.
2. Montier, 66–68.
3. "The Geeks Shall Inherit the Earth? Quantitative Managers' Recent Edge," Casey, Quirk, and Associates, November 2005, http://www.caseyquirk.com/docs/research_insight/05.11_RI_Geeks.pdf (accessed October 5, 2011).
4. Amir E. Khandani and Andrew W. Lo, "What Happened to the Quants in August 2007," MIT Laboratory for Financial Engineering, working paper, draft version, revised September 20, 2007.
5. Frank J. Fabozzi, Sergio M. Focardi, and Caroline Jonas, "Challenges in Quantitative Equity Management, The Research Foundation of CFA Institute, April 11, 2008 (corrected July 2008), http://web.mit.edu/alo/www/Papers/august07.pdf (accessed October 5, 2011).
6. Andrew W. Lo, Harry Mamaysky, and Jiang Wang, "Foundations of Technical Analysis: Computational Algorithms, Statistical Inference, and Empirical Implementation," *The Journal of Finance* LV, no. 4 (August 2000).
7. Xu-Shen Zhou and Ming Dong, "Can Fuzzy Logic Make Technical Analysis 20/20?" *Financial Analysts Journal* 60, no. 4 (July/August 2004): 54–73. This article also ups one's mathematical skills.

Chapter 14

1. An illuminating book on this topic is Roger Penrose, *Shadows of the Mind* (Oxford University Press, 1994). A more summary approach for investors can be found in John Palicka's article "Cyberanalysts Will Outperform Humans," *Equities Magazine*, December 1996.
2. Javier Estrada, "Black Swans in Emerging Markets," *Journal of Investing* 18, no. 2 (Summer 2009): 50–56, summarized in *CFA Digest* 39, no. 4 (November 2009): 111–112.
3. See "Ineluctable Assured Algorithms," *FTSE Global Markets*, July/August 2006, 54–58.

4. This study was reported for financial planners and other investment professionals interested in comparing these approaches. See Craig L. Israelsen, "What's In a Name?" *Financial Planning*, June 1, 2010, 139–141, http://www.financial-planning.com/fp_issues/2010_6/whats-in-a-name–2667032–1.html?zkPrintable=1&nopagination=1 (accessed October 5, 2011).

5. Morningstar, FundInvestor: Glossary, http://mfi.morningstar.com/Glossary.aspx (accessed October 5, 2011).

6. A good summary of these trends is found in Michael Santoli's "Requiem for Floor Traders," *Barron's*, November 20, 2006.

7. Simon Emrich, "Using Smarter Algorithms vs. Smarter Use of Algorithms," A Guide to Global Liquidity II, *Institutional Investor*, Spring 2010, 42.

8. Example based on example in Adam Bradbery, "Traders Fret Algorithmic Systems", *Wall Street Journal*, February 21, 2007, b11.

9. Max Palmer, "Dark and Lit Markets: A User's Guide," A Guide to Global Liquidity II, *Institutional Investor*, Spring 2010, 96.

10. Ibid., 97–98. This example is based on Palmer's example in his article.

11. Aaron Lucchetti, "Firms Seek Edge Through Speed as Computers Trading Expands," *Wall Street Journal*, December 15, 2006, A1, A12.

12. Ibid., A1.

13. Reported and adapted from Jeremy W. Peters, "From Reuters, Automatic Trading Linked to News Events," *New York Times*, December 11, 2006, C2.

14. Santoli, "Requiem for Floor Traders."

15. Ivy Schmerken, "CalPERS Crunches FX Data to Search for Alpha in Electronic Trading," *Wall Street & Technology*, June 10, 2010, http://wallstreetandtech.com/trading-technology/showArticle.jhtml?articleID=225600225&cid=nl_wallstreettech_daily (accessed October 5, 2011).

Chapter 15

1. Technical Outlook is found in the Flash section of my Web site, www.glgec.com.

Chapter 16

1. Rob Lati, "The Real Story of Trading Software Espionage," *Advanced Trading*, July 10, 2009, www.advancedtrading.com/showArticle. jhtml?articleID=218401501 (accessed October 5, 2011).
2. Eugene F. Fama and Kenneth R. French, "The Anatomy of Value and Growth Stock Returns," *Financial Analysts Journal* 63, no. 6 (2007).

Chapter 17

1. Belinda Goldsmith, "Most Women Own 19 Pairs of Shoes—Some Secretly," *Reuters.com*, September 10, 2007.
2. The described case was done actually near date on the chart (December 9, 2009). Hence I used the actual chart available for the class.
3. Equity value, means a price to cash flow. It is shown subsequently as a DCF.

Chapter 18

1. I am using Morningstar because the cost is very affordable for the average investor.
2. *CFA Program Curriculum*, Vol. 1, 2010, CFA Institute, p. 105.
3. Richard Fortin and Stewart Michelson, "The Earnings Forecast Accuracy of Analysts Who Are CFA Charterholders," *Journal of Investing* (Fall 2006): 19–24.
4. Gus De Franco and Yibin Zhou, "The Performance of Analysts with a CFA Designation: The Role of Human-Capital and Signaling Theories," *The Accounting Review* 84, no. 2 (2009): 383–404.
5. Fast Facts About the MTA, 2009 May Symposium, www.mta.org.

Conclusion

1. When I wrote this in 2008, we did not yet see the day of rage of GCC countries and of course, the Occupy Wall Street demonstrations of today. I maintain that these demonstrations will continue and even escalate…

2. For the past ten years as of this writing on October 14, 2011, per Russell Investments, global small-cap stocks have shown annualized total returns of 10.1 percent, compared to a 5.4 percent for global large cap stocks. In the United States for a recent ten-year period published on the Russell Investments internet site (as of September 30, 2011), United States small-cap stocks (Russell 2000 Index) showed annualized total returns of 6.1% per annum, compared to 3.3 percent for large cap stocks (Russell 1000).

3. So, this would offer great opportunities to investors. The last ten years have shown global small-cap stocks with about a total annualized return of 10%; therefore, this would imply that we can almost double these returns with my forecast of 18.5% per annum over the next ten years.

INDEX

ABOUT THE AUTHOR

V. John Palicka CFA CMT has been researching and managing global, emerging, and US small-cap stocks for more than 30 years. He helped generate high alpha returns during his 11-year career as Chief Portfolio Manager of small- and mid-cap stocks at The Prudential Insurance Company, where he managed over $1.5 billion. He is currently President and Chief Portfolio Manager at Global Emerging Growth Capital (GEGC). Palicka has done extensive training for major asset management firms around the world. He has provided advice to country presidents, leading banking officials, and wealthy investors, and he has taught finance courses at Columbia Business School, Baruch, and New York University. He earned his MBA at Columbia University. Palicka lives in New York City with his wife and three children.